Writing from Start to Finish

A Rhetoric with Readings

Writing from Start to Finish
A Rhetoric with Readings

JEFFREY L. DUNCAN
Eastern Michigan University

Harcourt Brace Jovanovich, Publishers
San Diego   New York   Chicago   Atlanta   Washington, D.C.
London   Sydney   Toronto

To my prize pupils,
Anne and John

Preface

Pianist Clifford Curzon has observed that in mastering a piece of music we learn the notes last. Every experienced musician agrees. We must grasp the whole piece—its form and dynamic—before mastering its parts. We cannot dwell on each note and phrase to get them just right. If we did, we would achieve nothing more than a jumble of assorted notes and phrases—never a whole piece of music.

Although this principle is fundamental to music education, in the teaching of writing it is traditionally assumed that we learn best one step at a time—from words to phrases, to clauses, to sentences, to paragraphs, to the complete piece and the entire skill. Michael Polanyi, the physician-turned-chemist-turned-philosopher, has demonstrated time and again that in the learning process we must have a sense of the whole before we can understand its parts. For example, if we had never seen a tree and were told only its chemical components, we could not possibly figure out what a tree looks or feels or smells or sounds like. We could have no idea how its various elements combine to form a harmonious whole.

I begin with a consideration of writing in general, discuss the unique opportunity it provides—"to be smarter than we actually are"—and proceed to its three main purposes: to explore, to explain, and to persuade. Then, chapter by chapter, I move through the writing process from start to finish: prewriting to writing, to rewriting, to editing a final product. I advocate no rigid formula—no compulsory sequence of steps (one dance and one dance only)—because no two people work exactly alike. Nevertheless, the chapter titles follow—sometimes roughly—the natural sequence of all writing:

Prewriting: We must think about what we are going to write. We make notes, read, talk to people—whatever it takes to define, organize, and launch the subject.

Writing: We then frame sentences, structure paragraphs (writers often produce only approximations the first time through), and complete a draft—something to work on and over.

Rewriting: We must now revise the sentences and paragraphs as many times as necessary to get them just right.

Editing: Ultimately the work must be presentable. We must make last-minute adjustments before the piece is typewritten and proofread to get usage, punctuation, and spelling in final form.

As Polanyi and Curzon argue, the whole is not simply the sum of its parts—the whole determines its parts, their order, and their form. Grammar and punctuation are meaningful only in terms of the sentences they support; sentences are effective only in relation to the paragraphs they compose; paragraphs work only in terms of the essay, the article, or the writing they constitute.

In short, I provide an overview—a concept of writing for a purpose and to an end. Then I deal with finding a subject and thesis, gathering and organizing information, writing it out, framing paragraphs, fashioning sentences, choosing words, employing figures of speech, and checking grammar and punctuation. Accordingly, I provide not only a concept of composition but the basic notes as well.

I include numerous student writings—promising, horrendous, indifferent—most of them from my freshman classes. I include only a sampling of advanced student writings, and always say so when I do. Students can learn a great deal from each other's work. Because they share common interests, they are eager to see what their peers have to say and how they say it. And in terms of writing, all students have much in common: similar problems, tendencies, mistakes, and—equally important—the same potential for success. This last point is especially significant. When students see how well professionals write, they often conclude that such skill is forever out of their reach. But when exposed to how well their peers sometimes write, they often come to believe they can write well too.

I include considerable professional writings to demonstrate prose at its best and to illustrate just how well words can work: perfectly. So that students may consider the passages in context, I take most of these writings from the essays that constitute the Reader section of this book. Although the Reader is organized thematically, I have furnished an alternative table of contents classified according to rhetorical strategies.

Professional essays on various aspects of writing follow each chapter of the Rhetoric section, most of which are directly concerned with the subject matter of that chapter. However, some are equally relevant elsewhere because they concern more than one phase of writing.

Generally, the essays chosen for the Reader are short and self-contained. Six of the essays are accompanied and complemented by postscripts—authors' commentaries on how and why they wrote the specific selection as they did. Some selections are followed by earlier drafts so that students may see firsthand the painstaking process of professional writing.

Because students must learn that writing is both *vision* and *revision*, many of the exercises involve revision. Some exercises involve writing bad prose intentionally so students realize that seeing with words means manipulating words—maneuvering them to achieve some particular effect.

Writing is a collaborative as well as a solitary effort. Consequently, the exercises often involve group discussion and sometimes group writing. For such activities I rely on the instructor to provide an infrastructure with specific assignment of roles and tasks.

The primary purpose of the exercises is to stimulate and provoke— not to drill. Accordingly, there are no exercises in Chapters One and Five. Given their content, exercises would be mere drill—busywork better left for actual writing.

The desire to stimulate and provoke also underlies many of the questions that follow the essays in the Reader. Students are directed to write their response to the selection in considerable detail, exploring the intellectual and emotional reactions aroused in them by the reading. To write, one must before all else respond to the world—to its shapes and forces. If this book—the Rhetoric and the Reader—encourages and helps students respond more ardently to the energy and grace of words used well, it will have accomplished its major task.

I owe many thanks. To Eunice Jordan, Russell Larson, and Frank Ross of the Writing Assistance Team at Eastern Michigan University— for hundreds of hours of intense discussion concerning the teaching and learning of composition. To John S. Nixon, John N. Snapper, and Karl Zender for thoughtfully critiquing the manuscript and causing me, in rewriting it, to work much harder than I wanted to. To Paul H. Nockleby, my acquisitions editor at Harcourt Brace Jovanovich, for a superb job—one that made all the difference. To Robert C. Miller, my house editor at HBJ, for his diligent attention to detail and valuable contributions. To Eleanor Garner, my HBJ permissions editor, for her heroic efforts. To my students—especially those whose work is so useful to the book. And to the Graduate School and the Board of Regents of Eastern Michigan University for a generous Faculty Research Fellowship.

Jeffrey L. Duncan

Contents

Writing from Start to Finish
A Rhetoric with Readings

I

RHETORIC

1
Introduction

I. WHAT WRITING CAN DO FOR YOU

Novelist Kurt Vonnegut observed that the great thing about writing is that it enables us to be so much smarter than we actually are. Put another way, we can consistently be at our smartest: witty, charming, logical, knowledgeable, commanding—all the things we would be in person if we only had the presence of mind.

When writing, we think of that turn of phrase, that illuminating quote, those exact statistics *in time* to use them (rather than thinking of them later when it's too late) because there *is* time to think of them, time to compose or find whatever we need to make our point with precise effect. When writing there is *time* to think of points to make, of something to say. There is *time* to think of the line "we can be so much smarter than we actually are," and, having thought of it, time to enjoy *being* so smart after all.

Writing, quite literally, enables us to make some of our dreams come true. One of our deepest dreams is to possess the power and skill to do things well, to accomplish objectives. Children yearn to be adults for precisely that reason: Adults can do things children can't. Adults know and understand things children don't. Superman and Wonder Woman are thrilling primarily because they are competent. They get the job done! And they perform their feats with the virtue Ernest Hemingway so admired—grace under pressure.

The hidden moral of those myths is that you can do the same. Just remember that Superman and Wonder Woman are *written*. In writing you too can perform breathtaking leaps of imagination and flights of fancy, dazzling displays of logic, compelling turns of phrase. In writing you too can be super-competent, wondrously effective.

I can hear the Doubting Thomases: "Me? Be serious!" But I am serious. I'm not selling snake oil or an instant fix for all your deficien-

3

cies. Writing is not a painless remedy for what ails you—but a skill that requires much time and more trouble. And speaking of trouble, you might as well know the rest of the bad news: Writing does not get easier the better you get at it; it gets harder. So I'm not promising you fun in the park. Yet, if you take the time and trouble, you can learn to exercise this difficult but powerful skill. These students did.

> On growing up:
> The more people I meet, the more cash I have to scrape up and dish out.

> On trichinosis:
> The worms like to lounge in muscle and intestine.

> On *Moby Dick*:
> Captain Ahab tried on divinity for size.

Many of you probably still doubt that you can learn to write well. You may think that, popular songs and slogans to the contrary, you cannot be whatever you want to be, do whatever you dare to do. Impossible dreams are just that: impossible. I agree. I cannot be a point-guard in the NBA, an astrophysicist, or a tenor at the Met, however ardent my desire. I haven't the speed or coordination to play that caliber of basketball, I've no gift for science and math, and I can't carry a tune—much less sing an aria. But I'm not basing my promise on mere desire.

Well-known educator John Holt remarked that anyone who learns to speak is a genius, because language is inconceivably complex. Holt is right. And anyone who knows how to speak a language can learn how to write. We speak without a second thought. Writing amounts to speaking *with* a second thought, a third if necessary, and a fourth—as many as it takes to get the "speaking" exactly right. That is how writing enables us to be so much smarter than we actually are.

Novelist Stanley Elkin has said that for each page of his that is printed he has written four, a ratio of 3:1. Ernest Hemingway rewrote the ending to *A Farewell to Arms* 39 times. Asked what the trouble was, he said, "Getting the words right." While you may not be an Elkin or a Hemingway—literary renown may not be in your future—you too can learn to write with force and grace if you expend that kind of time, painstaking time. I guarantee it.

I also guarantee the satisfaction that comes from acquiring and improving a skill. It is often a pleasure to play tennis, golf, bridge, flute, piano; to build bookcases and decks; to hang paper, lay brick, sling pots; to cook, dance, sing, ski, sail, and, yes, to write. Writing, however, offers something extra. Even when it is possible to earn a living from them, most other skills are ends in themselves. People play the piano to make music. People sling pots to make pots. People ski simply to ski. Writing, however, serves specific purposes beyond the pleasure of its performance, and in many respects you will find these purposes important.

II. WHAT YOU CAN DO BY WRITING

Several purposes are easily identified, but there are three major ones: to explore, to explain, and to persuade. These are *not* mutually exclusive. Rather, they complement and reinforce one another like old friends. And while one or another may occasionally predominate, they are *never* contradictory.

A. Explore

To *explore* means to search out. And even the most elementary act of writing involves exploration. To make a grocery list you must check the refrigerator and the cabinets and your memory to see what you need. To write a diary entry you must review your day to determine what is worth including. To write a letter you must rummage through your mind to locate just what you want to say and just how you want to say it.

Poets, playwrights, and fiction writers often consider exploration their central purpose in writing. At the start, the result is unknown. And that's as it should be, because the purpose of their writing is to *find out*. What if so and so should happen? What if such and such should be the case? What then? And how? And why? And off they go in pursuit of answers, meaning, form.

In this course you will write essays mainly, if not exclusively. *Essay* is a French word meaning "to attempt," to try something, to launch into the unknown. So exploration is at the very heart of the essay form. But exploration is a major component of virtually all writing: memorandums, reports, articles, proposals, presentations. Note this: *You cannot write effectively without engaging in exploration.*

There are two kinds of exploration: external and internal. For most writing, both are necessary.

Ordinarily writing involves some piece or other of the world. Unless you know everything about the subject—and I've never met anyone who knows everything about anything—you must explore it to some extent so that you will know what you are talking about. This exploration is *external* because it involves looking into the world outside of yourself. A more common word for it is *research*. If you don't do it, you will probably make a fool of yourself—as this student did in an essay on the New Testament.

> The books by Matthew, Mark, and Luke are known as the Synoptic Gospels because, of course, they present synopses or summaries of the Savior's life.

Well, there is no such *of course* to it. If the student had explored, he would have quickly (and easily) discovered that *Synoptic* describes different accounts of Christ's life from the same point of view. In the original Greek, the word is a compound of *syn* and *opsis*, and means "seeing together." (Compare *optical*.)

You may view research with a negative eye, as a burden. I urge that you view it with new eyes, in the spirit of *exploration:* an adventure to unknown reaches, a trip to new parts of familiar places—where you will likely find those nuggets of information and insight that produce an "Ah ha!" or "Eureka!"

Joseph Wood Krutch found that flowers, only one hundred million years old, are evolutionary youngsters. John McPhee learned that Hershey, Pennsylvania, has street names like Chocolate Avenue and streetlights resembling Hershey Kisses—including even the little pull strips. Jean George discovered that mayflies don't bite; they have no mouths. Gay Talese explored New York and gathered all sorts of goodies.

> In New York the Fifth Avenue Lingerie shop is on Madison Avenue; The Madison Pet Shop is on Lexington Avenue; the Park Avenue Florist is on Madison Avenue, and the Lexington Hand Laundry is on Third Avenue.

Wherever you look, if you really look, you will discover gold. The world is enormously rich, an absolutely fascinating planet.

Writing also involves an internal exploration, a journey within to discover how you think and feel about a particular subject. Novelist and essayist Harry Crews puts it this way.

> Knowing what you really think or feel about something would seem simple enough. But if you aren't careful, and above all, patient, you'll think and feel what your parents or your friends think and feel. Writing well demands that you be profoundly in touch with your unique self.

Not your social self, mind you—not the face you offer to all the faces that you meet—but the unique self that makes you *you* and not someone else.

Several years ago I attended a conference where eminent critic and historian of literature Geoffrey Hartmann was asked a question I've since forgotten. It's the answer I remember: "I don't know what I think about that yet." Like Crews, indeed like all writers, Hartmann assumed he already had an attitude about the issue. He knew he thought and felt something. He just didn't know what yet. To find out, he would have to write about it.

An important distinction arises here. Writing is thinking. Yet the purpose of thinking is not simply to *produce* thought. The purpose of thinking is to *discover* what your thoughts are, to find your attitudes and assess their relative values—to see where you really stand and who you actually are.

To write, therefore, you must explore—adventuring to the heights and depths of consciousness—and then report accurately and honestly what you find there. For example, Talese is intrigued by the oddities of the city. Should you write about the city, you might find you're not. But more importantly, you might discover *why* you're not. The oddities of the city might affect you differently. You might view them as symptomatic of our cultural brutality or perhaps as the signs of technological chaos and old night.

Exploring a subject and your relation to it may bring you to your very wits' end, as it did Lewis Thomas when he examined the medusa and the snail.

> Sometimes there is such a mix-up about selfness that two creatures . . . incorporate the two selves to make a single organism. The best story I've heard about this is the tale told of the nudibranch and medusa living in the Bay of Naples. . . . the nudibranch, a common sea slug . . . [has] a tiny vestigial parasite, in the form of a jellyfish, permanently affixed to the ventral surface near the mouth. . . . The attached parasite can still produce offspring. . . . They drift through the upper waters, grow up nicely and astonishingly, and finally become full-grown, handsome, normal jellyfish. Meanwhile, the snail produces snail larvae, and these too begin to grow normally, but not for long. While still extremely small, they become entrapped in the tentacles of the medusa and then engulfed within the umbrella-shaped body. . . . Soon the snails . . . begin to eat, browsing away first at the radial canals, then the borders of the rim, finally the tentacles, until the jellyfish becomes reduced in substance by being eaten while the snail grows correspondingly in size. At the end, the arrangement is back to the first scene, with a full-grown nudibranch basking, and nothing left of the jellyfish except the round, successfully edited parasite, safely affixed to the skin near the mouth.
>
> It is a confusing tale to sort out, and even more confusing to think about. Both creatures are designed for this encounter, marked as selves so that they can find each other in the waters of the Bay of

Naples. The collaboration, if you want to call it that, is entirely specific; it is only this species of medusa and only this kind of nudibranch that can come together and live this way. And, more surprising, they cannot live in any other way; they depend for their survival on each other. They are not really selves, they are specific *others*.
The thought of these creatures gives me an odd feeling. They do not remind me of anything, really. I've never heard of such a cycle before. They are bizarre, that's it, unique. And at the same time, like a vaguely remembered dream, they remind me of the whole earth at once. I cannot get my mind to stay still and think it through.

By such exploration, you not only learn something about the subject and your self, but also the limits of your learning and of your ability to comprehend your surroundings. And it always helps to know your limits.

Whenever and whatever you write, always explore the subject and your attitude towards it. You are invariably rewarded with something you didn't know or hadn't realized—at least one "Ah ha!" per outing. If you ignore exploration, you assume the risk and miss much of the excitement and pleasure of the entire enterprise.

B. Explain

Good writing demands exploration—but not necessarily in the essay itself. Although Thomas explores in his essay, he has good reason: To explain the limits of his knowledge, he must describe his mind running up against those very limitations. Explanation, then, is critical. *In everything you write for others to read, you are explaining something.* You present the subject—even when fictional—so the readers will understand.

To this end, you must explain the subject clearly and answer all pertinent questions. Consider the following example. A student of mine wrote, "I used to love yelling at my teachers, 'You retarded idiotic nincompoop!'" I had several questions but asked only one: How old were you? In revising the essay, he answered that question and others as well.

I enjoyed calling my teachers names at the top of my lungs. I didn't hate them. It just made me feel big in front of the other kids to yell "You retarded idiotic nincompoop!" at my teacher. I was especially fond of that phrase, probably because it was longer than any other I knew. I was only six at the time, and big words, especially big sarcastic put-down words, made a very big impression on me.

His statement was no longer limited to *what* he did because he explained *why* he did it. He revealed later that he was able to explain only because he had explored the causes underlying his behavior. And, yes, he experienced several "Ah ha's." Because he understood it more clearly, he could write the results of his exploration simply and accurately. Now the readers understand too.

Bureaucrats—public and private—and others of similar persuasion appear dedicated to defeating this purpose of writing. They write in a style that does not explain—it obfuscates. A case in point is from a newsletter of the Eastern Michigan University Federation of Teachers (EMUFT). Because this style is employed by persons and groups attempting to sound official, like the voice of authority, it is popularly known as "officialese."

> The EMUFT takes full cognizance of the fact that the suspension of the salary schedule at E.M.U. and the subsequent lack of any effective faculty voice in the determination of faculty remuneration has resulted in inequitable salary provisions for the total faculty. In order that these inequities may be remedied and in order to guarantee that divisiveness will not be associated with salary considerations at E.M.U., the EMUFT wishes to be guided on its final position related to merit pay by the faculty.

Did you take full cognizance of that? Apparently faculty members of the same rank and with equal years of service draw different salaries, and the EMUFT wants to know what the faculty thinks of merit pay.

That seems to be the message. Yet "inequitable salary provisions" could mean the opposite: that faculty members *are* drawing the same salary and, by implication, should not. Business and engineering professors can earn higher salaries elsewhere than English professors, hence they should get more from the University. That seems only fair. Perhaps merit pay can serve that precise purpose. But the EMUFT proposes, apparently, to remedy the inequity with or without merit pay—depending on faculty guidance—and thus avoid divisiveness. One wonders, though, how divisiveness can be avoided if the faculty (as is likely) is already divided.

Who knows what the EMUFT is saying? Will the real meaning please stand up? Or do you suppose that the writers (surely a committee composed this) don't know what they are saying because they haven't yet explored the matter to learn what they think?

Purple prose ("purple" for short) is another example of bad writing. You find it in the Sunday travel section of most newspapers. Purple is a literary notion, an attempt to sound colorful, vivid, emotional, poetic, like the very voice of the muse. Descriptions, like this one of Galilee, are frequent offenders.

> The azure of the sky penetrates the depths of the lake, and the waters are sweet and cool. On the west stretch broad fertile plains; on the east, the wild and desolate mountains contrast finely with the deep blue lake; and toward the north, sublime and majestic, Hermon looks down on the sea, lifting his white crown to heaven with the pride of a hill that has seen the departing footsteps of a hundred generations. Flowers bloom in this terrestrial paradise, once beautiful and verdant with waving trees; singing birds enchant the ear; the turtle-dove soothes with its soft note; the crested lark sends up its song toward heaven, and the grave and stately stork inspires the mind with thought, and leads it on to meditation and repose.

Ironically, although this aspires to be the exact opposite of officialese, it's the same thing: inflated nonsense. Consider how Mark Twain, in *The Innocents Abroad*, so easily punctures the inflation.

> Toward nightfall, the next evening, we steamed into the great artificial harbor of the noble city of Marseilles, and saw the dying sunlight gild its clustering spires and ramparts, and flood its leagues of environing verdure with a mellow radiance that touched with an added charm the white villas that flecked the landscape far and near. [Copyright secured according to law.]

This sort of stuff is a fake, a mere pretense. It does not describe; it emotes. Instead of explaining what something is like, writers of purple prose try (in vain) to prove what deep, noble, sensitive souls are theirs. Similarly, writers of officialese abandon explanation in favor of displaying their complex intellects.

To avoid these sorts of nonsense—and they are nonsense, literally—you must explore every subject to know what you are talking about. Then you must talk about it simply and concretely, clearly defining the ideas and spelling out the details. Remember this the way you remember your address and telephone number: To understand what you want to say, readers need *detail* and *idea*. To explain your subject satisfactorily, you must supply both.

Detail—examples, images, analogies, figures of speech, facts—is absolutely essential. Without it the reader has only a vague idea of what you are talking about. For example, a student of mine wrote about her weight problem. (That alone is vague.) She wasn't simply overweight or underweight; she was both—now one, now the other. Always going on radical food binges and then on equally radical crash diets, feasting or fasting, gaining or losing—she went up and down the scale like a yo-yo. (Now we begin to get the picture.) Consequently, she had four complete wardrobes: one for 120, 130, 140, and 150 pounds, respectively. (Now we understand.) What a difference some detail makes!

Now I'll share with you in greater detail a "before and after" written by one of my seniors, a description of student teaching in an elementary school.

Before:

> One of the worst times in student teaching comes when the university supervisor comes to inspect you. They never show up on time and usually have very little idea of what is going on. My supervisor spent a total of fifteen minutes in my classroom after I had prepared for her visit one week in advance. She was late, of course, and did not know what was happening even though I had supplied her with a lesson plan.

After:

> Universities hire supervising teachers to observe student teachers. They write evaluations on your performance during their visits, and make sure things are going well. For my first evaluation I prepared a very impressive math lesson on liquid measurement. I used water to show how many quarts make a gallon, how many pints make a quart, how many cups a pint, and so on. My supervisor showed up an hour late, as I was reading the spelling list for the week. On her evaluation of me she wrote that I didn't walk around the room enough. When I asked her about it, she said she thought I was doing well but she had to write something negative on the first evaluation.

The difference speaks for itself.

Now, idea is as essential as detail. Detail without idea is pointless, incoherent—like features without a face.

> A long way off, the surface looks perfectly smooth. Closer up, though, it looks like a blur of scratches. Up very close you can see the pits and mounds. Between the pits and mounds the surface looks comparatively smooth, as if sanded but not polished or painted. The pits and mounds are distributed irregularly, bunched here, widely scattered there.

This sounds like a riddle: What is it that has . . .? Except this riddle has several possible answers: the moon, maybe, or a concrete wall, or metal primered for painting, or a face afflicted with acne. But without a point of reference, an idea to explain and unify these details, they just don't add up. They are meaningless.

Here are some details from a student essay that do add up because they share something in common—a single and simple idea.

Instead of making his bed my brother asked a question: "Why make it if I'm just going to sleep in it tonight?" He had all his toys on the floor of his bedroom. Cars and dice were all over the place, cards were scattered everywhere, and little game pieces were stuck under his mattress and in the vent of the heater. In the bathroom he always left wet towels and washcloths on the floor. He always lost the cap to the toothpaste, and he never rinsed his spit out of the sink. He loved to squeeze a perfectly useful bar of soap between his fingers until it looked like a smashed banana.

However, an idea alone is not enough; you must explain it—as this student did—before citing the detail: "My brother was a mess." That way the idea makes sense of the detail and the detail makes sense of the idea. They make a perfect couple.

Isn't the main idea obvious—so obvious that it can go without saying? As anyone can see from the details alone, the kid was a mess. But that isn't the only obvious idea, is it? My brother was odd. My brother was unconventional. My brother was a free spirit. My brother was absentminded. Each idea may be reasonably inferred from the details, but each idea casts a different light on those details. So you mustn't assume the readers know what you are thinking. You must explain what you are thinking.

One thing: State your ideas simply and quickly. Broadway producer Joseph Papp warns that if you cannot write your basic idea on the back of his business card, you don't know what you think yet—and neither of course does he. The idea need not be profound—few ideas are—only *CLEAR*. Idea: My brother was a mess. Idea: I have a weight problem—I'm always gaining or losing 30 pounds.

Beginning writers are often afraid of stating their ideas as simply as possible, probably out of fear of looking simple themselves (as in simple-minded or simpleton). In fact, that very fear is an underlying motive for writing officialese and purple prose: If you use lots of big words in complex sentences, no one will suspect you or your idea of being unsophisticated. These styles are smokescreens, then—coverups of the plain truth—as well as misguided pursuits of literary elegance.

The motive is understandable. Psychologically, it is frightening to say what we think in simple language to people we don't know. No one wants to be considered a dum-dum, and we all know that stupid people are simple people. Yet ideas *are* simple, expecially profound ideas. You may doubt that, but it's true. Trust me—for a while at least—until you realize it's true.

Another fear leads to officialese: the fear of conflict. If we say what we *really* think, the readers may rise up in arms and overwhelm us in controversy. Most of us don't enjoy being attacked or being regarded as contentious loud mouths spoiling for a fight. If we muffle our ideas in the soft tepid mud of officialese, we'll blunt their edge and avoid the readers' wrath.

The fear of conflict is common and understandable—but unnecessary. If you state your real thought and feeling simply, as Harry Crews recommends, readers will respect you even though they may disagree. In the relationship between writer and reader, honesty is a supreme value—far more important than agreement.

So pluck up thy courage and gird thy loins. State your ideas simply, clearly, and quickly. Get to the point! And remember to provide sufficient detail to make the point concrete and specific. *Explain* your thoughts. You won't seem stupid. Neither will you seem contentious. On the contrary, you will seem intelligent, knowledgeable, confident, firm, dynamic—like Superman or Wonder Woman on the scene.

C. Persuade

Most often you will be writing not only to explore and explain a subject, but also to persuade the reader to do something about it. Some rhetoricians distinguish between argumentation and persuasion. *Argumentation* means convincing readers to adopt a point of view; *persuasion* means convincing readers to take a course of action. I regard them as two sides of the same coin. Action is thought in motion; thought is mind in action. Consequently, when I say persuasion I mean argumentation as well. I am talking about writing to move people and thus to make a difference in the world.

It is nearly impossible to exaggerate the importance of persuasion. When you apply for something—a scholarship, a job, a grant, a favor— you engage in persuasion. When you try to sell something—a product, a service, a new idea, the status quo—you engage in persuasion. When you promote something—a political candidate or program, a marketing strategy, a constitutional amendment, a concert—you engage in persuasion. When you propose, advocate, attack, defend—whenever you take a stand—you engage in persuasion.

In an argument once, playwright George Bernard Shaw explained, "All I want is to have my way in everything." Although we are not supposed to feel that way, much less admit it, it's what we all want. And the better we are able to persuade, the more we can have of what we want.

Effective persuasion requires effective exploration. You must know precisely what you want. Effective persuasion requires effective explanation. Your readers must know precisely what you want—and why. Finally, effective persuasion requires the use of pertinent *facts* and tight *logic*. Now your readers have little choice but to conclude that you ought to have what you want.

When you engage in persuasion you are trying to make a difference—trying to effect a change. To convince others of the need for change, you must present pertinent facts so they can see the situation clearly and understand why it needs changing. Everything you write must include detail. And in persuasive writing, the most important detail is matter-of-fact. In his "Letter from Birmingham Jail," Martin Luther King, Jr., who knew as much about persuasion as anybody, demonstrated the value of fact.

> We have waited for more than 340 years for our constitutional and God-given rights. . . . Perhaps it is easy for those who have never felt the stinging darts of segregation to say, "Wait." But when you have seen vicious mobs lynch your mothers and fathers at will and drown your sisters and brothers at whim; when you . . . suddenly find your tongue twisted and your speech stammering as you seek to explain to your six-year-old daughter why she can't go the the public amusement park that has just been advertised on television, and see tears welling up in her eyes when she is told that Funtown is closed to colored children, and see ominous clouds of inferiority beginning to form in her little mental sky, and see her beginning to distort her personality by developing an unconscious bitterness toward white people . . . when you take a cross-country drive and find it necessary to sleep night after night in the uncomfortable corners of your automobile because no motel will accept you; when you are humiliated day in and day out by nagging signs reading "white" and "colored"; when your first name becomes "nigger," and middle name becomes "boy" (however old you are) and your last name becomes "John," and your wife and mother are never given the respected title "Mrs." . . .—then you will understand why we find it difficult to wait.

King sought an end to racial discrimination. And partly because of his ability to base his case on the facts of the matter, he persuaded millions of the justness of his desire.

In addition to providing detail, you must define your ideas. In persuasive writing, you must define their *logic* as well. And you must refute the ideas you are opposed to by defining their lack of logic.

Read another paragraph from King's letter. Observe how skillfully he refutes an argument against (and simultaneously defends the logic of) civil disobedience.

In your statement you assert that our actions, even though peaceful, must be condemned because they precipitate violence. But is this a logical assertion? Isn't this like condemning a robbed man because his possession of money precipitated the evil act of robbery? Isn't this like condemning Socrates because his unswerving commitment to truth and his philosophical inquiries precipitated the act by the misguided populace in which they made him drink hemlock? Isn't this like condemning Jesus because his unique God-consciousness and never-ceasing devotion to God's will precipitated the evil act of crucifixion? We must come to see that, as the federal courts have consistently affirmed, it is wrong to urge an individual to cease his efforts to gain his basic constitutional rights because the quest may precipitate violence. Society must protect the robbed and punish the robber.

King paid as close attention to logic as to facts. In justifying the action he advocated—thereby persuading others to approve and join his cause— he paid scrupulous attention to the logic of his position. Because civil disobedience involves breaking allegedly unjust laws, an important question arises: How can we tell, objectively, whether a law is just or unjust?

An unjust law is a code that a numerical or power majority group compels a minority group to obey but does not make binding on itself. This is *difference* made legal. By the same token, a just law is a code that a majority compels a minority to follow and that it is willing to follow itself. This is *sameness* made equal.

By setting forth the logic of his position (and note how simply he did so, without the gobbledygook of officialese), King also refuted the idea that he approved of breaking laws on the basis of mere caprice. He based his case on logic and fact. And as a consequence he made a considerable difference in the world—a difference for the better and a difference for all.

King may seem an intimidating example—he *is* an imposing figure, to be sure—but you should not be intimidated. By concentrating on working out the logic of your position and by marshalling facts in its behalf, you can be just as clear and effective as he.

The following paragraph was written by a freshman student arguing against the position, advocated by neurologist Robert J. White, that animals do not feel pain.

When a planaria, a primitive flatworm, is in a container of water, and an electric shock passes through it, the organism balls up. It appears to feel pain. Some, including Dr. White, argue against this conclusion. They say that the balling up may be a mere reflex, or even a symptom of pleasure. To disprove these arguments, experimenters have repeatedly flashed a light before inducing the shock, and they have set up another container of water that the planaria can get to. Once the sequence of light and shock is established, and the planaria has found the other container, he knows that he has a choice: stick around after the flash for the pleasure of the shock, or deny himself the experience by swimming to the other container. The planaria consistently chooses to avoid the shock. If balling up is just a reflex, or a symptom of pleasure, why does he flee every time? Are we to suppose that planaria is an ascetic at heart? Hardly. He avoids the shock because it hurts. He feels pain.

Here the writer demonstrates that she has explored the subject. She explains her findings simply and clearly. Combining facts and logic, she not only refutes the opposition but makes a persuasive case for her position as well. She has done a good job.

And you can do just as well. This Freshman biologist did not always write like this. She learned by reading carefully to see how the pros do it and by *writing hard:* exploring the subject and her self, explaining with detail and idea, arguing with fact and logic, and writing it again and again until she got the words right. Now, if she did it—and she did, as you can see—so can you. You have my word on it.

JOAN DIDION

Why I Write

A Californian, Didion is a novelist, short story writer, screenwriter, and columnist, noted in all she does for her precision of observation, thought, and expression. Her collections of essays include Slouching Towards Bethlehem *(1968) and* The White Album *(1979). In the following she points out how writing is a process of learning because it is not just something that you do, it is an activity that does something to you.*

Of course I stole the title for this talk from George Orwell. One reason I stole it was that I like the sound of the words: *Why I Write.* There you have three short unambiguous words that share a sound, and the sound they share is this:

I

I

I

In many ways writing is the act of saying *I*, of imposing oneself upon other people, of saying *listen to me, see it my way, change your mind*. It's an aggressive, even a hostile act. You can disguise its aggressiveness all you want with veils of subordinate clauses and qualifiers and tentative subjectives, with ellipses and evasions—with the whole manner of intimating rather than claiming, of alluding rather than stating—but there's no getting around the fact that setting words on paper is the tactic of a secret bully, an invasion, an imposition of the writer's sensibility on the reader's most private space.

I stole the title not only because the words sounded right but because they seemed to sum up, in a no-nonsense way, all I have to tell you. Like many writers I have only this one "subject," this one "area": the act of writing. I can bring you no reports from any other front. I may have other interests: I am "interested," for example, in marine biology, but I don't flatter myself that you would come out to hear me talk about it. I am not a scholar. I am not in the least an intellectual, which is not to say that when I hear the word "intellectual" I reach for my gun, but only to say that I do not think in abstracts. During the years when I was an undergraduate at Berkeley I tried, with a kind of hopeless late-adolescent energy, to buy some temporary visa into the world of ideas, to forge for myself a mind that could deal with the abstract.

In short I tried to think. I failed. My attention veered inexorably back to the specific, to the tangible, to what was generally considered, by everyone I knew then and for that matter have known since, the peripheral. I would try to contemplate the Hegelian dialectic and would find myself concentrating instead on a flowering pear tree outside my window and the particular way the petal fell on my floor. I would try to read linguistic theory and would find myself wondering instead if the lights were on in the bevatron up the hill. When I say that I was wondering if the lights were on in the bevatron you might immediately suspect, if you deal in ideas at all, that I was registering the bevatron as a political symbol, thinking in shorthand about the military-industrial complex and its role in the university community, but you would be wrong. I was only wondering if the lights were on in the bevatron, and how they looked. A physical fact.

I had trouble graduating from Berkeley, not because of this inability to deal with ideas—I was majoring in English, and I could locate the house-and-garden imagery in *The Portrait of a Lady* as well as the next person, "imagery" being by definition the kind of specific that got my attention—but simply because I had neglected to take a course in Milton. For reasons which now sound baroque I needed a degree by the end of the summer, and the English department finally agreed, if I would come down from Sacramento every Friday and talk about the cosmology of *Paradise Lost*, to certify me proficient in Milton. I did this. Some Fridays I took the Greyhound bus, other Fridays I caught the Southern Pacific's City of San Francisco on the last leg of its transcontinental trip. I can no longer tell you whether Milton put the sun or the earth at the center of his universe in *Paradise Lost*, the central question of at least one century and a topic about which I wrote 10,000 words that summer, but I can still recall the exact rancidity of the butter in the City of San Francisco's dining car, and the way the tinted windows on the Greyhound bus cast the oil refineries around Carquinez Straits into a grayed and obscurely sinister light. In short my attention was always on the periphery, on what I would see and taste and touch, on the butter, and the Greyhound bus. During those years I was traveling on what I knew to be a very shaky passport, forged papers: I knew that I was no legitimate resident in any world of ideas. I knew I couldn't think. All I knew then was what I couldn't do. All I knew then was what I wasn't, and it took me some years to discover what I was.

Which was a writer.

By which I mean not a "good" writer or a "bad" writer but simply a writer, a person whose most absorbed and passionate hours are spent arranging words on pieces of paper. Had my credentials been in order I would never have become a writer. Had I been blessed with even limited access to my own mind there would have been no reason to write. I write entirely to find out what I'm thinking, what I'm looking at, what I see and what it means. What I want and what I fear. Why did the oil refineries around Carquinez Straits seem sinister to me in the summer of 1956? Why have the night lights in the bevatron burned in my mind for twenty years? *What is going on in these pictures in my mind?*

When I talk about pictures in my mind I am talking, quite specifically, about images that shimmer around the edges. There used to be an illustration in every elementary psychology book showing a cat drawing by a patient in varying stages of schizophrenia. This cat had a shimmer around it. You could see the molecular structure breaking down at the very edges of the cat: the cat became the background and the background the cat, everything interacting, exchanging ions. People on hallucinogens describe the same perception of objects. I'm not a schizophrenic, nor do I take hallucinogens, but certain images do shimmer for me. Look hard enough, and you can't miss the shimmer.

It's there. You can't think too much about these pictures that shimmer. You just lie low and let them develop. You stay quiet. You don't talk to many people and you keep your nervous system from shorting out and you try to locate the cat in the shimmer, the grammar in the picture.

Just as I meant "shimmer" literally I mean "grammar" literally. Grammar is a piano I play by ear, since I seem to have been out of school the year the rules were mentioned. All I know about grammar is its infinite power. To shift the structure of a sentence alters the meaning of the sentence, as definitely and inflexibly as the position of a camera alters the meaning of the object photographed. Many people know about camera angles now, but not so many know about sentences. The arrangement of the words matters, and the arrangement you want can be found in the picture in your mind. The picture dictates the arrangement. The picture dictates whether this will be a sentence with or without clauses, a sentence that ends hard or a dying-fall sentence, long or short, active or passive. The picture tells you how to arrange the words and the arrangement of the words tells you, or tells me, what's going on in the picture. *Nota bene:*

It tells you.

You don't tell it.

Let me show you what I mean by pictures in the mind. I began *Play It as It Lays* just as I have begun each of my novels, with no notion of "character" or "plot" or even "incident." I had only two pictures in my mind, more about which later, and a technical intention, which was to write a novel so elliptical and fast that it would be over before you noticed it, a novel so fast that it would scarcely exist on the page at all. About the pictures: the first was of white space. Empty space. This was clearly the picture that dictated the narrative intention of the book—a book in which anything that happened would happen off the page, a "white" book to which the reader would have to bring his or her own bad dreams—and yet this picture told me no "story," suggested no situation. The second picture did. This second picture was of something actually witnessed. A young woman with long hair and a short white halter dress walks through the casino at the Riviera in Las Vegas at one in the morning. She crosses the casino alone and picks up a house telephone. I watch her because I have heard her paged, and recognize her name: she is a minor actress I see around Los Angeles from time to time, in places like Jax and once in a gynecologist's office in the Beverly Hills Clinic but have never met. I know nothing about her. Who is paging her? Why is she here to be paged?

How exactly did she come to this? It was precisely this moment in Las Vegas that made *Play It as It Lays* begin to tell itself to me, but the moment appears in the novel only obliquely, in a chapter which begins:

> Maria made a list of things she would never do. She would never: walk through the Sands or Caesar's alone after midnight. She would never: ball at a party, do S-M unless she wanted to, borrow furs from Abe Lipsey, deal. She would never: carry a Yorkshire in Beverly Hills.

That is the beginning of the chapter and that is also the end of the chapter, which may suggest what I meant by "white space."

I recall having a number of pictures in my mind when I began the novel I just finished, *A Book of Common Prayer*. As a matter of fact one of these pictures was of that bevatron I mentioned, although I would be hard put to tell you a story in which nuclear energy figured. Another was a newspaper photograph of a hijacked 707 burning on the desert in the Middle East. Another was the night view from a room in which I once spent a week with paratyphoid, a hotel room on the Colombian coast. My husband and I seemed to be on the Colombian coast representing the United States of America at a film festival (I recall invoking the name "Jack Valenti" a lot, as if its reiteration could make me well), and it was a bad place to have fever, not only because my indisposition offended our hosts but because every night in this hotel the generator failed. The lights went out. The elevator stopped. My husband would go to the event of the evening and make excuses for me and I would stay alone in this hotel room, in the dark. I remember standing at the window trying to call Bogotá (the telephone seemed to work on the same principle as the generator) and watching the night wind come up and wondering what I was doing eleven degrees off the equator with a fever of 103. The view from that window definitely figures in *A Book of Common Prayer*, as does the burning 707, and yet none of these pictures told me the story I needed.

The picture that did, the picture that shimmered and made these other images coalesce, was the Panama airport at 6 A.M. I was in this airport only once, on a plane to Bogotá that stopped for an hour to refuel, but the way it looked that morning remained superimposed on everything I saw until the day I finished *A Book of Common Prayer*. I lived in that airport for several years. I can still feel the hot air when I step off the plane, can see the heat already rising off the tarmac at 6 A.M. I can feel my skirt damp and wrinkled on my legs. I can feel the asphalt stick to my sandals. I remember the big tail of a Pan American plane floating motionless down at the end of the tarmac. I remember the sound of a slot machine in the waiting room. I could tell you that I remember a particular woman in the airport, an American woman, a *norteamericana*, a thin *norteamericana* about 40 who wore a big square emerald in lieu of a wedding ring, but there was no such woman there.

I put this woman in the airport later. I made this woman up, just as I later made up a country to put the airport in, and a family to run the country. This woman in the airport is neither catching a plane nor meeting one. She is ordering tea in the airport coffee shop. In fact she is not simply "ordering" tea but insisting that the water be boiled, in front of her, for twenty minutes. Why is this woman in the airport? Why is she going nowhere, where has she been? Where did she get that big emerald? What derangement, or disassociation, makes her believe that her will to see the water boiled can possibly prevail?

> She had been going to one airport or another for four months, one could see it, looking at the visas on her passport. All those airports where Charlotte Douglas's passport had been stamped would have looked alike. Sometimes the sign on the tower would say "Bienvenidos" and sometimes the sign on the tower would say "Bienvenue," some places were wet and hot and others dry and hot, but at each of these airports the pastel concrete walls would rust and stain and the swamp off the runway would be littered with the fuselages of cannibalized Fairchild F-227's and the water would need boiling.
> "I knew why Charlotte went to the airport even if Victor did not.
> "I knew about airports."

These lines appear about halfway through *A Book of Common Prayer*, but I wrote them during the second week I worked on the book, long before I had any idea where Charlotte Douglas had been or why she went to airports. Until I wrote these lines I had no character called "Victor" in mind: the necessity for mentioning a name, and the name "Victor," occurred to me as I wrote the sentence. *I knew why Charlotte went to the airport* sounded incomplete. *I knew why Charlotte went to the airport even if Victor did not* carried a little more narrative drive. Most important of all, until I wrote these lines I did not know who "I" was, who was telling the story. I had intended until that moment that the "I" would be no more than the voice of the author, a 19th-century omniscient narrator. But there it was:

> "I knew why Charlotte went to the airport even if Victor did not.
> "I knew about airports."

This "I" was the voice of no author in my house. This "I" was someone who not only knew why Charlotte went to the airport but also knew someone called "Victor." Who was Victor? Who was this narrator? Why was this narrator telling me this story? Let me tell you one thing about why writers write: had I known the answer to any of these questions I would never have needed to write a novel.

RICHARD SELZER
Why a Surgeon Would Write

A surgeon and faculty member at Yale University School of Medicine, Selzer has also written four volumes of stories and essays, among them Mortal Lessons *(1977) and* Letters to a Young Doctor *(1982). In the former, at the same time that he demonstrates his dramatic gift for metaphor, Selzer shows how the practice of writing informs other practices.*

Someone asked me why a surgeon would write. Why, when the shelves are already too full? They sag under the deadweight of books. To add a single adverb is to risk exceeding the strength of the boards. A surgeon should abstain. A surgeon, whose fingers are more at home in the steamy gullies of the body than they are tapping the dry keys of a typewriter. A surgeon, who feels the slow slide of intestines against the back of his hand and is no more alarmed than were a family of snakes taking their comfort from such an indolent rubbing. A surgeon, who palms the human heart as though it were some captured bird.

Why should he write? Is it vanity that urges him? There is glory enough in the knife. Is it for money? One can make too much money. No. It is to search for some meaning in the ritual of surgery, which is at once murderous, painful, healing, and full of love. It is a devilish hard thing to transmit—to find, even. Perhaps if one were to cut out a heart, a lobe of the liver, a single convolution of the brain, and paste it to a page, it would speak with more eloquence than all the words of Balzac. Such a piece would need no literary style, no mass of erudition or history, but in its very shape and feel would tell all the frailty and strength, the despair and nobility of man. What? Publish a heart? A little piece of bone? Preposterous. Still I fear that is what it may require to reveal the truth that lies hidden in the body. Not all the undressings of Rabelais, Chekhov, or even William Carlos Williams have wrested it free, although God knows each one of those doctors made a heroic assault upon it.

I have come to believe that it is the flesh alone that counts. The rest is that with which we distract ourselves when we are not hungry or cold, in pain or ecstasy. In the recesses of the body I search for the philosphers' stone. I know it is there, hidden in the deepest, dampest cul-de-sac. It awaits discovery. To find it would be like the harnessing of fire. It would illuminate the world. Such a quest is not without pain. Who can gaze on so much misery and feel no hurt? Emerson has written that the poet is the only true doctor. I believe him, for the poet, lacking the impediment of speech with which the rest of us are afflicted, gazes, records, diagnoses, and prophesies.

I invited a young diabetic woman to the operating room to amputate her leg. She could not see the great shaggy black ulcer upon her foot and ankle that threatened to encroach on the rest of her body, for she was blind as well. There upon her foot was a Mississippi Delta brimming with corruption, sending its raw tributaries down between her toes. Gone were all the little web spaces that when fresh and whole are such a delight to loving men. She could not see her wound, but she could feel it. There is no pain like that of the bloodless limb turned rotten and festering. There is neither unguent nor anodyne to kill such pain yet leave intact the body.

For over a year I trimmed away the putrid flesh, cleansed, anointed, and dressed the foot, staving off, delaying. Three times each week, in her darkness, she sat upon my table, rocking back and forth, holding her extended leg by the thigh, gripping it as though it were a rocket that must be steadied lest it explode and scatter her toes about the room. And I would cut away a bit here, a bit there, of the swollen blue leather that was her tissue.

At last we gave up, she and I. We could no longer run ahead of the gangrene. We had not the legs for it. There must be an amputation in order that she might live—and I as well. It was to heal us both that I must take up knife and saw, and cut the leg off. And when I could feel it drop from her body to the table, see the blessed *space* appear between her and that leg, I too would be well.

Now it is the day of the operation. I stand by while the anesthetist administers the drugs, watch as the tense familiar body relaxes into narcosis. I turn then to uncover the leg. There, upon her kneecap, she has drawn, blindly, upside down for me to see, a face; just a circle with two ears, two eyes, a nose, and a smiling upturned mouth. Under it she has printed SMILE, DOCTOR. Minutes later I listen to the sound of the saw, until a little crack at the end tells me it is done.

So, I have learned that man is not ugly, but that he is Beauty itself. There is no other his equal. Are we not all dying, none faster or more slowly than any other? I have become receptive to the possibilities of love (for it is love, this thing that happens in the operating room), and each day I wait, trembling in the busy air. Perhaps today it will come. Perhaps today I will find it, take part in it, this love that blooms in the stoniest desert. . . .

. . . I would seek the soul in the facts of animal economy and profligacy. Yes, it is the exact location of the soul that I am after. The smell of it is in my nostrils. I have caught glimpses of it in the body diseased. If only I could tell it. Is there no mathematical equation that can guide me? So much pain and pus equals so much truth? It is elusive as the whippoorwill that one hears calling incessantly from out the night window, but which, nesting as it does low in the brush, no one sees. No one but the poet, for he sees what no one else can. He was born with the eye for it.

Once I thought I had it: Ten o'clock one night, the end room off a long corridor in a college infirmary, my last patient of the day, degree of exhaustion suitable for the appearance of a vision, some manifestation. The patient is a young man recently returned from Guatemala, from the excavation of Mayan ruins. His left upper arm wears a gauze dressing which, when removed, reveals a clean punched-out hole the size of a dime. The tissues about the opening are swollen and tense. A thin brownish fluid lips the edge, and now and then a lazy drop of overflow spills down the arm. An abscess, inadequately drained. I will enlarge the opening to allow better egress of the pus. Nurse, will you get me a scalpel and some . . .?

What happens next is enough to lay Francis Drake avomit in his cabin. No explorer ever stared in wider surmise than I into that crater from which there now emerges a narrow gray head whose sole distinguishing feature is a pair of black pincers. The head sits atop a longish flexible neck arching now this way, now that, testing the air. Alternately it folds back upon itself, then advances in new boldness. And all the while, with dreadful rhythmicity, the unspeakable pincers open and close. Abscess? Pus? Never. Here is the lair of a beast at whose malignant purpose I could but guess. A Mayan devil, I think, that would soon burst free to fly about the room, with horrid blanket-wings and iridescent scales, raking, pinching, injecting God knows what acid juice. And even now the irony does not escape me, the irony of my patient as excavator excavated.

With all the ritual deliberation of a high priest I advance a surgical clamp toward the hole. The surgeon's heart is become a bat hanging upside down from his rib cage. The rim achieved—now thrust—and the ratchets of the clamp close upon the empty air. The devil has retracted. Evil mocking laughter bangs back and forth in the brain. More stealth. Lying in wait. One must skulk. Minutes pass, perhaps an hour. . . . A faint disturbance in the lake, and once again the thing upraises, farther and farther, hovering. Acrouch, strung, the surgeon is one with his instrument; there is no longer any boundary between its metal and his flesh. They are joined in a single perfect tool of extirpation. It is just for this that he was born. Now—thrust—and clamp—and *yes*. Got him!

Transmitted to the fingers comes the wild thrashing of the creature. Pinned and wriggling, he is mine. I hear the dry brittle scream of the dragon, and a hatred seizes me, but such a detestation as would make of Iago a drooling sucktit. It is the demented hatred of the victor for the vanquished, the warden for his prisoner. It is the hatred of fear. Within the jaws of my hemostat is the whole of the evil of the world, the dark concentrate itself, and I shall kill it. For mankind. And, in so doing, will open the way into a thousand years of perfect peace. Here is Surgeon as Savior indeed.

Tight grip now . . . steady, relentless pull. How it scrabbles to keep its tentacle-hold. With an abrupt moist plop the extraction is complete. There, writhing in the teeth of the clamp, is a dirty gray body, the size and shape of an English walnut. He is hung everywhere with tiny black hooklets. Quickly . . . into the specimen jar of saline . . . the lid screwed tight. Crazily he swims round and round, wiping his slimy head against the glass, then slowly sinks to the bottom, the mass of hooks in frantic agonal wave.

"You are going to be all right," I say to my patient. "We are *all* going to be all right from now on."

The next day I take the jar to the medical school. "That's the larva of the botfly," says a pathologist. "The fly usually bites a cow and deposits its eggs beneath the skin. There, the egg develops into the larval form which, when ready, burrows its way to the outside through the hide and falls to the ground. In time it matures into a fullgrown botfly. This one happened to bite a man. It was about to come out on its own, and, of course, it would have died."

The words *imposter, sorehead, servant of Satan* spring to my lips. But now he has been joined by other scientists. They nod in agreement. I gaze from one gray eminence to another, and know the mallet-blow of glory pulverized. I tried to save the world, but it didn't work out.

No, it is not the surgeon who is God's darling. He is the victim of vanity. It is the poet who heals with his words, stanches the flow of blood, stills the rattling breath, applies poultice to the scalded flesh.

Did you ask me why a surgeon writes? I think it is because I wish to be a doctor.

2
Prewriting

I. CHOOSING A SUBJECT

A. Common Problems in Defining a Subject

Most often you don't just sit down and start writing. You face a specific problem that must be addressed in words. Many of your teachers give essay examinations and assign term papers. The campus newspaper runs a story falsely implicating your residence hall in drug traffic or your athletic team in vandalism. You are applying for a scholarship and must submit a 1000-word autobiographical statement. You are writing letters of application for employment. Your superior asks you to attend a computer seminar and to prepare a report for your colleagues. Your position includes writing memorandums to update other departments on developments in your own department. Before actually taking pen in hand, then, you must have a subject—something specific to write about—which the problem at hand precisely defines.

In composition courses, however, you are often faced with a different challenge. Teachers sometimes require essays without defining a problem or assigning a subject. Part of the assignment is for *you* to define a problem that needs addressing, to come up with a subject by yourself. And sometimes many of you—is this not so?—bring to the blank page a blank brain and draw a blank. Your mind is numb like a freezing foot and you limp along in a meaningless circle going nowhere. (Sound familiar?) You can understand the reason you are forced to choose a subject: You can't be told what to say and what to do for the rest of your life. But understanding the rationale of the assignment does not solve your immediate difficulty. To address the problem, it must be defined. How do you define a problem—choose a subject? How do you engage in the process commonly called *invention*?

27

But first, what is a subject? Many students think that unless it's *BIG*, a subject is not worth the effort. The economic effects of World War II on Western Europe. Communism in the Third World. Cancer. Abortion. San Francisco. Freedom. Bureaucracy. Crime. What do you know about such significant issues? You are against crime, bureaucracy, and cancer. Depending on your politics, you may be for or against abortion, communism, and San Francisco. You are for freedom and economics. And many of you, if we got right down to it, could not care less about World War II or Europe—Western *or* Eastern.

On these formidable issues, however, you've said all you have to say once you've stated your opinion. Anything else you write is filler, padding, malarkey. You have nothing new to say. What you know is common knowledge, and people don't want to read a lot of hooey they already know. And on any subject there are only a few ideas around. They are common knowledge, too, as familiar as French's Mustard, as the Surgeon General's warning on cigarette packs, as Smokey the Bear. And you have no new convictions to offer. There are fewer convictions around than ideas. You are either for or against—or you abstain. Besides, what difference might it make to a reader how you feel? So what? Instead of attempting an essay, then, why not cast a vote—preferably a secret ballot—and be done with it?

If you don't attempt something *BIG*, you're stuck with something small—something about as new and interesting as pavement. Your summer vacation. Your first date. Your last. Grades. Common complaints. Football. Pizza parties. Procrastination. You would settle for almost anything, yet nothing seems right. So why bother to write? Why not do everyone a favor, including yourself, and put down your pen? Silence is golden. Let us, therefore, be worth our weight in gold. Let us be utterly silent.

You have a point, a legitimate concern. You don't want to bore anyone. You don't want to be a jerk, a self-inflated windbag who drones on and on and lulls people to sleep. Fair enough. But refusing to write is not the way to remedy your concern. Write without being a windbag. *That's* the answer.

B. Find a Subject That Interests You

To find a subject of interest to readers, forget the readers and find a subject that interests you. For readers to be interested, *you* must be interested. Yet, at the beginning, perhaps you should dismiss all thought of *subject*. The word is abstract and intimidating. Instead, think of what interests you: some happening, some event—whatever comes to mind. Set your mind free—it has a will of its own—and follow its lead. Read how I follow the course set by my mind in the following:

> Follow the leader. We used to play that when I was a kid. In a lumberyard for God's sake. Scared hell out of the workers, a bunch of kids scrambling over the stacks of lumber, leaping from stack to stack, pretending they were buildings. Too dumb to realize what could happen. I loved my grandfather's tales about follow the leader. They were a lot bigger than my lumberyard episodes. A string of guys leaping off a cliff, breaking legs and arms. He was lying through his teeth, of course, to make legend, myth—the old times, the wild west, when men were real men and boys were real boys—Tom Sawyer, Huck Finn, the Lone Ranger. My kids, when they were little, three, four, five, liked to play follow the leader with me, only I was never the leader. Felt like an ass a lot, a man in his mid-thirties crawling under fences, over snowbanks, and through jungle-gyms. That was part of the point, probably—to equalize the situation— put me not *in* my place but *out* of it, in theirs.

This is called *free association*—here triggered by the phrase, "follow the leader." There may be one subject; there may be several; there may be none. It is simply the record of my mind musing, window-shopping, traveling—exploring. And the record is not an essay or a letter to any part of the world. It is a note to myself of my findings. Invention, then, is essentially a process of exploring and taking note of your findings.

Writing the actual note serves two purposes: 1) It slows down the mind as it explores, helping it focus on what catches its eye and encouraging it to speculate on origins, connections, implications; 2) it allows the mind to track itself, so it doesn't become lost in its own maze.

EXERCISES

1. Just before going to bed tonight, write a free association for 15 minutes. Forget grammar, spelling, punctuation, coherence and logic. Just free your mind and use Ruth's famous declaration as your sole guide: "Whither thou goest, I will go." *Wherever* your mind goes, tag along—but write a running account. Be as free as you like—no one else need ever see it. Then go to sleep with a clear conscience.

2. First thing tomorrow morning write a second free association for 15 minutes. Pick up where you left off or start anew. The idea is to free your mind—get it used to roaming freely.

3. Three hours later write again for 15 minutes, either continuing where you left off or starting afresh. By now, if you have really freed your mind, you'll find its behavior fascinating.

4. Three hours later continue the identical process for 15 minutes.

5. Before going to bed, read over everything you have written during the last 24 hours. Look for something you'd like to develop into a longer article. As you write once again for 15 minutes, focus on that subject. Then let it rest at least a day before taking it up again.

C. Keep a Journal

To help the mind focus and track itself, many writers keep a daily journal—a sort of professional diary—not necessarily recording what they have done that day, but what their minds do as they write the entry. For the same reasons, many teachers require students to do the same. If you have no such requirement, try it anyway. (We don't live by assignments alone. Seize the initiative! Take charge of your life!) You may be surprised by your work, how creative you are.

For instance, consider the following selection from the (unedited) journal of one of my students:

> Charlie asked me today what it was like being the only boy with three older sisters. A mess. Cant get into the bathroom. Cant get a turn on the phone. Can't get a word in edgewise. Can't hit back. Cant keep track of my razor or my tube socks or my tee shirts because theyre always borrowing them. It used to be worse though when I was little. Sometimes they would call me an animal and cage me up in the garage and throw scraps of food on the floor. The worst was when they used me as one of their dolls, when I was really little. They put their dolls clothes on me and made my face up like a doll's with lipstick and carted me around in a buggy and showed me off to the other kids in the neighborhood, the kids their age. I couldnt get out of it, I was outnumbered.

One of the best things about a journal is that it allows you a maximum of freedom with a minimum of effort. In the privacy of those pages you are totally free. You may, if you wish, defy convention, disregard rules, ignore commandments, violate taboos, break laws. Or, if you wish and if it helps, you may impose upon yourself the constraints of a courtroom, or a high mass, or a board of directors meeting. It's your journal.

Because it's yours, all yours, it's a good source of provocative subjects. This student reveals several provocative possibilities—items his mind might have missed if he had not stopped to write—and these memories deserve a second thought. There may be an interesting subject lurking in there. What else did I suffer at the hands of my three older sisters? What was the effect on my personality? Or, viewed differently, are there times when even adults turn each other into animals or dolls? "Oh, he/she's a doll!" we exclaim. What attitude does such an exclamation reveal? Do we want a doll or a person? Is there a difference? Is a doll *in the flesh* our ideal—warm and alive, yet with nothing to do but our bidding? Or do we prefer a creature with its own will, something we cannot *possess* because it is its own excuse for being? If so, do we want one that is our equal or one that is in certain respects inferior—an animal? The expression "He's an animal" is ambiguous, sometimes said in disparagement, sometimes in praise. What do we really think and feel about people who remind us of animals?

Questions, thoughts, toying with an idea—swirling it like a wine taster judging a new vintage—to decide whether to make it the subject of an essay.

The passage of mine contains several possibilities: the variations on follow-the-leader we continue to play all our lives, the reckless self-assurance of boys, the way personal history becomes legend, the postures that love can get a parent in. To determine if any is suitable for a subject, I would need to examine each as critically and patiently as I just did the student's journal.

Keeping a journal is the most effective way to explore your preoccupations, prejudices, attitudes, obsessions, passing fancies, convictions—whatever is on and in your mind. It should be a regular part of your workday, or at least of your workweek. If you find the task unappealing, consider keeping a journal as an exercise in intellectual aerobics: something that benefits your mind but only if you do it regularly several times a week. Writers are reputed to be wild, unpredictable creatures. In truth, when it comes to working, they keep hours as regular as bankers. They maintain a schedule, whether they feel like it or not, because they know the way they feel is no predictor of how they will do. Discovering treasure is not a function of feeling but of application—hard diligent effort. The excitement comes in the process: in discovering leads, following hunches, receiving insights, and finding solutions. So reserve certain times for your journal, for exploring your deep dark interiors, searching for suspects.

Then, when you locate possible suspects (for example, follow-the-leader or human dolls) shine the light squarely in their eyes. Give

them the third degree. And if they turn out to be subjects, don't let
up. Keep grilling them until you're satisfied they've given you all they've
got, so you know how you really think and feel about them.

D. Use Reverie and Analysis

I have described two processes: free association to locate ideas and
testing to determine their value. Free association is reverie: the mind
wandering over its terrain footloose and fancy-free. Testing is concentration: the mind operating consciously toward a specific goal—to
define something (in this case a subject). Testing is sometimes called
critical thought or analysis. Reverie and analysis are modes of thought.
Reverie makes connections, analysis takes things apart. The mind moves
from one mode to the other, sometimes rapidly, sometimes slowly.
Both are essential to defining a subject and to invention in general.
Now that you understand their importance, you can deliberately
use them (up to a point—the mind does have a will of its own) when
appropriate.

To persuade your mind to enter a specific mode, consider the following: To muse in the reverie of free association, begin by looking at
words in a dictionary. Glance around for those that catch your eye.
Then read about them. Don't overlook the etymologies! They are often-
times provocative. The word *subject*, for example, originally meant to
throw down or under. *Reverie* meant to wander. Free association, then,
means wandering around looking for something to throw down—to
analyze—which literally means to take apart. The entire process is a
hunt: a bloodhound's search for a scent, for a trail leading to a subject.

In addition to the dictionary, wander through basic references at
your local library: *The Reader's Guide to Periodical Literature, Winchell's Guide to Periodicals, The New York Times Index, The Monthly
Catalogue of United States Government Publications, Information Please
Almanac, Editorial Research Reports.* Ask the nearest librarian where
you can find one of these. Librarians love to help people in their searches
and researches. Then scan the subjects for something that piques your
interest. Something will. These references contain more subjects than
any one person can think of. (The government, incidentally, publishes
material about *every*thing.) While doing this, write down some of the
references. You may need them sooner or later.

You may find that looking through out-of-town newspapers helps
set your mind in motion—or leafing magazines, or listening to music,
or swimming or jogging or making love. Whatever it may be, if it gives

you something to write about, do it. Log the sights you see, the sounds you hear, the emotions you feel. Pursue your mind's fits and starts on paper. Write them down and write them out.

To set your mind on the critical path—to analyze and test the possibilities that emerge from free association—try mulling things over with friends or with anyone who may provide a different perspective, positive hints, token amendments, encouraging criticism. Indeed, talk to yourself, silently or aloud, perhaps into a tape recorder in front of a mirror (to force yourself to concentrate) as if you were on radio or television. Engage in formal dialogue with yourself on paper or with a computer. Interview yourself. Assume the roles alternately of prosecutor and defendant. Put your ideas on the witness stand; see if they talk back to you. If they do, you may have a story on your hands.

E. The Signs of a Subject

What is a good subject? How do you recognize one?

A good subject is, first, an idea that raises several peripheral questions you find interesting enough to explore and, second, an idea that you can deal with concretely: with details, facts, events, perhaps actual experience, each of which you find worthy of further exploration. If you enjoy playing racquetball—if you know the game inside out—but find it doesn't arouse your intellectual curiosity, you'd better write about something else. If you find the general idea of the stock market fascinating but have never played it, know nothing specific about it, and have neither the time nor the patience to learn—better write about something else.

If, however, you have played follow-the-leader many times and in many ways, and wonder what following and leading involve, whether the distinction always makes sense, what the complex roles of leadership and conformity mean to you and perhaps to your friends and community—when knowledge and wonder combine like that, with a neat click and a quick surge—then you know you have a subject.

Or if you have a hobby, an extracurricular activity, a friendly preoccupation—these are ready-made subjects. Think of how you spend your leisure time. Whatever your favorite pursuit, you find it fascinating and you know a good deal about it. Knowledge and wonder are combined in just the right way.

Go with your strengths, with your aptitudes, your expertise. When you have the opportunity, write about what you know and enjoy.

EXERCISES

1. Review the free associations you were assigned, looking for possible subjects. Locate three.

2. In your journal, analyze each possibility fully—perhaps two pages each—then rank them from most to least likely to succeed.

3. Share your ideas at random with a group of classmates. Ask them to rank your ideas from most to least likely to succeed. Then compare the rankings and the explanations. The goal is to determine what interests people (including yourself) and why.

F. Trust Your Own Interests

If you locate a subject, it's interesting by definition. (Did you just say that you can never find anything worth writing about? Come on. Only the dead find life a drag. You are probably thinking of readers instead of concentrating on the business at hand. Come on. Whatever interests you interests thousands, probably millions. Stamps. Sex. Stock cars. Dogs. Cats. Kitty litter. Litter along the highway. Graffiti. Soap. *The Edge of Night. Three's Company.* Two's a crowd. So forget *others.* Free your mind and follow the leader. Wherever it stops, fascinated, others will stop, fascinated too.)

G. How to Get Going on a Subject That Does Not Interest You

Let's try again. If you locate a subject, it's interesting by definition. If it's assigned, however—and if it bores you—how can you successfully engage in the process of invention? What do you do?

Don't try free association; your mind will just run away. Don't grit your teeth, close your eyes, and plunge in thrashing. You would plunge straight into resentment, anger, frustration—a state of being fatal to effective writing.

If you care about your grade and about the quality of your work, you cannot whip through an assignment in a few minutes with carefree abandon. Indifference is as fatal to effective writing as anger. If you don't care, it will show, and no one else will care, either. Murder may not always out, but in writing, carelessness, fear, and loathing are apparent in every fallacy and comma splice.

Assigned a subject that does not suit your fancy, you may postpone thinking about it. Then you get the guilts. You become testy, snarling and snapping at both friends and foes. And the longer you wait, the harder it is to begin. You've wasted so much time already, what difference will another hour, even another day make? Finally, absolutely unable to procrastinate any longer, you write in a tense, angry frenzy, knowing this *stuff* is far from your best. But there's no way out; it's too late. If only you had a decent excuse.

Sound familiar? Good writing requires time. That's why procrastination is a serious obstacle to good writing. Delay takes time too— the same time that should be used for writing.

What to do then? Whatever the subject, *get involved*. Make the subject personal. To achieve that, I have three suggestions.

First, contrive a connection between the subject and yourself: a point of relevance, an aspect that makes some difference in your life. Such a connection exists. Everything is related to everything in some manner. Poet Walt Whitman said that a leaf of grass is the journey-work of the stars. Scientist Jacob Bronowski observed that the salt in our blood is testimony of our kinship with the sea, the great mother of all life.

Football affects everyone, even those who despise the game. Its combination of complex strategy and simple brutality reflects our culture and our values. Any game—football, bridge, dungeons and dragons— raises the significant issue of games per se, their similarities to and differences from ordinary life, the needs they fulfill, the damage they do, the ambivalence they create. In the same breath we can discuss "the game of life" and declare that "life is no child's play."

Fashion is fascinating. Clothes don't *make* the woman or the man, but reveal much about their wearers. In fact, we often feel and behave differently because of our clothes. Take off your loafers and pull on some western boots. You will not only stand taller and walk differently, you may even alter your speech.

Manners often seem to be trivial considerations of form. Yet somehow they interact with morality and make a difference—sometimes a crucial difference—in the way we relate to each other. It is not *wrong* to wipe your nose with your sleeve, but to many people it *is* disgusting—more disgusting than some crimes.

We're all affected by *things* in our lives: physics, chemistry, political science, economics, business, insurance, retirement policies, investment plans, profit sharing, mortgage rates, fair housing laws, taxes, TV, MTV, day care, the ERA, the Third World, the Second, South Africa, gold, jewelry, frozen foods, thermos bottles, glass, tab-top cans, toothpaste, peanut butter, small change, big bucks, lotteries, bumper stickers, graffiti, church walls, Martin Luther, Martin Luther King, Jr., marches, drives, rent-a-cars, airline deregulation, the Boston Tea Party, rock music, Native Americans, rain dancing, fire walking, transcendental meditation, dreams, psychoanalysis, fairies and elves and gnomes and such, the Garden of Eden, the Promised Land, the Mormon Tabernacle Choir, Amway, pyramids, chain letters, franchise marketing, microwave ovens, silicon, computers, the telephone, the telephone operator, the ballpoint pen. We are touched by everything; we escape nothing. Therefore, anything and everything that we can think of or that anyone else can think of is potentially interesting if we use our imagination.

And don't say you have no imagination! You laugh at a joke, don't you? Then you have imagination, because you make leaps and connections.

To make an assigned subject interesting, use your imagination another way. Follow Hamlet's advice to his mother. "Assume a virtue if you have it not," he admonishes her; assume an interest if you have it not, I suggest to you. Act interested. Pretend to be. Throw yourself into the role completely. The line between imagination and reality can be extremely vague. We can change the way we think and feel by changing the way we act. (This is the basic principle of behavior modification therapy.) We can become the part we play: cry real tears, laugh real laughs, shout real anger, acquire real interest. Try it. It may work.

However, I hope you learn firsthand that writing can be fascinating as an end in itself, no matter the subject or the form. Whatever the requirements—a description of a technical process, an explanation of a policy, a letter of application, a presentation of sales strategy, a school bulletin, a union announcement—they are challenging. And challenges are exciting by nature.

Moreover, whatever the occasion, writing is an opportunity to put our best foot forward. Sometimes we must put our foot forward when the shoes are too tight or dyed a color we don't like. Actors are often given roles they don't prefer, but they accept them and do the best job they can—even if it means playing second banana in an underwear ad. In every profession, in every pursuit, we get stuck with tasks we'd rather not have. But the better we do them, no matter how unpleasant, the greater the satisfaction. That's a cliche, I know, but it's also a truth.

Consequently, if you're assigned a subject you'd rather not have, concentrate on the challenge. No matter the subject, pretend to be interested—as if performing on stage. And find a connection between the subject and your life, as if your life depended on it.

EXERCISES

1. From the following topics, choose the one that interests you least. Using the reference books listed earlier, gather sufficient information to write a five-minute presentation for your classmates describing your fascination with this topic.

bedspreads	sparkplugs
drinking glasses	eyeglasses
windowsills	curbs
paper clips	elastic
pencils	hog jowls

2. From the topics listed below, choose the one that seems remotest from your life. Prepare a five-minute presentation describing its relevance to you. To accomplish this, explore the library and yourself.

flannel	Paris fashions
instamatic cameras	jonquils
oxen	barbed wire
chain gangs	running shoes
whiplash	microscopes

II. DEFINING THESIS AND READER

Once you have chosen a subject or a subject is assigned, you must define a thesis to develop and a readership to address. The thesis guides your efforts; the readership determines the direction of that guidance. In other words, they provide the foundation that every successful enterprise requires: direction and purpose.

A. Define Your Thesis

The difference between *subject* and *thesis* is crucial. Before defining it, let me show it to you by citing several essays in the Reader.

In "The Santa Ana" Joan Didion's subject is the wind of that name. Her thesis is something else: "to live with the Santa Ana is to accept, consciously or unconsciously, a deeply mechanistic view of human behavior."

Yi-Fu Tuan's subject is the orientation of Chinese and Americans to the world they inhabit. His thesis is that the Chinese live in it as *place* while Americans live it in as *space*.

Gay Talese's subject is New York City. His thesis is that it is a city of things unnoticed.

C. W. Smith's subject is ironing. His thesis is that it's a pleasure.

Suzanne Britt Jordan's subject is fat and thin people (attitudes, actually). Her thesis is that fat is good, thin is bad.

Judith Viorst's subject is friends. Her thesis is that we have (and should have) various sorts of friends for various purposes.

Jacques Barzun's subject is capital punishment. His thesis is that sometimes it is fitting and proper.

The subject is the matter you write about: the thesis is the point you make about it. A thesis gives you something to do with the subject: make a case, take a position. Now the essay has a specific purpose in life and, along with that, a life of its own—drive and vigor.

Consider what an essay might be without a thesis. Joan Didion might have written on the Santa Ana forever, detailing the physics of the phenomenon from ions to sun spots, and recounting every recorded event in great detail. She would have put her readers to sleep, her publishers out of business, and her family and friends out of patience. And still her essay might go on and on—endlessly, formlessly, pointlessly.

Having a thesis, however, Didion has her massive and violent subject by the tail. Because she has a thesis, she knows how to deal with the subject—what to include and exclude, what organization to work out, what tone to take.

Thesis, then, is an element of the process and the product. You must have a thesis to write and your essay must have a thesis to work— whether your primary purpose is exploration, explanation, or persuasion.

1. Exploration

Henry David Thoreau made it his business to explore the countryside around his village at least four hours every day. He always hoped to find something new, some form of life that no one had seen there and that everyone assumed couldn't be there because of the weather, the soil, and the like. Early in his career Thoreau discovered that when he set out with nothing in particular in mind, he never found anything of note. On the other hand, when he set out with something specific in mind, he either found it or something else equally noteworthy.

Similarly, scientists don't just study stars or apes or chemistry. They explore nature by means of hypo*theses*: tentative or working theories

by which they set up specific experiments, conduct rigorous observations, and calculate reasonable inferences. In the course of their
studies, they often obtain results that require changes in the hypotheses.
But if they explored with no hypotheses, they would obtain no results.
Einstein said it's the theory that determines what we see. We can
also say it's the theory that enables us to see at all. If we looked at the
world with no idea in mind, we would see only booming buzzing
confusion. And as far as writing is concerned, any idea is better than
none.

To explore your subject with direction and purpose, you must define
a thesis right away. If the thesis is the pleasure of ironing your clothes,
you need not explore commercial cleaning operations. If the thesis is
the barbarism of capital punishment, you need not explore all the
modes of execution. If the thesis is the superiority of fat people, you
need not explore weight-loss programs.

Remember that initially the thesis is tentative, not absolute. It is not
a legally binding contract. Regard it as a hypothesis, a working theory
that you can change (or not) according to your findings.

In the essay itself, however, the thesis should be definite, even if the
essay's purpose is primarily exploratory. In "The Medusa and the Snail,"
for instance, the thesis is exactly as clear as the tale is confusing,
because that is the thesis: These two creatures utterly confuse our
understanding of the nature of self.

2. Explanation

Often the primary purpose of an essay is to explain something, not to
persuade others to believe it or to write their senators about it. Even
so, such an essay will benefit from a thesis for a reason discussed
earlier: A thesis is fuel for an essay—push, liftoff. As every lawyer and
politician and writer knows, making a case is more exciting than
explaining the facts.

In "A State of Grace," Don Ethan Miller's major purpose is to explain
the spiritual dimension of the martial arts. But look at how *he*
says it.

> . . . the martial arts have been for me a doorway into terrains of
> experience beyond the normal "limits," into other realms where the
> common assumptions about conflict and fear, effort and energy, and
> even the nature of physical reality may be overturned and completely
> reordered.

Such a claim is an implicit promise to challenge *our* assumptions
about basic things. It is a thesis, a point that Miller will have to prove.

Otherwise we won't believe it. And because the promise is intriguing and exciting, we read on.

In "Depths on the Surface" Rushworth Kidder doesn't merely describe ice skating on frozen ponds. He explains (after exploring the subject) the appeal of such skating. But he doesn't simply offer his conclusion as explanation. He presents an idea so strange it must be proved—a thesis. Read how Kidder does this.

> And as we skated that day, I began to grasp what it was that for so many years had appealed to me. It was not just that, like the skaters in a Breugel painting or a Currier and Ives print, we were carrying forward a tradition of almost classic purity, one that had changed hardly at all over the years. Nor was it simply that we were conquering the winter, turning to our advantage the dragon that defends New England from those who care only for warmth. It was more. We were, however accidentally, exploring the unknown.

The balance of the essay is a justification of his thesis.

Even if the primary purpose is not to persuade but to explain, the explanation should be constructed as a thesis. To do this, you must *have* a thesis. So define one right away. And if you determine later it must be changed, change it. But keep one on your person at all times, as you do your driver's license.

3. Persuasion

Do I need to persuade you that a thesis is central to persuasion? It is the very point you are arguing to your readers—the purpose of the persuasion. Barzun argues in favor of capital punishment. Anne Taylor Fleming argues in defense of flirting. Thomas Jefferson argues that citizens have not only the right but the duty to throw off oppressive governments and form their own. King argues that citizens have not only the right but the duty to disobey unjust laws. In persuasion the thesis is not simply the point of the subject; the thesis *is* the subject.

Remember this. When exploring the subject prior to writing a persuasive paper, be sure to review the evidence and arguments *for* and *against* the thesis. To prove a case, you are often required to disprove the opposition's. A passage from Barzun will show you what I mean.

> If I agree that moral progress means an increasing respect for human life, how can I oppose abolition [of capital punishment]?
> I do so because on this subject of human life, which is to me the heart of the controversy, I find the abolitionist inconsistent, narrow or blind. The propaganda for abolition speaks in hushed tones of the sanctity of human life, as if the mere statement of it as an absolute should silence all opponents who have any moral sense. But

most of the abolitionists belong to nations that spend half their annual income on weapons of war and that honor research to perfect means of killing. These good people vote without a qualm for the political parties that quite sensibly arm their country to the teeth. The West today does not seem to be the time or place to invoke the absolute sanctity of human life. As for the clergymen in the movement, we may be sure from the experience of two previous world wars that they will bless our arms and pray for victory when called upon, the sixth commandment notwithstanding.

Barzun, by the way, is just beginning. He spends the next several pages refuting the abolitionist position.

Another thing to remember. Review the evidence and arguments for and against the thesis with an open mind. As you explore the subject and examine your findings, you may discover you were wrong, or didn't understand, or didn't know. Determine how you really think and feel, of course. But don't press the opinion—right or wrong— simply because it's yours. If the thesis is weak on evidence and reason, admit it. You should be smart enough not to try to prove it anyway. Adopt this motto: Make the best case you can for the best thesis you can get.

EXERCISES

1. Write two theses for each of the following subjects. Make them more specific than just *for* and *against*. For example, no one is simply *for* abortion the way many are for nuclear disarmament. Briefly specify the terms or conditions of your thesis.

abortion	leash laws
three-way light bulbs	Amtrak
the ERA	required courses

2. Compare your theses with those of a group of classmates. Identify strengths and weaknesses. Note a particular problem in each thesis that the writer must address.

B. Define Your Reader

You may or may not be able to choose the type of readers you hope to write for—your readership. In either event, you must define *whom* you are going to address to know *how* to accomplish the purpose. Explaining time to school children or to physicists requires radically different approaches. Indeed, you probably couldn't *explain* time to physicists. You'd have to *explore* it by means of a hypothesis. The readers, then, not only make a difference in how you accomplish your purpose, in some instances they determine the purpose itself.

In defining your readership, you must observe three factors: experience, expertise, and attitude.

1. Experience

How old are the readers? How educated? How worldly-wise? The answers are extremely important in terms of purpose and preparation.

Let's suppose the subject is karate. More specifically, the benefits of karate. If the readers are young teenagers, you may want to convince them of the benefits of self-defense—protection against aggression. In preparation, you would search for instances when knowing karate helped particular people and not knowing it hurt. The purpose of the paper would be primarily persuasive.

If the readers are professional atheletes, there is little need to extol the virtues of self-defense. Professional athletes know all about that. You might focus instead on how karate can improve quickness, dexterity, body control, and the like. In preparation, you would search for specific information: experiments, measurements, facts, figures, expert testimony. The thesis might argue the superiority of karate over other physical disciplines.

Perhaps your readers are members of the clergy. You might focus on a psychological aspect of karate—its value as a form of meditation, as a means of attaining transcendental states. In preparation, you would analyze the significance of Zen Buddhism in the history and practice of karate. The purpose might be to explain, or persuade, or possibly even explore. A provocative thesis might address the desirability of requiring karate in the seminary.

Usually the readers won't fall into such neat, coherent groups. But as you see from the examples, you must consider the general sophistication of the intended readers. To do so, you must have *some* readers in mind. To discuss the specific physiology or the transcendentalism of karate when addressing young teenagers would be an exercise in pushing your rhetorical luck.

2. Expertise

In addition to gauging the readers' general experience, you must have an idea of how expert they are in the particulars of your subject. The less they know, the more elementary the paper must be. The more they know, of course, the more sophisticated the paper must be. A paper on karate written for a chamber of commerce requires different content and a different approach from a paper on karate written for a martial arts team.

If the readers are largely ignorant of the subject (however sophisticated in general they may be), don't dwell on technicalities. If some are necessary, present them simply and clearly. Always search for common denominators with which to explain the subject—things already known that may help readers understand. (Karate is like boxing in that. . . . Karate is like self-hypnosis in that. . . .)

If the readers are expert in the subject, they will expect a discussion of technicalities. Technicalities are their meat. You must gather fine detail and elaborate the intricate, complex structures necessary to render the detail coherent.

If the readers fall between the poles of ignorance and mastery, you must calculate just where, and adjust the preparation and approach accordingly. Often writing involves a rough approximation, and this is one of those times.

You may find this helpful: When the readers are ignorant of the subject, answer basic questions about it; when they are expert, answer sophisticated questions involving alternative explanations and possible weaknesses in your argument. In prewriting activities, then, prepare to answer the questions you expect the readers to ask and the objections they might raise as well.

3. Attitude

Consider how a group passionately devoted to the ideal of passive resistance might respond if you write on the peculiar effectiveness of a specific karate chop. Or suppose you write on the spiritual serenity karate can bring and it is read by a motorcycle gang. I don't mean to suggest that you cannot effectively make these points with such readers. But to do so requires overcoming a great deal of resistance. And determining how and securing the necessary material become major objectives of the preparation.

To understand how to do the job effectively, you must, then, determine the basic attitudes of your readers. Be aware early on that on any number of subjects the readers may have a calculable position, a stance or attitude that you can predict and that—whether you address it directly or not—you must consider in doing the subject justice.

Let's say that the purpose of the paper on the serenity of karate is to explain. If the readers are pacifists, you can simply get to work. By explaining your thesis that karate promotes peace and not violence, you will overcome any resistance you might meet. If, on the other hand, the readers are into sporting violence—if they enjoy cockfights and Australian football and war—you must, simply to get their attention, persuade them of the *value* of serenity before you can explain how to achieve it through karate (whether they want it for themselves or not).

As often as not—and maybe more often than not—the readers will have more than one basic attitude among them which must be considered. Assuming the primary purpose is not to persuade those opposed to your position—although it is reasonable to try because those who already agree with you won't be bored; on the contrary, they will approve and applaud the effort—what do you do? Anticipate the objections. Address them quickly, and move on *as if* the opposition is convinced beyond a reasonable doubt.

This point is so important, yet so subtle, that I want to show you what I mean. Although the example goes far beyond prewriting, the point in issue involves prewriting—the way you prepare. In her essay on friends, Judith Viorst begins by explaining how she once thought of friendship: all or nothing, intimate or not at all.

> In other words, I once would have said that a friend is a friend all the way, but now I believe that's a narrow point of view. For the friendships I have and the friendships I see are conducted at many levels of intensity, serve many different functions, meet different needs and range from those as all-the-way as the friendship of the soul sisters mentioned above to that of the most nonchalant and casual playmates.

Viorst acknowledges that many readers may not agree with her definition of friendship, and indicates that she understands. She once didn't agree herself. She states that she believes the view she once held is too narrow, because she now has something like a functional notion of friendship based on her experience and the experience of others. Then, whether the readers who are inclined to the narrow view have been talked out of it or not, Viorst continues *as if* they have. She has no intention of presenting a philosophical argument to convince them once and for all. That's not her purpose. Her's is a classification of the different sorts of women friends that women enjoy, and she must get on with it.

The moral is precise: Consider quickly the basic attitude of the readers. If resistance is likely, look for materials and methods to overcome it—facts, examples, anecdotes, arguments, whatever you can find. If resistance is unlikely, don't waste your time looking for ammunition. Spend it instead exploring the subject sufficiently to satisfy the friendly interest of sympathetic readers.

EXERCISES

1. Write a paragraph for an uncle explaining some aspect of college life. Rewrite it for college friends. Rewrite it for friends of the same age who have never attended college. Rewrite it for your eleven-year-old brother or sister.

2. Write a paragraph exploring a favorite activity for readers who share your passion. Rewrite it, justifying the activity to readers who might disapprove of it. Rewrite it for simultaneous presentation to both groups of readers.

III. GATHERING INFORMATION

A. Take Notes

You now have a subject that you know you can deal with, a thesis, and a readership clearly defined. Now what do you do? How do you keep the process of invention in gear?

Take notes. Take them in any form that you like—on 3 × 5, 5 × 8, or 6 × 9 cards; in bluebooks or shorthand tablets; on legal pads or scraps of paper. Use a pen, a pencil, a typewriter, or wordprocessor. Write sentences, fragments, phrases or single words. Do any of the above or—if you can think of alternatives—none. Just *take notes*. Take them sitting at your desk. Take them on the bus, in the car, in the field—whenever something comes to mind. Keep your mind's eye open at all times for information with a bearing on the purpose, the subject, the thesis, the reader. At every street and road, look right and left; cross to see what's on the other side. Then take note of what you have seen.

What kind of notes? Write down everything that pertains to the subject in the context of purpose and reader: ideas, facts, quotes, anecdotes, examples, questions. Write them out completely, if you like, or abbreviate; use shorthand, Morse code, whatever you like—so that later, when reviewing, you'll be able to reconstruct what you had in mind. For example, here's a page of notes for this book:

stylistic considerations should emphasize:
parallelism
motif
concrete intro
concrete conclusion that goes beyond summary into upshot
also the conclusion that comes full circle—and can do both
make syntax grammar form expressive of meaning—the fishing example
you and I—usage
alliteration
rhythm—*hear* your prose
most common figure of speech among young writers:
  hyperbole. Avoid.
pronoun agreement—everybody/their
effective fragments
active/passive
contractions
must play as well as work
be precise in relation to subject, not to every aspect of context
personify with extreme caution
let verbs do walking/acting—not nouns
writing as learning experience—making connections—Gestalt

Much of this probably doesn't make sense to you because it is so abbreviated, fragmentary, random, private. (If you want to see what became of these notes, read the entire book.) But that is the point, to show how informal notes can be.

When taking notes, concentrate on acquiring specific facts, examples, anecdotes, images, and the like—not on generalities. Most student writing does not suffer from a dearth of ideas but from a dearth of detail. As a matter of fact (not exaggeration) my students often feature more ideas and fewer specifics per square paragraph than a dialogue by Plato.

> In building a greenhouse several considerations must be taken into account. It must be able to withstand strong winds, snow loads, and gradual settling as well as human traffic. Materials must be able to handle more than the required amount of stress. The ridge and the eaves must be set at the proper height. The greenhouse must be located and positioned and designed so that it can obtain the most sunlight possible and maintain a stable temperature.

If some facts were forthcoming we could learn a thing or two. But they aren't and we don't. Instead we have questions. *How* do you make it strong enough? *What* materials do you use? What *is* the required amount of stress? What *is* the proper height, and *why*? *What* makes a good location? Position? Design?

This student knows his greenhouses. He just isn't sharing much of his knowledge. Consequently, we get a lot of generalities about the subject but very little specific information—and thus no reason to stay awake. For it is chiefly through detail that you stimulate interest, present proof, make the idea's case. It is said there are no new ideas under the sun. It's an exaggeration, but not by much. New ideas are rare, exceptional events, and most old ideas are common knowledge. There are, however, countless details, figures, and facts that are not common knowledge and that have the power to surprise, to inform, and to delight. That's why the point is so important it's worth repeating and remembering. So don't forget: It is chiefly through detail that you stimulate interest, present proof, make the idea's case.

Nature has created some fantastic characters, says Jean George— an idea as old as consciousness. But look at one of George's (and nature's) examples.

> The jucana, a bird of the American tropics . . . is endowed with spurs which unfold like a switchblade at the bend of the bird's wings and with which he can slash his enemies to shreds.

Another instance:

> When the ponds of Africa dry up in the arid season, the lungfish wrap themselves in mud and wait it out, sometimes for years. When the rains finally return, they resume their water life.

George produces many more examples to prove the point (the essay is in the Reader: read it), and it is the examples that keep us riveted— quite apart from whatever general point she wants to make.

Most subjects you choose will be ordinary. Consequently, the best strategy, once you have the subject in hand, is to concentrate on obtaining detail. Take notes on everything you consider pertinent. Ransack the library, friends' minds, telephone directories. If you happen across an idea, by all means jot it down. But keep on the lookout for specific, revealing details.

EXERCISES

1. Choose one of the subjects listed in previous exercises and list 25 details that pertain to it. Compare the list with those of your classmates who chose the same subject. As a group, select the 25 details

you judge most pertinent. Discuss the choices; air the disagree-ments. Thinking *about* detail helps you select pertinent detail—and helps you use it effectively.

2. Define *detail* as you understand it. Don't try to figure out the correct definition. Rather, try to figure out how the concept of detail applies to your writing situation. Compare your *private* definition with those of your classmates. Discuss differences of opinion. Try to work out a definition on which you all agree.

B. Do Research and Take More Notes

Sooner or later you will see that you need more information—facts. Do some more exploring, some more research. All writers spend long hours on research, even when they know a subject well and are explaining it in elementary terms for readers who know nothing about it. It is an integral and essential part of the process of invention. Joan Didion, for example, suffers from migraine headaches—so she knows the subject firsthand. Yet in writing about migraines for the general reader, she found it useful to do some research anyway.

> The chemistry of migraine . . . seems to have some connection with the nerve hormone named serotonin, which is naturally present in the brain. The amount of serotonin in the blood falls sharply at the onset of migraine, and one migraine drug, methysergide, or Sansert, seems to have some effect on serotonin. Methysergide is a derivative of lysergic acid (in fact Sandoz Pharmaceuticals first synthesized LSD-25 while looking for a migraine cure), and its use is hemmed about with so many contraindications and side effects that most doctors prescribe it only in the most incapacitating cases. Methys-ergide, when it is prescribed, is taken daily, as a preventive; another preventive which works for some people is old-fashioned ergotamine tartrate, which helps to constrict the swelling blood vessels during the "aura," the period which in most cases precedes the actual headache.

Clearly Didion did not have all of this information at her fingertips. She had to research it and take notes. I don't know where she found it. The information exists in many places: pharmaceutical journals, biochemistry textbooks, and the literature of psychology. But she might also have located it through several of the references I mentioned earlier: the *Reader's Guide to Periodical Literature, Winchell's Guide to Periodicals*, the *Monthly Catalogue of United States Government Pub-lications*, or the *New York Times Index*. As we see by their titles the first two are lists of articles on all manner of subjects in many magazines and periodicals. The third is a monthly list of government publications (the government publishes literature on just about everything). The last is a list of the authors and subjects in the *New York Times*, probably the most widely respected newspaper in the United States. (Two references I mentioned earlier—*Information Please Almanac* and *Editorial Research Reports*—are lists of various pieces of information and selected editorials of many major publications. The *Reports* is a valuable guide to opinion concerning the major issues of the day.)

Perhaps Didion began in the card catalogues of her local library and located the information in a particular book. Or she may have used a medical reference obtained by asking a librarian, or a physician, or a pharmacist.

The library is the major center for research; there you find information on almost everything. A good library is absolutely indispensable to the practicing writer.

But research does not mean simply reading in libraries; it means gathering information. And information exists everywhere: in laboratories, statistical studies, surveys, polls; on the street; at a friend's, an enemy's, a stranger's, a museum, a business or office. Wherever it is, go to the source. If you're writing about cars—see a mechanic. About modeling—visit an agency. About acne—talk to a dermatologist. About a chemical reaction—corner a chemist. About aging—go to a gerontologist and an old person or two. About hospitals—stay in one. About funeral homes—don't stay, take a tour. If the subject is crime, go directly to jail; do not pass through the library first to collect preconceived ideas. Wherever the information is, that is where you go to get it. Get as much of it firsthand as time permits. And always, always go to the library at some point or another to read what the experts have written. You'll be amazed at what you learn.

And remember: Wherever you do the research, take a notepad with you. Don't rely on memory. Memory is a fickle friend with interests of its own. Much that you consider major, it forgets in a flash. Much that you consider trivial or pointless, it remembers to the last detail. Play it safe. When you come across something that might prove useful, make a note of it.

Now, when it comes to researching large projects where there is a great deal of material to record and sort out and organize, most textbooks and teachers—including this book and me—recommend that you make one note only per card or page (depending on what you are using) rather than filling each page with several notes. This approach takes a little more time and a lot more paper. But when you are collating the notes, you'll be able to arrange and rearrange the information with ease and without recopying. By taking a little more time now, you save a great deal of trouble later.

Let's say you've chosen to write on the peculiar feeding patterns in nature, similar to Jean George's essay on astounding creatures. On one card or page you may note an instance you learned of from television.

> PBS documentary on Jane Goodall, Jan. 12, 1984:
> Goodall has recorded an episode of cannibalism among chimpanzees—a particular mother and one of her young (nearing maturity) kidnapped several baby chimps and ate them. This started abruptly and several months later ended just as abruptly.

Perhaps more information should be included in this note. However, you want only the information about this particular observation on one card or page. For example, the following does not belong on the same page with the chimps. It should have a page of its own.

> My aunt and uncle have a dog that eats firecrackers. When you are lighting them you have to keep him in the house so he doesn't blow his mouth up.

When the source is not personal, document it in the note. If you can't, separate the note and be sure to track down the source:

> On TV several years ago—a carnivorous plant in the Amazon forest with a blossom that gets up to 4 feet in diameter and that looks and smells exactly like rotten meat—in order to attract the flies it feeds on.

Then call your local botanist and request a reference for this remarkable flower's name and curriculum vitae. When you get it, put the information on the card and record the exact source.

Suppose you find just what you need in a book, but it's too long. Pretend it's the paragraph by Lewis Thomas describing the feeding pattern of the medusa and the snail. Your note might read:

> Lewis Thomas, "The Medusa and the Snail," in volume of same name; New York, Bantam Books, 1980, pages 3–4.
> In Bay of Naples a sea slug called nudibranch produces tiny larvae that are engulfed by a jellyfish called medusa. But instead of being digested, one of the nudibranches starts eating the medusa, and grows as the other reduces, until finally the jellyfish winds up a tiny little reproducing parasite attached near the mouth of the full-sized snail.

In making notes from printed material, you may quote, paraphrase, or both. Quote only that which is striking, catchy—that you might want to quote in your essay because it can't be improved. Paraphrase when you don't need all the information. From Thomas's paragraph, for instance, you don't need the observations about self because the subject is eating.

If you find something worth quoting, take it down exactly: word for word, puncuation mark by punctuation mark. And if you use the quote, punctuate it with quotation marks and note the source. To avoid committing plagiarism—the writer's unpardonable sin—you should also note the source for material you summarize or paraphrase.

If it seems you are taking down more information than you can possibly use, you're doing a good job. On most subjects, there is much more information than anyone can use. Writing (the next phase of this book) is essentially a process of selection. And by simply applying the law of averages, the more notes you have to select from, the greater your chances of making good selections.

All within reason, of course. There is such a thing as overdoing it, of too much of a good thing. For a two page report, you don't need 200 pages of notes: 100:1 is a ratio not of thoroughness but of paranoia.

C. Look for Revealing Detail

For most students the concept of detail is extremely troublesome. We teachers say, "Detail, detail, detail!" as if conducting drills or leading pep rallies. And you try to comply. Heaven knows you try. Yet time after time upon return of your assignment there's that frustrating legend in the margin: "Not enough detail." When the effort seems fruitless, you begin wondering what's the use.

Let me assure you the problem has nothing to do with ability. You use detail all the time in conversation without thinking about it—just as you use noun clauses without thinking about noun clauses, maintain balance without thinking about the equilibratory mechanisms in your ears, and use phonemes without being aware of phonemes. When you take pen in hand, though, language becomes conscious and deliberate. And now that you have to stop and think about it, you may find that like millions of others you don't really understand abstractly and conceptually what detail is. Therefore, you feel stuck. You don't know what to do first, much less second.

That may seem a curious paradox: that you don't grasp something you know perfectly well, well enough to do with ease and grace. But it's a paradox we live with every day. Much of what we know best we understand least. Thinking, for example. We all know how to think, how to run images and concepts and words through the mind. But we don't understand the process much at all. We have only the foggiest notion of how electrical impulses flash through the brain and then flash across the mind as images, concepts, and words. Therefore, not understanding detail doesn't prevent us from using it—any more than ignorance of the complete structure of a language prevents us from speaking it. For many activities—riding a bicycle, recognizing a voice, choosing a design—we employ a tacit knowledge that is acquired, not a formal knowledge that is learned.

Dictionary definitions of detail are of little help:

1. The act of dealing with things item by item [the *detail* of business]

2. a minute account; circumstantial story [to go into *detail* about a trip]

3. any of the small parts that go to make up something; item; particular [the *details* of a plan]

—*New World Dictionary*

Look up "specific" and you find the same sort of thing—"of a special, or particular, sort of kind" and "a distinct item or detail: particular," and so on. When I asked you for a definition, you probably came up with something resembling this. But defining in the abstract is one thing, understanding quite another. What do these definitions actually mean?

Part of the problem, I suspect, is that you simply cannot believe that anyone would ask you to put on paper the trivial stuff these definitions imply and that you include in conversations with friends.

1. Richard's white socks

2. Pamela's new roly-poly perm

3. Mr. Reynolds' bloodshot raspberry nose

4. the Smiths' old brass mailbox

This is gossip, not writing.

You're right—to a point. Readers—well, *most* readers—don't enjoy mere gossip. Writing must be informed by an idea, not just the news. Yet we still want items that make for gossip: the juicy tidbits we all relish, the perfect touches that put a subject forever in its place—

whatever the subject may be—animal, vegetable, or mineral; person, place, or thing; an event, a book, an argument. And it is precisely that kind of detail that teachers yearn for but rarely receive. Here's what we often see.

> The hot Florida nights offered as many activities as the days. But the one that most people my age enjoyed were the beach parties. No one really knew each other, but everyone was friendly because we all had something in common: we were all there to have as much "fun in the sun" as possible.

What activities? What happened at the beach parties? What all did they do? If you think the writer can't say because beach parties are too hot for paper and print, you're wrong. Not even the hottest pornography reaches 451 degrees Fahrenheit—the temperature at which paper catches fire. Now it may be true that the *writer* can't handle the lively detail without burning up with acute embarrassment. If that's the case, he should try writing about ice cream socials. The point is, if you are going to write about something, then write about it in particular. Satisfy the reader's curiosity, especially if you have managed to arouse it. A last question: How can you have "fun in the sun" in the dark of the night?

At the beginning of a semester, I often tell my students to describe a person they know by citing one fact, one telling detail. Often I hear things like: Angela is very casual; Fred is generous; George is neat; Mary is nervous, high-strung. But those are ideas. I'm asking for something physical. "Something *physical?*" they say, staring in disbelief, then looking at a loss.

But we need concrete facts, examples, anecdotes, and images to appreciate fully what someone is thinking. Casual could mean wearing Izod sweaters or sleeping on the floor. Generous could mean donating blood or offering a spouse to a friend. Neat could mean ironing underwear or merely making the bed. Nervous could mean habitually drumming fingers or picking cuticles until they bleed. The detail is the difference in the idea and in our understanding of it. For each of these ideas, moreover, I have offered only two details. Many more are possible.

Notice that not all detail is of equal value. Some is more effective because it catches the reader by surprise—it's not a tired old phrase or image the reader saw coming four blocks away—and better because it freshens the idea and defines it more precisely. Take the idea of neat: Frank makes the bed, combs his hair, trims his nails, edges the sidewalks, vacuums the garage, hangs his pictures with a carpenter's level, and color coordinates his closets. Some examples are much more informative than others. For instance, the line about ironing underwear is surprising and informative in quick and equal measure. If a man irons his underwear, you see, it goes almost without saying that he makes his bed, combs his hair, trims his nails.

Watch how a pro does it. The nineteenth-century American author, Herman Melville, describes a character in his famous story, "Bartleby the Scrivener."

> Nippers . . . was a whiskered, sallow, and, upon the whole, rather piratical-looking young man, of about five and twenty. I always deemed him the victim of two evil powers—ambition and indigestion. The ambition was evinced by a certain impatience of the duties of a mere copyist, an unwarrantable usurpation of strictly professional affairs, such as the original drawing up of legal documents. The indigestion seemed betokened in an occasional nervous testiness and grinning irritability, causing the teeth to audibly grind together over mistakes committed in copying; unnecessary maledictions, hissed, rather than spoken, in the heat of business; and especially by a continual discontent with the height of the table where he worked. Though of a very ingenious, mechanical turn, Nippers could never get this table to suit him. He put chips under it, blocks of various sorts, bits of pasteboard, and at last went so far as to attempt an exquisite adjustment, by final pieces of folded blotting-paper. But no invention would answer. If, for the sake of easing his back, he brought the table lid at a sharp angle well up towards his chin, and wrote there like a man using the steep roof of a Dutch house for his desk, then he declared that it stopped the circulation in his arms. If he lowered the table to his waistbands, and stooped over it in writing, then there was a sore arching in his back. In short, the truth of the matter was, Nippers knew not what he wanted.

You can describe things rather than people. Read how a modern writer, Rushworth Kidder, handles a familiar scene.

> Ice. It hung in spikes from the eaves. It gathered in great cobbled chunks in the downspouts. It grew in frosted thickets inside the storm windows, and rattled like broken bottles along the sidewalks, and lay in shattered panes over the places where puddles used to be.

Kidder illustrates an important point: To be original, you must provide detail to *reveal* the subject to the readers, to give them a good look so they get the picture. Kidder also demonstrates that if you pay attention to the subject, you can provide detail no less revealing than his. *You* can see that icicles hang in spikes, that frost on windows resembles thickets, and that the ice that forms on the surface of water looks like a pane of glass. So take the hint from Kidder: Pay attention and note what you see. Your readers will appreciate every bit of attention you've given.

EXERCISES

1. Take the 25 specifics you cited in the last set of exercises. On a scale of one to three (one being the highest), grade them for effectiveness. Ask some of your classmates to grade them. Compare grades. Discuss differences. (The point: to develop a sense for the kind of detail that interests, that works.)

2. Jot down 25 specifics concerning one person. Choose the five most revealing. How many of the 20 remaining can you imply from the five? In addition to the five, how many (if any) of the 20 remaining are necessary to adequately describe this person?

3. Give copies of your list to several classmates. Ask them to jot down the five they consider most revealing. Compare results. Discuss differences. (The point? Same as before.)

IV. GETTING FOCUSED

A. Work With the Specific

Textbooks and teachers usually tell you that any time now you should start "narrowing or limiting the subject." I know—I have said it myself. Beginners have great difficulty understanding this. How, they wonder, do you narrow or limit an idea? You may have wondered yourself, and for good reason. You cannot narrow or limit an idea. The idea of infinity is about the size of infinity. Limit it, and it's no longer the idea of infinity. Curiously, however, the idea of finitude is the same size. In truth, ideas have no size, no dimensions. Tape the figure of any idea and you come up with the same measurements: $0-0-0$.

But you can narrow or limit the focus. In the context of writing, focus is a metaphor, a principle borrowed from the visual arts. It means, quite simply, approaching the subject through specifics. To illustrate, let's look at a classic, E. M. Forster's "My Wood."

Forster defines the subject as "the effect of property upon the character." Now, that is a subject large enough to warrant a book (as we teachers often say to our students). So how can Forster examine this subject adequately in a relatively brief essay? The answer is implied in the very title: by examining the effect of property he owns on himself. (A "wood" is acreage in the countryside, specifically the English countryside, wooded or not.)

First, Forster says his property makes him feel heavy, reluctant to move, to change; owning property makes a person conservative. Second, owning the wood makes him wish it were larger. He wants to own more, and to own everything on it—including a bird he describes in amusing detail. In other words, owning property makes a person acquisitive. Third, owning the wood makes him want to change it—to "improve" it, as we say—even though he has nothing specific in mind. This urge he deems pseudocreative—a cheap counterfeit of genuine creativity—because genuine creativity means taking the pains to make something significant, not pottering about. Last, Forster discovers he doesn't want anyone else to have any of the blackberries on his land or to enjoy his wood in any way. He wants it all to himself. Owning property makes a person selfish.

By focusing on specific instances, we can deal with a large subject in the space of a brief magazine article. That is, in fact, what writers do. Annie Dillard writes about the fear of God by focusing on a childhood neighbor who played Santa Claus. E. B. White writes about the nature of time by focusing on a practice session at the circus. Roger Rosenblatt writes about human potential by focusing on the behavior of one man in a plane wreck. George Orwell writes about the brutality of capital punishment by focusing on one hanging. The instances that writers use may be personal or otherwise—the particular subject and the particular occasion determine whether personal experience is appropriate or not—but they are always specific.

Effective writing means dealing with the general in particular.

EXERCISES

1. List three different focuses for three of the following subjects. For each focus, list the primary purpose, the thesis, and the reader you have in mind.

nuclear energy	insecticides
aluminum	airplanes
sports	television
women's liberation	the sky
peace	money

2. List three of your own ideas for subjects. Define three different focuses for each, again specifying purpose, thesis, and reader.

3. Identify the one focus for each that you consider most interesting and promising. Ask friends to identify one focus for each that *they* consider most interesting and promising. Compare and discuss.

B. Continue to Gather More Specifics

Now that you've settled on a subject and explored it sufficiently to define a purpose, a thesis (or hypothesis), and readers, what's next? What does the process of invention entail at this point? What do you do now?

Well, now that you know exactly what you're doing, go exploring again to find the most revealing details about your subject. You want something (some *thing*) inherently interesting with which you can define with precision the idea and the problem it involves. I bought some property, and I wonder how owning it has affected me. You're searching for additional things through which you can specifically define and examine different implications and consequences of the main idea. Owning property makes me just want to sit there, loath to move or change. I feel heavy. I have become conservative. Owning property makes me want more. A bird that I assumed was mine flew next door; if I owned next door it would still be mine. I have become acquisitive. Owning property makes me want to do insignificant things to it, even though I don't know what. I've become pseudocreative. I find I don't like people picking my blackberries or using my property in any other way for their pleasure. I want it all to myself, for myself, by myself. I have become exceedingly possessive.

Or, let's use an earlier idea: follow-the-leader.

There's the lumberyard episode. There is my grandfather's episode, but that may get me into a different subject, the business of legend and truth, and I also have to decide whether I am going to use only personal examples or others as well. In junior high we used to play follow-the-leader off diving boards—that should work very well. In football we followed the lead of the quarterback, who called the plays himself. Troublemaking and hell-raising always involved follow-the-leader: there was the time we all went to school wearing our clothes inside out, and the time all the boys walked out of a class when one got kicked out, and the time we rode bicycles in the halls of the high school. Taking up smoking and drinking follows the follow-the-leader pattern. But doing good often seems to follow the pattern as well. Donating blood, doing volunteer work in hospitals or nursing homes or ghettoes, giving to Jerry Lewis and his kids, pledging to the United Fund, becoming born again—such things often take the form of fads, the in-thing to do no less than getting stoned or stealing hubcaps. Christianity itself is a follow-the-leader

sort of religion, especially in the Catholic branch. But not just Christianity—Islam, too, and others? Need to check that out. Call Schwartz
in the Religion Department.

And so on. This is not nearly complete, but it should be sufficient for
you to get the point. And although it's not complete, it still contains
more things than I can use. After all, I have yet to decide on a principle
of selection. Should I use only personal episodes? Should I use the
moral principle—good behavior and bad? Or should I focus on follow-
the-leader as political behavior? Or corporate behavior? Or military
behavior? Whatever the focus, I definitely need more specifics.

This technique is sometimes called "brainstorming," sometimes
"clustering." It involves getting ideas out of your system and down on
paper with the same pell-mell haste as free association, but with a
marked concentration on the primary subject you have defined. You
gain the wherewithal to decide on a principle of selection, a focus,
and enjoy sufficient specifics from which to choose. You may be sure
that Forster had more than four on his mind and in his notes. He chose
those four because they are particularly revealing and adequate in
number for him to make his point complete. Unfortunately, there is
no formula for adequacy. Generally, however (and this is true for every
kind of writing), figure three to five specifics for each idea. Sometimes
six or seven are necessary; sometimes two are enough. Once in a
while—if it's stunning—one is enough.

If you have a tendency to get stuck—to freeze at the first step because
you simply cannot think of what do do next—use this time to generate
more ideas and thus more detail. Let's say your initial idea focuses on
unusual forms of feeding in nature, and you have four specifics.

dogs eating firecrackers

medusas ingesting snails and snails digesting medusas

chimps eating chimps

rotten flowers eating flies

Now look into each specific for another idea.

dogs > domestic animals

medusas and sea slugs > marine animals

chimps > land animals

flowers > plants

Now, for each of those ideas dig up three or four specifics—three or four more creatures with bizarre feeding habits—and you will amass considerable material to work with.

Plants:

    1) rotten-meat flower

    2) _____

    3) _____

    4) _____

Marine animals:

    1) medusas and sea slugs

    2) _____

    3) _____

    4) _____

Etcetera:

If more is necessary, look into your latest specifics for additional ideas. Don't forget that you can always go to the library and rummage around. You can talk to friends and acquaintances, call the folks—find information wherever you can. You'll soon have exactly what you need and more material than you can use.

If you have a series of stunning specifics—as Talese does, for instance—you may want to use more than three or four. Often you can use a great many sparkling details without taxing the readers' patience or interest. If you have an incidental point—a point worth a paragraph, say, and no more—you often need no more than five specifics.

Once you have chosen the specifics, determine the order of their use. And the idea of order brings us to the subject of outlining.

EXERCISES

1. List one of the subjects and the three focuses for it that you defined in the last exercise.

    Subject: _____

    Focus 1) _____

Focus 2) _____

Focus 3) _____

Now list three specifics for each focus:

Focus 1:

    a) _____

    b) _____

    c) _____

Focus 2:

    a) _____

    b) _____

    c) _____

Focus 3:

    a) _____

    b) _____

    c) _____

2. For one of the specifics, list three ideas it suggests:

    1) _____

    2) _____

    3) _____

Now dig up three specifics for each of those ideas. Write them on note cards along with the other facts and ideas you have just listed, and keep them somewhere safe. You will probably find a use for them before the semester ends.

V. GETTING ORGANIZED

A. The Need to Organize

Textbooks and teachers sometimes urge students to prepare a formal outline before beginning to write. Many teachers require it. Students must hand in an outline for approval before writing the essay or submit an outline with their essay. We know that many students, a large majority, regard this requirement as busywork, a bother, an irritation, not a necessity. Consequently, if outline approval is required, many dash it off at the last minute. And if it must be submitted with the essay, they dash it off after completing the essay—again at the last minute. Right?

Let's face it, then. A formal outline for a short piece is not strictly necessary, not for everyone anyway, not even for most.

But textbooks and teachers have a point, too. Remember Joe Papp's remark about ideas? If you can't write yours on the back of his card, you don't know what you think. The same thing applies to larger projects: You must be able to distill them to a single outline on one sheet of paper to achieve simple conspicuous order and obvious sense. For instance, in this chapter it makes sense to discuss gathering materials first, and then to discuss their order. In this book it makes sense to discuss prewriting before writing itself and writing before rewriting. To discuss ordering before gathering, revising before writing, or writing before prewriting would make no sense—only nonsense. Yet teachers often—and I mean *often*—receive essays so disorganized they are nothing more than incoherent drivel.

> Nightmares occur toward morning. They are the most frightening of dreams. When you awake during a dream you will be able to remember it. Many people believe that nightmares are something we outgrow. They do become less frequent, but they do not disappear. Adults have more nightmares than people realize. One of the most common nightmares that appears throughout adulthood is about taking exams. Surveys taken at many schools, including Princeton and Harvard, indicate that a large percentage of students have nightmares about exams. The types of nightmares change as we grow older. Younger children usually have dreams and nightmares concerning something they are involved in, such as playing house and baseball. Old people worry about money to live on. Teenagers dream of gaining independence and establishing a career and settling down for marriage. When they get older they dream about raising the children and getting them off to college.

Not only has the author failed to establish any order, he doesn't even keep to the same subject.

But you may not have a subject with an inherent order, a logical or chronological structure that you can follow. You may, like Jean George or Gay Talese, have several examples to make a certain point or numerous facts to make a catalogue. Having no inherent structure, how do you order these items? Get them off to a rousing start; then list them in order of increasing interest. That is, to grab the readers' attention, begin with a compelling detail—a hook—next list the quietest, work your way to the most unusual, and end with a bang. Always save the best for last so you don't let down the readers with anticlimax. (You never want to let down the readers with anything.)

> Probably the most dumbfounding of nature's extraordinary creations is the horned toad of our Southwest. A herpetologist once invited me to observe one of these lizards right after it had molted. In a sand-filled glass cage I saw a large male. Beside him lay his old skin. The herpetologist began to annoy the beast with mock attacks, and the old man of the desert with his vulnerable new suit became frightened. Suddenly his eyeballs reddened. A final fast lunge from my friend at the beast and I froze in astonishment—a fine spray of blood shot from the lizard's eye, like fire from a dragon! The beast had struck back with a weapon so shocking that it terrifies even the fiercest enemy.

Thus Jean George winds up with the most dumbfounding example possible: saving the best for last.

How do you know if you have listed the items in order of increasing interest? *You can explain it.* You may not be able to explain this sort of order with the same exactitude as logical or chronological order, but you can come pretty close. At the very least, you can explain it so that it makes sense.

When it comes to writing, you don't muddle through. When you muddle in writing, you simply muddle, thrash around, stall in your tracks, and sink. To get through—through the subject and through to the reader—you must organize.

I prefer the word "organize" to the word "outline" because you may organize effectively without going through the formality of the conventional outline. You may simply list points one, two, and three. Under each number you may list items A, B, and C—or forego such designation. The particular form isn't important so long as you put things in order and *see* that you have put them in order.

B. Organize to Suit Yourself

Before beginning to write, you should have defined and arranged the major points. Most hikers in Glacier National Park or Yosemite carry a map of some kind. They also hike along a trail which has a beginning, a middle, and an end. Yet if they had to plan everything down to the last tree on the trail and tinkle in the bushes, I doubt many of them would have the time or the interest to hike. Nevertheless, as every hiker knows, preparation is everything. Plan ahead as much as you can without cramping your style.

It's a matter of psychology, not principle or logic. On each writing occasion, you must find out what works best for you. Sometimes you must organize in advance extensively, as if preparing a military campaign. Other times you can virtually improvise—you know so well what you have to say and how you ought to say it. Most of the time you'll be somewhere between the two extremes.

Each time out, then, calculate the extent to which you must plan ahead to do the best work. Then do it.

Whatever your needs are, however, you must have defined and arranged the main points before you begin writing. That *is* a matter of principle. You can begin a journey with no idea where you are going. You can, if you like, close your eyes and spin around until you get so dizzy you fall, and then take off in the direction your head is pointing. You can make whim your guide: go wherever you like, as far as you like, as long as you like, and to no end—for no purpose except the going. But you can't expect many people to go along, to follow your lead and enjoy your journey, your whimsies through time and space. They have their own journeys to take, their own whims to follow, their own things to do.

Every piece of writing is a journey of sorts—you saw that one coming, didn't you?—and to ensure readers go along, you have to take them somewhere they want to go and by a route they want to travel. And the trip must have a purpose they find significant. People resent having their time wasted; don't waste the readers' time by not knowing where you're going. Respect them as you expect other writers to respect you (the Golden Rule of prose). Give them solid reasons for taking the time and trouble to go along with you on the trip. Have a route and destination in mind. Before you begin, define and arrange the main points simply, sensibly, obviously. And whenever you deal with the minor points and details—in advance or as you go—define and arrange them the same.

C. Be Accountable for Your Organization

You may wonder how to determine if you have achieved clear and simple and sensible organization. I'll tell you: You know you have achieved effective organization if you can say, simply and clearly, what it is and why. You should be able to write the order and its rationale on the back of Joseph Papp's card. This applies to the minor points as well. When finished, you should be able to account for the structure of the piece—letter, report, memorandum, whatever its form and function—down to the last detail: why each thing is where it is and not somewhere else. If you cannot, you don't really know what you're doing—much less why. Because writing effectively means you know exactly what you're doing—and why.

The beauty of the conventional outline is that you can see the structure, large and small, and quickly determine if you can account for it.

I.
   A.
   B.
      1.
      2.
         a.
         b.
            (1)
            (2)
            (3)
               (a)
               (b)
   C.
II.

Note that each subdivision requires at least two parts. Otherwise there is no need to subdivide. Theoretically it is possible to subdivide further. But I have rarely seen the need to go even as far as I have. By the time you get to (1) and (2), you virtually have the piece itself. Ordinarily it is only for longer pieces—for monographs and books—that you may need to extend the conventional outline to the point of parentheses.

As a way of checking the structure's coherence or lack thereof, outlining may prove as useful after you have written as before.

EXERCISES

1. Use the focus for which you generated specifics in the last exercise. Arrange the ideas and their specifics. Then write a quick justification for the arrangement. (I told you that you might find them useful.)

2. The following paragraph is from a student paper. Explain what is wrong with its organization. Rearrange it, and explain the principle of the rearrangement:

Strength is a key factor in motocross. The entire arm works in operating the bike. The upper body maintains control of a two-hundred-
pound motorcycle while going up to seventy miles per hour over
jumps, bumps, and hills. The wrists work the throttle and support
the arms while steering. The fingers work the brakes and clutch.
The grip remains tight throughout the race, tiring even the strongest
forearms. The biceps, triceps, and shoulders are the most important
muscles in steering. They also absorb the shock transmitted through
the front of the bike.

D. Play It Loose

Journalist John McPhee specializes in writing best-selling books on all
sorts of subjects. Samples of his work are found in *The John McPhee
Reader* by William Howarth, who, in the "Introduction," describes at
length McPhee's elaborate method of composition. In his discussion
of McPhee's technique of organization, Howarth observes that "writers have infinite options for order, and McPhee delights in playing any
that do not violate his story's 'logic.'" Howarth then explains what
this means specifically:

> A book on tennis can imitate the game's back-and-forth, contra-
> puntal action; but it could also resemble a mountain climb, with an
> ascent, climax, and descent arranged in pyramidal form. The choice
> is McPhee's: either find an idea for order *in* the material or impose
> one *upon* it, selecting what Coleridge called the "organic" or
> "mechanic" principles of structure. McPhee has experimented with
> both: *Oranges* follows the life cycle of citrus fruit, while *Encounters
> with the Archdruid* was planned *a priori*, as a matrix into which he
> poured the molten confrontations of Brower and company. . . . McPhee
> wants to create a form that is logical but so unobtrusive that judg-
> ments of its content will seem to arise only in the reader's mind.
> And he also wants to stay loose himself, free to encounter surprises
> within the pattern he has formed.

There's a moral in this passage, and it applies to you.

Always remember that the outline you prepare before writing, no
matter how detailed, is not a binding contract you must strictly adhere
to. It is just a set of notes. As you get into the subject, you may, like
McPhee, realize things about it that you had not seen earlier. Like
McPhee, you may discover a better route to the destination. If so, revise
the itinerary—the organization—by all means. No one will sue you
for breach of contract. No one will invoke Islamic law and cut off
your hand or perform a lobotomy. No one will even know. But remem-

ber to make a note of the revision so you can keep track of what you're doing.

To write effectively you must know where you are going, where you are, and where you have been.

JAMES E. MILLER, JR.

The Maze of Many Tongues

A professor of English at the University of Chicago, Miller has written numerous books on various writers and sundry aspects of literature, among them Quests Surd and Absurd: Essays in American Literature *(1967) and* Word, Self, Reality: The Rhetoric of Imagination *(1972), from which the following piece is taken. In it Miller explains with eloquent precision the role of language in all we are and do.*

We live surrounded by language as by air, taking it in and releasing it as naturally as we inhale and exhale. We are bombarded on every side, assaulted at every hour, by language demanding, commanding attention; and we are forced to pick and choose, to tune in or tune out, to see and read or turn and depart, to say yes or no or maybe, to argue or agree or remain suspended in doubt. We thread our way through the maze of many tongues; we make money or we make love, we encounter the world, which shapes us as we shape it, we know life as it comes to know us—all through words, words, words.

Words do not simply accompany experience; more frequently they *are* the experience, or are its primary content. We live surrounded by language, inside and outside us. It can strangle and suffocate us, or it can connect and link, strengthen and renew us. Language, then, is far more than mere communication; it is indeed a kind of creation. With it we make our world and ourselves. Through our daily linguistic encounter with the world, we proclaim our identities, shape our lives, and (in some small or big way) leave our impress on the world. . . .

If we live daily in an external chaos of language which forces us to select and arrange, to place in context and put in order, we also feel something of the chaos of language churning inside use, welling up from depths, darting in from the dim sidelines, appearing and disappearing with a bewildering and uncontrollable rapidity. As we must come to terms with the language chaos without, so we must adjust to the chaos of language within. But we can do more than adjust. We can look upon the ceaseless flow of language within us as one of our most precious resources. We can view it as a great flood rolling rapidly along, floating on and in its waters the treasures of the world, to be snatched out and put to creative use.

All of us live rich inner linguistic lives, lives fantastically full of imaginative leaps and spurts; of language tangles that mass suddenly like barbed wire balls and barriers and dissolve as suddenly by a "pool" of fragmentary fantasy; of language explanations that build laboriously on successive solid bases that rise higher and higher to sway in linguistic breezes that laugh at the seriousness and the solidity, and that puff and puff until the great, ponderous, massive structure of pretentious thought comes crashing, tumbling down to disappear into the crevices and corners of the psyche; uninhibited emotional language that begins to grow in a shapeless, inflated mass, rising and proliferating in lumps and bumps and expanding to a huge suffocating monstrosity, only to be punctured by a sharp linguistic splinter of ridicule, to collapse with a great outrush of air and shrieking sound, and to drip finally away into the darkness beyond consciousness; of language games and language play, of language jokes and language hoaxes, of language hysteria and language outrage, of language sense and language nonsense.

All of this rich inner linguistic life goes on without our willing or wanting, encouraging or directing it. It is ours by right of being human, of being conscious and aware, of living and breathing in a linguistic environment. And it is an important part of what makes us individual human beings, each one different from all others. The interior stream of language is never duplicated from person to person, and never duplicated in the same person from day to day. Like a kaleidoscope of constantly shifting shapes and colors, with no single frame remaining for more than a moment, the linguistic flow offers a complex of ideas, words, phrases, and anti-ideas for a flash of contemplation, and then rushes on to another complex, the old one breaking into parts which rearrange or flow on into the deeper reservoirs of self. . . .

When we set forth in search of an idea, or set of related ideas, what we really begin with is a muddle—that eternal flow of irrational association through the mind. Where in the midst of all those vaguely related impressions and responses, fragmentary feelings, and aborted ideas—where is belief, commitment, conviction? Where indeed? If we are suddenly asked our opinion about God, or our view of socialism, or our thinking about the police, we can pluck at once something floating by in the stream and provide an answer, or we can await the surging to the surface of some old attitudes conditioned by forgotten or only dimly remembered experiences and offer the questioner sets of words and phrases whose meaning remains unexamined and possibly incoherent. Or we can let the question become a seine, arrange it in the stream for its catch, and then examine and sort through what the net has caught, using the experience as a way of finding out what we *really* think, what we *really* believe, what and who we really are, and what we might come to think and believe. Such examining or sorting through can no doubt be painful, as when we discover in the net an unrealized prejudice or irrational hatred; or it can be pleasant, as when we find unexpected generosities and impulsive kindliness. But painful or pleasant, the experience must prove valuable as a process of rediscovery and reshaping of the ever changing, always becoming, enigmatic self. . . .

To live an aware life, the individual must begin with an awareness of self. He must conduct a running examination and periodic reexaminations of the self—in language, the medium of furthest reaches, deepest diving, most labyrinthine windings. The sorting through might well begin with the ordinary, everyday experiences of life. A diary or journal enables one to sift through and evaluate experiences, as well as come to understand them and their significance—or insignificance. Most of us do this sifting and evaluation in moments of reverie or in that state of mental vagabondage just before sleep. There is some (even great) advantage, however, in subjecting ourselves to the discipline of written language, in which the vague and the mushy and the muddled must give way to the specific, the firm, the clearly formulated.

For writing *is* discovery. The language that never leaves our head is like colorful yarn, endlessly spun out multicolored threads dropping into a void, momentarily compacted, entangled, fascinating, elusive. We have glimpses that seem brilliant but quickly fade; we catch sight of images that tease us with connections and patterns that too-soon flow on; we hold in momentary view a comprehensive arrangement (insight) that dissolves rapidly and disappears.

Writing that is discovery forces the capturing, the retrieving, the bringing into focus these stray and random thoughts. Sifting through them, we make decisions that are as much about the self as about language. Indeed, writing is largely a process of choosing among alternatives from the images and thoughts of the endless flow, and this choosing is a matter of making up one's mind, and this making up one's mind becomes in effect the making up of one's self. In this way writing that is honest and genuine and serious (though not necessarily without humor or wit) constitutes the discovery of the self. It is not uncommon, before the choices are made, before the words are fixed on paper, to be quite unsure of which way the choices will go. Most people have experienced the phenomenon of their opinions or feelings changing, sometimes markedly, in the process of writing a paper which forces confrontations with language and choices among expressions. All people have experienced the clarification of their views and persepctives as they have worked through the process of placing them on paper. It is not at all unusual to find an individual who is uncertain and unclear about his feelings on a subject or an issue, but who, on discovering his attitude in the process of writing, becomes committed, often dedicated, and sometimes even fanatical: he has come to know himself. When this happens the individual is not being insincere, but is simply experiencing the discoveries of writing—discoveries that are often surprising and frequently exhilarating.

WILLIAM CARLOS WILLIAMS
How to Write

> *A practicing obstetrician who spent his life in Rutherford, New Jersey, Williams is one of the major writers in twentieth-century American literature. He wrote in virtually every genre—poetry (especially poetry, but also), fiction, drama, history, criticism—and he won virtually every major American literary award. In this essay on writing he stresses the happy play of spontaneity as a way of getting going.*

One takes a piece of paper, anything, the flat of a shingle, slate, cardboard and with anything handy to the purpose begins to put down the words after the desired expression in mind. This is the anarchical phase of writing. The blankness of the writing surface may cause the mind to shy, it may be impossible to release the faculties. Write, write anything; it is all in all probability worthless anyhow, it is never hard to destroy written characters. But it is absolutely essential to the writing of anything worth while that the mind be fluid and release itself to the task.

Forget all rules, forget all restrictions, as to taste, as to what ought to be said, write for the pleasure of it—whether slowly or fast—every form of resistance to a complete release should be abandoned. . . .

At such a time the artist (the writer) may well be thought of as a dangerous person. Anything may turn up. He has no connection with ordered society. He may perform an imbecility or he may by a freak of mind penetrate with tremendous value to society into some avenue long closed or never yet opened. But he is disconnected with any orderly advance or purpose.

It is now that artists stoutly defend themselves against any usefulness in their art. And it makes no difference whether it is a treatise on mathematics or a poem that is being written. *While* it is being written, as far as possible, the writer be he mathematician or poet, must with a stored mind no doubt, must nevertheless thoroughly abandon himself to the writing in greater or less degree if he wishes to clinch his expression with any depth of significance. . . .

But once the writing is on the paper it becomes an object. It is no longer a fluid speaking through a symbolism of ritualistic forms but definite words on a piece of paper. It has now left the region of the formative past and come up to the present. It has entered now a new field, that of intelligence. I do not say that the two fields do not somewhat overlap at times but the chief characteristic of the writing now is that it is an object for the liveliest attention that the full mind can give it and that there has been a change in the whole situation.

It is this part of writing that is dealt with in the colleges and in all forms of teaching but nowhere does it seem to be realized without its spring from the deeper strata of the personality all the teaching and learning in the world can make nothing of the result. Not to have realized this is the greatest fault of those who think they know something of the art.

All that the first phase of writing has accomplished is to place its record on the paper. Is this valuable, is it worthless? These questions it cannot answer and it is of no use for the poet to say: This is what *I* have done, therefore it is excellent. He may say that and what he has done may be excellent but the reasons should be made clear and they involve the conscious intelligence.

The written object comes under the laws of all created things involving a choice and once the choice has been made there must be an exercise of the will to back it. One goes forward carefully. But the first step must not be to make what has been written under a quasi-hallucinatory state conform to rules. What rules? Rather the writing should be carefully examined for the new and the extraordinary and nothing rejected without clear reason. For in this way the intelligence itself is corrected.

WILLIAM L. HOWARTH
The Method of John McPhee

Howarth is a professor of English at Princeton University. An expert on Henry David Thoreau—his publications include Thoreau in the Mountains *(1982) and* The Book of Concord: Thoreau's Life as a Writer *(1982)—Howarth has also edited* The John McPhee Reader *(1976) and contributed a number of articles to* National Geographic. *The following, taken from the "Introduction" to the McPhee Reader, is not a definition of the method you should use in writing but an illustration of the amount of detailed labor that writing usually involves and that professional writers are willing to do—and therefore that you should be willing to do.*

Travel occupies a large portion of McPhee's early work on a project. Not overly fond of junketing, however, he has logged only whatever mileage his stories have required. He prefers trains or cars over planes; a car with canoe strapped on top is his ideal vehicle. In the car he often takes along a tape player and several cassettes of his favorite Mozart or Brahms. When he arrives at a wilderness site, his ears and spirit are well massaged. Work has confined him largely to the eastern United States, north and south, although books on David Brower and Ted Taylor entailed journeys to the far West, as did "Ruidoso," a short piece on the world's richest horse race, held annually in New Mexico. Across the Atlantic he has concentrated on England and Scotland, but "Templex," a profile of the travel writer Temple Fielding, required a trip to Fielding's home in the Balearic Islands east of Spain.

When McPhee conducts an interview he tries to be as blank as his notebook pages, totally devoid of preconceptions, equipped with only the most elementary knowledge. He has found that imagining he knows a subject is a disadvantage, for that prejudice will limit his freedom to ask, to learn, to be surprised by unfolding evidence. Since most stories are full of unsuspected complexity, an interviewer hardly needs to *feign* ignorance; the stronger temptation is to bluff with a show of knowledge or to trick the informant into providing simple, easily digestible answers. Neither course is to McPhee's liking; he would rather risk seeming ignorant to get a solid, knotty answer.

As a result, some of his interviewees have mistakenly believed he is thick-witted. At times his speech slows, his brow knits, he asks the same question over and over. When repeating answers, he so garbles them that a new answer must be provided. Some informants find this manner relaxing, others are exasperated; in either case, they talk more freely and fully to him than they normally would to a reporter. While McPhee insists that his air of density is not a deliberate ruse, he does not deny its useful results. Informants may be timid or hostile, unless they feel superior or equal to their interviewer. By repeating and even fumbling their answers, McPhee encourages people to embroider a topic until he has it entire. In an ideal interview he listens without interrupting, at liberty to take notes without framing repartee or otherwise entering the conversation.

McPhee's stories often develop from interviews with a principal informant, a strong personality who provides skeletal framing for the work. Finding this character may be an act of serendipity; in *The Pine Barrens* he accidentally met the indispensable Fred Brown, who knew all the people and nameless sandy roads of his region. Profiles built around a single character, like Frank Boyden or Thomas Hoving, are inevitably more planned from the outset; but in the cases of Ted Taylor and Henri Vaillancourt, McPhee was led to his central figure on the advice of informants, who play minor roles in the stories. He never uses tape recorders when interviewing, for they inhibit some people and are too subverbal for his purposes. The writing process must begin with *words*—a scrap of talk, bits of description, odd facts and inferences—and only a pencil and notebook will answer these needs with literacy and economy.

In some interviews he may play mental chess, anticipating answers or plotting questions, but usually he builds on what he has already seen and heard. Although he writes in a clear, left-handed script, the notes are unintelligible to anyone but himself. Yet they are not indiscriminate jottings; items entered in a notebook are likely to get into his final text as well. McPhee has a passion for details, for they convince readers that he deals in actualities. Added to his journalist's reverence for facts is a novelist's propensity for symbols. His task is to burnish objects until they become reflectors of character and theme. Instead of sermonizing on thrift or prodigality, he notes that Donald Gibbie's teapot is plugged with fourteen wood screws, or that the light in Lt. Arthur Ashe's closet at West Point is always burning.

By examining things as they are, he converts familiar objects into *synecdoches*, mere particles of experience that represent its totality. Oranges seem less ordinary when McPhee has recited their botany and history. In writing about basketball, he wanted to develop "a sense of the game itself" around Bill Bradley by learning and projecting the player's knowledge. He modestly credits Bradley with the book's power of articulation, yet creating a true replica of his informant's talk actually demanded great artistry, rather like a ventriloquist's. In *The Deltoid Pumpkin Seed* McPhee more boldly pulls the narrative strings—his climax reports the inner thoughts of a test pilot in a tense situation—but always with an uncanny fidelity to outside facts like air speed, stability, angle of attack, and rate of climb.

When he starts to hear the same stories a third time, McPhee stops interviewing, returns to Princeton, and begins the tortuous process of composition. His working methods vary according to a project, but some steps are fairly constant. He first transcribes the notebooks, typing entries in order, occasionally adding other details or current thoughts as he goes. He likens this process to a magnet's attraction of iron filings; as the notes take shape, they draw from him new ideas about placement, phrasing, or possible analogies. When finished, he may have a hundred typed sheets of notes, enough to fill a large spring binder. He makes a photocopy of the original set and shelves it for later use. He then reads and rereads the binder set, looking for areas he needs to flesh out with research and reading at Firestone Library. The reading produces more notes, the notes more typed pages for his binder. Finally, he reads the binder and makes notes on possible structures, describing patterns the story might assume.

While its structure is forming, or when he senses how the story may end, McPhee often writes out a first draft of "the lead," a term journalists use to describe openings. In newspaper writing the lead is usually a single-sentence paragraph, designed to impart the classic who-what-where particulars of a story. In McPhee's work the lead is longer (fifteen hundred to two thousand words), more dramatic, yet rather more oblique. It establishes a mood, a setting, and perhaps some main characters or events, but not in order to put the story in a nutshell or even to hint at its full dimensions. One of his best leads is in "Travels in Georgia," where he manages to convey tone, style, characters, and theme in a few dramatic actions. Three people are riding in a Chevrolet across Georgia's back roads. They share some "gorp," exchange good-humored insults, and halt to eviscerate a turtle lying dead on the road. The action begins *in medias res* and continues without flashbacks or helpful exposition for several pages. When readers finally hit a backward loop, they already have a subliminal sense of who-what-where, and fulfilling this expectancy becomes McPhee's primary challenge in planning the rest of his story.

Having read the lead via telephone to an editor at *The New Yorker*, he goes back to the binder and begins to code it with structural notes, using titles like "Voyageurs," "Loons," or acronyms—"GLAT," "LASLE."

These are his topics, the formal segments of narrative, which he next writes on a series of index cards. After assembling a stack, he fans them out and begins to play a sort of writer's solitaire, studying the possibilities of order. Decisions don't come easily; a story has many potential sequences, and each chain produces a calculus of desired and undesired effects, depending on factors like character and theme. When he has the cards in a satisfactory arrangement, he thumbtacks them to a large bulletin board. The shade of Mrs. Olive McKee, his high-school English teacher, smiles upon this array. McPhee defines the outline that finally emerges, in deference to her training, as "logical," but its logic is of no ordinary, abecedarian variety, A to Z or 1 to 10.

Cards on the board, committed to their structure, he next codes the duplicate set of notes and then scissors its sheets apart, cutting large blocks of paragraphs and two or three-line ribbons. In a few hours he has reduced the sheets to thousands of scraps, which he sorts into file folders, one folder for each topical index card on the bulletin board. These folders are pre-compositional skeletons of the narrative segments he will refine when writing a first draft. With the folders squared away in a vertical file, he is ready to write. A large steel dart on the bulletin board marks his progress. He stabs the dart under an index card, opens a folder, further sorts scraps and ribbons until this segment also has a "logical" structure. Then, without invoking the muse, he begins to type his first draft, picking up where the lead ends. When he finishes a folder, he moves the dart, gets the next folder, sorts it out, and continues to type.

Outlined in this fashion, McPhee's writing methods may seem excessively mechanical, almost programmatic in his sorting and retrieval of data bits. But the main purpose of this routine is at once practical and aesthetic: it runs a line of order through the chaos of his notes and files, leaving him free to write on a given parcel of work at a given time. The other sections cannot come crowding in to clutter his desk and mind; he is spared that confusion by the structure of his work, by an ordained plan that cannot come tumbling down. The strategy locks him in, gives him no easy exits from the materials at hand, which he must confront with that humorless partner, the typewriter.

Structural order is not just a means of self-discipline for McPhee the writer; it is the main ingredient in his work that attracts his reader. Order establishes where the writer and reader are going and when they will arrive at a final destination. As the reader begins a piece, he can be certain that McPhee always knew how it would end. He also knew where the center was, and how that middle would span its opposite structural members. At the center of *The Pine Barrens* stands a chapter on Chatsworth, "The Capital of the Pines," and Chatsworth itself stands but six miles from the region's geographical center. The dead-even spot of *Levels of the Game* is not at dead center, however, but twenty pages from the end. Ashe and Graebner have each won ninety-three points at that moment; McPhee rushes on to a swift denouement—"the next four points they play will decide it all." His closing chapters are usually antiphonal, setting poignant echoes from the past against ominous future rumbles. New Jersey's wild, legendary pines steadily shrink before the press of urban development. The fresh citrus market of old Florida wanes, a booming industry in concentrate rises. Atlantic City crumbles, but Monopoly goes on forever. One of his best endings is in *Encounters with the Archdruid*, where Brower and his opponent Dominy ride through the Colorado River's Lava Falls, their ceaseless quarrel silenced momentarily by the roar of the pounding water.

McPhee is a craftsman; he understands that his work must always have inherent form. A potter knows that, and so do carpenters; it was Aristotle who said writers should have a similar goal. But writers have infinite options for order, and McPhee delights in playing any that do not violate his story's "logic." A book on tennis can imitate the game's back-and-forth, contrapuntal action; but it could also resemble a mountain climb, with an ascent, climax, and descent arranged in pyramidal form. The choice is McPhee's: either find an idea for order *in* the material or impose one *upon* it, selecting what Coleridge called the "organic" or "mechanic" principles of structure. McPhee has experimented with both: *Oranges* follows the life cycle of citrus fruit, while *Encounters with the Archdruid* was planned *a priori*, as a matrix into which he poured the molten confrontations of Brower and company. He has a certain preference for mechanic form, since it arises from human logic, but he trusts the organic principle enough not to condone formal manipulation for its own sake. Too much shuffling of those cards leads to fussy and baroque patterns, reflecting the self-indulgent mind of their maker. Yet he is also wary of simple organicism, where subject matter dictates a work's form. The story of a horse race need not run in an oval, nor must a canoe trip curve at its ends—those limited formal objectives are dull and pious, like the "shaped" verse of seventeenth-century poets.

McPhee wants to create a form that is logical but so unobtrusive that judgments of its content will seem to arise only in the reader's

mind. And he also wants to stay loose himself, free to encounter surprises within the pattern he has formed. He is quite willing to manip-
ulate contexts; in recounting Thomas Hoving's discovery of an ivory
cross, McPhee cuts and reshapes time as though he, too, were a carver
in ivory. In *The Deltoid Pumpkin Seed* he repeatedly digresses from the
story's forward motion; his aim is to suggest an experiment in progress, lurching ahead ten yards and then around in circles. The pattern
makes readers oscillate, too, between serious and satiric estimates of
the experiment's probable fate. Despite his attraction to making these
forms, he never trims evidence to fit a narrative pattern. When trouble
begins on a canoe trip, "it comes from the inside, from fast-growing
hatreds among the friends who started." That pattern an artist cannot
control; McPhee accepts it with the "logic" of an athlete who respects
the impartial rules of his game.

Writing a first draft is painful work for any writer, whether it moves
like lightning or like glue. McPhee spends twelve-hour stints at his
office, not writing constantly, but "concentrating" and distilling his
research into prose. Some authors overwrite and later boil down; he
culls before ever typing a phrase. He likens this method to the sport
of curling, where great effort is spent sweeping the ice clean to advance
each shot. With writing comes the need for endless decisions, mostly
on what *not* to say, what to eliminate. The process is nerve-racking
and lonely. His family sees less of him, he also cuts off most visitors
and phone calls. Sometimes he talks to editors or friends about problems, but then generally follows his own counsel. Facing the typewriter for long stretches, he generates excess energy like a breeder
reactor. A fly buzzing at sun-struck windows is not more manic, and
often hard physical exercise is a welcome distraction. Tennis, squash,
and basketball are favorite outlets; he professes to play at a level that
"attracts ample company and no attention." In fact, he is capable of
great intensity on the court, but he dislikes opponents who are arrogant or childish. Arthur Ashe plays in McPhee's preferred style, unpre-
dictably full of contours and strata. Writing is the same sort of game:
he has spent a long time learning to move *against* a habitual thought
or phrase, which is always the easiest, oldest rut to follow.

The resulting prose style, rare in modern journalism, is fresh, strong,
unaffected, and yet entirely idiosyncratic. His phrases and sentences
come in many guises. A basic mode is simple declaration, arranged
in strings of laconic grace: "Every motion developed in its simplest
form. Every motion repeated itself precisely when he used it again."

This description of Bill Bradley also describes McPhee's prose: taut, impersonal, yet carrying values like endurance, precision, solitude, success. He can write with eloquence, whether on his own or by hearing and reporting a character like Tom Hoving, who talks of his adolescence in a kind of poetry: "At noon, we ate sandwiches and field tomatoes, and drank iced tea; then we slept off lunch in the cool earth of the corn furrows. The corn had a kind of mystery. You were out there and it was very high, all around you." On his students' papers at Princeton, McPhee often writes in the margins: "Busy." The terse comment defines that clarity and purity for which he constantly strives. Nothing could be less "busy" than his description of Havasu Canyon, a chain of deep, cold pools set amid baking desert scenery: "The pools were as much as fifteen feet deep, and the water in them was white where it plunged and foamed, then blue in a wide circle around the plunge point, and pale green in the outer peripheries." A good part of his style rests on knowing the professional "lingo" of a subject. He masters its vocabulary and syntax, even the jargon of atomic destruction—ploot, shake, jerk, kilojerk, megajerk. "A cross-section for neutron capture was expressed in terms of the extremely small area a neutron had to hit in order to enter a nucleus—say, one septillionth of a square centimetre—and this was known as a 'barn.' " But mostly the prose succeeds because its imagery is solid and expressive. The images do not just profess his values; they incarnate them. Here is a description of Clark Graebner's neighborhood: "The houses of Wimbledon Road appear to be in the fifty-to-seventy-thousand-dollar class and almost too big for the parcels of land allotted to them. They are faced with stratified rock, lightened with big windows, surrounded with shrubbery, and lined up in propinquous ranks like yachts at a pier."

Persistent good humor—of course the Graebners would live on "Wimbledon Road"—is another strong aspect of McPhee's style. He can paint a serio-comic scene, like the unforgettable Carranza Day ceremony in *The Pine Barrens*, replete with an Army band, beery Legionnaires, and a speaker who "had recently spent 'an unprecedented hour with the President of Mexico.' " The events are explicit yet improbable; their hilarity precipitates from a wicked trace of acid. Certain touches of *The New Yorker*'s elegance often grace his witty lines. Like the magazine, he uses trademark names—L.L. Bean, Adidas, The Glenlivet—but not to sell shoes or whiskey. Names specify a scene, sharpen the focus of his observation. This fascination with names produces a long monologue in *The Crofter and the Laird:* two full pages of Gaelic place names, each with an English translation, like "Sguid nam Ban Truagh (the Shelter of the Miserable Women)."

His best jokes are little asides that puncture a character's hyperbole. One chap, awestruck at having met David Brower in the desert, sparks McPhee's fire: "I wondered if the hiker was going to bend over and draw a picture of a fish in the sand." Later on, the name of Upset Rapid rests heavily on his companion rafters' tongues: "People say it is as if they were being wheeled toward it on a hospital cart." "Travels in Georgia" has an unusual touch, an ironic motif established by the repeated acronym, "D.O.R." Carol Ruckdeschel, an environmental biologist, collects specimens of animals accidentally killed by autos and found Dead on the Road, or "D.O.R." Barely explained in the story's lead, McPhee gradually transfers "D.O.R." to other contexts, like a traffic jam around Newark Airport: "thousands and thousands of murmuring cars, moving nowhere, nowhere to move, shaking, vibrating, stinking, rotting, *Homo sapiens* D.O.R." By the end of his piece, the joke has become a powerful emblem of cultural decay: "D.O.R. gas station. It was abandoned, its old pumps rusting; beside the pumps, a twenty-year-old Dodge with four flat tires." In his moments of greatest hilarity, McPhee divines extreme analogies that provoke shock, laughter, and truth. One scene in *The Deltoid Pumpkin Seed* depicts John Kukon's frantic efforts to win a model airplane race. With time running out, he must find some means of gaining greater speed for a tiny aircraft. In his equipment box are four bottles of high-energy fuel, and one is the ultimate secret weapon: "Blend 4 had never been used. Kukon had never actually expected to use it. He had conceived of it as a fuel for a situation of extreme and unusual emergency. Its characteristics were that it would almost certainly destroy the engine that burned it, but meanwhile the engine would develop enough thrust to drive a sparrow to the moon."

Moving beyond a first draft, McPhee generally picks up speed. He makes few changes in his original structure, mostly just prunes sentences and polishes their style. The laborious planning and composing pay off here; his hardest stretches of work are over. A typist makes clean copies and off they go to *The New Yorker.* No official deadlines are set, but he usually meets self-imposed goals. Editors Shawn and Bingham read the final draft, rarely suggesting changes. McPhee has previously settled troublesome points with them; his copy gets its closest reading from three *New Yorker* institutions. The grammarian provides a meticulous parsing of every sentence and point of English usage. The legal office looks for potential libel. The "checkers" independently verify every assertion of fact. McPhee strives for total accuracy, hoping the checkers will not catch a flat-footed error. Few Ph.D. dissertations are read this carefully. The checkers retrace McPhee's steps, contact his informants, look up the books he read.

Exactly when his work appears in *The New Yorker* depends on many factors, including the magazine's current backlog and the seasonal aspects of the piece. "Firewood" cannot run well in July, for example, but is fine in early March. Like most writers, he endures the chore of proofreading with no visceral pleasure. His work is published in a single issue or in a series, depending on the length, usually under the rubrics "Profile" or "A Reporter at Large." Stories on white-water canoeing or enriched uranium have a nice incongruity in those glossy pages; the copy is bordered with ads for expensive gadgets and imported porcelain rabbits. *The New Yorker* copyrights everything, but transfers ownership to McPhee when he has arranged for book publication. To date, Farrar, Straus and Giroux have published all his books. The later texts are virtually unrevised; on a few occasions he has altered or added minor factual details. He also proofreads these works, even when caught up in the travel and interviewing for his next project.

3
Writing

According to myth, the Sphinx held the city of Thebes hostage until someone answered her riddle: What has four legs at the beginning of life, two legs in the middle, and three legs at the end? Oedipus answered—humankind. Us. We have four legs at the beginning because we crawl. Then we learn to walk and get by on two. In old age, however, we fall victim to various ailments and use a walking stick, a crutch, or a cane to keep from falling down. So at the end we have three legs.

Beginning, middle, and end: That's the way we like our lives, our stories, our games, our wheels and deals, our classes, our essays. You don't throw readers into the middle of an essay and let them swim for it. You lead them to it—that's the introduction. You take them through it—that's the body or development. Then you give them a last look, a parting thought or two, and send them onward and upward—that's the conclusion.

Every essay—indeed virtually everything we write, even letters, memos, and reports—must have a beginning, a middle, and an end. There must be an introduction to announce the subject, a body to develop the subject, and a conclusion to provide the point of it all. Without an introduction, the readers feel lost. Without a body, the readers feel shortchanged. Without a conclusion, the readers feel left hanging in midair. When you write, therefore, you owe the readers all three parts.

Now, to complete an essay—all three parts, all finished—writers work in various ways. Some write and rewrite successive drafts, working through the entire piece each time. Others write and rewrite a section or a paragraph at a time, not beginning the next until this one is finished. Still others write and rewrite a sentence at a time, finishing each before beginning the next. Experienced writers often combine these three approaches.

81

On the other hand, most beginning writers hope the first thing they write will be the last—avoiding rewriting altogether. They try to do everything at the same time: determine the subject, purpose, and reader; marshal the necessary detail; organize the material; plan the rhetorical strategies; structure the paragraphs; form the sentences with just the right words; and edit the grammar and punctuation—all at once. It's too much to do. Even God took six days to compose the world. And as evolution suggests, it's been in revision ever since.

To overcome this fond hope and to do the best work, beginning writers are usually wiser to write successive drafts. In this way they *expect* to write and rewrite *the whole thing* several times. In this chapter, then, I deal with *writing* in the sense of laying down a first draft: getting the introduction going, working out the rhetorical strategies of development in the body, and formulating a conclusion. The idea is to get the entire piece written, however roughly, so there is something tangible to work over in the next phase of the process. Chapter 4, "Rewriting," covers the finer points of composition: paragraphs, sentences, diction, and the like.

I. THE INTRODUCTION

A. How Not to Write an Introduction

When I was a student, I was always told to write the introduction last, usually for two reasons. First, it is the hardest part. If you begin by trying to write the introduction, you may get hung up—a case of arrested development. Second, you can't really write the introduction until you know what you have to say. And you won't really know that until you have written the essay through to the end at least once.

So you begin writing just where the introduction will end. And after concluding, you write the introduction. In it you define the subject, the focus, the thesis, and the plan—all in a series of precise generalizations. In effect, you summarize the essay so the reader will know exactly what you are up to, why you are up to it, and how you intend to go about accomplishing it. Here is a sample of such an introduction from a master's thesis. It's long, but there's a payoff at the end.

> The hero of James Fenimore Cooper's Leatherstocking Tales elects for very conscious reasons to spend his life in the wilderness rather than in the society of his fellow men. "Society" may be defined as any group of people constituting a community of related, interdependent individuals, ranging in number from several to an entire civilization. The story of Natty Bumppo revolves around the com-

parison and conflict of these two modes of life, and since Natty is
the moral hero, the life spent in society suffers in the comparison.
To understand the full meaning of Natty's story, it is important to
know why he repudiates society.

The purpose of this thesis is to examine civilized society as Cooper
pictures it in these Tales and to see what effect it has upon its individual members. At the same time we shall analyze this society
according to Cooper's morality, as that morality is expressed through
Natty Bumppo. Although Natty's interpretation of both nature and
society is a part of Cooper's general view and therefore does not
represent precisely the judgment that the author would render necessarily, it is clear, nevertheless, that Natty's point of view is at least
a possible interpretation according to Cooper, especially since Natty
is the moral hero of these Tales. The analysis will reveal Cooper's
feeling or sense that societal man is caught up in a dilemma. By
cutting him off from the morally benign influence of nature, society
corrupts him. An important result of this situation is that man bases
his behavior upon legality rather than moral principle; in fact, moral
principle is of no consequence. However—and this is the crux of the
dilemma—despite this corruption, man is compelled to live in society because of the nature of woman.

Now you get the payoff. This is the introduction to *my* master's thesis,
written according to the prescription I am urging you to avoid and
showing you why. The results are dreadful. The reader is not invited
in but rather turned away. In fact, I bet a good many of you did not
read it all the way through. If it does not generate anger, such an
introduction merely puts people to sleep.

To reinforce the lesson—so you will never (again) write such an
introduction—let me show you these, both written by freshmen.

Water is one of the most important chemical compounds in our
life. Besides its numerous industrial uses, its participation in life
makes it essential for every form of life. There is much concern
about the need for clean water among environmentalists. They point
out that the time is gone when we can take good water for granted.
Water is a necessary source of energy for all life. However, all too
often its importance is forgotten by those who pollute our aquatic
supplies. Although the problem of water pollution is not new, people
must begin to realize that the water supplies which we depend on
are in great danger.

The prescription for this sort of introduction actually *induces* bad
writing—stilted, pedantic, pompous, redundant, sloppy, vague.

A review of college entrance requirements shows an attempt to
be fair to all students and shows an attempt to recognize all fields
of knowledge. Along with these democratizing ideas, there was an

attempt to unify and control requirements. At times requirements reflected a need to limit or select enrollment and at other times reflected a need to increase or encourage enrollment. As defects or abuses were recognized, changes were made to effectuate the idea of fair and equal opportunity to all students.

These pieces are not stupid. But they flounder because the writers rely on generalizations, cliches, big words, and complicated sentences to express ideas that are in and of themselves fairly decent. The ideas are drowning in the form; the prose is thrashing around aimlessly; the writers are powerless to come to the rescue. I know. As you've seen, I've been there.

Professional writers never write introductions of this sort. Read the essays in the Reader and you will see what I mean. In any magazine— Harper's, Atlantic Monthly, The National Review—you will search in vain for such an introduction. On a recent flight I looked through American Way, the magazine that American Airlines provides its passengers. It contained several quite good articles on a wide variety of subjects: Milton Berle, San Diego Sea World, "The Odd Couple," fund raising, Scrabble, weeds, and others. None of them—not one—began with an abstract definition of subject, thesis, purpose, and plan.

By now you should be wondering how you *should* begin an essay.

B. How to Write an Introduction

1. Start with the Specific

As discussed earlier, the introduction is where you must catch readers by their attention and then entice them to stick around to take the ride. You do this—catch and hold them—by announcing and defining the subject in specific terms. By detail, with detail, and in detail.

Compare Joan Didion's introduction to the subject of the Santa Ana with the student's introduction to the subject of water pollution. (Didion could have done it as the student did: Both essays are concerned with the relation of people and nature.)

> There is something uneasy in the Los Angeles air this afternoon, some unnatural stillness, some tension. What it means is that tonight a Santa Ana will begin to blow, a hot wind from the northeast whining down through the Cajon and San Gorgonio Passes, blowing up sandstorms out along Route 66, drying the hills and the nerves to the flash point. For a few days now we will see smoke back in the canyons, and hear sirens in the night. I have neither heard nor read that a Santa Ana is due, but I know it, and almost everyone I have

seen today knows it too. We know it because we feel it. The baby frets. The maid sulks. I rekindle a waning argument with the telephone company, then cut my losses and lie down, given over to whatever is in the air. To live with the Santa Ana is to accept, consciously or unconsciously, a deeply mechanistic view of human behavior.

By common consent, Didion is one of the best practicing essayists around. Watch how she works. In the introduction to "In Bed," she focuses on something specific in the first-person singular.

> Three, four, sometimes five times a month, I spend the day in bed with a migraine headache, insensible to the world around me. Almost every day of the month, between these attacks, I feel the sudden irrational irritation and flush of blood into the cerebral arteries which tell me that migraine is on its way, and I take certain drugs to avert its arrival. If I did not take the drugs, I would be able to function perhaps one day in four. The physiological error called migraine is, in brief, central to the given of my life. When I was 15, 16, even 25, I used to think that I could rid myself of this error by simply denying it, character over chemistry. "Do you have headaches *sometimes? frequently? never?*" the application forms would demand. "Check one." Wary of the trap, wanting whatever it was that the successful circumnavigation of that particular form could bring (a job, a scholarship, the respect of mankind and the grace of God), I would check one. "*Sometimes*," I would lie. That in fact I spent one or two days a week almost unconscious with pain seemed a shameful secret, evidence not merely of some chemical inferiority but of all my bad attitudes, unpleasant tempers, wrongthink.

Beginning by focusing on something specific is not a strategy unique to Didion, an invention that she patented and that by law no one else may use. It's a convention that belongs to the public domain. So we all may use it—and most writers do. And they use it because, as Didion's examples demonstrate, it works.

Starting with the specific does not have to mean focusing on a first-person singular condition or event. Notice how George Will begins his essay, "On Her Own in the City."

> When police, responding to her call, arrived at her East Harlem tenement, she was hysterical. "The dog ate my baby." The baby girl had been four days old, twelve hours "home" from the hospital. Home was two rooms and a kitchen on the sixth floor, furnished with a rug, a folding chair, and nothing else, no bed, no crib.
> "Is the baby dead?" asked an officer. "Yes," the mother said, "I saw the baby's insides." Her dog, a German shephard, had not been fed for five days. She explained: "I left the baby on the floor with the dog to protect it." She had bought the dog in July for protection from human menaces.

> She is twenty-four. She went to New York three years ago from a small Ohio community. She wanted to be on her own. She got that wish.

Beginning with the specific does not have to mean starting with an anecdote. Although an anecdote is an effective item with which to begin—we all love a story, and that's why so many writers indulge us at the outset—you may, like Jean George in "That Astounding Creator—Nature," begin with specific facts, questions, and assertions.

> A bird that eats feathers, a mammal that never drinks, a fish that grows a fishing line and worm on its head to catch other fish. Creatures in a nightmare? No, they are very much with us as co-inhabitants of this earth.
>
> Nature has fashioned most animals to fit the many faces of the land—moose to marshes, squirrels to trees, camels to deserts, frogs to lily pads. Give nature an environment or situation and she will eventually evolve a creature, adapting a toe here, an eye there, until the being fits the niche. As a result of this hammering and fitting, however, some really unbelievable creatures circle the sun with us.

Starting with a quote is a popular method among professional writers. Suzanne Jordan begins by using a quote for the title. In Shakespeare's play, Caesar tells Brutus that they may have a rival in their midst: "Yon Cassius," he says, "hath a lean and hungry look." Jordan entitles her essay "That Lean and Hungry Look," and takes off.

> Caesar was right. Thin people need watching. I've been watching them for most of my adult life, and I don't like what I see. When these narrow fellows spring at me, I quiver to my toes. Thin people come in all personalities, most of them menacing. You've got your "together" thin person, your mechanical thin person, your condescending thin person, your tsk-tsk thin person, your efficiency expert thin person. All of them are dangerous.

Note that Jordan engages in generalizations with a vengeance. She gets away with it by couching her generalizations (each of them comically outrageous) in the specific: the famous quote, her first-person-singular adulthood study.

You do not, by the way, have to quote Shakespeare. You may quote anybody: politician, athlete, scholar, preacher, cabdriver, nurse. You find gems everywhere. The only requirements are that somehow you define the subject by the quote and that you explain how.

Now, have I persuaded you that the best way to begin is to be particular? If so, read on. If not, I don't know what to recommend. Forget it? Read it again? Go bowling?

2. Do the Introduction First

You may find it difficult to believe, but beginning an essay with something specific not only works—it is relatively easy to do. Of course, writing is never absolutely easy, never unadulterated fun, even for the pros. But beginning with something concrete is much easier than beginning with a string of generalizations, a statement of thesis, a definition of purpose, and a blueprint of your itinerary. Beginning like that is so difficult that professional writers don't even try. Besides, it's boring.

The best thing for you, then, as beginning writers—no, the *only* thing for you, since you are beginning writers—is to start with something specific. And I do mean *start*. Don't wait until you have written the first draft. Lay down your detail, your anecdote, your line of facts, your quote—whatever you have—and then explain how it defines your subject.

Sometimes when you explain the subject, you also define the thesis: the particular focus you wish to develop, the argument you wish to make, the point you want to prove. For instance, Talese announces the subject, focus, and thesis in the first sentence—"New York is a city of things unnoticed"—all in one. (In eight words no less!) If you haven't clearly expressed the thesis yet, give it a sentence of its own. Return to George's introduction and see how she wraps it up with an express statement of thesis: "As a result of this hammering and fitting, however, *some really unbelievable creatures circle the sun with us*" (italics mine).

For an object lesson, consider how Didion begins her essay, "Why I Write."

> Of course I stole the title for this talk from George Orwell. One reason I stole it was that I like the sound of the words: *Why I Write.* There you have three short ambiguous words that share a sound, and the sound they share is this:
>
> I
> I
> I
>
> In many ways writing is the act of saying *I*, of imposing oneself upon other people, of saying *listen to me, see it my way, change your mind.*

Didion first explains how the title, a quote, defines the subject: why she writes. Then she explains how it implies the thesis: Writing is an imposition of oneself upon others.

In the course of writing an essay, you may find that you want or need to revise the thesis. Fine. Go back and revise it.

Beginning with small but tasty morsels gives a good start to the essay, much as good hors d'oeuvres are an appetizing start to a meal. If the introduction is right, you'll not only hook the reader into the essay but you'll also have a good running start at writing the essay. You may have to try several introductions until you find one that gets you going, that sets the tone and leads quickly and vigorously into the development. Keep trying. Because the right introduction can be the difference between an essay that is alive and an essay that is barely breathing. Think of it this way: Imagine trying to write an essay that is alive using the sort of introduction I wrote for my master's thesis. It can't be done.

But you can get off to a running start even though you're not a professional writer. Remember the awful introduction concerning college entrance requirements? The following is by the same writer.

> I remember always feeling picked on when I was a little girl. During the school year all the other kids were allowed to stay outside until eight o'clock, but I had to be inside when the street lights went on. My sister was always allowed to stay up late and watch T.V. when I had to go to bed. My sister always got a bigger serving of dessert than I did. I was always saying how unfair everything was and Mom would always reply, "Teri, one thing you're going to learn: *Life isn't fair*." Those words have stuck in my mind, and the older I get the more I realize that she was right and they are true: life's not fair.

The same writer. See why you have to define the subject? Out of the specifics cited, the subject could just as well be self-pity, proverbs, parents, or moms and daughters—to name a few. Note also how in this case defining the subject simultaneously defines the thesis: Life is not fair.

Here's another freshman sample.

> Some nights I have a difficult time falling asleep. Most of the time I feel tired, but I can't relax enough to fall asleep. I lie on my stomach for five or six minutes, then realize *that's* not working, so I turn to my side. That doesn't work, either, because I feel narrow and about to lose my balance. I toss myself onto my back, but that also proves futile because I can never fall asleep while lying on my back. I don't know why, maybe because I don't feel comfortable with my toes sticking up in the air.
>
> Recently, though, I have found several drug-unrelated aids to relaxation, little tricks of the mind that help me get to sleep and that, if you ever suffer the same plight, may help you.

The essay could just as well have been about insomnia. Either way, it's off to a lively wide-awake start. And the writer didn't have to write the balance of the essay before writing the introduction.

Here is another, by yet another freshman.

> I was totally lost. The crowd of runners in front of me disappeared into a confusing maze of trees and trails. My only guides were colored flags that appeared when I didn't expect them. I couldn't remember whether a red flag meant to turn right or left. I just guessed. If I didn't see another flag later on, I would know that I had taken a wrong turn.
>
> This was my first cross country race. When I had stood at the starting line, I thought that competitive distance running was only a test of endurance. I quickly found out that it also takes much planning, strategy, and skill.

Incidentally, starting with something specific works as well for formal as for informal essays. The following, also written by a freshman, is the introduction to a term paper.

> All day long Tommy sits by the window and watches people and cars come and go from the institution. He has lived in an institution for twelve years, ever since he was born in 1970. Tommy is there because he has a disease, and cannot function properly in society. At least that is what his parents say. But as time passes maybe they will change their ideas, along with those of many other people.
>
> Today many children like Tommy are out in the open. Children like Phillip Becker, who has a hole between his two ventricles, or Ellen Grietzen, who at age four still wears diapers, talks baby gibberish, and needs constant watching, or even Lee Ann Grady, an eighteen-year-old who is now sterile: these are the ones who in the past were locked up but are now acknowledged. People with special problems need special understanding and help to overcome the handicaps of their disease. Phillip, Ellen, and Ann all suffer from the same one: Trisomy 21, Down's Syndrome, Mongolism. People know it by one name or another, but unfortunately that is just about all they know about it.

Now that she has hooked our attention, the writer goes on to tell us about the disease. You can hook the readers' attention, too, just as effectively. All you have to do is find something specific, really specific, and to the point.

3. Forget Statements of Purpose and Plan

Unless forcibly required to do so, make no formal statement of purpose. Imagine wrapping up the introduction to the term paper on Mongolism with such a statement.

> People with special problems need special understanding and help
> to overcome the handicaps of their disease. Phillip, Ellen, and Ann
> all suffer from the same one: Trisomy 21, Down's Syndrome, Mon-
> golism. People know it by one name or another, but unfortunately
> that is just about all they know about it. The purpose of this paper
> is to describe the primary causes and effects of mongolism, the major
> problems it involves, and the steps that may be taken to help over-
> come these problems.

Such statements are always awkward, redundant, unnecessary, and
offensive. We already know the subject of the essay, and that's all we
need. Imagine such a statement in any of the other introductions we've
studied.

> She is twenty-four. She went to New York three years ago from a
> small Ohio community. She wanted to be on her own. She got that
> wish. This essay explores the plight of those who, lacking adequate
> preparation and any sort of support system, attempt to live by their
> own resources in large metropolitan areas such as New York, the
> problems they encounter, and the prospects they face. It explores,
> in short, the condition of anonymity, poverty, and powerlessness in
> the city.

Or:

> Give nature an environment or situation and she will evolve a crea-
> ture, adapting a toe here, an eye there, until the being fits the niche.
> As a result of this hammering and fitting, however, some really
> unbelievable creatures circle the sun with us. In the remainder of
> this essay I will describe, one by one, a representative sample of the
> strange creatures evolved by that astounding creator—nature.

Or:

> This was my first cross country race. When I had stood at the starting
> line, I thought that competitive distance running was only a test of
> endurance. I quickly found out that it also takes much planning,
> strategy, and skill. In this essay I will analyze the planning, the
> strategy, and the skill that are involved in competitive distance run-
> ning. I will, moreover, analyze them in the order just cited.

That last sentence helps to point out the next prohibition. You may
have been taught (as I was) to define the plan of your essay, its overall
organization, so the readers will know not only *what* they are about
to read but the order in which they will read it. Such remarks are
often part of statements of purpose: "In this essay I will analyze, in
this order, the planning, the strategy, and the skills that are involved
in competitive distance running."

Such statements are commonly found in prefaces to books. In scale, books are similar to long trips. An itinerary is almost indispensable on a long trip. But we rarely, if ever, need a map to go around the block. So forget explicit statements of plan. They are even more awkward and redundant and intrusive and offensive than statements of purpose.

EXERCISES

1. Choose two of the introductions I cited as good models for you to follow. Revise them. Make them bad. Get rid of specifics. String together some generalizations. Make explicit statements of thesis, purpose, and plan. (Take this assignment seriously. Do your best job of writing a bad introduction. You must learn firsthand how difficult such introductions are, and why. Also, turning something good into something bad will help you see how good it really is.)

2. Choose two of the introductions I termed regrettable as poor examples to follow. Revise them. Make them good. Be particular. Begin with something specific (which for the purposes of this assignment you may simply invent). Include revealing detail. Define the subject, the general idea that the specific leads up to—simply and clearly. Define the thesis as simply and clearly as the subject. In one, focus on the first-person-singular, as Didion does in the introduction to "In Bed." In the other, focus on the subject only and without using the first-person, as Will does in "On Her Own in the City."

II. THE BODY OF THE ESSAY

A. Anticipate Your Readers

To anticipate literally means to take before. It means to look ahead or to take care of something in advance. It means looking out the window before leaving home to see if you need a down jacket, a raincoat, or suntain oil.

In developing the subject—in advancing its cause—you must always anticipate the readers' response to what you are saying. Actually, you must anticipate the readers' response to everything you write. But anticipation is especially important in the body, because there you are trying to make the subject make perfect sense to the readers. Most readers are willing to suspend disbelief or critical judgment during the introduction, just as we are upon being introduced to a stranger. But you cannot expect the readers' continuing good will if they do not find the body of the paper worth their while. To keep their good will, then, when you make a statement you must ask yourself how they are likely to respond. As I noted in the last chapter, you must be on the lookout for objections and questions, and you must answer them if you are going to keep your readers satisfied and keep them reading to the end.

Think of it this way. In casual conversation, as we make a point, our listeners are likely to interrupt us now and then with all manner of protests, requests, and commands. "Who says?" "Aw c'mon!" "Can you elaborate on that?" "Gimme an example! Just one!" Listeners often don't even have to speak. They can ask, protest, request, and command with expressions and gestures: a raised eyebrow, a shrug of the shoulders, a tilt of the head, a frown. By these cues we are alerted to questions, objections, hesitations, doubts, and the like which must be answered. And as we try to answer, we receive more cues letting us know if we are satisfying our customers or not: smiles, smirks, scowls, harumphs. Even when one person holds the floor, informal conversation is a give-and-take exchange.

On the other hand, writing is a one-way proposition. Our readers cannot provide us with cues. We are not within seeing and hearing distance of one another. When we write, therefore, we must both listen and talk simultaneously. We must put ourselves in the reader's place to anticipate their responses and alert ourselves to their cues. We must foresee questions and objections to answer them. And we must answer them to hold the readers' attention and their favorable opinion of the case we are making. Here's what happens when we don't.

> The sun is wonderful for the skin. People always look healthier with a tan.

Thud. The writer foresees none of the questions sure to arise: What about sun burn? What about sensitive skin? What about dry skin? What about premature wrinkling? What about skin cancer? Is the appearance of a sun-drenched coppertone body the same thing as a healthy body? Is fashion out of synch with good sense? These questions must be answered in any discussion of sunbathing. And if the writer cannot answer these questions satisfactorily, he or she should choose another topic.

Remember the student who called his teachers names? I am going to reprint his drafts because they are perfect examples of the point under discussion.

> I loved to call my teachers names at the top of my lungs. My all time favorite was, "You retarded idiotic nincompoop!"

As it stands, more questions are raised than answered. In the margin I asked the writer, you may recall, how old he was. In answering that question, he went ahead to answer another more important one I didn't ask: *Why* did he love to call his teachers names?

> I enjoyed calling my teachers names at the top of my lungs. I didn't hate them. It just made me feel big in front of the other kids to yell "You retarded idiotic nincompoop!" at my teacher. I was especially fond of that phrase, probably because it was longer than any other I knew. I was only six at the time and big words, especially big sarcastic put-down words, made a very big impression on me.

First he sets aside a conclusion we might leap to immediately: that he called his teachers names because he hated them. No, he didn't hate them. Then, in one sentence, he answers two more questions that we could reasonably ask: If not out of hate, then why? And what names did you call them? He goes even further by anticipating the question, Why that name? And then, to explain his fondness for big put-down words, he tells us his age.

I cannot think of a pertinent question the writer has not foreseen and not answered in his second draft. I can think of all kinds of nonpertinent questions: How old were you when you learned to talk? What was your favorite food? What was your mother's maiden name? What size shoe did you wear? What was the name of your school? Did you have a pet? A pug nose? A patchwork quilt? I could go on with questions *ad infinitum* (forever) and *ad nauseam* (to the retching point). But the writer is not obligated to satisfy my impertinence. He or she need answer only those questions germane to the subject and beneficial to my understanding. Everything else is beside the point.

Another thing to note: The answers do not have to be exhaustive. Unlike the three-year-old child who keeps asking "Why?," readers are not interested in infinite regress. Readers are more easily pleased than three-year-olds on a philosophical spree. They are usually as satisfied with a "probably" or a "maybe" as with a truth carved in stone.

> I was especially fond of that phrase, *probably* because it was longer than any other I knew.

Or, to cite another passage we have already seen:

> I toss myself onto my back, but *that* also proves futile because I can
> never fall asleep while lying on my back. *I don't know why, maybe*
> because I don't feel comfortable with my toes sticking up in the air.

She doesn't know why, so she attempts an explanation: Her toes stick
straight up in the air, at attention, which is no position for sleeping.
Her hypothesis seems reasonable, and that satisfies most readers. We
don't demand that she undergo psychoanalysis and disclose the reason
behind her discomfort.

As you write, list on a separate sheet the objections and questions
you anticipate. Decide which are relevant, toss the rest. Then weave
the answers into the essay. Unfortunately, there is no foolproof formula
for determining relevance. Some of the objections and questions you
choose will be on the borderline of relevance. When in doubt, keep
them. For in the beginning, it is better to err on the side of too much
than on the side of too little. Most beginners err on the side of too
little. Their work is skimpy. They put their readers on a starvation
diet. You must resist that tendency immediately, before it becomes an
ingrained habit. If you include too much, you can always remove the
superfluous objections and answers at a later date.

As you become a more practiced writer, you will develop a sense,
an intuitive feel, for the readers' needs that will be your formula—
though it will never be foolproof.

Now that you know which questions and objections to anticipate,
answer them.

EXERCISES

1. Prepare a list of the questions and objections that the student writer
   raises in the following opening.

   > I like being young. Young people can be as free as they want to
   > be. They have goals, and if they don't like them they can change
   > them, because they have time.

   Compare your list with the lists of your classmates. Working as a
   group, decide which questions and objections must be answered.

2. Rewrite the passage, answering the common objections and questions. Compare your passage with the revisions prepared by other
   members of the group. Note the variety of ways to deal with the

same questions and objections. Consider the approaches (the strategies) that are most effective. File them in your memory bank for
later use.

B. Develop Your Subject

Development is like pumping iron: expanding muscle, building bulk.
It's like developing a photograph: bringing a negative into view, into
positive reality. It's like doing math: solving a problem step-by-step.
It's like performing a striptease: disclosing (disclothesing) the subject
little by little. It's like a seed growing into a mature thriving plant.

In the body of an essay (article, memo, report), you develop the
subject. You body-build the outline by working out the idea with logic
and detail. You bring out the shapes and colors from the negative of
the thesis until it becomes a picture. You systematically solve the problems the subject involves one by one. You reveal the subject an item
at a time, so it can be seen at last in its entirety. You cultivate the idea
of the subject, so it grows into a form that is easily read from beginning
to end.

In writing, then, development means transforming the intangible
into the tangible—fleshing out the original idea into a specific form—
something that readers can peruse and comprehend. Development
means making an idea make sense in two respects: You make it physical by supplying concrete, sensuous detail; you make it intelligible by
explaining the logic of its structure.

In developing the subject, therefore, practice two familar principles:
Spell out both detail and idea; anticipate the readers. In this way, you
will be forced during exploration to determine just what the subject
means. You will also be forced to plan the rhetorical strategies necessary to enable the readers to know exactly what you are talking
about when you are explaining the subject, to persuade them by the
thesis, and—if it happens to be the purpose—to motivate them to
take the action you advocate.

Let's get down to hard cases before we're mired in explanation. A
student of mine wrote an essay on how to get rich quick. Here is how
he starts it.

> I got another notice from the bank the other day letting me know
> that one of my checks bounced. That's the third this month. It has
> been a tough semester. My car's on the fritz, my dog's got worms,
> my girl friend's got taste, and my brother wants his money back—

the money he lent me to get the car, the dog, and the girl. For the
first time in my life I began to think seriously about how to make a
lot of money fast, and while I was watching an ad for Jordache jeans
I got this idea.

How to make a lot of money fast is the basic idea to be developed.
but it's too big and too vague. He must have a particular slant—an
angle, as get-rich-quick artists would say, or a thesis, as English teachers would say—and that's what he means by "this idea." Having indicated that he has an angle, he defines it in the next paragraph.

The big money these days is in fads. People are getting rich on
everything from designer jeans to Pac-Man to cartoon cats. But it's
not easy to create a fad. That means coming up with a new idea,
which can take time as well as genius and luck and trouble. But if
you're no genius, and you're out of time and luck, and you prefer to
stay out of trouble, you can still get rich quick. All you have to do is
combine two or more fads and you'll have a hit on your hands and
money in your pocket.

He locates the big money (it's in fads), cites three quick examples as
cases in point (designer jeans, Pac-Man, and cartoon cats), explains
the difficulties in getting to this lucrative spot, and then offers us his
inspiration, his angle—the thesis of his essay. He could have offered
it at the top, but he would have tipped his hand and spoiled the fun.
Moreover, by explaining the advantages and rationale of his angle
before defining the angle itself, he creates suspense and keeps the
readers' interest.

Having defined the angle, the writer must spell it out in detail and
with specifics.

For instance, there has been much speculation recently about the
material of the future. Aluminum? Zinc? Plutonium? All wrong. It's
nerf. Everything's going nerf. Already we have nerf balls, nerf cars,
nerf ping-pong—all big sellers. Take advantage of this. Combine it
with another fad: Nerf Pac-Man, Nerfy the Cat, Smurf-Nerf, nerf
unicorns, nerf rainbows to hang on rear-view mirrors, nerf vanity
plates that say "I'd Rather Be Nerfing," nerf picket signs, nerf pocket
cameras.

First the writer justifies (not seriously, of course) the material he recommends by discounting other theories and explaining the advantages
of nerf: It's *in*, an established fad. Thus, it will remain *in*, thus it will
sell. Then he's ready to get down to hard cases, to particular fads
merged with other fads in an order of increasing improbability.

Note how the writer, in anticipation of the reader, is spelling out
not only detail but logic. He recommends nerf because it will sell.

And it will sell because it's a growing fad in the present and thus the wave of the future. The logic isn't actually logical because this essay is humorous. But such as it is, it still must be spelled out. Otherwise the reader would ask, "Why nerf?"

Coupling nerf with other fads is only one example of the writer's idea, however, and one is not enough. He must develop it more; he does in the next paragraph.

> The other day I was in a bakery and noticed a couple of possibilities in the cookie department. One was a normal everyday round cookie, but it had "Happy Barmitzvah," or something like that, written on it in frosting, and it sold for $3.50. Not a bad idea: charge a whole lot more for only a little extra. Next to it, however, was a much better idea: a Pac-Man cookie. It, too, was just a normal everyday round cookie, but with about one-fifth of it sliced out, and it sold for $4.00. And I realized: *people will pay more for less.* They will pay 12 1/2 percent more for 20 percent less, to be exact. Then I got an idea. You can make a Pac-Man out of anything round and make 32 1/2 percent more for your trouble than you otherwise would. Take three slices out and you have a Pac-Man pizza. Eliminate a wedge and you have Pac-Man apple pie, Pac-Man pineapple upside-down cake, Pac-Man hamburgers. But you don't have to stick to food. Why not Pac-Man frisbees? Pac-Man hockey pucks? Why, after a little tinkering with the technology we can have Pac-Man records and Pac-Man floppy disks. Any way you turn there's a future there.

Again, the writer develops the thesis by writing it out in detail in order of ascending improbability and by detailing its logic: Increase the sales and profits by removing a wedge from anything round.

Now we have two good examples of the essay's main premise—that a good way to get rich quick is to combine fads. As a rule—one that I have cited already—two is not enough, and here the rule applies. The essay on fads would benefit from a third example. The writer thought so, too, and provided one.

> Soap operas have always been popular, but in the last few years they have achieved the status of fad. It is no longer just the lonely housewife who watches them, but students and shopkeepers and barflies and harlots. On any weekday afternoon, walk into a dorm or any store or the neighborhood bar or your local bordello and you will find a television set tuned into *General Hospital* or *Days of Our Lives* or *The Young and the Restless.* With the likes of *Dallas* and *Dynasty* and *Falcon's Crest,* the soaps have successfully invaded prime time TV, too. Fans read soap opera digests and call soap opera hotlines to get the latest on their favorite shows, the characters and the stars.
>   A more recent fad of intensity is the Cabbage Patch doll. It is a soft and cuddly baby doll, so homely it's cute, that you do not just

buy, but adopt. Each doll comes with a name of its own and adoption papers complete with pledges and oaths that you solemnly swear and sign. Last Christmas the demand for the Cabbage Patch doll reached such fervor that grown people stood in line overnight in zero degree weather for the *chance* to buy one for their children and nieces and nephews and girl friends. They fought, they rioted, they bribed, they sued, and in the midst of a melee myself, as I was wondering how J. R. would get his hands on one of these things, the question occurred to me, "Why not a cabbage patch doll for adults?" And then another question: "Why not a cabbage patch doll *of* adults?" Not just of adults in general, but of adults in particular, specifically, the popular characters of soaps? A Holly Scorpio cabbage patch doll, and a Robert Scorpio cabbage patch doll, and a Luke Spenser, a Monica and an Allen Quartermane, and a Roman and Bear Brady, a Joe Novak, an Alexis Colby, a Pamela Ewing—my God, Victoria Principal out of a cabbage patch!—and J. R. himself! Instead of adoption papers you could offer a whole array of documents, depending on how the customer feels about the character: marriage licenses, divorce agreements, injunctions, lawsuits, death certificates. Different dolls for different relationships, to make the owner's life with them complete and thus more life-like, and to expand the market at the same time. And to make these dolls as up-to-date as possible, you could *manufacture them out of nerf.*

But I have changed my mind. I'm no longer saying *you.* I know a good thing when I see it. I'm taking this idea myself. But I'll tell you what I'll do. When the soap-opera cabbage-patch dolls hit the market, I'll let you have first dibs. If you stay in line, that is.

The final example is the most complicated and perhaps the weirdest. The first two have certain possibilities. A nerf rainbow for the rearview mirror is feasible. So is a Pac-Man pizza. But a Luke Spenser cabbage-patch doll is as out of the question as a Marilyn Monroe teddy bear. The writer has prepared the reader for such impossibility, though, by the way he has ordered his ideas in each example: from feasible to outrageous. On the possibility scale, a nerf pocket camera and a Pac-Man record album seem further out of reach than a cabbage-patch Victoria Principal. We don't care if any of these ideas are even remotely doable, though. The essay is not a feasibility study, and doability is not the point.

The lesson in this paper is that to develop a thesis, you spell it out in sufficient detail and logic so the reader *gets* the idea and needs no more to get it any better. Then you stop. This student could have discussed other, stranger examples and continued for many more pages. But by the end of the third example the point is made—fads and get-rich-quick schemes are frivolous and fun—and he neatly concludes by pretending to take the last idea seriously.

And now I'm going to let you in on a secret. The paper we have just gone through is a slight variation on a classic freshman composition formula, the five-paragraph essay. This particular essay has seven paragraphs, two for the introduction and two for the soap-opera cabbage-patch dolls. If they weren't so complicated, each would have required one paragraph only. But in basic structure, this essay follows the formula.

The formula is simple: The essay is introduced in the first paragraph, expanded in the next three—the body—and concluded in the fifth. Preparing means finding a good specific with which to begin, devising three major ideas with which to develop it, and working up a conclusion. The essay about get-rich-quick fads—nerf novelties, Pac-Man products, and soap-opera cabbage-patch dolls—works exactly this way.

If you experience difficulty organizing and developing a subject, you may find the five-paragraph formula useful. And don't look down upon it simply because it is a formula. So is syntax a formula, and it must be used. If you don't use it, you don't make sense. And you can use it in a way that is not mechanically formulaic. In fact, that is what good writing is all about: coming up with something new out of the same old material (words) and the same old formulas (syntax). The same is true of the five-paragraph formula. As is clear from the student paper, you can use the formula and still write with such originality and flair that no one notices the formula.

EXERCISES

1. Using three to five examples, develop in a paragraph one of the following ideas.

    The proper care of plants.

    The pleasures of dorm life.

    What to do about the blues.

    Disgusting habits.

    City slickers.

2. Meet with a group of classmates who developed the same idea. Compare paragraphs. Brainstorm together. Then outline a five-paragraph paper developing the same idea.

3. In the privacy of your quarters, write the essay.

4. Meet with the same group. Compare results.

C. The Basic Rhetorical Strategies

In developing the subject, at every step along the way you must decide the rhetorical strategy best suited to meeting anticipated reader response. Responses will vary, of course, depending on the purpose and the readers.

If the purpose is primarily to explore and explain, responses will consist mainly of questions you must answer: the *what how where when why* that journalists face daily. Readers rarely object to exploration and explanation, and when they do the objection is often to the subject itself. "Why," journalists are asked, "do you write only about disasters and catastrophes? Why do you always write just about bad news?" The only way to meet the objection is to write about something else—not the war in the Mideast but the benefit ball in Boston. However, if the purpose is primarily to persuade, the responses will include, in addition to questions, objections you must try to satisfy. "You say that fraternities and sororities ought to be outlawed. But wouldn't that abridge the First Amendment right to freedom of assembly? And what's next—denying freedom of speech?"

If the readers are knowledgeable about the subject, anticipate sophisticated questions and objections concerning fine points, subtle distinctions, and alternative approaches. If the readers are not knowledgeable about the subject, anticipate questions and objections concerning elementary principles and facts. There are, of course, degrees of knowledge between expertise and ignorance. Economists discuss and debate trade deficits one way in a professional conference of peers, another way at the committee hearing before senators, and quite another still on a televison talk show aimed at a mass audience.

Consequently, you must have an idea of who the readers are so you can anticipate the sorts of questions and objections to be answered. Ask yourself, "In this paragraph (or section) will they want to know what the subject looked like or sounded like? Must I define a certain concept at length, relate certain events in story form, analyze the process under discussion in detail, sort out the main types or categories of the topic?" The answers to questions such as these involve using certain techniques or strategies traditionally called *rhetorical modes.*

Since Aristotle addressed the subject some 2,500 years ago, teachers of rhetoric have classified these modes into eight to ten categories. I favor nine myself: description, narration, illustration, classification, comparison and contrast, process analysis, definition, cause and effect, and argumentation. These modes are not distinct species as though

fixed from on high. Few essays conform exclusively to the characteristics of one mode. Most essays are like most dogs: They are mongrels.
You cannot be commanded to keep the strains pure; they never have
been pure. They have always mingled, mated, and produced all manner of offspring.

However, these modes are useful as descriptions of the tendencies
of nonfiction prose written to explore, explain, or persuade a public
through essays, articles, reports, memos, and the like. Most expository
writing favors one mode or several modes more than others, just as
mutts favor one breed or several—but not all.

As indicated, these modes are most useful as descriptions of the
basic strategies involved in writing all expository prose, of organizing
material, and executing purpose. To point writing in the direction
you've chosen—to realize that goal—you must learn the principles
and characteristics of the rhetorical modes. Therefore, I will define
them one at a time, and demonstrate how they work by citing examples that relate to a subject I introduced in the last chapter—one which
affects our lives in various forms every day—leading and following.
In this way you can *see* what a difference the modes make.

1. Description

Description satisfies the readers' desire and need to perceive the physical aspects of the subject.

> They were all dressed much the same, five young men wearing
> aviator sun-glasses, black leather jackets studded with silver brads
> and tasseled zippers, Levi jeans, and heavy black steel-toed boots.
> They all walked with a menacing swagger in slow motion. They all
> stared through everyone who happened into their field of vision.
> They all smoked without using their hands. They seemed five of a
> kind, mirror images out of one movie, until I watched them very
> closely. Then I noticed that one of them, the guy without whiskers,
> was always a split second, just a frame or two, ahead of the others.
> When he moved, they moved. When he stopped, they milled to a
> stop. When he laughed—a brief snort, usually, expressing scorn—
> they shared his amused contempt. He was the director as well as
> the star of the show, and he got the script directly from Hollywood.

When describing, keep your mind buttoned on the subject. Use
adjectives and adverbs that refer directly to it, not to you or your
responses. ("The disgusting young men were wearing sleazy jackets
with tasteless tassels and zippers"—that sort of thing.) You may be
the subject, of course, or part of it. In that case, describe yourself as
you were involved. ("I was standing on the corner wearing a three-

piece suit and a haircut. I could watch them because they pretended I wasn't there.") But be careful not to shift the focus—yours or the readers'—from the subject to you. ("I usually wear three-piece suits. I get my hair cut every week. I'm a pretty straight fellow. I go to church twice a week, belong to the Junior Chamber of Commerce and take tennis. . . .")

Through description you provide something the readers can get their senses on—usually their eyes. Most description is concerned with appearances. When it comes to writing, the eyes usually have it. Set forth specifics, concrete detail with precision: the type of sunglasses, the brads and zippers on the coats, the pace and air of the swagger. But keep in mind that appearances aren't everything. In the description of the gang, the type of laughter adds a meaningful note.

Use images for comparison, to help readers perceive and understand. Comparing the young men's walk to slow motion gives a sense of their pace. Comparing the brief delay between the leader's initiative and the others' response to a frame or two of movie film gives a sense of the subtlety of their relationship. Moreover, the image of movies—especially when it is extended to direction and script—helps the readers understand that these guys are not just behaving, they are performing, and their leader is himself following the example of many movies and television programs.

In other words, through images you not only describe, you *interpret* the subject, revealing to the reader what you think (these guys are all copycats) without shifting the focus from the subject.

One thing you must know from the outset. The purpose of description is to provide a fair idea of the subject but not a complete one. You cannot describe anything completely—there is too much to comprehend. You don't even want to describe anything completely. Imagine describing the five toughs for 150 pages. That would constitute reader abuse, a felony in any book. Rather, you must exercise discretion: Choose the most telling detail and put it to work for the subject.

Next, organize the detail of the description clearly and coherently. There must be direction: from top to bottom (sunglasses to boots) or bottom to top, from right to left or left to right, from inside out or outside in, from beginning to end or (rarely but possibly) from end to beginning. Or it must have psychological order: Follow the logic of perception, the movement of the perceiver's awareness (from manner of walking to manner of smoking). And you must not only discern the order and follow it to the letter, you must also know why you have chosen it. In other words, it must be appropriate to the particular subject. If you are describing how a city looks as you drive into it, order the detail from the outside in. If you are describing a sunrise, take it from beginning to end.

EXERCISES

1. Consider the opening paragraph of "A Hanging" by George Orwell.

> It was in Burma, a sodden morning of the rains. A sickly light, like yellow tinfoil, was slanting over the high walls into the jail yard. We were waiting outside the condemned cells, a row of sheds fronted with double bars, like small animal cages. Each cell measured about ten feet by ten and was quite bare within except for a plank bed and a pot for drinking water. In some of them brown, silent men were squatting at the inner bars, with their blankets draped round them. These were the condemned men, due to be hanged within the next week or two.

Define the principle of Orwell's order. Try rearranging the paragraph. Discuss with a group of classmates the difference that various arrangements make.

2. List five different orders possible in describing a car. Define the logic of each.

2. Narration

"Tell me a story!" children cry. We get hooked on stories at a tender age—about the same time we begin making sentences—and we never outgrow them.

> The summer that I learned to dive I also learned that taking a dare can involve courage *and* cowardice in about equal measure. I was thirteen. A couple friends and I went to the pool one afternoon. We ran into several older guys we knew a little and admired very much. They were stars on the high school football team. They invited us to join them in a game of follow-the-leader off the high board, an honor we had not expected and could not turn down.
> First they did some simple stuff: a jump, a cannon-ball, a straight dive, a jackknife, a swan. Following suit, we were feeling pretty smug, the envy of our peers. Then one of them did a one-and-a-half and our hearts fell in fear. None of us had ever done a flip before, much less more than one. The others followed the first's lead, all of them grinning, and we knew we had been suckered.
> It was our turn. We hesitated.
> "Well, who's gonna go first?" one of them challenged.
> We just stood there, dumb with terror.

"You're not chicken, are you?" another smirked.

It was the question that we dreaded, the accusation that put honor on the line. We found out that we feared losing it more than suffering the pain of a flop from on high. Cowards all, lacking the courage to quit, we pretended to be eager and clamored to be first.

Because we were so scared, when we survived we were perfectly exhilarated, and afraid no more. By the end of the summer we could do a back double flip with a full twist.

First, observe that a story is not just a series of events in time. When I recount a trip to the supermarket to buy oranges, then apples, then lettuce, then celery, and so on, I am not telling a story. A story is a series of events that leads to a single outcome. And the outcome must involve this principle: *As a consequence of those events, the main character (or characters) can never be the same again.* In other words, the events must make a real difference, large or small, for better or for worse, in the main character's life. As a result of taking the dare, the boys forever lost their fear of diving.

Next, you do not simply cite events in chronological sequence. You explain their connections, the way each event is the consequence of something else. The older boys invited the younger boys to play because they wanted to set them up. The younger boys accepted because they felt flattered. They took the dare because they feared losing a certain image more than getting hurt. And so on.

Bear in mind that explaining connections and consequences may mean combining events *out* of sequence. If, for example, a humiliation of three years earlier had been a factor in the boys' decision to dive, it should have gone in the narrative *there*, at the pool, not three years earlier.

Keep in mind (no one said narrating is simple) the difference between *showing* and *telling.* Remember show and tell? You held up a hamster or a fire truck or a doll or whatever and told your classmates all about it? The two activities are distinct but go together like law and order. Narrative has something of the same distinction and the same principle. Relating an anecdote or a story involves showing and telling. Sometimes the distinction between the two is as obvious as noon and midnight; other times it is as vague as dusk. But to narrate, you must understand the difference between the two and the principle of each. Because you must at times show and at times tell and at times do some of both—and you must constantly choose which it's going to be.

When the older boys challenge the younger, the narrator is showing the action. The lines are verbatim; the descriptions of tone, expression, and response detailed. The narrative takes about the same time to read as the action depicted took to occur. At the very end of the anecdote, when he summarizes the rest of the younger boys' summer in a sentence, he is telling. Telling involves considerable summary with little or no detail. It takes far less time than the action related took to occur. The narrative preceding the patch of dialogue and response is a combination of both. It is more detailed than the last sentence and less than the dramatic crisis. It takes much less time to read than the action related took to occur. Yet it isn't disposed of nearly as quickly as the pure telling of the last sentence.

Obviously, showing is more dramatic than telling. So the question arises, why tell instead of show? Telling is much quicker than showing. Telling keeps the narrative moving swiftly by conveying information that is necessary but that doesn't require dramatic treatment. If you show everything, you'll never get the story told.

Next question: When should you show? Answer: when, to understand the story, the readers must *experience* the events as the characters did: emotionally and intellectually. You should *always* show the crucial scene, the moment of pressure and decision that makes the permanent difference in the character's life. And blend show and tell when you don't need a full-stage production but you do need more than a simple summary.

Another thing to keep in mind is *point of view*, the *person* in which you narrate the story. In the preceding example, the point of view is *first* person: *I* and *we*. It could have been in *third* person: "*They* ran into several older boys they knew a little and admired very much." In narrative, be consistent: Once you establish the point of view, stick to it. Further, if the point of view is first person, respect its limits: You cannot tell the readers what's in the heads of the other characters. If your story requires such knowledge—if it requires that the readers know what's in the heads of more than one of the characters—you should narrate in the third person.

Bear in mind: In a short story, a novel, or a play, the story exists for its own sake. It is its own reason for being. In expository writing, on the other hand, a narration must have a point beyond itself: Taking a dare can involve cowardice *and* courage.

But what is "point"? Have you ever begun a story to illustrate an argument or point of view and then, in the middle of the story, forgotten your "point"? You remember the story—you always remember the story—but you panic because you can't remember the connection between the story and the discussion. What's the point? they ask. If you're lucky, you remember it. If you're not, you feel like an ass. In an essay, any narration must have such a point, and it must be explicit. The value of narrative in an essay is simple and profound. A story can convey complexity—such as the relationship of courage and cowardice involved in taking a dare—more quickly, concretely, and dramatically than any other mode. If your subject involves such complexity, use the narrative mode for at least part of your essay. And don't be surprised if narrative constitutes virtually the whole of it, as we see (looking at the Reader) in the pieces by Rivera, Kingston, Emerson, Will, and Stadtfeld.

EXERCISES

1. The following is from "Take the Plunge . . ." by Gloria Emerson.

> Two of us boarded a Cessna 180 that lovely morning, the wind no more than a tickle. I was not myself, no longer thin and no longer fast. The jump suit, the equipment, the helmet, the boots, had made me into someone thick and clumsy, moving as strangely as if they had put me underwater and said I must walk. It was hard to bend, to sit, to stand up. I did not like the man with me; he was eager and composed. I wanted to smoke, to go to the bathroom, but there were many straps around me that I did not understand. At twenty-three hundred feet, the hateful, happy man went out, making a dumb thumbs-up sign.

In this passage identify all events that are consequences of other events. Identify the chronology of events. Show when the order of consequence and the order of chronology are not the same.

2. Try rearranging the paragraph. See if another order works. See if another order works as well. Discuss the results with a group of classmates.

3. Read the essay "Trapping Days" by Stadtfeld. Identify the parts that tell and those that show and those that do some of both. Explain the rationale for Stadtfeld's choices.

4. Write a short anecdote twice, once in first person and once in third. Read both to a group of classmates to determine what difference the two points of view make to them. Describe any difference you perceive as writer and as reader.

3. Illustration

Sometimes known as exemplification, illustration is a basic strategy to all writing. Because it involves spelling out the point in detail, with fiction or fact or true confessions—whatever will serve as an example of what you are talking about—illustration is often blended into narration. Whenever you state an idea, provide specific instances. That way you develop the idea by illustrating it, which means (literally) illuminating it, lighting it up so the readers can see it as clearly as possible.

> Talk about keeping up with the Jones's! Marge and Harold keep up so close that at times it seems they even get ahead. They are on top of every fad. When large station wagons became the official family car of suburbia, they were the first or second on their street to have one, a Buick, no less. When economy cars became the thing, economy cars became their thing: a Rabbit and a Chevette. Now that sporty cars are in, they have a brand new aerodynamic Turbo-driven Mustang.
>
> In their professionally landscaped yard they have all the right trees: a flowering crab, a flowering plum, a weeping cherry, a couple of hawthornes, a couple of birches, and a corkscrew willow. Before vegetable gardens were the thing to do, backyards were for games. Marge and Harold had croquet, badminton and volleyball, horseshoes, even a putting green. (That put them way ahead of the Jones's in that department.) Now they have the largest garden on the block, and every fall they pickle, preserve, and can. And I heard just the other day that they have been looking into the possibility of chickens, a move so far out that it could put them beyond even the vanguard of the suburban back-to-nature trend. Instead of following fad, they may fashion one!

There are three basic ways to illustrate a point. One way—such as we have just seen and as we saw in the student's paper on fad combining—is to cite several major examples and to illustrate each of them with a number of quick examples. Another way is by multiple example: citing one after another without distributing them under the headings of major categories. For examples of this technique, look at Gay Talese's "New York" and Jean George's "That Astounding Creator—Nature."

The third way is the extended illustration, a single lengthy example to make a single point—the sort of thing that George Will does in "On Her Own in the City." Stories are willing and able examples of extended illustration. (You want to know how taking a dare can involve courage *and* cowardice? Let me tell you about the time I took up diving.) If you choose a story as your example, organize it according to the strategies of narration described in the last section. Remember to stick to the main line and to get to the point. Don't digress. Don't dawdle. Don't pick up any hitchhikers. The readers are waiting, and they don't like stories that end up being late.

For multiple illustration, whether you include narrative or not, follow simple and clear principles of organization so the reader can make sense of the subject. For example, Buick to Mustang and yard games to chickens follow a chronological order not only simple but appropriate—because time is a major factor of fads. Whatever the organizational principle may be, make the first item sufficiently arresting to grab the readers' attention. Then, as much as possible, put the rest of the items in order of increasing interest, from least to most (for instance, from croquet to putting green). Now the readers stay tuned and experience greater and greater pleasure.

As with description, many orders are possible. But if you force yourself to find one and to define what it is—if you *explain* to yourself why it is appropriate to the thesis and how it intensifies in interest— you may be sure that it will work.

EXERCISES

1. Define the order of examples in the following passage. While doing so, explain the principle of selection—why choose *these* figures to illustrate the point?

    > But though I was initially disappointed at being categorized as an extremist, as I continued to think about the matter I gradually gained a measure of satisfaction from the label. Was not Jesus an extremist for love: "Love your enemies, bless them that curse you, do good to them that hate you, and pray for them which despitefully use you, and persecute you." Was not Paul an extremist for the Christian gospel: "I bear in my body the marks of the Lord Jesus." Was not Martin Luther an extremist: "Here I stand; I cannot do otherwise, so help me God." And John Bunyan: "I will stay in jail to the end of my days before I make a butchery of my conscience." And Abraham Lincoln: "This nation cannot survive half slave and half free." And Thomas Jefferson: "We hold these truths to be self-evident, that all men are created equal. . . ."
    >
    > —*King, "Letter from Birmingham Jail"*

2. Choose one of the following theses and list seven examples to illustrate it. Arrange them and explain the principle of the arrangement to a group of classmates. As a group, consider whether the arrangement can be improved or not. While doing so, consider whether the examples can be improved.

    Girls have more fun than boys.

    Boys have more fun than girls.

Bald is beautiful.

Bald is ugly.

Rock music is good for you.

Rock music is bad for you.

4. Classification

Classification is one of the most fundamental powers of the brain:
breaking down something into parts, categories, or types so we recognize differences as well as similarities. And we do it from the first
moment of intellect. We teach little ones the different kinds of creatures: fish, fowl, mammals, bugs; the different kinds of plants: trees,
shrubs, flowers, weeds, grass; the different kinds of vehicles: cars,
trucks, busses, motorcycles, bicycles. And how quickly they learn.

Classification comes naturally. We all do it, all the time, and enjoy
it. The different types of dates:

The Fox

The Squirrel

The Gorilla

The Pig

The Rat

The Nerd

The different types of teachers:

The Fuddy-Duddy

The Drone

The Clown

The Preacher

The Egghead

The Lecher

The different types of students:

The Jock

The Good-Timer

The Grind

The Brownnose

The Slide-Rule

The Misfit

You classify when providing an orderly overview of a subject. To classify effectively, you must anchor the categories to deep footings in reality—real-life examples.

> The Fuddy-Duddy is the teacher who insists that students follow his instructions to the letter, and he makes his instructions as fine and complex as a contract. On every paper, name and date go in the upper right-hand corner, last name first, date written in full beneath the name. Page numbers go at the bottom, centered, with a hyphen on each side. (Not a dash!—a hyphen.) The left-hand margin must be one-and-one-quarter inches, the other three one inch. The paper itself must be twenty-weight bond, non-erasable, and corrections must be made with Liquid Paper. For every breach of these specifications the paper shall be docked half a grade point.
>
> I had a teacher who assigned one-and-a half page papers. I handed in one that was one-and-three-fifths. At the bottom she wrote, "I *said* one-and-a-half," and she docked me an entire grade point.
>
> "I don't know what's wrong with these students," a colleague of mine recently remarked. "I told them to indent paragraphs five spaces, and some indented ten, some seven, some three—it was a mess."
>
> I guess we all may have at least a little fuddy-duddy in us. I have to be honest: I won't accept an exam unless it's written in a small blue-book.

Real-life examples make the categories credible. Such examples don't have to be personal. In a well-known essay, "The Technology of Medicine," Lewis Thomas cites actual episodes in medical history—not personal history—to support the case for his classification of medical technology. The subject does not need the stamp of personal experience to ring true; medical hisotry is rich in significant, compelling examples. On the other hand, the category of fuddy-duddy teacher is so obviously whimsical and subjective that without the support of personal examples it would be considerably weakened. The writer *knows* some fuddy-duddies. In a way, he is one himself.

When classifying, as a rule define three to nine categories—certainly no less, probably no more. Each category should be simple, clear, and distinct from all others, even though in reality individuals will slop all over the neatly drawn boundaries. (In a famous psychological classification, three types of persons are established: endomorphs, ectomorphs, and mesomorphs. I've yet to meet anyone belonging exclusively to one type.) So arrange the categories as simply and clearly as you define them. Observe how Judith Viorst arranges hers in "Friends, Good Friends—and Such Good Friends"—from more distant and specialized friends to more intimate and all-around friends. Be able to explain the principle of the arrangement in a short sentence or two. For each category develop at least three specifics, and arrange them in order of increasing interest.

EXERCISES

1. Outline Susan Allen Toth's classification in "Cinematypes" (in the Reader). Explain their order.

2. Develop three to five categories for each of the following topics.

   dogs

   parents

   lamps

   chewing gum

   rock music

   Compare the classifications with those of a group of classmates. Observe how differently the same thing can be analyzed by following different principles. (Classification is relative and flexible, not absolute: It satisfies many needs.)

3. As a group, pool resources and work out the best classification for each subject. As part of the task, define and defend what "best" means to you.

5. Comparison and Contrast

Ask a twelve-year-old car freak the difference between a 1977 and a 1978 Corvette, and you will hear as fine an exercise in comparison and contrast as can be imagined. Comparison and contrast is one of the basic strategies of intellect. We use it virtually every time we go shopping, every time we make a choice, every time we merely state a preference (you may be sure the car freak likes one model more than the other). Whenever we combine two or more items, noting the similarities and differences, we are engaging in comparison and contrast.

Because comparison and contrast is such a valuable aid to understanding, writers use this strategy all the time and in every sort of

writing. Let's say we are classifying basic attitudes concerning obedience. (Such a classification is useful when assigning various organizational positions.) Some comparison and contrast is required.

> The blind zealot follows orders unquestioningly, enthusiastically, and
> courageously. His not to question why, his but to do and die. He
> loves action, especially in the form of doing his duty. He believes in
> order, discipline, and sacrifice, in his country right or wrong, in
> hierarchy and chain of command. In a war you want him on your
> side. G. Gordon Liddy, the former CIA agent implicated in the Water-
> gate scandal, who went to prison rather than betray his superiors,
> is a perfect example of the blind zealot.
>
> The thoughtful critic, on the other hand, questions leaders and
> orders on principle and by instinct. He accepts nothing on authority,
> but examines everything for himself, and he regards scepticism as
> a duty. He enjoys action when it accords with his sense of reason
> and justice. He believes in critical analysis, in intellectual freedom,
> in values that transcend the time and place of patriotism. At all
> times you need him, whether he's on your side or not. Henry David
> Thoreau, the author of "Civil Disobedience" who went to jail rather
> than pay taxes supporting the Mexican-American war, is a prime
> example of the thoughtful critic.

To achieve a clear and sensible classification, we would have to compare and contrast many types. But you get the idea.

We compare and contrast to understand better than we otherwise
would one or both of the terms under consideration. Finding similarities helps: This is like that, we say, in order to explain *this*. Playing
the stock market is like gambling: it's a game of chance, a dicey
proposition. But finding differences is of equal help. We must always
discriminate, distinguish between things, lest we become confused
and make a fundamental error. Not all mushrooms are the same; the
differences are often, quite literally, a matter of life and death. Further,
we know what something is partly by knowing what it is not. Accordingly, writers often employ contrast to clarify a point.

> What is the effect of property upon the character? Don't let's touch
> economics; the effect of private ownership upon the community as
> a whole is another question—a more important question, perhaps,
> but another one. Let's keep to psychology. If you own things, what's
> their effect on you? What's the effect on me of my wood?

By stating specifically what he is *not* writing about, Forster offers a
clearer understanding of what he *is* writing about.

In comparison and contrast, two structures are available. One we
see in the paragraph on zealots and critics. You discuss one term

completely—the zealots, then the other—the critics. You may indicate likeness and difference in the latter half as you discuss the second term or in a third section after discussing the second term. The second structure compares and contrasts the two terms point by point.

> The blind zealot follows his leaders unquestioningly, enthusiastically, and courageously, whereas the thoughtful critic, with a different sort of courage, accepts nothing on authority but questions all leaders and all orders on principle and by instinct. Not the zealot to question why, his but to do and die. He loves action, especially in the form of doing his duty. The critic, on the other hand, enjoys action only when it accords with his sense of reason and justice, and considers scepticism as a duty. The zealot believes in order, discipline, and sacrifice; in his country, right or wrong; in hierarchy and chain of command. The critic believes in analysis, in intellectual freedom, in values that transcend the space and time of patriotism. In a war you want the zealot on your side. At all times you need the critic, whether he's on your side or not. G. Gordon Liddy, the former CIA agent implicated in the Watergate scandal, who went to jail rather than betray his superiors, is a perfect example of the blind zealot. Henry David Thoreau, the author of "Civil Disobedience" who went to jail rather than pay taxes in support of the Mexican-American War, is a prime example of the thoughtful critic.

If the two terms of the comparison and contrast are lengthy, go point by point. Otherwise the reader must skip back and forth to keep the terms clearly in focus. If the two terms are short, use either structure. Go with the one that feels easier.

A final note: Comparison and contrast is easy to abuse. You can compare and contrast *any* two things, even apples and oranges. But many couples are not worth the trouble of analysis. We all know how shag carpet and grass are much alike. We all know how garbage disposals and roofs are radically different. We have nothing to learn from comparing and contrasting such couples.

Don't abuse it, then. Compare and contrast only when you have an interesting couple and when, by using it, you (and therefore the readers) learn something.

EXERCISES

1. Identify the comparison and contrast structures in the following works (in the Reader): "Diogenes and Alexander" by Highet, "That Lean and Hungry Look" by Jordan, "American Space, Chinese Place" by Yi-Fu Tuan.

2. Look at "My Wood." Identify every instance you find of comparison and contrast. Compare your findings with those of your classmates. Discuss differences to ensure you understand the principle of comparison and contrast and the extent of its use in all writing.

3. Organize an essay comparing and contrasting your mother and father term by term. Change the theme—say from your parents as parents to your parents as professional people—and organize a second comparison and contrast essay on the same pair point by point. Observe how you can compare and contrast the same pair from different vantage points.

6. Process Analysis

Perhaps the most familiar use of this strategy is the common explanation of how something is done—how to cook your goose, how to catch a smallmouth bass, how to operate a computer, how to make a million, how to win friends and influence enemies, how to make love, how to make war, how to build a greenhouse, how to play a game.

> A good basketball game for sharpening shooting skills is called *Horse*. You can play it with any number of people beyond one, but I don't recommend it for more than five because the individual players then have a long wait between turns and the game gets slow.
>
> It makes no difference who starts or what order of turns the players follow—this is a game of skill, not luck, and everyone will have an equal chance. Whoever leads takes any shot she wishes—a layup, a hook, a fade-away jump shot—whatever. If she makes it the other players have to try to duplicate the shot. Anyone following who misses gets a letter, H first, then, if and when she misses another, O, then R and so on. When anyone gets all five she's a HORSE, and horses can't shoot baskets so she's out of the game.
>
> If and when the leader misses her shot, the next player in turn becomes the leader, so the rotation always stays the same.
>
> The player left holding the ball with less than five letters to her name is the winner.
>
> There is nothing magical about the name *Horse*, only traditional. In theory, the game by any other name would be as fitting. If you are the least bit superstitious, I suggest you stick with tradition.

The word "process" means a going forward, an activity that proceeds. Analysis means dissolving, taking apart. In process analysis, we take apart a complex, forward-going activity to view its constituent components and their structural composition. We learn how something works. Much technical and scientific writing is process analysis.

Other streets (Lagos, Accra, Para) are named for the places the beans come from: quotidian freight trains full of beans that are roasted and, in studied ratios, mixed together—base beans, flavor beans, African beans, American beans—and crushed by granite millstones arranged in cascading tiers, from which flow falls of dark cordovan liquor. This thick chocolate liquor is squeezed mechanically in huge cylindrical accordion compressors. Clear cocoa butter rains down out of the compressors. When the butter has drained off, the compressors open, and out fall dry brown discs the size of manhole covers. These discs are broken into powder. The powder is put into cans and sold.

—*John McPhee, "The Conching Rooms"*

As McPhee illustrates, process analysis consists mainly of description and narration—but instead of telling a story, you tell a process. The principles of organization are similar. Sequence—the chronological order of events—must be maintained; consequence—events resulting from other events—must be accounted for. Often sequence and consequence are identical, as you might infer from their names. But when they aren't, make explanation the guide to organization. That is, interrupt chronology only where and when you must insert additional factors to make the process clear.

You often deal with technical terms in process analysis. When you write for the general reader, use only essential terms; when you introduce them, define them. For example, in the first two paragraphs of his essay, McPhee defines the technical term in the title: *conching* means "granite rollers rolling through the chocolate over crenellated granite beds at the bottoms of the pools." If he didn't, *every time he referred to the process* he would have to use a phrase instead: the rolling of the chocolate on granite beds by granite rollers. How awkward. So he uses the technical word, but is careful to define it simply and clearly. Do likewise. Of course, if the readers are expert in the subject, you may use the language of the trade—commonly known as shoptalk.

EXERCISES

1. Write an analysis of the most technical process you can do. (If you know a lot, choose one *part* of the process.) Write it for those who already understand the discipline as well as you do. Read it to some of them; see if they find it effective and sensible.

2. Read the analysis to some classmates who do not understand the discipline. List what they don't understand. Rewrite the analysis focusing on their concerns. Read it to them again; see if you've done the job. Keep doing it until you *have*.

7. Definition

To define literally means to set a limit, a boundary. It is what I am doing with these rhetorical modes. By fixing bounds and providing individual attention, we define what something is—or at least what we think it is. Consequently, the readers, whether they agree with the definition or not, know what we are talking about. And, just as importantly, so do we.

> *Following* means coming after something else, voluntarily or involuntarily, whether in pursuit or not. Hounds chasing a fox are following it. Prisoners of war marching at gun-point behind the captors' commanding officer are following him. The man who opens the door for a woman follows her in. The class of '84 follows the class of '83. The cars of a train, and their cargo, follow the engine and the engineer, and the engineer follows a schedule. The conscientious objector follows the dictates of her conscience, the conscientious ambassador follows the policy of his government, and, conscientious or otherwise, children follow the example of their parents. Always, then, following means coming after something—a person, an event, a plan, whatever—that precedes in space or time or both.
>
> Following a leader is simply a little more specific. It means coming after some*one*, whether in the flesh or in the form of orders. It should not, however, be equated with obedience. When we obey we follow voluntarily. But sometimes we follow a leader involuntarily, under duress, at the point of a bayonet, for instance, or under the influence of some drug, or in a cloud of tear gas. Nevertheless, if we come after a leader we are following, by definition.

Note the use of the multiple illustration and comparison and contrast in this definition.

To understand certain concepts, phenomena, places, times, events, we must define them in great detail and at great length—sometimes far greater than I have defined *following*. Indeed, some essays are nothing more than detailed (extended) definitions. We could write such an essay on *following*. It would (as detailed definitions often do) probably involve using several rhetorical strategies in addition to illustration and comparison and contrast: some description, for instance, and some narration; classification, perhaps, and quite probably one we haven't discussed yet—cause and effect.

Because one of the major motives for reading and writing is to understand what something is, definition is an important strategy. Detailed definition is particularly useful for working out what certain compelling but vague abstractions—love, honor, generosity, self-interest, and the like—mean specifically to us. Two essays in the Reader—"My Wood" and "Democracy"—are excellent cases in point. Reading what possession and democracy mean to Forster and White (respectively), even if we don't agree, helps us understand what they mean to us.

Definition is also an important local strategy. Most beginning writers don't realize how important it is to define key terms. They assume the readers will know what is meant because the terms are ordinary, perhaps as ordinary as the word "definition." But ordinary terms often mean different things to different people. One person's tragedy may be another's farce. Once couple's love may be another's lust. One nation's boundary may be another's grounds for war. And terms are often ambiguous in our own minds—in ways we barely realize. In one frame of reference, *following* may mean voluntary behavior; in another it may mean "coming after." To use the word in an essay, therefore, it must be defined. Then both writer and readers know the meaning.

For any type of expository writing, for any purpose, and for any group of readers, define the major terms—the key concpets—quickly and clearly.

> When I say *follow*, I mean choosing to do what another does or says to do. I do not mean compulsory obedience such as we find in prisons.

If you write about osmosis, define it. If you write about divorce, define it. If you use words such as tragic, pathetic, comic, sentimental, anxious, glad—look them up to see if they are at all ambiguous and whether you must define them.

EXERCISES

1. Following the example of E. B. White's "Democracy," define love. Make the definition no longer or shorter than White's.

2. Compare the definition with the definitions of several classmates. Note fundamental differences and similarities. As a group, fashion a collective definition using something from each student's definition.

3. To lighten the mood, fashion the worst collective definition possible.

8. Cause and Effect

Use the strategy of process analysis when explaining how something is done—the process. When analyzing reasons for and consequences of events, use the strategy commonly called *cause and effect*. This strategy often involves sophisticated levels of abstraction.

> In political life leaders do not simply lead and citizens do not simply follow. If they did so, overthrows of governments would be unheard of because revolutions would never happen. Presidents would never fail to get what they want, elected officials would never be unseated, rascals would never be thrown out, judges defrocked, preachers ridden out of town on a rail.
>
> In political life, leading and following are complex and paradoxical in nature. The effective leader actually follows the will of the citizens *by anticipation*, by knowing what their will is sometimes even before they do and thus being able to articulate and enact it in advance. The North's engagement in the Civil War under Lincoln, and the nation's engagement in World Wars I and II under Wilson and Roosevelt respectively, are cases in point.
>
> Thus the leader precedes the citizens in time yet follows them in effect. And thus the citizens, without intending to, actually lead their leaders, especially when, as we say, the leaders have a *following* because the citizens are *behind* them, giving their support.

In analyzing the nature of leading and following in politics, we must consider cause and effect. The specific point of the analysis is that—contrary to appearances—leading is effect, not cause, and following is cause, not effect. Thus the paradox. The general point of the analysis is that when we analyze the nature of anything, we must consider cause and effect.

Cause and effect is an important strategy because—as writers *and* readers—we often must consider the nature of something to understand how to deal with it. For example, is crime the result of environment and heredity or of free will and choice? The answer to the question necessarily involves considerations of cause and effect, and the answer we adopt means a significant difference in the way we handle the subject. The answer is itself, then, a cause with important effects. And even though it cannot be answered to everyone's satisfaction, we *must* answer the question—because we have crime and criminals to deal with.

You must pay attention to explanation as well as sequence when employing the strategy of cause and effect—even more than with narrative and process analysis. There is often more than one cause for each effect and more than one effect for each cause. Separate them.

And continually review the logic and sequence of the events. Ask if a certain effect necessarily results from a certain cause. You must be able to explain the connection.

However, watch out for the fallacy of *post hoc, ergo propter hoc* (after this, therefore because of this): assuming that when a happening follows another it must be the result. Say I watch a lift-off of the space shuttle, then have some breakfast. I don't eat breakfast *because* of the lift-off; I'd have eaten anyway. Sequence doesn't necessarily mean consequence.

Be alert for paradox: causes that are effects and effects that are causes. Look for inversions: apparent causes that are actual effects and vice versa. Remember that apparently small causes can become large effects. Napoleon may have been defeated at Waterloo in part because of hemorrhoids. Don't be intimidated by such a discrepancy if you can explain the connection. (What is the connection between hemorrhoids and Waterloo? Just wait till you get them; you'll see.)

A final word. As kids delight in proving by asking "Why?" until we quickly run out of answers, there is no ultimate explanation of anything. So don't shy away from using cause and effect because you doubt your ability to provide a definitive explanation. All explanations arrived at by using this strategy are provisional—the best our minds can do with the problems we face. That they cannot be definitive, however, means neither that all explanations are created equal nor that they deserve equal treatment. Don't even think of thinking that. Getting up on the wrong side of the bed does not account for mass murder. Neither does indigestion. As explanations go, those should be cited for contempt and thrown out on their ears.

EXERCISES

1. Choose one of the many things you've done without understanding why. Describe it in terms of what and how—narrate it and analyze it as a process.

2. Read it to a group of classmates. Ask them to suggest possible causes for the behavior. Consider the suggestions, contemplate your own, and rewrite it—paying attention to the causes as well as the what and how.

3. Read the rewrite to the same group. If they are satisfied with the account, fine. If not, ask them to discuss what's wrong with the explanation. Rewrite it again, until they are satisfied.

4. As a group, try to define what constitutes a satisfactory explanation of cause and effect.

9. Argumentation

Virtually every time you write, you engage in the business of trying (with varying degrees of intensity) to persuade readers to accept the thesis. That is what rhetoric is: the art of persuasion. As Didion puts it, writing amounts to saying, *"listen to me, see it my way, change your mind."* Now, when you practice the art of persuasion—when you try to convince readers to think and act a particular way—you are using the strategy called *argumentation*.

In Latin the verb *argutare* means to prattle and *arguere* means to make clear, to prove. Today the word "argument" has a similar ambiguity: It may mean quarreling—and nothing leads to prattle as quickly as a quarrel—and it may mean proving a point by means of persuasion.

For purposes of rhetoric, avoid quarreling. You cannot quarrel in print without appearing small, catty, snide, sarcastic, petulant, and whiney—like a twerp. Argue only in the sense of making a case—supporting your point of view.

There are two basic ways to make a case: by appealing to reason and by appealing to emotion. On occasion only one approach is useful. An emotional appeal in a chemistry paper is an exercise in futility. (Please, sir, I need the grade.) Stick to evidence and logic. When raising money to feed the starved of Africa, do not construct arguments from intricate logic. (The moral imperative of this crisis is so startling it fulfills the criteria of both the intuitionist and the utilitarian schools of ethics. According to intuitionist ethics. . . .) Instead, appeal directly to human compassion and generosity.

More often than not, try to persuade readers by appealing to reason *and* emotion—both. In truth, the two are as inseparable as thinking and acting, as form and content, as law and order. For the purposes of analysis, however, let's consider them separately for a few pages—then put them back together again where they belong.

a. *Appealing to Reason*

The word *logic* means reasoning correctly, sensibly, and without contradiction. Contradiction—he was nice but mean—makes no sense because it cancels itself, like a self-dismantling machine.

Logic does not exist in a vacuum, however. We don't just think. We must have something to think about and something to think with. In argumentation, the things are the facts of the matter.

It is common to distinguish between voluntary and involuntary obedience. Voluntary means *choosing* to obey, *willingly* following this or that leader, this or that order or instruction or policy. I chose to go to college, to take the courses I studied, to fulfill the requirements of the classes, and so on. I followed the curriculum willingly, not because I had to. I could at any time have quit.

Involuntary obedience means *having* to follow this or that leader, order, instruction, under *compulsion*, without the choice to do otherwise. In prison I would have to conform to the institutional regimen. I would have to keep to my cell at certain times, have to eat what was dished up on schedule, have to work where and when assigned at the job decreed, and so forth. I could not quit or leave. I would be stuck.

So we commonly distinguish. But I deny the validity of the distinction. There is no such thing as involuntary obedience. We are always free, and everything we do—everything—is by choice. Say I am a prisoner-of-war and am tortured for information. As some prisoners in that situation have proved, I do not have to give the information. I can die first. Religious martyrs demonstrate that freedom every time they are threatened: they refuse to forswear themselves. They would rather die first. I do not have to pay taxes, to cooperate with the draft, to answer to a summons, to obey or disobey the law, to follow my superior's orders or the dictates of my conscience.

In dire circumstances our freedom of choice can be restricted, radically, but it cannot be abolished. Anytime we obey, therefore, we obey voluntarily, by choice. We are always responsible for what we do. *We are what we make of ourselves.*

Making a case involves setting forth the facts and logic. Moreover, you must set them forth simultaneously so the facts make sense of the logic and the logic makes sense of the facts. Some people have *in fact* refused to obey authority. Because they were free to disobey (even on threat of death), then I, as human as they, am also free to disobey or to obey, as I choose.

Argumentation often requires refuting the facts or logic—or both—of the opposing view. Don't attack the person or persons whose views you disagree with. Never call names. Avoid adjectives. Address the facts and logic of their position. As to the facts, reveal how they are inadequate, distorted, false, missing, or—if you have no quarrel with the facts—how they don't lead to the conclusions claimed. As to the logic, show why it isn't. See how King refutes the argument advanced by various ministers and rabbis that civil disobedience is wrong because it is illegal. He cites certain historical facts they don't, and by doing so reveals the fallacy of their logic concerning the value of civil law.

We should never forget that everything Adolf Hitler did in Germany was "legal" and everything the Hungarian freedom fighters did in Hungary was "illegal." It was "illegal" to aid and comfort a Jew in Hitler's Germany. Even so, I am sure that, had I lived in Germany at the time, I would have aided and comforted my Jewish brothers. If today I lived in a Communist country where certain principles dear to the Christian faith are suppressed, I would openly advocate disobeying that country's anti-religious laws.

Incidentally, notice how King uses historical facts of special significance to Christian ministers and Jewish rabbis.

1. *Deductive Logic:* There are two kinds of logic: deductive and inductive. Deductive, like the rhetorical strategies, comes from Aristotle's tent—thus it is termed Aristotelian logic. It features the syllogism, which consists of a major premise, a minor premise, and a conclusion.

Major premise: All mammals are warm-blooded.

Minor premise: Whales are mammals.

Conclusion: All whales are warm-blooded.

Or:

Major premise: All who have choice are responsible for their behavior.

Minor premise: Everyone always has the choice to be or not to be.

Conclusion: Everyone is always responsible for his or her behavior.

In other words, you reason from the general to the particular.

We use deductive logic all the time, usually without being aware of it. Be aware of it. Watch for it all the time. If there is a flaw in any part of the syllogism, the entire argument fails—even if basically sound—because you lose credibility with the reader.

2. *Inductive Logic:* In contrast, inductive means reasoning from particular facts or individual cases to general conclusions. You use it, at least the appearance of it, when you cite fact after fact or instance after instance, and then advance the only logical conclusion.

Certain prisoners of war refuse to give information, even under torture. Martyrs refuse to forswear their faith even on pain of death. Many people—such as the freedom fighters in the civil rights movement and the abolitionists before the civil war—have refused to obey certain laws even though refusal meant imprisonment. These people prove that we do not *have* to obey any command, and that therefore all obedience is voluntary.

Be sure the facts are relevant and the conclusion is reasonable. Consider other conclusions: Certain people possess courage beyond the ordinary, so their behavior cannot be made the norm. If other conclusions don't follow reasonably, be sure you know why. If they do, be sure you explain why. (Courage is a matter of choice: We choose whether or not to act courageously.)

b. *Appealing to Emotion*

There is a suspicion lurking about that appealing to emotion is illegitimate—not quite cricket. Ideally, persuasion, like behavior, should be entirely rational—an exercise of logic based strictly upon fact.

Not so. We don't live by intellect alone. Nor can we, nor should we. Logic and facts alone often charge us emotionally, and they ought to. Consider the numbers of deaths caused by drunk drivers—just the numbers, just the facts—and let them sink in. You'll soon see what I mean. Ask a mathematician how he or she responds to a particularly fine proof; you'll hear what I mean.

Except in instances such as scientific papers, *appeal* to the readers' emotions. Don't leave out relevant facts because they are moving: on the contrary, their emotional impact is crucial. Likewise, don't decline a stretch of logic because it might arouse the readers; on the contrary, it can win the day.

The following paragraph from Didion's essay, "In Bed," is a legitimate appeal to emotion.

> It was a long time before I began thinking mechanistically enough to accept migraine for what it was: something with which I would be living, the way some people live with diabetes. Migraine is something more than the fancy of a neurotic imagination. It is an essentially hereditary complex of symptoms, the most frequently noted but by no means the most unpleasant of which is a vascular headache of blinding severity, suffered by a surprising number of women, a fair number of men (Thomas Jefferson had migraine, and so did Ulysses S. Grant, the day he accepted Lee's surrender), and by some unfortunate children as young as two years old. (I had my first when I was eight. It came on during a fire drill at the Columbia School in Colorado Springs, Colorado. I was taken first home and then to the infirmary at Peterson Field, where my father was stationed. The Air Corps doctor prescribed an enema.) Almost anything can trigger a specific attack of migraine: stress, allergy, fatigue, an abrupt change in barometric pressure, a contretemps over a parking ticket. A flashing light. A fire drill. One inherits, of course, only the predisposition. In other words I spent yesterday in bed with a headache not merely because of my bad attitudes, unpleasant tempers and wrongthink, but because both my grandmothers had migraine, my father has migraine and my mother has migraine.

Didion is trying to persuade us that migraine is not psychosomatic but physiological, not imaginary but hereditary. By citing Jefferson and Grant, Didion disabuses us of the notion that migraine is confined to nervous hypochondriacal females. By describing her first experience with migraine, she helps us realize the pathetic yet brutal insensitivity of the belief that migraine is all in the head, and she coincidentally shows us the need for change. In both instances she appeals to emotion: Jefferson and Grant are images of American strength; childhood is an image of tender vulnerability. By including family history, Didion convinces us with logic that is moving. We must conclude that migraine is, regrettably enough, visited upon the heads of succeeding generations in accordance with genetic determinism.

There is, however, such a thing as illegitimate appeal to emotion: when you do it *at the expense* of logic and fact. Like using code words and slogans ("pro-life," "pro-choice") instead of genuine argument. Like trying to persuade an all-white jury to convict a man because he's black. Or trying to persuade a nation to exterminate a people because they're Jewish. Or arguing against certain legislation by calling its backers communists or fascists. Or trying to persuade readers that migraine is neurotic and sissy because more women than men suffer from it.

Didion uses facts that appeal to emotion, and these facts do not contradict other facts or the logic. On the contrary, they fit together neatly and inform the logic. Such an appeal is not just legitimate, it is desirable. She demonstrates the way we ought to go and helps *move* us in that direction. Now that we understand migraine, we will behave toward its victims with understanding.

When the purpose is primarily persuasive, gather facts helpful to making the case: facts that appeal to emotion and reason. And note the logic of the arguments for *and against* the position you advocate. For in making a case in support of your position, you must not only answer the readers' questions so they will understand, you must also answer their objections so they may agree.

c. *A Case in Point—The Declaration of Independence*

Depending on the need, you must vary the several rhetorical strategies when arguing a thesis. Sometimes a description of a scene is necessary, sometimes a narrative, sometimes a process analysis. You must always define the terms and illustrate the points. You may need to analyze cause and effect or to classify categories. To determine which strategy to use, bear in mind that you are making a case. Imagine what it might take to convince a judge or jury. Act sceptical and convince yourself.

So you may see an argument from start to finish—to acquire a feel for the kinds of considerations involved in argumentation—here's a quick analysis of one of the most successful persuasion pieces ever written: The Declaration of Independence. Jefferson begins by stating the reason for the document.

> When in the course of human events, it becomes necessary for one people to dissolve the political bands, which have connected them with another, and to assume among the powers of the earth, the separate and equal station to which the Laws of Nature and of Nature's God entitle them, a decent respect to the opinions of mankind requires that they should declare the causes which impel them to the separation.

Jefferson cites the reason, and thereby implies the thesis: In this instance political revolution is justified by the laws of Nature and God. Jefferson assures the readers that this revolution does not signify revolution against civilized norms: He writes because he feels accountable to the opinions of others. Thus, rather than disaffecting the readers, he proceeds to establish common ground and common cause while engaging in treason. After all, what manner of person will argue against living in accordance with the laws of Nature and God?

Then Jefferson defines those laws so the readers will know exactly what he is talking about.

> We hold these truths to be self-evident, that all men are created equal, that they are endowed by their Creator with certain unalienable Rights, that among these are Life, Liberty and the Pursuit of Happiness,—That to secure these rights, Governments are instituted among Men, deriving their just powers from the consent of the governed,—That whenever any Form of Government becomes destructive of these ends, it is the Right of the People to alter or to abolish it, and to institute new Government, laying its foundation on such principles and organizing its powers in such form, as to them shall seem most likely to effect their Safety and Happiness.

He points out that these laws need not be established with empirical proof because they are "self-evident," like two and two are four and love-thy-neighbor-as-thyself. They are principles, and principles need only be reasonable to be true. Therefore, Jefferson carefully sets forth these principles and employs deductive logic: from major premise (the self-evident truths) to conclusion ("the Right of the People" to establish new government).

Jefferson then anticipates a compelling objection.

> Prudence, indeed, will dictate that Governments long established
> should not be changed for light and transient causes; and accord-
> ingly all experience hath shewn, that mankind are more disposed
> to suffer, while evils are sufferable, than to right themselves by abol-
> ishing the forms to which they are accustomed. But when a long
> train of abuses and usurpations, pursuing invariably the same Object
> evinces a design to reduce them under absolute Despotism, it is their
> right, it is their duty, to throw off such Government, and to provide
> new Guards for their future security.

Jefferson uses the strategy of cause and effect to assure his readers
that the self-evident truths he defines won't lead to revolution for
insufficient reason. Revolution is so drastic, he argues, that people
turn to it only as a last resort—when conditions have become absolutely intolerable and nothing less will suffice. Then he turns the objection to advantage by asserting that under such conditions people have
not only the right but the duty to revolt. To do otherwise would per-
petuate injustice and evil.

Having set forth the principle, Jefferson moves to specifics—the
present situation.

> Such has been the patient sufferance of these Colonies; and such is
> now the necessity which constrains them to alter their former Sys-
> tems of Government. The history of the present King of Great Britain
> is a history of repeated injuries and usurpations, all having in direct
> object the establishment of absolute Tyranny over these States. To
> prove this, let Facts be submitted to a candid world.

He then illustrates the charge of deliberate tyranny by following with
three pages of facts. The catalogue serves not only as proof but as
emotional appeal—an accumulation of abuse upon abuse intended
to outrage the readers and win sympathy for the cause.

Jefferson next employs inductive logic, draws the only conclusion
possible, and anticipates an important question.

> A Prince whose character is thus marked by every act which may
> define a Tyrant, is unfit to be the ruler of a free people. Nor have We
> been wanting in attentions to our Brittish brethren. We have warned
> them from time to time of attempts by their legislature to extend
> an unwarrantable jurisdiction over us. We have reminded them of
> the circumstances of our emigration and settlement here. We have
> appealed to their native justice and magnanimity, and we have con-
> jured them by the ties of our common kindred to disavow these
> usurpations, which would inevitably interrupt our connections and
> correspondence. They too have been deaf to the voice of justice and

of consanguinity. We must, therefore, acquiesce in the necessity, which denounces our Separation, and hold them, as we hold the rest of mankind, Enemies in War, in Peace Friends.

Viewed in the context of the entire argument, the logic is deductive, inductive, and inescapable: As a result of principle and facts, the colonists have no choice but to declare independence. And in the next paragraph, the last, that is precisely what they do.

However, Jefferson does not use all the rhetorical strategies available. For example, he does not include any description. He tells no tales, devises no classification, analyzes no process. He uses only those strategies that suit the occasion. Different occasions require different strategies.

But he does certain things that are almost always required for successful argumentation. He establishes a common ground with the readers. He sets forth ideas and facts not only to appeal to the readers' reason but to their emotions as well. He anticipates important objections and questions, thereby refuting potential opposition. And through deduction and induction, he draws logical conclusions.

EXERCISES

1. Define the syllogism implicit in the following assertion (from "In Favor of Capital Punishment" by Jacques Barzun): "a man's inability to control his violent impulses or to imagine the fatal consequences of his acts should be a presumptive reason for his elimination from society." Explain if the syllogism is logically valid or not, and why.

2. From the same essay:

> The victims [of violence] are easy to forget. Social science tends steadily to mark a preference for the troubled, the abnormal, the problem case. Whether it is poverty, mental disorder, delinquency or crime, the "patient material" monopolizes the interest of increasing groups of people among the most generous and learned. Psychiatry and moral liberalism go together; the application of law as we have known it is thus coming to be regarded as an historic prelude to social work, which may replace it entirely. Modern literature makes the most of this same outlook, caring only for the disturbed spirit, scorning as bourgeois those who pay their way and do *not* stab their friends. All the while the determinism of natural science reinforces the assumption that society causes its own evils. A French jurist, for example, says that in order to understand crime we must first brush aside all

ideas of Responsibility. He means the criminal's and takes for granted that of society. The murderer kills because reared in a broken home or, conversely, because of an early age he witnessed his parents making love. Out of such cases, which make pathetic reading in the literature of modern criminology, is born the abolitionist's [i.e., he who favors abolishing capital punishment] state of mind: we dare not kill those we are beginning to understand so well.

Explain the inductive logic Barzun uses. Does the conclusion logically follow? Are other conclusions possible? Are they more or less logical, more or less persuasive? Explain.

3. From the same:

The remote results [of violence] are beyond our ken, but it is not idle to speculate about those whose death by violence fills the daily two inches at the back of respectable newspapers—the old man sunning himself on a park bench and beaten to death by four hoodlums, the small children abused and strangled, the middle-aged ladies on a hike assaulted and killed, the family terrorized by a released or escaped lunatic, the half-dozen working people massacred by the sudden maniac, the boatload of persons dispatched by the skipper, the mindless assaults upon schoolteachers and shopkeepers by the increasing horde of dedicated killers in our great cities. Where does the sanctity of life begin?

Identify the emotional appeals in this paragraph. Analyze each instance to determine if it is compatible with fact and logic. Compare the analyses with those of some of your classmates.

4. Identify the logic in the following passages from student papers. Analyze each instance to determine if the logic is reasonable. Revise each instance, where necessary, to clarify the logic—if logic there is. Identify the emotional appeals. Analyze each to determine if it is consistent with the logic, contradicted by the logic, or indeed sustituting for logic.

Capital punishment is wrong. The death penalty is the most premeditated of murders, and is as bad as any criminal's deed. Nothing can be worse than this penalty. Both murders and executions are ugly, because both kill people.

Older people feel as if they are running out of time. They feel as if they have led their lives and their end is near. That's why most older people lead lonely lives. They sit in the house with no one to visit them but their children and grandchildren.

You should think before you drink. If not for your own safety, think of the innocent who might get hurt, a passenger in your car or a stranger in the street. Why should you jeopardize an innocent person's life just so you can get drunk?

III. THE CONCLUSION

A. How Not to Write a Conclusion

Never begin a conclusion by saying "In conclusion" or "In summary." And never conclude with a mere summary. (Exception: a memorandum or report in which a summary is specifically required for quick reference.) When you fashion a summary conclusion, the readers learn nothing new. As long as they must read more, they prefer to learn more. When you conclude summarily, the readers infer you've run out of gas before the finish or don't know how to finish.

"In conclusion," conclusions are as awkward and dull as introductory statements of purpose. I'll write one for Forster's essay so you can see what I mean.

> In conclusion, I have found that owning property has had four major psychological effects on my character. It has made me feel heavy, so to speak, which is to say extremely conservative, grounded in my possession. It has made me avaricious, always wanting more. It has made me pseudo-creative, always wanting to make meaningless changes. And it has made me selfish, wanting my property all to myself. In sum, property has had essentially a negative effect on my character.

Dreadful, isn't it? Terribly anticlimactic? Flat? Limp?

A conclusion, then, must not be a mere recapitulation; it must drive the point home again—but anew.

EXERCISES

1. Here is the conclusion to Amiri Baraka's "Streets of Despair."

> The old folks kept singing, there will be a better day . . . or, the sun's gonna shine in my back door some day . . . or, I've had my fun if I don't get well no more. What did they want? What would that sun turn out to be?
>
>   Hope is a delicate suffering. Its waste products vary, but most of them are meaningful. And as a cat named Mean William once said, can you be glad, if you've never been sad?

Read the entire essay; then rewrite the conclusion, making it the "In conclusion" variety.

2. Compare the revision with revisions of a group of classmates. Then compare revisions with the writer's original. Explain its superiority. Try to discern *all* that Baraka accomplishes in his conclusion.

B. A Model Conclusion

Let's study how Forster writes a conclusion. He begins it, oddly and interestingly, in midparagraph. I start with the "conclusion" portion of the paragraph, as if it were a separate paragraph—as it could easily be.

> There is a wood near Lyme Regis . . . where the owner has . . . built high stone walls each side of the path, and has spanned it by bridges, so that the public circulate like termites while he gorges on the blackberries unseen. He really does own his wood, this able chap. Dives in Hell did pretty well, but the gulf dividing him from Lazarus could be traversed by vision, and nothing traverses it here. And perhaps I shall come to this in time. I shall wall in and fence out until I really taste the sweets of property. Enormously stout, endlessly avaricious, pseudo-creative, intensely selfish, I shall weave upon my forehead the quadruple crown of possession until those nasty Bolshies come and take if off again and thrust me aside into the outer darkness.

This is fancier than ordinary: dives, Lazarus, a gulf traversed by vision, a quadruple crown of possession, Bolshies (Bolsheviks), outer darkness. Forster piles allusion on allusion so fast it is difficult to keep up. But he does it with great fun and with specific purpose: to poke fun at himself in order to keep certain personal problems in reasonable perspective. Forster knows it's best not to take oneself *too* seriously.

Structurally, however, Forster's conclusion is straightforward, even elementary. He launches it with fact: "There is a wood near Lyme Regis. . . ." And the conclusion proper begins when Forster relates the specific to himself: "And perhaps I shall come to this in time." But Forster cannot begin the conclusion without first presenting the specific. By the specific, therefore, he prepares the way for the conclusion. The point: The specific is the foundation of the conclusion.

Forster does summarize, but quickly. It's a reminder before his parting shot: Knowledge has comic value. Because even though he knows better, Forster will keep his wood to the bitter end—till death or the Bolshies do them part. Implicitly and quietly, Forster also returns to the beginning where he says that owning property is his "shame." Now he says he may be thrust into outer darkness as a consequence of his "shame."

Starting with a specific, returning to the beginning, positioning for a parting shot—these three techniques are often found in effective conclusions. Two of them—the specific and the parting shot—always are.

C. Begin with Something Specific

Just as you should begin the introduction with something specific—anecdote, example, quote—so should you begin the conclusion, and for the same reason: It's the easiest way to get one off to a flying start. And it precludes even the possibility of an "In conclusion"-type conclusion.

Forster begins with an example. Except for paragraphing, it is typical. He talks about preventing others from eating his blackberries, and without even so much as a transitional "For instance" he refers to the fellow in Lyme Regis. Actually, the example is itself the transition: It completes Forster's discussion of selfishness; it shows conclusively the extreme to which possession can go; and it enables Forster to make the final application to himself, the four-fold effect of property on *his* character. Furthermore, he can now go beyond mere summary, and take the conclusion as far as it can possibly go: the outer darkness. Which is either pretty far or pretty near, depending on your theology.

Gloria Emerson also jumps to a conclusion in midparagraph, immediately after describing her single experience with a parachute.

> I landed on my feet in the pit with a bump, then sat down for a bit. [Now the conclusion:] Later that day I was taken over to meet General James Gavin, who had led the 82nd Airborne in the D-day landing at Normandy. Perhaps it was to prove to him that the least promising pupil, the gawkiest, could jump. It did not matter that I stumbled and fell before him in those boots, which walked with a will of their own. Later, Mr. Istel's mother wrote me a charming note of congratulations. Everyone at the center was pleased; in fact, I am sure they were surprised. Perhaps this is what I had in mind all the time.

Emerson demonstrates that even a quick summary may be unnecessary. Instead, you may cite specific events—an episode or two—if they are meaningful to the subject of the essay. It is not just any general she later meets, but General James Gavin—parachutist par excellence. And she meets him, not with the grace you might associate with one who literally floats but with a pratfall caused by the very boots that she had landed in earlier that day.

Emerson also demonstrates that you must explain the meaning of the episodes and not leave the reader to guess. Why was she introduced to Gavin, of all people?—perhaps to prove that anyone can jump. Why mention the note and unanimous pleasure and surprise?—to drive home what she may have had in mind all along.

Finally, Emerson demonstrates how, even when the conclusion consists of events that occurred *after* those developed in the body, you can still return to the beginning: The note and the surprise are answers to the question with which she began the essay.

Ending on a specific note does not have to involve the first-person, either in the form of "I" or in the form of a moral with personal application. Gay Talese's conclusion has nothing to do with him personally, only with the city he loves.

> New York is a city in which large, cliff-dwelling hawks cling to skyscrapers and occasionally zoom to snatch a pigeon over Central Park, or Wall Street, or the Hudson River. Bird watchers have seen these peregrine falcons circling lazily over the city. They have seen them perched atop tall buildings, even around Times Square. About twelve of these hawks patrol the city, sometimes with a wingspan of thirty-five inches. They have buzzed women on the roof of the St. Regis Hotel, have attacked repairmen on smokestacks, and, in August, 1947, two hawks jumped women residents in the recreation yard of the Home of the New York Guild for the Jewish Blind. Maintenance men at the Riverside Church have seen hawks dining on pigeons in the bell tower. The hawks remain there for only a little while. And then they fly out to the river, leaving pigeons' heads for the Riverside maintenance men to clean up. When the hawks return, they fly in quietly—*unnoticed*, like the cats, the headless men, the ants, the ladies' masseur, the doorman with three bullets in his head, and most of the other offbeat wonders in this town without time.

Talese shows how specific we can be, all to the readers' delight. *Name* the objects, the places, the creatures you describe, whether well-known or not. Names are more specific, more effective. *Date* the specific events you refer to, well-known or otherwise. When facts are rooted in geography and history, they seem more substantial to the readers—more specific, more real—than when they drift namelessly in space and time.

In the catalogue of the last sentence, Talese shows how to summarize quickly and selectively. He also reveals the proper function of summary: not to review what has been written but to indicate how everything in the essay falls neatly into place according to the theme (in this essay, that New York is a city of strange phenomena—usually unnoticed).

One other point: By beginning the conclusion with the hawks, Talese proves the virtue of saving the most spectacular example for last. He also shows us how the skillful use of example helps to maneuver the essay to the upshot, a parting shot at the point of it all. In their quiet inconspicuous return, the hawks lead to the conclusion that New York is as wonderful and timeless and awesome as nature herself.

Imagine how an "In conclusion" conclusion would read. Imagine, if you can, how such a conclusion would compromise the wondrous example of the hawks.

Starting a conclusion with a quote is a common practice among professionals because it is usually effective. Roger Rosenblatt uses this technique in reaching the point about the man who lost his life by helping others save theirs.

> The odd thing is that we do not even really believe that the man in the water lost his fight. "Everything in Nature contains all the powers of Nature," said Emerson. Exactly. So the man in the water had his own natural powers. He could not make ice storms, or freeze water until it froze the blood. But he could hand life over to a stranger, and that is a power of nature too. The man in the water pitted himself against an implacable, impersonal enemy: he fought it with charity; and he held it to a standoff. He was the best we can do.

When you use a quote, even if it's a generalization like Emerson's, it has the feel of a specific. Incidentally, you don't have to quote from a philosopher, a king, or poet for the technique to work. If the subject reminds you of a line from a song, a friend, a proverb, or an ad, consider using it. If you find its connection with the subject curious yet enlightening—like the connection between Emerson's statement and Rosenblatt's subject—and if by using it you learn something new about the subject, then by all means use it. Just remember to *explain* the connection so the readers are enlightened as well.

Quoting is effective for another reason: You convey the message that the point of view is shared by others—that you have company, and sometimes impressive company at that.

Finally, it may be effective now and then to begin the conclusion with a quote so you may disagree with it—when by such disagreement you lead the reader to the final point. Say you're writing on some of the challenges of being in love. There's a song with the refrain, "Love is the answer." You might begin the conclusion by quoting it, then begging to differ. Love, in fact, is not the answer—it's the *problem*. And in explaining, you arrive at the upshot—the parting shot at the thesis.

EXERCISE

The following is the conclusion to Anne Taylor Fleming's essay, "In Defense of Flirting."

> I've discovered that I really don't want to talk to, let alone touch, most people, and flirting is a way of being affable, even affectionate, even slightly wicked without having to do either. It's a way of saying maybe, and I've always been a sucker for the romance of the near miss.

Read the essay, then rewrite the conclusion *three* times using an anecdote, a quotation, and an example to set it in motion. The specifics may be actual or imaginary; the point is to practice launching a conclusion with something specific. You need not make the same point as Fleming in your conclusion. Different specifics can lead to different conclusions. But be sure the conclusion is consistent with the essay in general.

D. Go Back to the Beginning

It isn't always necessary—but it's almost always effective—to refer somewhere in the conclusion to the beginning. Although the opportunity may lie in the first sentence of the conclusion, it doesn't have to be there. The reiteration may come later, perhaps in the last sentence. Wherever you place it, it's an effective strategy.

Annie Dillard begins "The Death of a Moth" by referring to her life alone with her two cats, one by the name of Small. This is her last paragraph:

> I have three candles here on the table which I disentangle from the plants and light when visitors come. The cats avoid them, although Small's tail caught fire once; I rubbed it out before she noticed. I don't mind living alone. I like eating alone and reading. I don't mind sleeping alone. The only time I mind being alone is when something is funny; then, when I am laughing at something funny, I wish someone were around. Sometimes I think it is pretty funny that I sleep alone.

E. B. White begins his short essay on democracy with this sentence:

> We received a letter from the Writers' War Board the other day asking for a statement on "The Meaning of Democracy."

He ends it with this:

> Democracy is a request from a War Board, in the middle of a morning in the middle of a war, wanting to know what democracy is.

William G. Wing begins his essay here:

> The Christmas sun rises first, in America, on trawlermen fishing the undersea meadows of Georges Bank.

He ends in the same place:

> Christmas came first to men on lonely meadows. It will come first again to the men on the lonely meadows offshore, fishing the Bank in boats wreathed by seabirds.

Far more often than not essayists knit together beginnings and endings; they do it because it is effective. Returning to the point of departure means coming full circle. The reader senses that you have examined the point from every angle—from all 360 degrees of angle.

However, please note that you don't merely go right back where you started from—period. Now that you've been around the world, you'll never view the point of departure through the same eyes. In the thirties, American writer Thomas Wolfe wrote the novel *You Can't Go Home Again*. The title has become virtually a proverb. With five easy words he states a multilevel truth: We can't go back to the beginning— as it was and as we were. Everything changes. Home is different, we are different—perhaps not in essence but in sufficient ways to make a complete return impossible. Returning, then, becomes a way of gauging how far we have come. If you have visited your old elementary school recently, you know what I mean. (If you haven't, you owe yourself the experience.) Returning to the beginning at the end of an essay serves precisely that purpose, figuratively or literally, as Judith Viorst points out. She begins her essay on friends with this sentence:

> Women are friends, I once would have said, when they totally love and support and trust each other, and bare to each other the secrets of their souls, and run—no questions asked—to help each other, and tell harsh truths to each other (no, you can't wear that dress unless you lose ten pounds first) when harsh truths must be told.

At the end she returns to the beginning, but with a significant difference.

> The best of friends, I still believe, totally love and support and trust each other, and bare to each other the secrets of their souls, and run—no questions asked—to help each other, and tell harsh truths to each other when they must be told.
>
> But we needn't agree about everything (only 12-year-old girl friends agree about *everything*) to tolerate each other's point of view. To accept without judgment. To give and to take without ever keeping score. And to *be* there, as I am for them and as they are for me, to comfort our sorrows, to celebrate our joys.

In a word, she grew up.

Through homecomings, reunions, and conclusions to most essays, we confirm our sense of stability and measure our sense of change. Such events, then, are paradoxical: The two senses are contradictory yet mysteriously coexist. People dislike contradiction. "He's a nice guy, basically, but he's mean." The two terms cancel each other, so the statement makes no sense. Rather, it makes us impatient with its non-sense. Although *paradox* literally means contradiction, it is commonly used to mean something else: an apparent contradiction, one that really isn't. "Nice guys finish last." In a Christian culture, where the meek are said to inherit the earth, the adage is a paradox. Just as in a dog-eat-dog world, the proverb that the meek shall inherit the earth is a paradox. And that's the very reason it's so popular. People dislike contradiction, but they love paradox because it induces wonder. So if the conclusion is paradoxical, it's almost sure to succeed.

If done skillfully, going back to the end serves a third purpose, also paradoxical: We can go beyond. I don't mean beyond the beginning—but beyond the end. Wing's conclusion is a case in point. He begins the essay with the Christmas sun rising on the fishermen—simple as that. He ends with the men falling asleep after a long night's work and the Christmas sun rising on them. Only now they resemble the shepherds of Bethlehem—the first to be touched by Christ's special blessing for the humble and the lonely—marked by the miraculous in the ordinary, a wreath of ravenous seabirds.

EXERCISES

1. Write an ending to E. B. White's "A Report in Spring," returning to the beginning but going beyond. You may have to replace the ending entirely or you may be able simply to modify it by adding yours.

2. Write an essay about your return to the past—a place (literal or metaphorical) where you had once been. First, describe the place: what transpired there, what it meant. End the essay with the return and what you learned from it. (You may learn only now what the place and the return meant. This is one reason people write: to find out.)

E. Define the Point of It All

Whether or not you return to the beginning in the conclusion, you must always go beyond the mere conclusion to an upshot, the simple but final point of it all. What a punchline is to a joke or anecdote, this sentence is to the *entire* essay. It's the snapper, the clincher—the parting shot at the point of the essay.

However, there is a major difference between the point of an *entire* essay and the point of a joke or anecdote. When you relate an anecdote, you already have the point in mind. And without a punchline, there is no joke. But when you write an essay, even if you have defined the subject, organized its development to the last detail, and have a thesis clearly in mind and on paper—you may not yet have the point of it clearly in mind. You are rarely aware of it so early on. To discover the point is reason enough to begin writing in the first place: your edification and delight as well as the readers'.

Let me show you what I mean. In the last section of her essay "Cinematypes," Susan Allen Toth describes the sort of movies she goes to alone, when she's not with her friends Aaron or Pete or Sam. She likes old musicals and comedies.

> Before I buy my ticket I make sure it will all end happily. If necessary I ask the girl at the box office. I have never seen *Stella Dallas* or *Intermezzo*. Over the years I have developed other peccadilloes: I will, for example, see anything that is redeemed by Thelma Ritter. At the end of *Daddy Long Legs* I wait happily for the scene when Fred Clark, no longer angry, at last pours Thelma a convivial drink. They smile at each other, I smile at them, I feel they are smiling at me. In the movies I go to by myself, the men and women always like each other.

Toth knew before beginning the essay that she liked old movies with happy endings. That's why she goes to them. But in the last clause of her last sentence—"the men and women always like each other"—she defines what she may not have known at the outset or even upon completion of the first draft (see the revisions in the Reader): exactly *why* she likes them. Because she wrote and revised—she knows and we know. And she also knows something more about herself: how important it is to her that men and women simply like each other. And the readers learn how important this is to them.

To put it another way, when you guide the readers through a piece of writing and approach the end, they'll ask the same question you ask: "So what?" You say you like it when Thelma and Fred smile at each other. So what? The answer to that question—I like the idea of men and women *liking* each other—is the punchline that answers the question, defines the point, and satisfies the reader.

Letting another define the upshot works nicely. Watch just how nicely Will does it as he finally reckons the horrible force underlying this life that is not really ours.

No metropolis can provide a floor of support solid enough to prevent the bewildered—like the woman from Ohio—from falling through the cracks.

Through those cracks you get an occasional glimpse of what George Eliot meant: "If we had a keen vision and feeling of all ordinary human life, it would be like hearing the grass grow and the squirrel's heartbeat, and we should die of that roar which lies on the other side of silence."

Or put it in your own words. And if they are simple, specific, and to the point—like Jefferson's in the Declaration—they too may be sublime.

And for the support of this Declaration, with a firm reliance on the protection of divine Providence, we mutually pledge to each other our Lives, our Fortunes and our sacred Honor.

You do not achieve sublimity like this by reaching for it. You achieve it by answering, specifically and clearly, the question "So what?" Concentrate on that. If the answer is sublime, fine. But don't worry about it. Answers that are funny, sad, straightforward, or matter-of-fact may also work. And in my book, an answer that works is by definition sublime.

Now let's review an essay by a student who concludes with every technique I have defined: It is specific, it returns to the beginning, and it ends with an upshot.

Directions by direction are best left to geographers and gas station attendants and Boy Scouts. A man or a kid who gives directions like "Head due south until you reach Ivansville, then head east by northeast on the third dirt road" obviously got a compass for Christmas. It does not take people with compasses long to discover the sadistic joy of directing a lost soul onto the path of total disorientation. They soon become expert at accurate misdirection by direction, no mean feat. The ability to get a person lost by telling him exactly where to go is distantly related to a lawyer's ability to make a statement vaguer by clarifying it.

That is why I like my directions simple. I like them left and right. This eliminates the need for a pathfinder or tour-guide in order to get where I'm going. I no longer have to wait until the sun sets in the west or until the northstar appears so that I can get a bearing. And I know that if my relatives give me directions by the compass they don't really want me to show up at all. I don't need to look for moss on the north side of a tree; I can find my own way, easy as left and right. I don't need maps, atlases, or sophisticated radar screens. It wouldn't bother me if the world were to suddenly shift under my feet, if the north star were to head south for the winter, if the sun were to set in New Jersey.

Why, with left and right on my hands, I can even handle hick gas station attendants and geographers and Boy Scouts. So let the roads roll on! Horace Greely said, "Go west, young man!" and I'm ready! I can count on myself, and if I'm not mistaken, west is thataway.

EXERCISES

1. Identify the three techniques (cited earlier) in the conclusion of the student essay.

2. Take a break.

WILLIAM STAFFORD

Writing

Stafford teaches at Lewis and Clark College in Portland, Oregon, and writes poetry of the first rank: Stories That Could Be True (1977), for instance, and A Glass Face in the Rain (1982), and the volume that received the National Book Award, Traveling Through the Dark (1962). In this essay Stafford explains the importance of discovery in writing.

A writer is not so much someone who has something to say as he is someone who has found a process that will bring about new things he would not have thought of if he had not started to say them. That is, he does not draw on a reservoir; instead, he engages in an activity that brings to him a whole succession of unforeseen stories, poems, essays, plays, laws, philosphies, religions, or—but wait!

Back in school, from the first when I began to try to write things, I felt this richness. One thing would lead to another; the world would give and give. Now, after twenty years or so of trying, I live by that certain richness, an idea hard to pin, difficult to say, and perhaps offensive to some. For there are strange implications in it.

One implication is the importance of just plain receptivity. When I write, I like to have an interval before me when I am not likely to be interrupted. For me, this means usually the early morning, before others are awake. I get pen and paper, take a glance out the window (often it is dark out there), and wait. It is like fishing. But I do not wait very long, for there is always a nibble—and this is where receptivity comes in. To get started I will accept anything that occurs to me. Something always occurs, of course, to any of us. We can't keep from thinking. Maybe I have to settle for an immediate impression: it's cold, or hot, or dark, or bright, or in between! Or—well, the possibilities are endless. If I put down something, that thing will help the next thing come, and I'm off. If I let the process go on, things will occur to me that were not at all in my mind when I started. These things, odd or trivial as they may be, are somehow connected. And if I let them string out, surprising things will happen.

If I let them string out. . . . Along with initial receptivity, then, there is another readiness: I must be willing to fail. If I am to keep on writing, I cannot bother to insist on high standards. I must get into action and not let anything stop me, or even slow me much. By "standards" I do not mean "correctness"—spelling, punctuation, and so on. These details become mechanical for anyone who writes for a while. I am thinking about what many people would consider "important" standards, such matters as social significance, positive values, consistency, etc. I resolutely disregard these. Something better, greater, is happening! I am following a process that leads so wildly and originally into new territory that no judgement can at the moment be made about values, significance, and so on. I am making something new, something that has not been judged before. Later others—and maybe I myself—will make judgments. Now, I am headlong to discover. Any distraction may harm the creating.

So, receptive, careless of failure, I spin out things on the page. And a wonderful freedom comes. If something occurs to me, it is all right to accept it. It has one justification: it occurs to me. No one else can guide me. I must follow my own weak, wandering, diffident impulses.

A strange bonus happens. At times, without my insisting on it, my writings become coherent; the successive elements that occur to me are clearly related. They lead by themselves to new connections. Sometimes the language, even the syllables that happen along, may start a trend. Sometimes the materials alert me to something waiting in my mind, ready for sustained attention. At such times, I allow myself to be eloquent, or intentional, or for great swoops (treacherous! not be be trusted!) reasonable. But I do not insist on any of that; for I know that back of my activity there will be the coherence of my self, and that indulgence of my impulses will bring recurrent patterns and meanings again.

This attitude toward the process of writing creatively suggests a problem for me, in terms of what others say. They talk about "skills" in writing. Without denying that I do have experience, wide reading, automatic orthodoxies and maneuvers of various kinds, I still must insist that I am often baffled about what "skill" has to do with the precious little area of confusion when I do not know what I am going to say and then I find out what I am going to say. That precious interval I am unable to bridge by skill. What can I witness about it? It remains mysterious, just as all of us must feel puzzled about how we are so inventive as to be able to talk along through complexities with our friends, not needing to plan what we are going to say, but never stalled for long in our confident forward progress. Skill? If so, it is the skill we all have, something we must have learned before the age of three or four.

A writer is one who has become accustomed to trusting that grace, or luck, or—skill.

Yet another attitude I find necessary: most of what I write, like most of what I say in casual conversation, will not amount to much. Even I will realize, and even at the time, that it is not negotiable. It will be like practice. In conversation I allow myself random remarks—in fact, as I recall, that is the way I learned to talk—, so in writing I launch many expendable efforts. A result of this free way of writing is that I am not writing for others, mostly; they will not see the product at all unless the activity eventuates in something that later appears to be worthy. My guide is the self, and its adventuring in the language brings about communication.

This process-rather-than-substance view of writing invites a final, dual reflection:

1. Writers may not be special—sensitive or talented in any usual sense. They are simply engaged in sustained use of a language skill we all have. Their "creations" come about through confident reliance on stray impulses that will, with trust, find occasional patterns that are satisfying.

2. But writing itself is one of the great, free human activities. There is scope for individuality, and elation, and discovery, in writing. For the person who follows with trust and forgiveness what occurs to him, the world remains always ready and deep, an inexhaustible environment, with the combined vividness of an actuality and flexibility of a dream. Working back and forth between experience and thought, writers have more than space and time can offer. They have the whole unexplored realm of human vision.

JACQUES BARZUN
A Writer's Discipline

Born in France, Barzun spent his career as a student and a history professor and dean at Columbia University in New York City. Among his many publications are books on history (European, American, and intellectual), on education, on music, on literature, on writing, on scholarship, and on science. In this selection Barzun discusses not only the value but the necessity of discipline in getting one's self to work.

No writer has ever lived who did not at some time or other get stuck. Even the great producers such as Scott and Dickens suffered from the professional malady of being "for no good reason" (as we all say) unable to write. And for every writer in working trim there may be a dozen persons of great ability who are somehow self-silenced. At long intervals they turn out remarkable fragments—half-essays or embryo stories; but they cannot seem to pull themselves together and finish anything, much less begin at will.

Now writing is not an art in which one can succeed by the production of interesting ruins, and since the total or partial paralysis of the writer's will is a fearsome and mysterious blight, most writers come to recognize the need of a discipline, a set of ritual practices which will put the momentum of habit behind their refractory ego and push them over the obstacle. Scott confessed that he used his divided self in order to rule: hating the thought of commitment, he hardly ever wrote anything except to flee the necessity of writing something else. And Dickens tells of long mornings when he forced himself to stay at the desk making false starts, lest by giving up he should give up forever. For all his books already in print, he might just as well have been the common schoolboy who is told to write of his visit to Aunt Julia and who honestly finds nothing to say except that he arrived on Friday and left on Sunday.

It may be partly because we were all coerced in this fashion that writing on demand comes so hard later on. If so, the old experience contains its own corrective, provided we are willing to look into it, that is to say, look into ourselves. If we ask what is the literary impulse par excellence we are, I think, bound to say that it is a desire to pull together one's conscious self and project it into some tangible constructed thing made up of words and ideas. The written thing may serve ulterior ends, as in exposition or polemic, but its first intention is to transfer a part of our intellectual and emotional insides into an independent and self-sustaining outside. It follows that if we have any doubts about the strength, truth, or beauty of our insides, the doubt acts as an automatic censor which quietly forbids the act of exhibition. Johnny cannot write about the visit to his aunt not merely because he did not initiate the literary idea, but because he feels like a fool relating the trivial things that happen every weekend: "They don't want to hear about that." Generalizing from his dominant conviction, we may say that the antiliterary emotion par excellence is fear. It acts precisely as when one attempts to speak a foreign language; one feels too damn silly for words—and one shuts up.

Obviously, if one were starving or in danger of assault, words would come fast enough, the inner censorship lifted and all sense of affectation gone. This, then, is the desirable situation to create for oneself every morning at nine, or every evening at five. The hopelessly stuck would find it expensive but worth it to hire a gunman to pound on the door and threaten death as a spur to composition. Ideas would come thick and fast and yet be sorted out with wonderful clarity in that final message to one's literary executors.

The sober application of this principle suggests that the writer needs an equivalent of this urgency, this pressure. It cannot help being artificial, like any pulmotoring; but although it need have nothing to do with danger, it must generate some form of excitement. Most of those who have written extensively under varying conditions would say that the true healthful pressure and excitement come from a belief that the things one wants to say form a coherent whole and are in some way needed; that is, the urge is a mixture of the aesthetic and the utilitarian impulses. This seems to be borne out by the observation frequently made that if one can only get something down on paper— anything—one feels no further hindrance to working. The final product may not contain a single sentence of the original, but in the successive drafts one has only a sense of pleasure at molding a resistant lump of clay—cutting away here and adding there in the double light of utility and harmony. It is at the outset, before the matter exists, that the great void paradoxically objectifies one's fear, one's conviction that "they don't want to hear about it."

To know how to begin, then, is the great art—no very profound maxim—but since in any extended piece of work one must begin many times, this is the art which it is essential to master. There is only one way: to study one's needs and quirks, and circumvent one's tricks for escape. The guidebooks will tell you that you should be full of your subject—a very good notion but too abstract. Fullness requires moral and mechanical aids and stout controls. For nothing is more common than to feel a stream of excellent ideas racing past and never a hook to lure them out into the open. This is especially true if one has previously tried to capture them and failed. We may say that our ideas feel like a whole world which is too big and whirling too fast to be pulled out in one piece. True, and this is why first aid at this point consists in not trying to have it born whole. Convince yourself that you are working in clay not marble, on paper not eternal bronze: let that first sentence be as stupid as it wishes. No one will rush out and print it as it stands. Just put it down; then another.[1] Your whole first paragraph or first page may have to be guillotined in any case after your piece is finished: it is a kind of "forebirth." But as modern mathematics has discovered, there can be no second paragraph (which contains your true beginning) until you have a first.

The alternative to beginning stupidly, with a kind of "Er-ah," is to pick out during the earliest mental preparation for the work some idea which will make a good beginning, whether for intrinsic or topical reasons, and let it pull the rest along. Thus I began this essay on the cheering note that those mighty engines, Scott and Dickens, also stalled, and I had this in mind long before I knew what would come next. The danger of this procedure is that a picturesque idea can lead one too far back of the true starting line, and the cleverness or the charm of the idea makes one unwilling to sacrifice it. Burke was rightly accused of beginning every speech by inviting the Speaker of the House to dance a minuet with him. Ruthless decapitation is the remedy; but note in passing that the error confirms our analysis of the writer's insidious desire to put a cozy padded vest between his tender self and that vague, hostile, roaming animal known as the audience.

Having begun, the writer of even moderate gifts will feel a certain warmth creeping into his veins and rising, as it should, to his head. (In writing, always keep your feet warm, unless you are a full-blooded Indian accustomed to thinking great thoughts while walking barefoot in icy streams.) This genial current, which might prove genius, must

---

1. Another "painful" writer, André Gide, makes the same remark in another way: "Too often I wait for the sentence to finish taking shape in my mind before setting it down. It is better to seize it by the end that first offers itself, head or foot, though not knowing the rest, then pull: the rest will follow along" (*Journal*, 4 June 1930).

be maintained and a physical and mental circulation established, in which blood, ink, and thoughts perform their appointed roles. It is now more than ever important not to let the vigilant censor within freeze everything on a technicality. I refer to that sudden stoppage due to the lack of the right word. Some writers, it is true, are able once started to shape their sentences whole in their heads before putting them down—Gibbon was one of those. But most, I believe, do not. Hence it is fatal for them to feel the entire system of ideas, feelings, and tenuous associations which is now in motion come to a dead stop because some adjective which means "boring" and begins with n eludes them. Don't look for it. Leave it blank. The probability is that there is no such word; if there is, it will come up of itself during revision or be rendered unnecessary by it. This sets the rule, by the way, for revision itself: keep going at a reasonable pace to the end, skipping the impossible; then start afresh until you have solved the true problems and removed the insoluble. Remember Barrie's schoolboy who chewed a pencil to splinters and failed the examination because he sought a word halfway between mickle and muckle.

The same law of momentum applies to the search for transitions, to perfecting the rhythm and shape of sentences, even occasionally to the ordering of paragraphs. Don't haggle and fuss but reassure yourself with the knowledge that when you come back to settle these uncertainties and fill these blanks you will still have your mind with you. Especially for young writers who have experienced difficulty and discouragement, the proper aim is that of the learner on the bicycle—keep going, which means a certain speed. Cutting slow capers will come later.

More serious than being stopped by a word is the breakdown in ideas. This has to be judged and treated with an even sharper eye for evasion and fraud on the part of the writing self. For the possibilities are several: one is that you have written enough for one day and reached a natural stopping place. It is wise therefore to have not simply a set time for writing—it need not be daily and yet be regular—but also a set "stint" for the day, based on a true, not vainglorious estimate of your powers. Then, when you come to a natural stop somewhere near the set amount, you can knock off with a clear conscience.

Another cause of stoppage is that the work has reached a point of real difficulty—an intellectual decision has to be made, a turning taken, and your mind is balking at it from fatigue or other causes. Or again, it may be that by reason of faulty arrangement there is no obvious bridge from where you are to where you want to go. If the former is true, you must fight it out sooner or later, on the same principles that enabled you to make a beginning. If the latter, devices may help: go back to the beginning, or to some convenient break in the development and read ahead, making but few corrections—just enough to warrant the expense of time and eyesight, but not enough to bog you down. As you approach the halting place, you may suddenly see where you lost the true way and how to bypass the evil spot altogether; or conversely you may find that your fresh running start carries you straight on and over the hump.

Why not an outline? Well, for my taste, outlines are useless, fettering, imbecile. Sometimes, when you get into a state of anarchy, or find yourself writing in circles, it may help to jot down a sketchy outline of the topics (or in a story, of the phrases) so far covered. You outline, in short, something that already exists in written form, and this may help to show where you started backstitching. To be sure, a memorandum listing haphazardly what belongs to a particular project is useful. In fact, if you would be a "full" man as you undertake a new piece of work, you should have before you a little stack of slips bearing the ideas that have occurred to you since the subject first came to life in your mind. Otherwise the effort and sense of treasures just out of reach will be a drain and diversion of writing power. It is jottings of this sort that fill the "Notebooks" at the tail end of "The Works." When I say slips or notebooks, I mean any congenial form of memorandum, for I doubt whether a self-respecting man with a lively flow of ideas can constrain himself to a uniform style and shape of note taking until the sacred fires have begun to cool—say around the age of fifty-one.

In all such matters, I believe in humoring to the greatest extent the timid and stubborn censor which stops work on flimsy pretenses. Grant, by all means, its falsely innocent preferences as to paper, ink furnishings, and quash its grievances forever. We know that Mark Twain liked to write lying in or on a bed: we know the Schiller needed the smell of apples rotting in his desk. Some like cubicles, others vasty halls. "Writers' requisites," if a Fifth Avenue shop kept them, would astound and demoralize the laity. Historically, they have included silk dressing gowns, cats, horses, pipes, mistresses, particular knick-knacks, exotic headgear, currycombs, whips, beverages and drugs, porcelain stoves, and hair shirts. According to one of Bernard De Voto's novels, writing paper of a peculiar blue tint has remarkable properties, about which the author makes an excellent point very subtly: he shows his writer-hero as neurotically exigent on this "trivial" matter, but after we have mocked and put him down as a crank, his work turns out to be a masterpiece. Quite simply, by yielding on such apparently irrational details, the writer is really outwitting his private foe—the excuse-maker within each of us who says: "I can't work today because I haven't any blue paper." Nor is this weakness limited to the literary artist, whether genius or duffer. Before me is a letter just received from a distinguished scientific friend who says: "I have got down to honest work on my article, drawing up elaborate typed notes in what may be a desperate attempt to avoid the actual writing."

That is the true spirit: suspect all out-of-the-way or elaborate preparations. You don't have to sharpen your pencils and sort out paper clips before you begin—unless it be your *regular* warming up. Give yourself no quarter when the temptation strikes, but grab a pen and put down some words—your name even—and a title: something to see, to revise, to carve, to do over in the opposite way. And here comes the advantage of developing a fixation on blue tinted paper. When you have fought and won two or three bloody battles with the insane urge to clean the whole house before making a start, the sight of your favorite implements will speak irresistibly of victory, of accomplishment, of writing done. True, you are at the mercy of the paper mills, as Samuel Butler was the slave of a certain thick book which he used to prop up his writing board at the exact slope of his desire,[2] but such attachments are changeable once they have become a way of tackling work. Even fundamental routines may be recast. I used to wonder how Jane Austen could possibly write in the midst of family conversation, when to me Crusoe's solitude was scarcely adequate. But I learned under necessity to compose (first drafts at least) while keeping a chattering and enterprising child out of mischief in my workroom. The one thing needful is to have an anchorage in some fixed habits and to deal with writer's cowardice precisely as one would with other kinds—facing pain or going over the top. For it is never the specifically literary faculty which balks; it is the affection for one's dear self seeking to protect it against the fearful dangers of laughter, criticism, indifference, and reprints in digest form.

Since habits are rooted in the physical part of us, some writers find it serviceable to begin by doing some act requiring no special thought but which insensibly leads to composition. This doing may be as simple as answering correspondence or (with Butler) "posting one's books"—

2. It was Frost's *Lives of Eminent Christians*, as he tells us in "Quis Desiderio?"

i.e., transcribing notes. But most writers prefer not to spoil the day's freshness by a reminder that relatives exist, nor distract themselves with the scattered subject matter of their notes. The ideal situation perhaps is to awaken with the grand design in mind (it was the last thing thought of before falling asleep), to shave while a matching throng of ideas lathers up within, and to go straight to the blank sheet without exchanging words with anyone.

Here a natural analogy with other arts suggests a few scales and runs on the typewriter, and it may well be that the writer's lack of anything so pleasantly muscular is a real cause of his frequent impotence; even the painter can busy his hands, craftsmanlike. The momentous question behind this comparison is of course the familiar one—pen or typewriter? It is no hedging answer to say, take your choice. But your choice (as I keep repeating) must be thoroughly considered. Is it possible, for instance, that like me you find it discouraging not to see whole paragraphs at a time and not be able to cross out whole sentences at a time? If so, stick to the pen and use the typewriter to do your first revision as you transcribe. The plastic aspect of written matter is important, and the best revision is undoubtedly made from a clean copy embodying previous revisions. One reason why so much nineteenth-century work is good is that printers' revises were cheap and the writer carved direct on cold print.

Many writers' liking to compose on the typewriter has to do with the clean look of near-print. Hence persons whose fingers are clumsy and whose typed odes are full of fractions and dollar signs should give up the instrument. According to biographers, what they usually take up instead is a short stubby pencil. I do not know why it must be stubby; I mention it only to be fair. Let us by all means have poems, even if written with skewers in goose fat: the point is: Suit Thyself, but pay for it, i.e., *work!*

Numberless other facts, tricks, and generalities could be added to this already overlong set of hints. Writers young and old who take an interest in the bare processes of their art (as painters more frequently do) would be well advised to read at large in the considerable literature of exhortation and confession about writing. Nine-tenths of it is pedantic or platitudinous, but the other tenth is often amusing and likely to contain particles of illuminating truth, especially if written by a practicing writer. But again, the reader's object being ultimately to make personal applications, he should be on the watch for statements—there must be more than one in the present essay—which make him exclaim: "What an idea! why, it's just the opposite." The writer must indeed turn everything into grist for *his* mill and no other, as a result of which he acquires both self-knowledge and self-command. His last consideration is therefore his first: what is he afraid of? Only, after he has disciplined himself, he puts the question differently and asks: Whom am I writing for? The century of the common man makes this no easy question to answer, for the common man is a social and political ideal, admirable in the spheres indicated. As a buyer and reader of books he does not exist; one finds humanity instead, which is diverse. One will write for different kinds of people at different times but at any one time there must be some imagined interlocutor, some animated ear trumpet, into which we pour our words. This may be posterity or the children aged eight to ten, but either must be represented in our minds. In judging our own work, we "suit" this mythical person, and our original verdict, "they don't want to hear about that," takes on another meaning—critical yet productive—a kind of ideal collaboration.

This endless conversation in which the writer's censor turns into a helping representative of a given public, is of course most pleasantly realized when the writer has in truth "a reader"—a relative or friend whose judgment he can use. Notice I did not say "whose judgment he will take." For the last step in the writer's liberation through discipline is the discovering of judicial distance—distance from himself, from his work, from his critic, and even from that fickle tiger, his audience.

The practical rules that follow are obvious. Do not read what you have written—much less what you are writing—to whoever will listen; indeed never read unpublished work (except perhaps poems), but give it to be read at leisure. Never show a first draft—except to an old and tried reader who knows from the crude signs what your work may become. Above all, do not talk yourself out of good ideas by trying to expound them to haphazard gatherings. In general, never choose your critic from your immediate family circle: they have usually no knowledge of the processes of writing, however literary they may be as consumers; and in their best-natured act of criticism one may hear the unconscious grinding of axes sounding like a medieval tournament.

No, your special reader (or two or three at most) must be chosen from those who care for writing as much as for you—no writer wants his work to shine in a *charitable* light. And even from your critic-by-appointment you must take only what goes with the grain of your thought and intent. This calls for delicate decisions, since it is always easy to cut off dead tissue and always hard to cut into the living cells that are not true flesh but tumor. The basic principle here as always is to protect the work and not the self.

There is one thing more. A man who writes, as Hardy said, stands up to be shot at, but Hardy was wrong to resent the shooting. So-called established writers who after years of work still wince at criticism are certainly not established in their own souls. Nor does one have to be callous or stubborn about reproof in order to feel solid and to accept one's errors and limitations with a composure which one can then extend to the errors and injustices of critics. Doing so habitually makes one more and more able to *see the work*, which is the prerequisite to producing it, pruning it, and preserving it against the ravages of time.

ROBERT A. DAY
What Is a Scientific Paper?

A biologist, Day has been a member of the Council of Biology Editors and of the Publications Board of the American Society for Microbiology. His book How to Write and Publish a Scientific Paper *(1979) is widely regarded as the definitive treatment of the subject. The following selection, an excerpt from the book, defines the essential criteria of scientific writing.*

A scientific paper is, or should be, highly stylized, with distinctive and clearly evident component parts. Each scientific paper should have, in proper order, its Introduction, Materials and Methods, Results, and Discussion. Any other order will pose hurdles for the reader and probably the writer. "Good organization is the key to good writing". . . .

This prescribed order is one that I have taught and recommended for many years. Until recently, however, there have been several somewhat different systems of organization that were preferred by some journals and some editors. The tendency toward uniformity has increased since 1972, when the order cited above was prescribed as a standard. . . .

This order is so eminently logical that, increasingly, it is used for many other types of expository writing. Whether one is writing an article about chemistry, archeology, economics, or crime in the streets, an effective way to proceed is to answer these four questions, in order: (i) What was the problem? Your answer is the *Introduction*. (ii) How did you study the problem? Your answer is the *Materials and Methods*. (iii) What did you find? Your answer is the *Results*. (iv) What do these findings mean? Your answer is the *Discussion*. . . .

In short, I take the position that the preparation of a scientific paper has almost nothing to do with writing, per se. It is a question of *organization*. A scientific paper is not "literature." The preparer of a scientific paper is not really an "author" in the literary sense. In fact, I go so far as to say that, if the ingredients are properly organized, the paper will virtually write itself.

Some of my old-fashioned colleagues think that scientific papers should be literature, that the style and flair of an author should be clearly evident, and that variations in style encourage the interest of the reader. I disagree. I think scientists should indeed be interested in reading literature, and perhaps even in writing literature, but the communicatin of research results is a more prosaic procedure. As Booth . . . put it, "Grandiloquence has no place in scientific writing."

Today, the average scientist, to keep up in his field, must examine the data reported in hundreds or even thousands of papers. Therefore, it seems obvious to me that scientists and, of course, editors must demand a system of reporting data that is uniform, concise, and readily understandable.

I once heard it said: "A scientific paper is not designed to be read. It is designed to be published." Although this was said in jest, there is much truth to it. And, actually, if the paper is designed to be published, it will also be in a prescribed form that can be read, or at least its contents can be grasped quickly and easily by the reader.

Language of a Scientific Paper

In addition to organization, the second principal ingredient of a scientific paper should be appropriate language within that organization. In this book, I keep emphasizing proper use of English, because it is in this area that most scientists have trouble.

If scientific knowledge is at least as important as any other knowledge, then it must be communicated effectively, clearly, in words of certain meaning. The scientist, to succeed in this endeavor, must therefore be literate. David B. Truman, when he was Dean of Columbia College, said it well: "In the complexities of contemporary existence the specialist who is trained but uneducated, technically skilled but culturally incompetent, is a menace."

Although it is recognized that the ultimate goal of scientific research is publication, it has always been amazing to me that so many scientists neglect the responsibilities involved. A scientist will spend months or years of hard work to secure his data, and then unconcernedly let much of their value be lost because of his lack of interest in the communication process. The same scientist who will overcome tremendous obstacles to carry out a measurement to the fourth decimal place will be in deep slumber while his secretary is casually changing his micrograms per milliliter to milligrams per milliliter and while the printer slips in an occasional pounds per barrel.

Language need not be difficult. In scientific writing, we say: "The best English is that which gives the sense in the fewest short words" (a dictum printed for some years in the "Instructions to Authors" of the *Journal of Bacteriology*). Literary tricks, metaphors and the like, divert attention from the message to the style. They should be used rarely, if at all, in scientific writing. Justin Leonard, assistant conservation director of Michigan, once said: "The Ph.D. in science can make journal editors quite happy with plain, unadorned, eighth-grade level composition" (*Bio-Science*, September 1966).

4
Rewriting

I. FROM WORDS TO THE WORD

You now have a draft—a beginning, a middle, and an end—to work on and over. It will probably require a great deal of working over, perhaps even a complete overhaul or two. Let me show you an example of revision from William Howarth's "Introduction" to *The John McPhee Reader*. First:

> Certain touches of *The New Yorker*'s elegance often grace his witty lines. He has an amusing propensity for dropping trademark names, as though references to L. L. Bean, Adidas, or The Glenlivet were enough assurance of solid value.

Then:

> Certain touches of *The New Yorker*'s elegance often grace his witty lines. Like the magazine, he uses trademark names—L. L. Bean, Adidas, The Glenlivet—but not to sell shoes or whiskey. Names specify a scene, sharpen the focus of his observation.

Here Howarth alters the structure of the second sentence to add information. He makes the comparison with the magazine's style explicit, and points out a reason McPhee does *not* use trademark names. Then Howarth adds a sentence explaining the reason McPhee does. The point of the revision is to make his meaning explicit and clear.

Often revision involves subtraction, not addition, to eliminate unnecessary words and sometimes unnecessary information.

> When he has the cards in satisfactory order, he codes them in standard outline fashion, with Roman numerals or capital letters, and thumbtacks them to a large bulletin board.

> When he has the cards in a satisfactory arrangement, he thumbtacks them to a large bulletin board.

153

Rewriting means adding, subtracting, and rearranging to say exactly what you want to say. That you must rewrite it, however, doesn't mean the original draft was wasted time. It's something tangible to rewrite— to work on and over.

So now look at the first draft and ask if it's beginning to say what you want it to say. Of course, to know the answer you must have determined what you wanted to say when you defined the purpose and thesis long ago. But purpose and thesis—especially thesis—are themselves subject to revision. When writing and reviewing the first draft, you may discover another purpose suits the material in a way you had not realized. Now that you understand the material more fully, you may find it necessary to change or refine the thesis. If so, make the changes (unless you are writing specifically to someone's order and therefore cannot).

Next, make the other changes that are necessary. You may have to discard some of the material in the first draft; you may have to discard a lot. In either case, you will need additional material: information from your notes, newly researched information, interviews, memory. You may have to reorganize your material radically, quite a bit, only a little.

You won't enjoy reading this—it's not what you want to see or hear—but you may have to perform several overhauls before you get the right introduction, the right development, and the right conclusion. Just remember that conducting such extensive exploration is *not a waste of your time.* The process of invention involves trial and error. Often you can't know that something doesn't work until you try it. And trying it helps you think of further possibilities, new ideas, alternative approaches. Of course it's possible you may get the right beginning, middle, and end on the first or second draft. Not probable—but possible.

Let's assume you ultimately write a satisfactory draft. The introduction is specific; you have liftoff. In the body you have material, structure, and rhetorical strategies sufficient to do the job. The conclusion contains a specific to help tie things together and clarify the point of it all. In other words, the house is up and roughed in: the walls are standing; the roof's on; and the windows, wiring, and plumbing are in. Now you're ready to do the finish work: fashion the paragraphs and sentences just so and attend to diction, figures of speech, and tone. You want it right—down to the last detail.

A. The Paragraph

A paragraph is a piece of prose, indented at the outset, that focuses on a single topic. You are at this very moment reading a paragraph about the paragraph.

1. The Three Main Patterns

Because of this indention you are now reading a new paragraph. This one focuses on the three main patterns of paragraph.

1. Topic/Restriction/Illustration
2. Question/Answer
3. Problem/Solution

To emphasize the three patterns, I indented even farther; yet by beginning *this* sentence at the left-hand margin, I clearly indicate the patterns do not constitute a separate paragraph but form part of this one. Quoted material of more than five lines is indented in the same manner.

a. *Topic/Restriction/Illustration*

Interestingly, I can write the first two paragraphs of this section as one and simultaneously demonstrate the first pattern cited.

> A paragraph is a piece of prose, indented at the outset, that focuses on a single topic. In fashioning a paragraph there are three main patterns from which to choose: 1) Topic/Restriction/Illustration, 2) Question/Answer, and 3) Problem/Solution.

The first sentence in the example is commonly termed the *topic sentence*. (The first sentence of a paragraph often is, but need not be, the topic sentence.) In it you state the topic of the paragraph—the focal point toward which everything gravitates. In the topic sentence you define the principle of the paragraph's unity. The main clause of the second sentence in the example *restricts* the topic. In discussing the topic, you might consider a number of different directions. In the restriction you define the one direction of choice from the three main patterns of paragraph—and exclude any others. Having defined and restricted the topic, you then *illustrate* it. In the example, the citation of the three patterns is the illustration.

Now I'm going to explain why I'm discussing the paragraph in the chapter on *re*writing. I have already shown one instance when, with minor adjustments, you can fashion one or two paragraphs out of the same piece of prose. I want to show you another. In the discussion just concluded, I dealt with the topic sentence, the restricting sentence, and the illustration all in the same paragraph. Because the topic is the paragraph and the restriction is one pattern of paragraph and I discuss that pattern—my paragraph is as coherent and unified as a piece by Mozart. (I didn't say as artistically profound—only as coherent and unified.) Yet I could have divided the discussion into three paragraphs: topic, restriction, and illustration. You have great latitude in paragraphing—freedom—which means you must consider and try (and try again) various arrangements to determine which is best for your purposes.

Let's see some possibilities by studying a student topic/restriction/ illustration paragraph.

> I know that you are supposed to sit up straight, but for me sitting like that for long is literally a pain in the back and a pain in the neck. The back goes first. It feels like my arms when I hold them straight out in front for any length of time: fine for a while, then numb, then aching and sore. The neck goes next. The strain in my back pushes my neck forward and pulls my shoulders down and back, and if I stick with it long enough—if I insist on sitting up straight—my neck finally gets a charley horse.

As this conventional paragraph demonstrates, you don't have to have a formal topic sentence, an announcement like a wedding invitation. You can combine it with restriction and still make it relatively implicit. As established in the first sentence of the student paragraph, the pain of sitting up straight is the topic—the pain in the back and the neck is the restriction. The balance of the paragraph illustrates the topic.

But you could rewrite the paragraph into two or even three paragraphs. For two, you might start a new paragraph about the neck. The topic sentence—"The neck goes next"—would also serve as the restriction. For three, you might make the back a single paragraph. If you should, the first paragraph would contain no illustration. However, because the topic would be illustrated so quickly and clearly in the following two paragraphs, the absence would make no difference.

b. *Question/Answer*

Here's a paragraph in the question/answer pattern. Notice the available options

> A bird that eats feathers, a mammal that never drinks, a fish that grows a fishing line and worm on its head to catch other fish. Crea-

tures in a nightmare? No, they are very much with us as co-inhabitants of this earth.

—Jean George, "That Astounding Creature—Nature"

The first sentence—a particularly long fragment, by the way—is in statement form. Although matter of fact, it contains such outlandish facts that we are prompted to ask the question that follows—which becomes a part of it by virtue of the word "Creatures." The last sentence answers the question and *could* form a separate paragraph—if George should want to emphasize the point almost melodramatically—just as the next paragraph might be made part of the first.

> Nature has fashioned most animals to fit the many faces of the land—moose to marshes, squirrels to trees, camels to deserts, frogs to lily pads. Give nature an environment or situation and she will evolve a creature, adapting a toe here, an eye there, until the being fits the niche. As a result of this hammering and fitting, however, some really unbelievable creatures circle the sun with us.

Actually, both paragraphs concern the same topic. Separating them gives the question and answer an emphasis that might be lost were they combined—and that emphasis is important. Rather than satisfying our curiosity, the answer arouses it.

However, these options don't mean you have complete freedom to indent on impulse or whim.

> A bird that eats feathers, a mammal that never drinks, a fish that grows a fishing line and worm on its head to catch other fish.
> Creatures in a nightmare? No, they are very much with us as co-inhabitants of this earth. Nature has fashioned most animals to fit the many faces of the land—moose to marshes, squirrels to trees, camels to deserts, frogs to lily pads.
> Give nature an environment or situation and she will evolve a creature, adapting a toe here, an eye there, until the being fits the niche. As a result of this hammering and fitting, however, some really unbelievable creatures circle the sun with us. [While we are at it, let's include the first sentence of the next paragraph:] One summer in Maine I saw a sleek mother horned grebe herding her three bobbing young to supper among the green pickerelweed.
> Suddenly I noticed through my binoculars that she was feeding her babies quantities of feathers from a deserted duck's nest.

That isn't paragraphing, it's caprice, license—a spin-the-bottle approach to indenting a stretch of text. It doesn't work. Whether or not you give the paragraph a separate, formal, explicit topic sentence, you must center it in a single topic. Otherwise it's pointless.

c. *Problem/Solution*

The problem/solution pattern of paragraph offers options.

> Perhaps flirting is only possible in a society of definite limits and
> thwarted lusts, the kind of society, for example, that nurtured the
> Southern belle. Obviously, I don't want to have the limitations back.
> I'm as grateful as any woman for my new freedoms. But now that
> my body is somewhat unbuckled and my consciousness reasonably
> raised, I would very much like to be able to flirt with immunity
> again. Flirting is evocative of tenderer times in all of our lives and
> of tenderer times in the lives of our marriages. I miss those times. I
> still think making goo-goo eyes (there is no dignified way to say it)
> at someone and having them made back at me is nicely sexy—and
> safe.
>
> —*Anne Taylor Fleming, "In Defense of Flirting"*

What's the problem? Flirting with immunity in these unrepressed,
uninhibited times. What's the solution? By describing what she would
like, Fleming implies what she might do, if only for the sake of nostalgia: make goo-goo eyes. Thus she disposes of the problem without
saying what she will or won't do—she doesn't know—but only how
she feels.

As the paragraph stands, the topic sentence sits right in the middle.
"I would very much like to be able to flirt with immunity again."
Actually, not the entire sentence—the main clause. When you write
question/answer and problem/solution paragraphs, you might consider locating the topic sentence somewhere after the beginning—
perhaps even at the end. For instance, you could divide Fleming's
paragraph, ending the first with the topic sentence (*clause*) and using
the next sentence to begin the next paragraph:

> Flirting is evocative of tenderer times in all our lives and of ten-
> derer moments in the lives of our marriages. I miss those times. I
> still think making goo-goo eyes (there is no dignified way to say it)
> at someone and having them made back at me is nicely sexy—and
> safe.

Notice what has happened. By means of simple division, you have
fashioned a topic/restriction/illustration type of paragraph. Likely you
will lead off with the topic sentence when writing such paragraphs.
However, as demonstrated in the preceding paragraph—not necessarily and not always. In this instance, the topic sentence—"I miss
those times"—occupies the center. The restriction comes before, the
illustration after.

In determining how to paragraph a piece, remember that readers are like Biblical shepherds and priests. We want signs: burning bushes, handwriting on the wall, arrows pointing the way. So make sure the topic sentence of each paragraph is clearly in control, and that everything else in the paragraph explains and supports the main topic.

Now that you understand the latitude in paragraphing, you are probably wondering *how* to exercise it. What factors must you consider in determining where to indent? There are several.

2. The Transition Paragraph

The preceding paragraph is known as a *transition paragraph*. Its purpose is simply to move the discussion from one subject to another— here from types of paragraphs to criteria for paragraphing. When you make a major shift, do it by means of a transition paragraph so the readers remain on track. As a rule, the more rapid the transit, the better—short and quick. (And don't follow it with a parenthetic discussion of what you've just done!)

3. The Uses of the Paragraph: Development and Emphasis

Basically, paragraphs serve two purposes: either to *develop* a point or to *make* a point. A longer paragraph is required for effective development. A shorter paragraph—usually limited to emphasis—makes a point. I will show you a paragraph you've seen earlier because it's a perfect example of development.

> Three, four, sometimes five times a month, I spend the day in bed with a migraine headache, insensible to the world around me. Almost every day of every month, between these attacks, I feel the sudden irrational irritation and flush of blood into the cerebral arteries which tell me that migraine is on its way, and I take certain drugs to avert its arrival. If I did not take the drugs, I would be able to function perhaps one day in four. The physiological error called migraine is, in brief, central to the given of my life. When I was 15, 16, even 25, I used to think that I could rid myself of this error by simply denying it, character over chemistry. "Do you have headaches *sometimes? frequently? never?*" the application forms would demand. "Check one." Wary of the trap, wanting whatever it was that the successful circumnavigation of that particular form could bring (a job, a scholarship, the respect of mankind and the grace of God), I would check one. "*Sometimes*," I would lie. That in fact I spent one or two days a week almost unconscious with pain seemed a shameful secret, evidence not merely of some chemical inferiority but of all my bad attitudes, unpleasant tempers, wrongthink.

Didion takes her readers on a grand tour of her detail and idea to a logical conclusion. It's a lengthy trip, covering (for many) new terrain—not like running next door for a cup of sugar and a chat. You see, she must prove the point. If she were not compelled to prove the point—to dispel the false mythology of migraine and persuade us of the truth—she could, if she wished, have used shorter paragraphs.

By paragraphing we interrupt the flow of text (this one just did) and, sometimes, the flow of thought. You pause, breathe, and read on. Parents teach children that it's rude to interrupt, but in prose, interruptions can be a courtesy. Readers need breaks. A long uninterrupted stretch of prose is discouraging in prospect and often tiresome in transit. But don't interrupt just anywhere—in midsentence or midthought. Paragraphing has much in common with punctuation: It is a graphic aid to interpreting the meaning of text. So give the readers a *meaningful* break. Interrupt now and then by indenting. Allow them to catch their breath while pondering your drift.

The shorter the paragraph, the less you *develop* the point and the more you *emphasize* it. Consider what Didion might have done if she had wanted above all else to emphasize the main point.

> The physiological error called migraine is, in brief, central to the given of my life.

As a single paragraph, it's a showstopper—but for a brief moment only. One of the most famous paragraphs in western literature works on this principle. It occurs in *The Scarlet Letter* by Nathaniel Hawthorne.

> The scarlet letter had not done its office.

That's it, the whole thing. And coming as it does in the midst of long paragraphs developing a complex and subtle analysis of the heroine, Hester Prynne, it has the stopping force and volume of heavy metal.

You may be asking why you shouldn't use lots of short paragraphs—a series of showstoppers. You can—if the paper is not too long, if the paragraphs contain strong points, and if you don't overdo it. In this excerpt from *Chicago: City on the Make*, novelist Nelson Algren carries this kind of paragraphing—not to mention the sentence fragment—about as far as it can go.

> To the east were the moving waters as far as eye could follow. To the west a sea of grass as far as wind might reach.
> Waters restlessly, with every motion, slipping out of used colors for new. So that each fresh wind off the lake washed the prairie grasses with used sea-colors: the prairie moved in the light like a secondhand sea.

Till between the waters and the wind came the marked-down
derelicts with the dollar signs for eyes.
Looking for any prairie portage at all that hadn't yet built a jail.
Beside any old secondhand sea.

The style is closer to poetry than to essay. It's a special case, to be
admired but not emulated. Remember that if there are too many
interruptions, emphases, and exclamations, the readers tire of the
herky-jerky progress much the same as if they had *no* breaks at all.
Both extremes lead to the same conclusion: fatigue.

Determine the length of the paragraphs according to the requirements of each topic. Avoid paragraphs that seem endless. Avoid too
many paragraphs that appear, comparatively, no wider than a set of
exclamation points. For variety, alter the length from time to time.
Sameness of length wearies the mind.

Whatever its length, be certain each paragraph makes sense of the
topic. This one doesn't.

> Randy's softball uniform consisted of shorts and t-shirt. Randy
> liked a uniform that was simple, thus creating the more relaxed
> softball player.

More than what? And how does a uniform create any sort of softball
player? On the other hand, the following paragraph makes lovely,
lively, and coherent sense.

> Aunt Stella is a kick to play poker with. She was a nun at one
> time, but left the religious life to run away with an insurance sales-
> man. She still wears a crucifix around her neck, though, and she
> kisses it every time she wins a pot. She also carries a lucky rabbit's
> foot and a coin she won in Vegas from a slot machine. She stashes
> her money in her thigh-high nylons, which she twists in a knot just
> above her knees. Several times during a bad evening she lifts a leg
> on top of the table in order to dig out more money. When such
> evenings get worse, this ex-nun aunt of mine cusses the dealer and
> spits on the floor.

Be sure the logic is logical, and develop the topic through detail.

There is another basis for determining the appropriate length for
paragraphs: the *format* of the particular piece. By format I mean the
physical properties—shape and length—of a work. For example, journalists write short paragraphs because their work is printed in narrow
columns. In a newspaper column even a medium-length paragraph
looks endless. On a letter-size sheet, a journalistic paragraph resembles a stutter. If you're writing a 500-word essay, you don't want long
paragraphs. You'd only have one or two—three at the most. (There is

an exception in the Reader: "Take the A Train" by Maeve Brennan. Read it and consider whether it's justified and if it proves the rule.) If you're writing a lengthy piece—for example, a term paper—you don't want a lot of short paragraphs. The precise purpose of term papers is to develop, not to jump and shout. So most paragraphs should run medium to medium-long.

Finally, how do you know that the paragraphs are the appropriate length? Use the test you now recognize as universal: If you can explain the length simply and clearly in a short sentence or two, chances are their length is appropriate.

EXERCISES

1. The following paragraphs are from Edward Rivera's "First Communion." Combine them into longer units. Then compare the revision with the original (in the Reader)—with which I have taken considerable liberties.

> I closed my eyes and did as he said. Then Father Rooney delivered his Latin lines:
> "*Corpus Domini nostri Jesu Christi custodiat animam tuam,* etcetera. Amen."
> Father Matt had his paten under my chin—cold metal—and I felt a familiar warm dribble working its way down my thigh, spoiling my fresh pair of First Communion shorts. The whole place was looking on, except possibly Papi and Mami, who must have been staring down at their hands in embarrassment.
> Then the worst of all possible things happened: the Host broke in half on my nose.
> I still had my eyes shut, so I didn't see just how Father Rooney managed to do it but I could figure it out. I must have made him nervous, and instead of slapping It down on the tip of my tongue, he caught the tip of my nose, and the presence broke in two.
> One half stayed in Father Rooney's fingers, and the other floated past my tongue, bounced off the railing, missing Father Matt's paten altogether, and came to a stop on the symbol-crowded rug on their side of the railing, between Father Matt's shoes, which were barely visible under his alb, as Sister Felicia had called that fancy undergarment.

2. In days of yesteryear, when heroes and legend thrived, readers must have developed greater attention spans than we to deal with lengthy paragraphs—lengthier than any contemporary editor would tolerate. Yet times may not have changed that much after all. We can still read those monumental paragraphs with far less trouble and

with far greater pleasure than we might predict. The following is from Mark Twain's *Roughing It*, an account of his days in the wild West. Consider how you might divide the paragraph into smaller (coherent) paragraphs in keeping with modern practice.

I had already learned how hard and long and dismal a task it is to burrow down into the bowels of the earth and get out the coveted ore; and now I learned that the burrowing was only half the work; and that to get the silver out of the ore was the dreary and laborious other half of it. We had to turn out at six in the morning and keep at it till dark. This mill was a six-stamp affair, driven by steam. Six tall, upright rods of iron, as large as a man's ankle, and heavily shod with a mass of iron and steel at their lower ends, were framed together like a gate, and these rose and fell, one after the other, in a ponderous dance, in an iron box called a "battery." Each of these rods or stamps weighed six hundred pounds. One of us stood by the battery all day long, breaking up masses of silver-bearing rock with a sledge and shoveling it into the battery. The ceaseless dance of the stamps pulverized the rock to powder, and a stream of water that trickled into the battery turned it to a creamy paste. The minutest particles were driven through a fine wire screen which fitted close around the battery, and were washed into great tubs warmed by super-heated steam—amalgamating pans, they are called. The mass of pulp in the pans was kept constantly stirred up by revolving "mullers." A quantity of quicksilver was kept always in the battery, and this seized some of the liberated gold and silver particles and held on to them; quicksilver was shaken in a fine shower into the pans, also, about every half hour, through a buckskin sack. Quantities of coarse salt and sulphate of copper were added, from time to time, to assist the amalgamation by destroying base metals which coated the gold and silver and would not let it unite with the quicksilver. All these tiresome things we had to attend to constantly. Streams of dirty water flowed always from the pans and were carried off in broad wooden troughs to the ravine. One would not suppose that atoms of gold and silver would float on top of six inches of water, but they did; and in order to catch them, coarse blankets were laid in the troughs, and little obstructing "riffles" charged with quicksilver were placed here and there across the troughs also. These riffles had to be cleaned and the blankets washed out every evening, to get their precious accumulations—and after all this eternity of trouble one third of the silver and gold in a ton of rock would find its way to the end of the troughs in the ravine at last and have to be worked over again some day. There is nothing so aggravating as silver milling. There was always something to do. It is a pity that Adam could not have gone straight out of Eden into a quartz mill, in order to understand the full force of his doom to "earn his bread by the sweat of his brow." Every now and then, during the day, we had to scoop some pulp out of the pans, and tediously "wash" it in a horn spoon—wash it little by little over the edge till at last nothing was left but some little dull globules of quicksilver at the bottom. If they were soft and yielding, the pan needed some salt or some sulphate of copper or some other chemical rubbish to assist digestion; if they were crisp to the touch and would retain a dint, they were freighted with all the silver and gold they could seize and hold, and consequently the pans needed a fresh charge of quicksilver. When there was nothing to do, one could always "screen tailings." That is to say, he could shovel up the dried sand that had washed down to the ravine through the troughs and dash it against an upright wire screen to free it from pebbles and prepare it for working over. The process of amalgamation differed in the various mills, and this included changes in style of pans and other machinery, and a great diversity of opinion existed as to the best in use, but none of the methods employed involved the principle of milling ore without "screening the tailings." Of all recreations in the world, screening tailings on a hot day, with a long-handled shovel, is the most undesirable.

B. The Sentence

Standing alone on two feet, words are relatively useless. Their meaning is elementary at best. A child says tree, dog, cat, car, run—one at a time and without any context or connections. And we all know you can't get very far in this life without connections, not even in English composition. (*Especially* in English composition.)

To make sense, words must be joined—not in random order or disorder—but according to the laws of the language. "Tom I when black ran have green are book been brush aardvark analyzed"—a collection of words respecting no laws—makes no sense. "The tree is green" and "The dog is running after the car"—collections of words conforming to the letter and the spirit of the laws of the language— make perfect sense. The words connect to each other and to our minds.

When words are combined to make sense, the product is a *sentence*. Technically, a sentence is defined as a group of words containing a subject and a predicate combined to express a complete thought. Let's explore those components one at a time.

The *subject* is a noun or pronoun that the predicate is all about.

> *I* drove downtown yesterday. *Traffic* was heavy. *The stores* were crowded.

These sentences say something about *I*, *traffic*, and *stores*. The italicized words are the subjects of the discourse in each sentence.

The *predicate* is the discourse about the subject.

I *drove downtown yesterday.* Traffic *was heavy.* The stores *were crowded.*

The verb *to predicate* means to make a statement or declaration. Grammatically, that is exactly the function of the predicate.

And finally, the *complete thought.* You have heard the phrase and have probably wondered what it is. Philosophically, I don't know; for purposes of writing, it doesn't matter. The test is whether the group of words can stand alone on two feet, and the determination is technical—not philosophical. There can be no word signifying dependency (something we'll get to in just a minute). There must be a subject and predicate, and the predicate must contain a *verb.*

Verbs are words that make connections—"The tree *is* green"—and that get nouns going somewhere: "The tree *is growing.*" Without the verb, a predicate could not predicate. The verb is the heart of the sentence, the muscle that makes it go.

It is time for some specialized vocabulary. A *clause* is a group of words containing a subject and a verb. A *phrase* is a group of words containing a subject or a verb—but not both. Because a clause is by definition a sentence, you may wonder why it isn't called a sentence. Let me show you.

I drove downtown yesterday.

When I drove downtown yesterday.

The first is a sentence. Whether or not it is, philosophically, a complete thought is irrelevant; it satisfies us as if it is. It does not feel incomplete. It does not leave us hanging in midair. Therefore, it is an *independent clause* (in Latin, *independent* literally means *not hanging*). It needs nothing more to complete its sense. It stands on its own two feet.

The second clause, however, leaves us hanging. "Go on," we say, "then what?" It needs something more to complete its sense. Therefore, it is a *dependent clause* (in Latin, *depend* means *to hang*). Even though it has a subject and a verb—the same ones as its independent cousin—it cannot stand on its own. "When" is the difference. Its purpose is twofold: to introduce the clause and to subordinate it to the main clause, where we find the point of the sentence.

When I drove downtown yesterday, traffic was heavy and the stores were crowded.

As thoughts go it's not much, but it's all that's required. Now the period puts us at ease, content with syntax and the world. We're no longer dangling in space, wondering about the point of it all.

Now to keep a promise of four paragraphs ago: When words such as *when*, *after*, *before*, *because*, *since*, *that*, *which* introduce a clause, they also subordinate it. They serve, therefore, as signs of the clause's status.

EXERCISES

1. Identify the dependent and independent clauses in the following sentences.

   a. Last night we went dancing at the Stardust.

   b. After dancing we decided to take a drive to Strawberry Lake.

   c. Before we got to the lake we had a flat tire.

   d. We had to hitchhike back home because we didn't have a spare.

   e. Since then, having nothing to do, we haven't done a thing.

2. In the preceding sentences, make the independent clauses dependent, the dependent clauses independent, and the phrases clauses of either sort.

1. Simple, Compound, and Complex Sentences

There are three kinds of sentences: *simple*, *compound*, and *complex*. A simple sentence is a single independent clause.

> I went downtown yesterday.

The clause may have more than one subject and verb.

> John and I worked and played downtown yesterday.

If we split up the subject and verbs—making them into two sets—we have a compound sentence.

> John worked and I played downtown yesterday.

A compound sentence consists of two or more independent clauses linked by conjunctions, semicolons, or—if the clauses are short—commas.

> John worked, Mary slept, Janie studied, and I played.

> I went downtown yesterday; I bought a hat.

> I went downtown yesterday, and I bought a smock.

> I went downtown yesterday, but I didn't get a thing.

All you have to do is add on independent clauses, and compound sentences reach monumental proportions.

> I went downtown yesterday, and I bought a hat and a smock, and a big orange drink, and I jaywalked and was run over by a truck and spilled my orange drink, so an ambulance came and picked me up and in the excitement of the moment I forgot my hat and smock but I didn't notice: My broken bones and smashed organs were killing me and I didn't have any consciousness to spare for my purchases.

My example reveals why you must compose compound sentences with care. They often are endless, mindless meanders—boring to the point of sleep.

A complex sentence consists of at least one dependent and one independent clause. It is called complex because it expresses a more complicated relationship than a mere collection of parts. It may involve before and after, cause and effect, simultaneity, logic.

> When I went downtown yesterday, I bought a hat and a smock and a big orange drink. As I was sipping the juice, my mind on my drink, I inadvertently jaywalked and was run over by a truck, which made me spill my drink. An ambulance came and picked me up and, in the excitement of the moment, I forgot my hat and my smock, but I didn't notice: Because my broken bones and smashed organs were killing me, I didn't have any consciousness to spare for purchases.

By adding dependent clause to dependent clause, you can make complex sentences as unmanageable as compound ones.

> Inasmuch as these United States hold certain truths to be self-evident, namely, that all citizens are entitled to life, liberty, and the pursuit of happiness, and inasmuch as many nations do not regard these great principles to be truths at all, much less self-evident, but instead hold that the state and only the state has the right to liberty, and that the citizens should pursue virtue rather than happiness, and that life is a privilege, not a right, we frequently find ourselves in international hot water, embroiled in disputes that arise out of conflicting policies which in turn are the result of these different views and values.

This example reveals why you must compose complex sentences with care. As with compound sentences, you can easily ramble on and on until through increasing complexity you overload circuits and short out the readers. Unlike politicians, the mind can handle only so many relationships at one time. How many is too many? How many digits can you remember after a single glance?

EXERCISES

1. In the following paragraph from Orwell's "A Hanging," identify the simple, compound, and complex sentences. Because there may be more than one way to analyze them, compare your analysis with those of some classmates. Discuss differences.

> We set out for the gallows. Two warders marched on either side of the prisoner, with their rifles at the slope; two others marched close against him, gripping him by arm and shoulder, as though at once pushing and supporting him. The rest of us, magistrates and the like followed behind. Suddenly, when we had gone ten yards, the procession stopped short without any order or warning. A dreadful thing had happened—a dog, come goodness knows whence, had appeared in the yard. It came bounding among us with a loud volley of barks, and leapt round us wagging its whole body, wild with glee at finding so many human beings together. It was a large woolly dog, half Airedale, half pariah. For a moment it pranced round us, and then, before anyone could stop it, it had made a dash for the prisoner and jumping up tried to lick his face. Everyone stood aghast, too taken aback even to grab at the dog.

2. Rewrite the sentences in the paragraph by altering their structure. Combine simple sentences to form compound and complex sentences; reduce some of the compound and complex sentences to simple sentences. Consider the difference your revision makes.

2. Make Your Sentences Express Your Sense

And now a consideration of the utmost importance: the reason you must understand these basic kinds of sentences. When you write, really write, *the sentence structure reflects its meaning*. In other words, you fashion the *how* of the statement to complement the *what*—the *form* to express the *content*.

A student of mine recently wrote a short piece on fishing. It begins, "Fishing is a lazy sport"—a topic sentence if there ever was one. Shortly thereafter he continues:

> You bait your hook, and you drop it in the water, and you wait for a bite, and you get a bite, and you pull out a fish, and you take the fish off the hook, and you bait your hook again, and you drop it in the water, and you wait for a bite.

A compound sentence, right? And the clauses are short enough to be treated as items in a series. And as another student pointed out, items in a series are ordinarily divided by commas, the conjunction used only between the next-to-last and the last items.

> You bait your hook, you drop it in the water, you wait for a bite, you get a bite, you pull out a fish, you take the fish off the hook, you bait your hook again, you drop it in the water, and you wait for a bite.

Generally the rule applies—you do treat items in a series as described—but notice what happens to the sentence by removing the conjunctions. It is speeded up; it's now hurried. But fishing, the writer says, is lazy. And after the conjunction-laden sentence, he ventures into what many would deem heresy: "Fishing is boring." By making the sentence slow and repetitious—all those *ands*—he expresses exactly that sense of boredom. If the pace of fishing resembled that suggested in the conjunction-free sentence, he would probably enjoy it.

If the main idea were the *complexity* of fishing, the structure should be markedly different.

> After baiting your hook, you drop it in the water and wait for a bite. While waiting, you must focus your attention on the bobber and on the feel of the rod in your hands. Watch for the bobber to go under suddenly and for a good sharp jerk. When that happens, give a good yank up on the rod in order to hook the fish securely. . . .

As the name implies, the complex sentence is designed to deal with complexity—with various relationships involving judgments of relative importance. Because some aspects of the subject are relatively minor (subordinate), they become dependent clauses. Because others are major, they become independent clauses. The compound sentence is designed to deal with sequences of events or ideas of relatively equal importance, sufficiently related to be joined in the same structure by conjunctions. The simple sentence is designed to emphasize a single idea.

As an accomplished writer, you will be able to explain the structure of each of your sentences: simple, compound, or complex. You will be able to explain the order of elements in each sentence and the order of sentences in each paragraph. And you will be able to justify every decision.

To understand more fully, look at the opening paragraphs of Curtis Stadtfeld's "Trapping Days."

> Muskrat pelts were worth three or four dollars in the late 1940s, a practical fortune for a farmboy—enough money to set him multiplying it and dreaming. There simply was no real money. Even in

the relative prosperity of the war years, income had not reached past three or four thousand dollars per year for us, and there was a long list of hungry needs lingering from the depression, snapping away every scrap of cash to repay an ancient debt, replace an old piece of furniture or machinery, or buy a bracelet for one of the girls who had never had one.

There was no money yet for a speedometer for a boy's bike, or a Gene Autry shirt, or a compass or telescope or any of the other useless things that a boy needs with such desperation when he is twelve or so.

If you were to interview Stadtfeld, he could explain why the two paragraphs instead of one. He could explain why the sentence "There simply was no real money" is in the middle instead of at the end. He could explain why the long compound (third) sentence instead of two or three short and simple ones. And he could explain why the items are in the present order: debts, furniture, machinery, bracelet; why the items of the next sentence are in the present order—why they weren't included in the previous sentence—and why they don't appear before those items. He could say why he put the prepositional phrases where they are, chose the adjectives, selected the verbs, and used the nouns. In other words, he could justify his preference for the present form and not, for example, this one:

In the late 1940s muskrat pelts were worth three or four dollars. That was enough money to set a twelve-year-old farmboy like me dreaming of a speedometer for his bike, of a telescope or compass, of a Gene Autry shirt. It was a small fortune, because we didn't have real money then—no more than three or four thousand a year— even though those were relatively prosperous times. We still had needs from the Great Depression: furniture and machinery to replace, a bracelet for one of the girls, old debts.

EXERCISES

1. Explain the superiority of Stadtfeld's form to my revision.

2. Identify the simple, compound, and complex sentences in the following paragraph (written by a student in an advanced composition class).

I can still remember my first solo flight on a bicycle. I probably looked like a colt learning how to run, but I felt as if the world was mine. After a couple of tentative passes by my proud but concerned Pop and my cheering brothers I decided that it was time to explore the block. I took the first corner slow and easy, still unsure of the wobbly world presented by a bike. I took the second turn with a bit more gusto, and when I was halfway around the block I felt that I could make it halfway around the world. On the third turn I picked up a bit of speed and leaned into the turn; to a trained observer I was no more than a child trying to master a bicycle; *I* felt that I was the essence of elegance. The excitement was building as I came to the end of my Tour de Block; I knew that my dad and brothers would be spectators for my recent mastery of the turn. I pedalled like mad and whipped by the turn, more intent on my spectators than on my bike. The conclusion was inevitable: I crashed. I did not know whether I had crashed because of an excess of speed or because of lack of concentration, nor did I care. I only knew that I had scraped my knee. The scrape hurt, of that there was no doubt. But what hurt me much more was what the scrape signified: defeat. I was a pre-school washout. I was a failure in a world that my innocence had assumed was wonderful. I was a lone wipe-out artist in a world of perfect turns. The scrape pointed out my imperfections to an accusingly perfect world.

3. Restructure the sentences. Fashion new sentences from phrases and clauses from other sentences. Compare the rewrite with those of a group of classmates. Be prepared to justify the construction (the form) of each sentence and clause you frame.

3. Vary Your Sentences

In addition to suiting the form of the sentence to its content, remember to vary its length and type to prevent monotony. Like all truths, the importance of variety bears repeating. I want to point out, however, that it is often possible to combine several sentences of similar length and type before boredom sets in.

> I can't handle warm weather. It makes me feel sick and irritable. I also sweat a lot. My hair droops. Perspiration streams down my face. My cheeks become flushed. I usually look as if I had just run a mile without the benefit of being in shape.

She fashions six short simple sentences in a row before a longer complex one. And had additional detail been necessary, she could have included more. How many more? That is hard to say—there is no simple formula—but more than you probably think (just as it is possible to combine several short paragraphs to form an effective whole). Consider the first paragraph of a student paper explaining how to flunk out of college.

> Drink heavily the night before. Don't get up before 11:00. Decide you're not feeling well enough to go to class. Have a cigarette. Drink some pop and take last night's taste out of your mouth. Do some bong tokes to get rid of your hangover. Get really stoned and go to lunch. When you get back to your room do some more bong tokes.

Take a shower. Leave all your clothes lying on the bathroom floor. Stay in the shower forty-five minutes. Sing "Stairway to Heaven." Ignore the people pounding on the door. Use up all the hot water. When you're done, put on a towel and walk around the room. Smoke another cigarette. Call up all your friends and try to get them to skip class with you. Sulk because they won't. Complain to your roommate that there's nothing to do. Decide to get dressed. Lay all your wardrobe out on your bed. Decide you have nothing to wear. Do the same thing to your roommate's wardrobe. Get depressed and chain smoke. Listen to all your hard rock albums.

To be sure, there is variety—but not much. Of 25 sentences, 16 are simple, 6 are complex, and 3 are compound. (It can be argued that 19 are simple, 6 complex and none compound—even less variety.) But all are short, and the paragraph works.

If you require several similar sentences in a row, keep them short and simple. Several compound sentences in a row quickly become monotonous. And several complex sentences in a row—characteristic of officialese—is certain death.

How long is long? How short is short? A sentence may be as short as one word. And in certain novels by William Faulkner and Samuel Beckett, there are sentences several pages in length. Each. I don't recommend you write one. Instead, always write the shortest sentence possible, and say exactly what you have to say. If what you have to say is complex, the sentence will be complex and lengthy. Just don't make it any longer and more complex than necessary. And remember that you don't have to say it all in just one sentence.

One of the commonplace mistakes of beginning writers is trying to say everything at one time and, in the process, sacrificing coherence. Consider the following sentence from a paper on the Supreme Court decision that bussing as a means of school desegregation is constitutional.

When the Supreme Court warned that compulsory bussing might be administratively awkward, inconvenient, and even bizarre in some instances, and might impose burdens on some, were the justices just being naive, or did they realize the truly astounding and far-reaching ramifications that their decision would produce, with the violence, the increased animosity between blacks and whites, not to mention that the additional financial burdens that such a measure imposed on the affected communities and states as it assuredly did?

The sentence is not simply long. It's involved—so involved that by the time we reach the end, the question mark is a complete surprise. We have forgotten the sentence poses a question. It's so long the writer forgets the initial syntactical pattern and changes in midcourse, condemning the sentence to grammatical incoherence. The moral is that when you write a long sentence, keep its constituent parts short and keep their relationships simple. Include only essential relationships. When possible, write separate sentences. You can't say everything at one time, so don't even try.

> In deciding compulsory bussing is constitutional, the Supreme Court acknowledged that the measure might prove administratively awkward, inconvenient, and bizarre in some instances, and burdensome in others. But did the Justices realize the truly astounding and far-reaching ramifications of their decision? Did they have any idea of the violence and the increased animosity between blacks and whites their decision would likely produce? Did they anticipate the extent of the financial burdens faced by states and communities where such measures are implemented?

See how much easier that is? Give the readers a break. Explore the subject a step at a time.

4. Transitions

Transitions—words like *thus, then, moreover,* and the repetition of words and phrases—maintain a coherent flow from one sentence to the next. Beginning writers have little trouble with transitions. When they do have trouble, it's usually a case of too much for fear of having too little:

> In deciding compulsory bussing is constitutional, the Supreme Court acknowledged that the measure might prove administratively awkward, inconvenient, bizarre in some instances and burdensome in others. But did the Justices *of the Supreme Court, in their deliberations on compulsory bussing,* realize the truly astounding and far-reaching ramifications of *their decision? Moreover,* did *the Justices, in contemplating the implementation of forced bussing to the end of racial equality,* have any idea of the violence and the increased animosity between blacks and whites *their decision* would produce? *Finally,* did *the Supreme Court* anticipate the extent of the financial burdens *their decision mandating compulsory bussing* would have on many communities and states?

Excessive transitions are surplus baggage: economy is the ideal. You must connect each sentence to the next. But as seen in the earlier paragraph, you can usually accomplish the transition with a word or two: *but, the justices, their decision, they, bussing.* Make the transitions brief. *Rapid* transit—that's the ticket.

EXERCISES

1. The following sentence is from a student paper. Divide it into several. Make the passage coherent and meaningful.

> By A.D. 160, while Roman emperors conducted their lives according to astrology and their subjects followed their example since astrology had become very complicated, each aspect being associated with different parts of the body and it being recognized that no two people are exactly alike (e.g., a person who is commanding had the sign of the ram associated with his head), and according to various forms of magic as well, the Christians rejected astrology as being an invention of demons and therefore immoral, so that for the next three hundred years until the fall of Rome (A.D. 410), at which time for all intents and purposes astrology vanished, there were constant disputes and riots between the Christian and the pagans.

2. Compare the revision with those of several classmates. As a group, produce a quality revision.

C. The Fragment

A fragment is a word or group of words with the earmarks of a sentence—a capital at one end and a period at the other—that is not a sentence. It is missing a subject or a verb (sometimes both), or it has a subordinator which makes it a dependent clause.

Textbooks and teachers ordinarily warn against using fragments. Here is why.

> We spent hours lying on the beach soaking up the sun's rays. Thus, this turning your skin color into a beautiful tan.

Here is another.

> In later life Socrates questioned public officials and private men. Proving them wrong if their statements were untrue.

And another:

> Recently while debating with another person on the subject of the legal drinking age, pointing out that eighteen to twenty is the prime age for military service because people are then in their physical prime, able to risk their lives, in other words, but not to get a drink.

Generally, readers want their money's worth of sentence—subject, verb, whatever is necessary for complete sense—and they expect complete satisfaction. If you leave out the subject or the verb (or both), they notice the absence. Like a chair with a missing leg, the sentence

is off balance, and the readers sit at an uncomfortable tilt. The fragment interrupts their concentration—diverting it from topic to structure. As a rule, then, give readers complete sentences: subject, verb,
and all.

However, you can use fragments occasionally to great effect. Stadtfeld,
after describing his family's financial straits, begins the third paragraph with one.

Thus, the lure of the muskrat skins.

Like Jean George, Rushworth Kidder begins his essay with one, only
much shorter—about as short as can be:

Ice.

Don Ethan Miller ends with one.

They tell us that all our personal limits—and by extension, our
destructive social and historical patterns—can be transcended.
Beginning with the next breath, drawn deeply.

E. M. Forster heard a twig snap on his property.

On coming nearer, I saw it was not a man who had trodden on the
twig and snapped it, but a bird, and I felt pleased. My bird.

You don't have to be a professional writer to fashion an effective fragment. The same student who wrote the poor fragment about Socrates
also wrote a good one.

He must have been a real bother to his teachers. Always testing their
knowledge.

Another student described making a cup of tea.

It is advisable to pour the water nice and slow. Real slow.

By using fragments we set apart and emphasize. But if they're lengthy,
they often lose their snap. Occasionally, however, a longish fragment
can be effective (like the first sentence of Jean George's essay) if it's
composed of short, snappy elements.

Just because it's snappy, of course, does not guarantee fragment
success. It must be short—as in shortcut—to reach the point faster
than otherwise. A complete sentence would dilute it. Too many words.

Finally, use fragments sparingly. Too much emphasis and the reader
gets punchy. When you shout people down, you turn them off—lose
them.

Effective fragments are gems. Their value is a reflection of their
rarity. Use them wisely. The more formal the occasion, the less suitable

they are. For example, don't use them in a laboratory report, in proposed legislation, or when speaking before the United Nations. If you are not certain of their suitability, write complete sentences. If the occasion is suitable but you are not convinced a particular fragment is effective, leave it out.

Fragments are delicate and temperamental. They backfire easily. Use them only when you *know* they work.

EXERCISES

1. Following are five fragments in some context. If the context is insufficient, review them in the Reader. Change them to complete sentences. Then discuss the effect of the fragment with a group of classmates.

> Even now I wonder: if I meet God, will he take and hold my bare hand in his, and focus his eye on my palm, and kindle that spot and let me burn?
>   But no. It is I who misunderstood everything and let everybody down.
>
> —*Annie Dillard, "God in the Doorway"*

> "Walk, Ssantoss Malanguezzz, don't run!" Sister hizzed behind me. Too late. I was already kneeling at the railing, hands joined under my chin. She'd get me tomorrow morning. Maybe in the auditorium. Special assembly for the execution. Organ music and chorus.
>
> —*Edward Rivera, "First Communion"*

> You'd think, to read about it, that we'd only just now discovered selves. Having long suspected that there was *something alive* in there, running the place, separate from everything else, absolutely individual and independent, we've celebrated by giving it a real name. My self.
>
> —*Lewis Thomas, "The Medusa and the Snail"*

> Like historical friends, our crossroads friends are important for *what was*—for the friendship we shared at a crucial, now past, time of life. A time, perhaps, when we roomed in college together;

or worked as eager young singles in the Big City together; or went together, as my friend Elizabeth and I did, through pregnancy, birth and that scary first-year of new motherhood.

—*Judith Viorst, "Friends, Good Friends—and Such Good Friends"*

Pools and pools and pools of chocolate—fifty-thousand-pound, ninety-thousand-pound, Olympic-length pools of chocolate—in the conching rooms in the chocolate factory in Hershey, Pennsylvania. Big aromatic rooms. Chocolate, as far as the eye can see. Viscous, undulating, lukewarm chocolate, viscidized, undulated by the slurping friction of granite rollers rolling through the chocolate over crenellated granite beds at the bottoms of the pools.

—*John McPhee, "The Conching Rooms"*

Generally, fragments should be short. McPhee proves the exception. Remember, in writing there are no absolute rules.

2. Don't *practice* fragments. If one comes along and you know it's good, by all means use it. But do practice the complete sentence for as long as it takes to master it.

D. Diction

Diction means choice of words—each word you write. The goal is to get the right word in the right place at the right time. To achieve it, you must logically weigh the effectiveness of each word by considering alternatives, pondering implications, and respecting context.

The principle of diction is simple. The problem lies in practice. What is "the right word"? How is it distinguished from the wrong?

These are important questions—and fair ones. As you may suspect, there is no definitive answer, no formula. You must rely on intuition. You can develop intuition through careful reading and writing. You can *learn* to choose the right word with considerable precision. In fact, you can probably already determine the right word better than you realize. Just as southern Californians know a Santa Ana is brewing, you know a word is right—because you *feel* it. It's like knowing the notes of a musical phrase are right—they *sound* right. It's much like recognizing faces and voices: You can't define either in the abstract but you know them when you see them and hear them.

To know when a word is right requires, therefore, an honest look and listen. Don't settle for the word that "comes close," that "will do." It won't. Insist on the one word that says *exactly* what you mean and says it with dispatch, with originality, and a pinch of surprise.

For example, one of my students wrote of a man who was balding.

> His hair threads across the top.

Read it again. Need I point out to you that "threads" is the perfect word? You know it as surely as I do.

Another student, describing Paul Newman, wrote:

> His chin has a dent in it.

Not a dimple or a cleft—they're too weak. And dimple is the wrong shape. Moreover, "dent" suggests wear and tear, a sure sign of maturity. And it's surprising, too. We rarely see it associated with a chin.

Another student described falling asleep in class.

> My head slowly dropped forward, then it suddenly lurched back, which startled me and woke me up.

As we know—from watching others fall asleep while sitting up—the head nods forward slowly, then lurches, and then jerks back. But when it's *our* head that does this, it seems only to jerk back because that's the moment we awaken. The student said it exactly right: "then it suddenly lurched back."

A few paragraphs ago I described a Santa Ana "brewing." I chose "brewing" because of its associations with magic and witchcraft and drinking. It often spells trouble. In Didion's essay that is precisely what the Santa Ana means: trouble—trouble of a spooky irrational nature. And I just chose the word "spells" because—well, you tell me.

You choose a word, then, for two reasons: *denotation* and *connotation*. Denotation is its exact explicit meaning; connotation is its inexact implicit meaning, the suggestions it offers. I chose *brew* because its denotation and connotation work together in the context of the sentence. To praise a man in public office, call him a *statesman*. To express reservations about him, call him a *politician*. In other words, be sure the connotations and denotations of the word you choose are compatible. If, intending amorous praise, you describe skin as *smooth as fine mud*, the denotation and the connotation are incompatible—a match written by a comedian.

Always use the simplest word that does the job. This fundamental principle of diction has two bases: simplicity and function. Both are essential. Just because a word is simple is no reason to use it. And just because a word is complex is no reason to reject it. The word must, of course, work. But again, just because a word works doesn't necessarily mean you should use it. If a simpler one works equally well, it's the right word.

The principle carries across the board. Don't use a foreign word or phrase if a domestic one works as well. Don't use a technical word or phrase if an everyday one works as well. Don't use jargon if mainstream language works as well. To repeat: Always use the simplest word that does the job.

EXERCISE

The following sentences contain optional words. In each case choose one and justify the choice. Consider denotation and connotation. Compare the choices to the original in the Reader.

> The [bodies; corpses; remains; dearly departed] appear to be mostly sow bugs, those little [armored; hard-shelled; armadillo; turtle-like] creatures who live to travel flat out in houses, and die round. In addition to sow bug [after effects; bodies; husks; remains], hollow and [emptied; sipped; bled; drained] of color, there are what seem to be two or three wingless moth bodies, one new [flake; piece; chunk; corpse] of earwig, and three spider [corpses; bodies; remains; carcasses] crinkled and clenched.
>
> —*Annie Dillard, "The Death of a Moth"*

> There was nothing to do but be [affected; struck; punched; impacted] by the wind, which knocked the [saliva; spittle; spit; moisture] from my mouth, reach for the wing strut, hold on [hard; tight; for dear life; for safety's sake], kick back the feet so [heavy-feeling; clumsy; country-like; weighted] and helpless in those boots, and let go. The parachute opened with a [noise; flash; plop; relief], as Istel had sworn to me that it would.
>
> —*Gloria Emerson, "Take the Plunge ..."*

> New York is a town of thirty tattooists whose interest in mankind is [superficial; flashy; skin-deep; abiding], but whose [works; impressions; scars; tattooes] usually last a lifetime.
>
> —*Gay Talese, "New York"*

II. MATTERS OF STYLE

By style I don't mean fashion—the in-thing—but the manner of saying what there is to say. To a great extent we have been concerned with style already. But we come now to the fine points of writing: the subtle touches that readers may not consciously notice but that they respond to nevertheless, the little things you can do to make a big difference in the effect—and thus the effectiveness—of your writing.

So don't confuse considerations of style with superficial concerns—like the trim on your car. It's more like fine-tuning an engine: not conspicuous but essential to the purr of the prose.

A. Use the Active Voice

This is a technical term you must know. It has a mate, the *passive voice*. To understand them, you must learn three others first.

1. Linking, Transitive, and Intransitive Verbs

There are three types of verbs: *linking*, *transitive*, and *intransitive*. *Linking verbs* (in bawdier times, "copulative" verbs) simply connect two different terms.

> My dog is brown.

> I feel sad.

> My tea tastes sweet.

> My car is junk.

The basic linking verb is *to be* and its variants: am, are, is, was, were, will be, have been, and so on. With these you connect noun with noun or noun with adjective. A few verbs—feel, taste, and become, for example—can function as linking verbs because a *to be* verb may be substituted without affecting the meaning.

> I feel (am) sad.

> My tea tastes (is) sweet.

Transitive verbs do something to an object.

> I hit the ball.

> The ball hit me.

The word *transitive* literally means to go across. With a transitive verb you move the action from the subject (the doer) across to the object (the receiver).

Intransitive verbs also do something—but not to an object. They don't make the crossing.

> I am going to go walking.

> I am walking.

> A mugger is coming my way.

> I am running.

Transitive verbs take direct objects; intransitive verbs don't. But remember that some verbs may be transitive or intransitive.

> I am walking.

> I am walking the dog.

2. Active and Passive Voice

Sentences in which the subjects of the verbs perform the action of the verbs are in *the active voice.*

> I hit the ball.   I see that mugger again.

> The ball hit me.   See Duncan run.

> I am walking.   See Duncan jump and run.

As you see, both transitive and intransitive verbs can be in the active voice.

In *the passive voice*, the subject of the verb does not perform the action of the verb, but instead is acted upon.

> I was hit by the ball.

> Duncan is being jumped by the mugger.

> This subject is being acted on by definition.

In the passive voice, the agent of the verb is always stated or implied by the word *by.*

> It is recommended (by the committee) that . . .

> It has been suggested (by yours truly) that . . .

> We have been advised (by the President) that . . .

Sentences with linking verbs have the same effect as sentences in the passive voice—in both the subject of the verb does nothing.

> I was helped by him a great deal.

> He was very helpful to me.

The first is passive, the second linking; both are static.

3. Get Verbs to Do Your Work

At last we arrive at the moral: To write effective prose, use the active voice as often as possible. The verb is the heart of the sentence—where the action is. If it is not active, the sentence is motionless. If it is active, the sentence is literally on the move. It moves, and thus it moves the reader. *So use active verbs.*

In much of today's prose—especially officialese and its kin—we see the major action of the sentence in the noun instead of the verb.

> I am *cognizant* of the fact that he was very *helpful* to her and she was very *supportive* of him.

Put it where it belongs—in the verb.

> I *know* that he *helped* her very much and that she *supported* him.

That way you make a statement more effective in every sense: shorter, simpler, clearer, livelier.

The passive voice also enjoys great popularity. Officialdom finds it particularly attractive because it allows action to be taken without responsibility.

> We have been informed that a decision has been made that troops shall be sent into combat.

Who informed? Who decided? Who's sending?

> It is recommended that the food stamp program be terminated.

> It has been suggested that compensation for the unemployed should be increased by 20 percent.

> It is widely believed that immigration should be limited and quotas imposed according to education, race, color, and creed.

Who knows, with the passive voice you just might get away with murder.

> It is to be hoped that methods can be devised so that certain undesirable elements of the population can be effectively eliminated.

When is the passive voice appropriate? When the focus of the sentence is the subject and the subject is acted on by the verb.

What happened to you?

I was hit by a truck.

The focus is not the truck but the subject "I" and what happened to the subject "I." In those circumstances, use the passive voice. It is the proper voice to express the meaning of the sentence.

Jacques Barzun uses the passive voice rather extensively in the opening paragraph of his essay on capital punishment:

> A passing remark of mine in the *Mid-Century* magazine has brought me a number of letters and a sheaf of pamphlets against capital punishment. The letters, sad and reproachful, offer me the choice of pleading ignorance or being proved insensitive. *I am asked* whether I know that there exists a worldwide movement for the abolition of capital punishment which has everywhere enlisted able men of every profession, including the law. *I am told* that the death penalty is not only inhuman but also unscientific, for rapists and murderers are really sick people who *should be cured, not killed. I am invited* to use my imagination and acknowledge the unbearable horror of every form of execution.

Barzun uses the passive voice appropriately because he is the focus of the letters—the target of the questions, the assertions, and the pleas—yet he does nothing. By using the passive voice regarding the rapists and murderers, Barzun implies the letter writers regard *them* as passive people who won't cure themselves and so who must *be* cured, by others—an attitude that Barzun questions throughout the essay.

Sometimes, then, the passive voice is appropriate to express the very point of the sentence. But every textbook, teacher, and writer recommends the active voice for most sentences and the passive voice *only* when *demonstrably* appropriate. And they are right. It is impossible to exaggerate the importance of the principle. Make the heavy majority of sentences move. Put verbs to work. Use the active voice.

EXERCISES

1. Identify the linking, transitive, and intransitive verbs in the following two paragraphs. Identify the active and passive constructions, and explain whether they are appropriate or not.

   > The real value of martial arts study, in other words, has nothing to do with physical feats such as brick-breaking; in fact, it is not even

primarily concerned with fighting. In our modern technologized society, it would be easier to buy a gun, or carry a can of mace. Their real value lies in what the martial arts tell us about ourselves: that we can be much more than we are now; that we have no need of fear; and that our capacities for energy, awareness, courage, and compassion are far greater than we have been led to believe. They tell us that all our personal limits—and by extension, our destructive social and historical patterns—can be transcended. Beginning with the next breath, drawn deeply.

—*Don Ethan Miller, "A State of Grace"*

Milton Hershey's native town was originally called Derry Church, and it was surrounded, as it still is, by rolling milkland. Hershey could not have been born in a better place, for milk is twenty percent of milk chocolate.

—*John McPhee, "The Conching Rooms"*

2. Revise the preceding paragraphs, putting them in the active voice. Compare the revisions with the originals. Decide whether, in these instances, the passive voice really is better.

B. Practice Parallelism

Also known as *coordination*, *parallelism* means expressing coordinate ideas in coordinate structures. Translated—express ideas that are alike and equal in the same structure. E. B. White does it nicely.

> It [democracy] is the feeling of privacy in the voting booths, the feeling of communion in the libraries, the feeling of vitality everywhere.

Because each feeling is of equal value, White repeats the entire phrase to give each the same structure. Note what happens when we remove the phrase:

> It is the feeling of privacy in the voting booths, communion in the libraries, vitality everywhere.

Communion and vitality slip a little in value because we haven't given them the same introduction, the same fanfare. By dropping "the feeling of" we also upset the rhythm of the sentence. With the introduction of the phrase, there emerges an expectation we want fulfilled—like the first phrase of a song. Sing the first phrase of "Tommy." Note how the phrase demands a companion—a mirror image of itself—and how, if you don't provide it, you are frustrated. You *need* the next phrase. And after the first two, you want more of basically the same structure. And it's there, with some variation, as it always is. The conventional structure of song satisfies the need for rhythmical repetition and variety. Think of the songs you know. Is there even one exception?

That same need exists when reading prose. Observe how Jefferson satisfies the need in assigning the King responsibility for the following:

> For quartering large bodies of armed troops among us:—For protecting them, by a mock Trial, from punishment for any Murders which they should commit on the Inhabitants of these States:—For cutting off our Trade with all parts of the world:—For imposing Taxes on us without our Consent:—For depriving us in many cases, of the benefits of Trial by Jury:—For transporting us beyond Seas to be tried for pretended offenses:—

Even now, over two hundred years later, the rhythm of the prose arouses our passions in protest of these grievances.

Professional writers apply the principle of parallelism to larger units, weaving it into elaborate patterns.

> The richness of the scene was in its plainness, its natural condition—of horse, of ring, of girl, even to the girl's bare feet that gripped the bare back of her proud and ridiculous mount. The enchantment grew not out of anything that happened or was performed but out of something that seemed to go round and around and around with the girl, attending her, a steady gleam in the shape of a circle—a ring of ambition, of happiness, of youth. (And the positive pleasures of equilibrium under difficulties.) In a week or two, all would be changed, all (or almost all) lost: the girl would wear makeup, the horse would wear gold, the ring would be painted, the bark would be clean for the feet of the horse, the girl's feet would be clean for the slippers that she'd wear. All, all would be lost.
>
> —E.B. White, "The Ring of Time"

Often, beginning writers fail to realize the importance of parallelism, how essential it is to prose. White's example is not extreme; it's typical. Every writer includes it in virtually every paragraph. Consider these opening paragraphs:

> Ice. It hung in spikes from the eaves. It gathered in great cobbled chunks in the downspouts. It grew in frosted thickets inside the storm windows, and rattled like broken bottles along the sidewalks, and lay in shattered panes over the places where puddles used to be.
>
> —Rushworth Kidder, "Depths on the Surface"

Don't spread it around, but I love to iron. Every Sunday evening
when the *60 Minutes* clock starts ticking, I haul my folding board
out of the hall closet, mantle it upright about five paces from my
television set, get out a week's worth of shirts, trousers, and jeans
(ironing jeans is an old cowboy tradition), and press the bejesus out
of everything while Ed, Morley, Harry, and Mike yammer away about
problems far more serious than wrinkled fabric, and far less easily
remedied.

—*C. W. Smith, "Pumping Iron"*

New York is a city of things unnoticed. It is a city with cats sleeping
under parked cars, two stone armadillos crawling up St. Patrick's
Cathedral, and thousands of ants creeping on top of the Empire
State Building. The ants probably were carried up there by wind or
birds, but nobody is sure; nobody in New York knows any more
about the ants than they do about the panhandler who takes taxis
to the Bowery; or the dapper man who picks trash out of Sixth
Avenue trash cans; or the medium in the West Seventies who claims,
"I am clairvoyant, clairaudient and clairsensuous."

—*Gay Talese, "New York"*

Two of these are quoted earlier for other reasons. Now I want you to
see them with new eyes—a different perspective. I also want you to
begin searching for parallelism and for the active voice in everything
you read.

I have provided several examples to emphasize that parallelism is
as important as the active voice. Using the active voice gives writing
vigor; using parallelism gives it grace. Without grace, vigor is all brawn
and no brain: thrashing and flailing, lurching and skidding. With grace,
vigor is efficient, effective, beautiful: a dancer, a gymnast, a basketball
player, a well-turned phrase.

EXERCISES

1. Review the quotes in this section. Identify every instance of parallelism. Compare the findings with those of a group of classmates.
   Discuss differences that occur. Be certain you understand parallelism.

2. The following passages are ill. They suffer from a serious deficiency
   of parallelism. Aid them through revision.

   The people I met in public school were from many different
   backgrounds. I had a friend from Texas, one was Jewish, there

was another from New England. In private school all of my friends
were from middle and upper-middle class families and some
were Protestant and others practiced Catholicism.

Between employer and employee, the employer is the one who
has the power. She's in control, the woman who gives the orders
to the people working for her, while the employer is given orders
and must perform them. The employer gets to decide whom she
will hire to work for her, who does what job, and how she wants
those jobs done. She can set the rate of pay. She is the one who
can decide when to fire you.

In high school the hoods were the crazy guys. They acted bizarre.
They were dangerous. They were feared. They were the ones who
wore cut-off shorts to swim in at the public pool, along with
white T-shirts. Parents and teachers heard little but filthy language from them. They vandalized public property. They were
thieves. Old ladies had reason to fear them, because they did not
respect age in choosing people to hurt. They made young girls
pregnant, often by raping them.

C. Figures of Speech

A figure of speech is a nonliteral use of language. Like a skater, writers
cut figures with words. But not only writers. We all use figures of
speech all the time. Language works literally only to a point. Then we
have to play tricks with it to say precisely what we want to say. We
are constantly comparing, implicitly and explicitly, one thing with
another:

What's it doing?
  Raining.
Soft or hard?
  Hard.
How hard?
  It's raining cats and dogs.
To beat the band?
  To make hair grow on your chest.
I'm a girl.
  Dare to be different.
That would be a revolution.
  It would be the change of your life.

And so on. We have conversations like this all the time, not to obscure
communication but to clarify—and to enjoy the clarification. For fig-

ures of speech are not only useful for clarifying, they can be exciting and pleasing as well. The better the figure of speech, the better our expression.

The number of figures of speech floating around is staggering. Classical rhetoricians researched and classified wagon loads. But if we learn just the major ones—what they are and how they work—we'll have all we need to make prose a treat.

1. Metaphor

A student wrote of the troubles she had on the highway with truckers. They would stare down at her, wave, leer, blast their air horns, laugh. They would also scare her, tailgating at 65, roaring past at 70.

Once she was in the right lane minding her business when she was startled by a loud horn.

> I looked in my rearview mirror. All I could see was the grin of a huge grill.

"The grin of a huge grill"—*that* is a metaphor. It's the combination of two very different things for purposes of comparison, absent the introductory words "like" and "as." Hence it is termed an *implicit* comparison.

In structure it amounts to an identification. Trucker *is* truck, truck *is* trucker; the grin of one is the grill of the other and vice versa. The physical resemblence of grin and grill is the basis of the metaphor— that which the two very different things have in common. Yet in a metaphor the identification of the two terms goes beyond mere physical resemblence—it also *explains* by enabling readers to *experience* the meaning. By "the grin of a huge grill," we know exactly how the writer feels about truckers.

Understanding essentially involves seeing connections—the kinds that make us say "Ah ha!" Consequently, metaphor is particularly effective in helping us understand: It reveals connections we had not seen earlier. Here is a longer metaphor, also by a student.

> I like the kind of breeze that blows your hair but doesn't mess it up. It just sort of shifts it across your forehead. I like the breeze that lifts your shirt off your skin and slips its fingers under to run up your spine and give you goose bumps.

Ah yes, we say, a breeze like a lover!

When explaining even something as everyday as a breeze, search for an image to couple it with in metaphor. You don't need one in every sentence—that would make the prose too thick to wade through. But watch for good ones. A good metaphor is *the* most powerful figure of speech, the single most effective punch in writing.

EXERCISES

1. Examine the following metaphors and explain the connections:

    > There is no great sorrow dammed in my soul, nor lurking behind my eyes.
    >
    > —Hurston, *"How it Feels to Be Colored Me"*

    > The birds revolving about the boat have made themselves not only guests at the feast but have formed the wreath as well.
    >
    > —Wing, *"Christmas Comes First on the Banks"*

    > But now that my body is somewhat unbuckled and my consciousness reasonably raised I would very much like to be able to flirt with immunity again.
    >
    > —Fleming, *"In Defense of Flirting"*

    > I'm drinkin' t.n.t., I'm smokin' dynamite, I hope some screwball starts a fight.
    >
    > —Baraka, *"Streets of Despair"*

    > In the days before steam irons my mother had to douse her clean wash in a cooked starch solution, dry it on a clothesline, and sprinkle each piece with water from a huge Coca-Cola bottle stoppered with a perforated aluminum nozzle shaped like a flower. She'd roll each piece and place it in a plastic bag to let it marinate for a time. Then she'd unfold the items one by one and cook them just short of scorching, until they were stiff as canvas.
    >
    > —Smith, *"Pumping Iron"*

2. When we are *sad* we have the blues; we are in the dumps. Create another metaphor for sadness, one you've never seen before. Do the same for the following:

    > When we are *happy* we are high: life is a bowl of cherries.

When we're *hot* we're hot; when we're not we're not.

When we *think*, we ride on a stream of consciousness.

2. Simile

A simile is *like* a metaphor, except that the comparison is made *explicit* by using "like" or "as." Simile doesn't make as tight a connection as metaphor. It doesn't identify the two terms; it holds them at arm's length.

> And then this moth-essence, this spectacular skeleton, began to act as a wick.

Thus Annie Dillard describes the moth caught in her candle. And she uses other similes to explain the event.

> The wax rose in the moth's body from her smoking abdomen to her thorax to the shattered hole where her head should have been, and widened into flame, a saffron-yellow flame that robed her to the ground like an immolating monk.

Simile—to a greater extent than metaphor—respects the differences in the terms. As a result it lacks some of the punch of metaphor. The preceding quote contains a simile and a metaphor for the same image. It's obvious the introductory metaphor "robed" is more intense than the simile "like an immolating monk." In another sentence, Dillard again combines simile and metaphor, and again we see (and feel) the difference.

> She burned for two hours without changing, without swaying or kneeling—only glowing within, like a building fire glimpsed through silhouetted walls, like a hollow saint, like a flame-faced virgin gone to God, while I read by her light, kindled, while Rimbaud in Paris burnt out his brain in a thousand poems, while night pooled wetly at my feet.

The metaphor is not only more powerful than the simile, but more complex: The difference between burning up and writing poems is as much the point as the similarity. But power and complexity are not always necessary. If the point is simple, metaphor may be an exercise in overkill. Try a simile because of its relative simplicty. Dillard chose simile over metaphor when writing that the moth's "heaving mouth-parts cracked like pistol fire." When describing simply how you looked and felt, try simile—as one of my students did.

> After working two hours in the sun, my hair stuck to the back of my neck like a dirty, old, matted carpet.

What a lovely, icky simile. If you have one you've never seen—an enlightening connection like the student's in the preceding quote or like Dillard's—don't dismiss it because it's not a metaphor. It's too good to waste.

Look for images that you can make into either similes or metaphors or both. For both enable you to explain the point according to the data of experience—something that readers can specifically relate to and thus truly understand.

EXERCISES

1. Examine the following similies. Review them in the Reader if you need more context than is provided. Explain whether or not they work. If so, how? If not, why not?

> Then she let go of my arm, and it was as if she had pressed a button or released a spring I didn't know I had. I took off for that railing like a hungry dog tearing ass for a bowl of chow.
>
> —*Rivera, "First Communion"*

> That, of course, is the problem with New England ice: a lot of the time there's snow. So the skates, exuding an air of hurt rebuke like dogs you have forgotten to feed, hang in a thousand woodsheds and chimney corners for weeks on end, awaiting that rare season when the freeze comes smoothly across a still night and the cold stands snowless for days.
>
> —*Kidder, "Depths on the Surface"*

> While some New Yorkers become morose with rain, others prefer it, like to walk in it, and say that on rainy days the city's buildings seem somehow cleaner—washed in opalescence, like a Monet painting.
>
> —*Talese, "New York"*

> I had a deep fear of ending up in bed with someone for whom I felt no passion or desire. That to me was really dirty. And flirting, it seemed, was a say of protecting myself from that kind of non-passionate sex, a way of trying out my lust before bedding—like trying out a play in Boston before opening on Broadway.
>
> —*Fleming, "In Defense of Flirting"*

> They crowded very close about him, with their hands always on
> him in a careful, caressing grip, as though all the while feeling
> him to make sure he was there. It was like men handling a fish
> which is still alive and may jump back into the water.
>
> —*Orwell, "A Hanging"*

2. Create new similes for these old ones:

   I feel like hell.

   She is as old as Methuselah.

   He fought like a tiger.

3. Analogy

Some rhetoricians regard analogy as a rhetorical strategy rather than
a figure of speech. I view it as somewhere in between, but closer to a
figure of speech than to full-blown strategy. It's a means of explaining
a remote subject by comparing it to something familiar and concrete.
For example, I recently read a piece explaining how to maneuver a
plane by comparing the process to steering a boat.

Analogy is a metaphor or simile of sorts: an extended comparison
of two things having several points in common. Scientists often use
analogy to explain findings to those unfamiliar with their working
language. We all know that biologists and physicians explain the human
body in terms of a machine: pump for heart, computer for brain,
electronics for nervous system, pipes for urogenital tract, and so on.
We have all seen the eye compared in detail to a camera. The response
of the human body to disease is sometimes compared to a nation
marshaling its defenses against invasion.

In perfect reverse, politicians, historians, and sociologists often
compare social phenomena to biological phenomena. An invading
army is likened to an epidemic the homeland must ward off. Urban
blight is a cancer of which the body politic must rid itself. Organized
crime is a plague the nation must cure.

Be wary of useless analogies. They're easily framed. But as disasters
go, they're unmitigated.

> The basic-studies courses at most colleges are like a smorgasbord—
> a variety of foods to be sampled in search of what is best for you.
> There are the salads of the social sciences, the cold cuts of the hard
> sciences, the cheeses of the humanities, and finally the relishes of
> the arts. For salad you may sample the lettuce of psychology, the
> cucumber of sociology, the green pepper of anthropology. . . .

I can't go on; I have a weak stomach. And yet, it's no worse than some I've seen in print.

Guard against false analogy as well, especially if the analogy is to be used as argument. A false analogy is one where the unacknowledged *dis*similarities between the two terms of comparison are so great they outweigh the logic of the similarities. The basic studies/ smorgasbord analogy is not only nonsense, it's false and unpersuasive. If it's anything, it's *dis*suasive.

Unless it's an extremely precise analogy, use this figure of speech primarily to illustrate a point—not to argue it. The following is proof of just how brilliantly a good analogy can serve as illustration of an unfamiliar subject.

> One cannot easily realize what a tremendous thing it is to know every trivial detail of twelve-hundred miles of river and know it with absolute exactness. If you will take the longest street in New York, and travel up and down it, conning its features patiently until you know every house and window and door and lamppost and big and little sign by heart, and know them so accurately that you can instantly name the one you are abreast of when you are set down at random in that street in the middle of an inky black night, you will then have a tolerable notion of the amount and the exactness of a pilot's knowledge who carries the Mississippi River in his head. And then if you will go on until you know every street-crossing, the character, size, and position of the crossing stone, and the varying depth of mud in each of these numberless places, you will have some idea of what the pilot must know in order to keep a Mississippi steamer out of trouble. Next, if you will take half of the signs in that long street, and *change their places* once a month, and still manage to know their new positions accurately on dark nights, and keep up with these repeated changes without making any mistakes, you will understand what is required of a pilot's peerless memory by the fickle Mississippi.
>
> —*Mark Twain, Life on the Mississippi*

EXERCISES

1. Define as many dissimilarities between basic-studies courses and a smorgasbord as you can. Explain the shortcomings of the analogy.

2. Write an analogy comparing getting an idea to catching a fish. If you've never fished, compare it to some form of hunting.

3. If exercise two resulted in nonsense, write a serious analogy of your own invention. If it resulted in serious work, write a foolish analogy of your own invention.

4. Hyperbole

Also known as exaggeration, this figure of speech is a favorite of beginning writers because it's easy and it looks impressive. It *is* impressive. But more often than not it makes a poor impression because its use is heavy-handed.

> I was sweating so much I felt like a saturated sponge that had just finished soaking up the Pacific Ocean. If I had had a bar of soap and a towel, I could have taken a salty shower standing right where I was.

Because it seems so easy, effective hyperbole is deceptively difficult. Regard it as a temptation, something to avoid. Concentrate instead on other more precise figures of speech.

5. Irony

Another favorite of beginning writers, irony is saying the opposite of what is meant. Say an earthquake has struck, followed by a tornado, a flood, and another crash on Wall Street. You turn to the person on your right and say:

> Ain't life grand?

Say a movie put you to sleep.

> A real thriller.

Say someone has decidedly put you down.

> Can't resist me.

Like hyperbole, it's as easy as poking ribs and winking. If it's subtle and sure, irony is extremely effective. For instance, in the opening sentence of Jane Austen's *Pride and Prejudice*, the irony is as invigorating as a cup of coffee.

> It is a truth universally acknowledged that a single man in possession of a good fortune must be in want of a wife.

That's no truth. It's the wish of those who seek a profitable marriage and who assume everyone feels the same—as Austen implies with irony and demonstrates throughout the novel.

Irony of this order is delicate and difficult—too difficult for most beginning writers. Their irony often falls prey to its cheapest form, sarcasm.

> So this poor guy—he was worth only a few mill—moved into that
> pit of civilization known as our town, and when word got out that
> he was not only cursed with a fortune but unblessed by a wife, well,
> the local maidens and damsels proved their undying love by disown-
> ing their sweethearts, and they demonstrated their disdain of mere
> money by posting themselves all over the guy's porch.

This is not the writing of a wit—but of a nitwit.

Like hyperbole, avoid irony. Save it for later. Not for retirement—
it's not social security—but for maturity, when you've mastered the
fundamentals.

6. Cliches

Cliches are not just figures of speech, they are *old* figures of speech—
so old they've lost their figures. Whatever punch they once enjoyed has
turned to paunch. Avoid them like the plague. They're as dead as a
doornail. (Have you ever seen a doornail? Have you ever avoided the
plague? Have you even wondered what a doornail and the plague are?)

In "Politics and the English Language" (Reader) George Orwell
recommends never using an image—a figure of speech—commonly
seen in print. To that add anything commonly heard on the airwaves.
Invent your own. They may not always work, but there is always a
chance. Whereas cliches are *doomed from the outset.*

There's an exception. In certain situations you may be able to pump
new life into a cliche. I had a student who wrote about always being
the only Jewish kid in her neighborhood and in her school.

> I was in a class by myself,

she observed. Suddenly the cliche is as fresh and new as an infant's
first word. It works because in that specific context its meaning is
entirely original. It's witty. If you have an opportunity to revive a tired
old phrase—to make it youthful again—do. Otherwise, don't.

So much for figures of speech. Onward to stylistic considerations.

D. Motif

After once using a figure of speech or a phrase, you may later have an
opportunity to use it again—with or without variation. And later still
you may see another such opportunity. If you repeat the figure or
phrase, you create what is known as *motif.*

In "The Ring of Time," E. B. White uses the image of the circle or
ring as a motif. After using it in the title, he begins developing it
immediately in the description of a *circus* event: putting a horse through

its paces in a practice *ring*. Horse and trainer, he says, "seemed caught up in one of those desultory *treadmills* of afternoon from which there is no apparent escape."

> The long rein, or tape, by which the woman guided her charge *counterclockwise* in his dull career formed the radius of their private *circle*, of which she was the *revolving center;* and she, too, stepped a tiny *circumference* of her own, in order to accommodate the horse and allow him his maximum scope.

A few pages later, with the young girl now on the horse, White continues the circle imagery.

> Everything in the hideous old building seemed to take the shape of a circle, conforming to the course of the horse. The rider's gaze, as she peered straight ahead, seemed to be circular, as though bent by force of *circum*stance; then time itself began running in circles, and so the beginning was where the end was, and the two were the same, and one thing ran into the next and time went round and around and got nowhere.

Then White envisions the girl in the center of the ring "caught in the treadmill of an afternoon long in the future." Yet for the present, he points out, the ring of time was perfectly formed "like the ring in which she was traveling at this moment with the horse that wallowed under her."

When you create such a motif, you develop the full meaning of the figure of speech or phrase by weaving it into different contexts. Consequently, the motif must be fashioned from good stock; a provocative figure of speech like the circle, a richly significant phrase like the ring of time.

A motif works for two reasons: It surprises by means of repetition, providing readers a paradoxical pleasure, and it adds a sense of coherence—of everything relating to everything else.

Be alert for the chance to create a motif. But don't force it. It's not an essential element of the effective memorandum, laboratory report, letter, or essay.

EXERCISES

1. Locate and define the motifs in Dillard's "Death of a Moth," Wing's "Christmas Comes First on the Banks," and Highet's "Diogenes and Alexander."

2. With a group of classmates, discuss the relative effectiveness (or ineffectiveness) of the motifs.

E. Alliteration

Take this on faith and remember it well: Alliteration—using words that begin with the same sound—is music to readers' ears, consciously or subconsciously. So if there's a choice—when two or several words can serve your meaning equally well—select the one that alliterates with another word or two in the same sentence or the one next door.

> There is something uneasy in the Los Angeles air this afternoon, some unnatural stillness, some tension. What it means is that tonight a Santa Ana will begin to blow, a hot wind from the northeast whining down through the Cajon Pass, blowing up sandstorms along Route 66, drying the hills and the nerves to a flashpoint.

For purposes of alliteration, treat all vowels that begin words as one sound only (*u*neasy, *a*ir, *u*nnatural). The consonants Didion alliterates most are S and H. The two B's—begin to blow—are obvious. The T's and W's—tension, tonight, will, wind—barely qualify.

To see that Didion's alliteration is deliberate—a matter of choice— consider a revision of the first sentence.

> There is something disquieting in Los Angeles this afternoon, a perverse quiet, a genuine tension.

The revised sentence is inferior to Didion's in several respects, but perhaps the most important weakness is the absence of alliteration. (note: *i*nferior, *i*mportant, *a*bsence, *a*lliteration.)

A word of caution: Don't overdo it, especially with harder sounds such as B, P, F, and S.

> The snake slithered silently and stealthily through the slush of the swamp scanning the slimy surface for small spoils to seize, subdue, and swallow.

In short, exercise restraint and discretion.

EXERCISES

1. Rewrite the snake sentence. Reduce the S alliteration and alliterate one or two other sounds. Compare the revised sentence with those of a group of classmates.

2. Read the first ten paragraphs of the first essay in the Reader. Note the alliteration. List ten nonalliterative alternatives the writer might have selected.

F. Rhythm

Listen to your writing; read the words aloud. Feel the rhythm. If it doesn't flow—if it bumps and lurches and stops and staggers and tangles the tongue—revise it.

But when is rhythm rotten? Just *listen*.

> In many cases, the employer is not only the boss, but also is employed as well himself. He is superior, as employer, to those who work for him, but he is inferior to his employees, those he works for to whom he must report. At McDonald's this is the case where they have head managers and there are also swing managers, who are crew members who are in charge of the store when no regular manager is there.

Through parallelism you may ensure swinging, rhythmic prose.

> In many cases, the boss is not only the employer but is also an employee.

Using active verbs may help.

> For example, McDonald's has both head managers and swing managers.

While listening to the rhythm, listen to the sounds as well. Phrasing like "He is superior, as employer" constitute noise pollution—an offense for which your efforts may be sentenced to the wastebasket.

EXERCISES

1. Compose an awkward paragraph about writing awkwardly. Compare it with those of a group of classmates.

2. Revise the following, paying particular attention to the rhythm:

> However, after standing there in ribbons and patent leather Mary Janes and I sweetly explained what had happened, my innocence of it, all my excuses, to the principal, his punishment was lessened from one week of no recesses and staying after school, to only one day.

Compare yours to the revisions of some others.

G. Humor

Few pleasures are more satisfying than saying something humorous and hearing others agree with laughter. Few pains are greater than listening to something supposedly humorous which isn't.

Because the pleasure is so real, it's understandable you'd like to write something funny. But understand that when it isn't, the readers suffer real pain. And remember that when you *try* to be funny, you rarely are.

> So there was yours truly, boogieing to beat the band, when along comes this dish in a dress so bright it was burning my candle at both ends and cut so low it should have had a sign warning of dangerous curves ahead, and so I says to myself, "Jeff, my boy," says I, "CHARGE!"

This is the stuff of beginners—strained and pained. It's probably based on a mistaken belief that humor lies in *words*. It rarely does. Few words are inherently funny. Perhaps puck or honk or smorgasbord or booboisie are intrinsically humorous—but they're few and far between. So take note: Look for humor in bizarre situations, incongruous events, and surprise happenings. If you encounter such an occurrence, get the words *out of the way:* Frame the structure clearly and simply. Allow *it* to get the laugh because *it* is where the humor really lies.

> One day before class I took the drawers out of my chemistry teacher's desk. I turned the desk upside down, put the drawers back in, and put the desk right side up. When he opened his drawers and everything spilled out, everyone laughed. He laughed. I laughed. Even the principal laughed. My parents didn't laugh.

The prank is funny, I suppose, if you like practical jokes. But the sudden—so sudden it's not even introduced with a "but"—refusal of the parents to be amused *is* amusing. Not one adjective, one hyperbole, one trace of ironic phrasing is necessary. The turn of events, in and of *it*self, is where the humor lies.

The moral: Don't *try* to be a comedian. Concentrate instead on writing exactly what you have to say. If some of it—perchance all of it—happens to be funny, fine. Get out of the way and *let* it be funny. If nothing funny appears, don't worry about it. Writing doesn't have to be funny to be effective.

H. Pathos

Just as beginning writers often strain to get a laugh, they sometimes overwork to wring a tear or two and break the reader's heart. For instance, here the writer describes an experience in a nursing home.

> As I walked down the hall there seemed to be a lot of confusion around one room. As I stood outside in the hall I could hear two females and one male talking.

The man had apparently misplaced his wrist watch. He was very
excited about this because he said his grandchildren had given it to
him. He kept saying this over and over to the women. They were
trying to reassure him that they would find it, but I also heard them
say softly that this was the seventh thing stolen this week. Very soon
the man broke into tears and cried, "There is no reason to live! First
they take my wife, now my precious grandchildren!" One of the
women was desperately trying to console him. She said, "Mr. Wilson,
I will find your watch for you!"

As I walked into the room I felt like life was not worth living. Mr.
Wilson is my grandfather.

The writer knew from the beginning who the man in the room was.
So why wait until the very end to tell us? To hit us where it hurts. But
instead of crying tears, we cry "Foul"; he's trying to move us with a
trick, not with the facts.

More commonly, beginning writers resort to adjectives and adverbs
and such.

The puppy lay piteously in its cage, its thin bony little frame racked
by kennel cough and hunger, whining feebly for a bite of food, its
eyes pleading as well for love if only a morsel, just a tidbit of affection, ma'am, sir, please. . . .

Remember purple prose? This is a form of it. It's written to make us
admire the writer's compassion as much as to make us pity the puppy's condition. Don't indulge in this drivel. It's tacky.

If you know a touching situation, let *it* do the touching. Cut out the
adjectives and the fancy figures of speech. Cut out the syrupy appeals
to emotion. Stick to facts. If the situation is moving, let it move on its
own. It it's not, even a tow truck won't move it.

I. The Element of Surprise

Essential for humor, surprise is *always* effective if it genuinely results
from the logic of the situation.

Consider the joke. Its structure consists of two basic parts: the situation and the punch line. The punch line must logically result from
the situation, and yet not be obvious or easily anticipated. It must also
be a surprise.

Use the basic structure of the joke for more than just a laugh. Most
everyone loves a surprise, funny or not. If you make the point with a
surprise, you make it doubly effective. This student did.

December 3, 1982:
> Every year around this time the radio stations all start to play the same songs. Some of the top stations even try to coax you to listen to them with hour-long specials, and interviews free of commercials. No, it's not Christmas. They do this every year on the anniversary of John Lennon's death. Sometimes I think they carry the thing too far. Yesterday the *Free Press* had an interview with Sean Lennon, John's son. He's only seven years old. He talked about his gym class.

Of course the kid talked about his gym glass. "He's only seven years old." But how many of you anticipated that? I didn't. And what better way to make the point that the media "carry the thing too far"? Reporters have no legitimate business talking to a seven year old—much less interviewing one—no matter whose son he is.

I hope you noticed that Sean's discussion is the *second* surprise of the paragraph. The first is the occasion for the media antics: not Christmas but Lennon's death. You are not restricted to one surprise per paragraph. Conversely, you are not required to have at least one per paragraph. The number of surprises you spring depends on how many lurk within the subject.

In developing the subject, watch for the surprise that flows naturally from the situation. If you have such a structure, write it simply and clearly. *Never build such a structure when a surprise does not exist.* That's what the grandson did: The punchline did not flow from the events—it preceded them. That's why we feel manipulated and cheated. It's not honest.

J. Honesty Is the Best Policy

It really is. Good old Huckleberry Finn has the reason: "You can't pray a lie." A piece of writing is a prayer of sorts: It's a statement launched with the hope it will be favorably received. And readers are almighty: They can accept or reject the statement as they please. They can smell a fib a page away, and they will not be mocked. So whatever you give them, give it to them straight.

What does it mean, though, *to be honest*? Before becoming a saint, Augustine was a notorious lech. In time he desired to be otherwise. This prayer follows:

> Give me continence and chastity.

He needed help to be chaste, so he asked for it. Simple. Yet not so simple. If *all* he wanted was to be chaste, he would have been chaste.

As a matter of fact, then, continence and chastity were not the sum of Augustine's desire. The prayer was not quite complete, not quite honest—and not Augustine's actual prayer. What he really said was:

> Give me continence and chastity, but not yet.

Augustine was an honest man; he had the makings of a saint.

A student wrote about driving a Porsche when she was 16. At 125 miles an hour, she totaled it in a ditch. She was unhurt but shaken.

> After the wreck, for the first time in my life, I felt mortal. And I realized, just as I hope my close call, my brush with death will help you realize, that driving dangerously is a losing game. We must buckle up and drive safely. We really can die, with just a flick of the wrist, a hole in a tire, a nod of the head, so the lives we save really can be our own. Since that day I have never exceeded the speed limit.

Do you believe that? Or do you believe this?

> After the wreck, for the first time in my life, I felt mortal. It lasted only a few days, though, and if I had been given the chance I would have done it again.

In the first version she describes the way she *should* have responded: according to the principles of common sense and responsibility. In the second version she describes the way she actually responded: according to the principles of teenage human nature. It rings true; we know it's the one she wrote.

All of us—6, 16, 60—occasionally think and feel and act at odds with conventional wisdom. However we happen to think and feel and act, our job as writers is to know it and—when relevant to the subject—to let the reader know it. We must not kid anybody, least of all ourselves. We must not pretend to be better than we actually are.

Wait a minute! Haven't I said from the start that the great thing about writing is that we can be so much smarter than we actually are? More charming, witty, commanding, profound? Well, why not better?

There's good reason. The great thing about writing is that we can be so much more honest than we usually are—and *therefore* better—by stripping ourselves of all pretense. Readers are turned off by pretense faster than by anything else.

So don't pretend to be better than you actually are. That's hypocrisy. Instead, be honest. You may not secure the readers' agreement, but you'll have something much more important—their respect, their understanding, and their appreciation. That's a promise.

Following arrest for allegedly trafficking in cocaine, automobile tycoon John DeLorean reportedly declared:

I have never done anything illegal or immoral in my life.

If indeed he made the statement, DeLorean is better than Saint Augustine, as good as Jesus, and the worst liar since the serpent of Eden.

Don't try to pray a lie; tell the truth. You'll be the better for it—not better than you are, but as good as you can be. Which for the readers is exactly good enough.

DONALD M. MURRAY
Internal Revision: A Process of Discovery

A writing teacher at the University of New Hampshire, Murray has been an editor of Time *and in 1954 received a Pulitzer Prize for his editorials in the Boston* Herald. *He has also published fiction, poetry, and a textbook on the teaching of writing, from which the following is selected. In it Murray shows how revision is an activity that goes on in the writer's head as well as on the writer's page.*

Writing is rewriting. Most writers accept rewriting as a condition of their craft; it comes with the territory. It is not, however, seen as a burden but as an opportunity by many writers. Neil Simon points out, "Rewriting is when playwriting really gets to be fun. . . . In baseball you only get three swings and you're out. In rewriting, you get almost as many swings as you want and you know, sooner or later, you'll hit the ball."

Rewriting is the difference between the dilettante and the artist, the amateur and the professional, the unpublished and the published. William Gass testifies, "I work not by writing but rewriting." Dylan Thomas states, "Almost any poem is fifty to a hundred revisions—and that's after it's well along." Archibald MacLeish talks of "the endless discipline of writing and rewriting and rerewriting." Novelist Theodore Weesner tells his students at the University of New Hampshire his course title is not "Fiction Writing" but "Fiction Rewriting."

And yet rewriting is one of the writing skills least researched, least examined, least understood, and—usually—least taught. The vast majority of students, even those who take writing courses, get away with first-draft copy. They are never introduced to the opportunities of serious revision.

A search of the literature reveals relatively few articles or books on the rewriting process. I have a commonplace book which has grown from one thin journal to 24 3-inch-thick notebooks with more than 8,000 entries divided into prewriting, writing, and rewriting. Yet even with my interest in the process of rewriting—some of my colleagues would say obsession—only four of those notebooks are labeled rewriting.

I suspect the term rewriting has, even for many writers, an aura of failure about it. Rewriting is too often taught as punishment, not as an opportunity for discovery or even as an inevitable part of the writing process. Most texts, in fact, confuse rewriting with editing, proofreading, or manuscript preparation. Yet rewriting almost always is the most exciting, satisfying part of the writing process.

The Writing Process

The most accurate definition of writing, I believe, is that it is the process of using language to discover meaning in experience and to communicate it. I believe this process can be described, understood and therefore learned. Prewriting, writing, and rewriting have been generally accepted as the three principal divisions of the writing process during the past decade. I would like to propose new terms for consideration, terms which may emphasize the essential process of discovery through writing: *prevision*, *vision*, and *revision*.

Of course, writing will, at times, seem to skip over one part of the writing process and linger on another, and the stages of the process also overlap. The writing process is too experimental and exploratory to be contained in a rigid definition; writers move back and forth through all stages of the writing process as they search for meaning and then attempt to clarify it. It is also true that most writers do not define, describe, or possibly even understand the writing process. There's no reason for them to know what they are doing if they do it well, any more than we need to know grammatical terms if we speak and write clearly. I am convinced, however, that most writers most of the time pass through the following distinct stages.

Prevision. This term encompasses everything that preceeds the first draft—receptive experience, such as awareness (conscious and unconscious), observation, remembering; and exploratory experience, such as research, reading, interviewing, and note-taking. Writers practice the prevision skills of selecting, connecting, and evaluating significant bits of information provided by receptive and exploratory experience.

Prevision includes, in my opinion, the underestimated skills of title and lead writing, which help the student identify a subject, limit it, develop a point of view towards it, and begin to find the voice to explore the subject.

Vision. In the second stage of the writing process, the first draft—what I call a discovery draft—is completed. This stage takes the shortest time for the writer—in many cases it is written at one sitting—but it is the fulcrum of the writing process. Before this first draft, which Peter Drucker calls "the zero draft," everything seems possible. By completing this vision of what may be said, the writer stakes out a territory to explore.

Revision. This is what the writer does after a draft is completed to understand and communicate what has begun to appear on the page. The writer reads to see what has been suggested, then confirms, alters or develops it, usually through many drafts. Eventually a meaning is developed which can be communicated to a reader. . . .

The Two Principal Forms of Revision

The more I explore the revision process as a researcher and the more I experience it as a writer, the more convinced I am that there are two principle and quite separate editorial acts involved in revision.

Internal revision. Under this term, I include everything writers do to discover and develop what they have to say, beginning with the reading of a completed first draft. They read to discover where their content, form, language, and voice have led them. They use language, structure, and information to find out what they have to say or hope to say. The audience is one person: the writer.

External revision. This is what writers do to communicate what they have found they have written to another audience. It is editing and proofreading and much more. Writers now pay attention to the conventions of form and language, mechanics, and style. They eye their audience and may choose to appeal to it. They read as an outsider, and it is significant that such terms as *polish* are used by professionals: they dramatize the fact that the writer at this stage in the process may, appropriately, be concerned with exterior appearance.

Most writers spend more time, *much* more time, on internal revision than external revision. Yet most texts exmphasize the least part of the process, the mechanical changes involved in the etiquette of writing, the superficial aspects of preparing a manuscript to be read, and pass over the process of internal revision. It's worth noting that it is unlikely intelligent choices in the editing process can be made unless writers thoroughly understand what they have said through internal revision.

Although I believe external revision has not been explored adequately or imaginatively, it has been explored. I shall concentrate on attempting to describe internal revision, suggesting opportunities for research, and indicating some implications for the teaching of writing.

The Process of Internal Revision

After the writer has completed the first draft, the writer moves toward the center of the writing process. E. M. Forster says, "The act of writing inspires me," and Valery talks of "the inspiration of the writing desk." The writer may be closer to the scientist than to the critic at this point. Each piece of writing is an experiment. Robert Penn Warren says, "All writing that is any good *is* experimental: that is, it's a way of seeing what is possible."

Some pieces of writing come easily, without a great deal of internal revision. The experience is rare for most writers, however, and it usually comes after a lifetime of discipline, or sometimes after a long night of work, as it did when Robert Frost wrote "Stopping by Woods on a Snowy Evening." The important thing to understand is that the work that reads the most easily is often the product of what appears to be drudgery. Theodore Roethke wisely points out that "you will come to know how, by working slowly, to be spontaneous."

I have a relatively short 7-part poem of which there are 185 or more versions written over the past 2 years. I am no Roethke, but I have found it important to share with my students in my seminar on the teaching of writing a bit of the work which will never appear in public. I think they are impressed with how badly I write, with how many false starts and illiterate accidents it took for me to move forward towards some understanding of the climate in a tenement in which I lived as an only child, surrounded by a paralyzed grandmother and two rather childlike parents. The important thing for my students to see is that each word changed, each line crossed out, each space left on the page is an attempt to understand, to remember what I did not know I remembered.

During the process of internal revision, writers are not concerned with correctness in any exterior sense. They read what they have written so that they can deal with the questions of subject, of adequate information, of structure, of form, of language. They move from a revision of the entire piece down to the page, the paragraph, the sentence, the line, the phrase, the word. And then, because each word may give off an explosion of meaning, they move out from the word to the phrase, the line, the sentence, the paragraph, the page, the piece. Writers move in close and then move to visualize the entire piece. Again and again and again. As Donald Hall says, "The attitude to cultivate from the start is that revision is a way of life."

Discovery and Internal Revision

The concept of internal revision is new to me. This essay has given me the impetus to explore this area of the writing process. The further I explore the more tentative my conclusions. This chapter is, indeed, as I believe it was meant to be, a call for research, not a report of research. There are many things I do not understand as I experience and examine the process of internal revision. But in addition to my normal researches, I am part of a faculty which includes seven publishing writers, as well as many publishing scholars and critics. We share our work in process, and I have the advantage of seeing them discover what they have to say. I also see the work of graduate students in our writing program, many of whom are already publishing. And I watch the writing of students who are undergraduates at the university, in high school, in middle school, and in elementary school. And I think I can perceive four important aspects of discovery in the process of internal revision.

The first involves *content*. I think we forget that writers in all forms, even poetry, especially poetry, write with information. As English professors and linguistic researchers, we may concentrate on stylistic differences, forgetting that the writer engaged in the process of internal revision is looking through the word—or beyond the word or behind the word—for the information the word will symbolize. Sitting at a desk, pausing, staring out the window, the writer does not see some great thesaurus in the sky; the writer sees a character walking or hears a character speaking, sees a pattern of statistics which may lead toward a conclusion. Writers can't write nothing; they must have an abundance of information. During the process of internal revision, they gather new information or return to their inventory of information and draw on it. They discover what they have to say by relating pieces of specific information to other bits of information and use words to symbolize and connect that information.

This naturally leads to discoveries related to *form and structure*. We all know Archibald MacLeish said that a poem should not mean but be, but what we do not always understand is that being may be the meaning. Form is meaning, or a kind of meaning. The story that has a beginning, a middle, and an end implies that life has a beginning, a middle, and an end; exposition implies that things can be explained; argument implies the possibility of rational persuasion. As writers bring order to chaos, the order brings the writers toward meaning.

Third, *language* itself leads writers to meaning. During the process of internal revision (what some writers might call eternal revision), they reject words, choose new words, bring words together, switch their order around to discover what they are saying. "I work with language," says Bernard Malamud, "I love the flowers of afterthought."

Finally, I believe there is a fourth area, quite separate from content, form, or language, which is harder to define but may be as important as the other sources of discovery. That is what we call *voice*. I think voice, the way in which writers hear what they have to say, hear their point of view towards the subject, their authority, their distance from the subject, is an extremely significant form of internal revision.

We should realize that there may be fewer discoveries in form and voice as a writer repeats a subject or continues to work in a genre which he or she has explored earlier and become proficient with. This lack of discovery—this excessive professionalism or slickness, the absence of discovery—is the greatest fear of mature, successful writers. They may know too much too early in the writing process.

RICHARD A. LANHAM

Who's Kicking Who?

> *Lanham is a professor of English at U.C.L.A. who has written a number of scholarly works and articles and, in addition, two superb books on writing:* Style: An Anti-textbook *(1974) and* Revising Prose *(1979). This chapter from the latter demonstrates Lanham's knack for explaining how and why you should do what he tells you to do.*

No student these days feels comfortable writing simply "Jim kicks Bill." The system seems to require something like "One can easily see that a kicking situation is taking place between Bill and Jim." Or, "This is the kind of situation in which Jim is a kicker and Bill is a kickee." Jim cannot enjoy kicking Bill; no, for school use, it must be "Kicking Bill is an activity hugely enjoyed by Jim." Absurdly contrived examples? Here are some real ones:

This sentence is in need of an active verb.

There is a great deal of feeling and involvement in his description.

Another noticeable feature of the passage is the use of nouns, not only in reference to the name of things present, but in achieving a more forceful description of the scene.

See what they have in common? They are like our Bill and Jim examples, assembled from strings of prepositional phrases glued together by that all-purpose epoxy "is." In each case the sentence's verbal force has been shunted into a noun and for a verb we make do with "is," the neutral copulative, the weakest verb in the language. Such sentences project no life, no vigor. They just "are." And the "is" generates those strings of prepositional phrases fore and aft. It's so easy to fix. Look for the real action. Ask yourself, who's kicking who? (Yes, I know, it should be *whom*, but doesn't it sound stilted?)

In "This sentence is in need of an active verb," the action obviously lies in "need." And so, "This sentence needs an active verb." The needless prepositional phrase "in need of," simply disappears once we see who's kicking who. The sentence, animated by a real verb, comes alive, and in six words instead of nine. (If you've not paid attention to your own writing before, think of a lard factor [LF] of ⅓ to ½ as normal and don't stop revising until you've removed it).

In "There is a great deal of feeling and involvement in his description," where is the action? In "description" obviously. And so, "He describes the scene feelingly." Out go the "of" and "in" prepositional phrases. We've five words instead of twelve, even though I've added two ("The scene") as a direct object for "describes." And notice how the rhythm improves? The original galumphs, every cadence about the same length:

There is/a great deal/of feeling/and involvement/in his description.

The "is"-plus-prepositional-phrase pattern aborts any possible shape or rhythm. Now for the third example.

"Another notable feature of the passage is the use of nouns"—stop right there. Notice how long this sentence takes to get going? Again, who's kicking who? The "passage" is "using" nouns. When you omit the opening tautology—you have proved that the passage is notable by noting it—it reads "The passage uses nouns." We've eliminated two prepositional phrases and gotten the sentence off to a snappier start. Now we get rid of three more by locating the action—in "naming."

So. "The passage uses nouns not only to name things present . . .". Since "but in achieving a more forceful description of the scene" obviously wants to say "but to describe the scene more forcefully," two more prepositional phrases bite the dust. And the parallelism of "to name" and "to describe" now comes clear since they can get closer together.

So: "The passage uses nouns not only to name things present but to describe the scene more forcefully." (Ignore, for the time being, that "more forcefully" is an indefinite comparative—more forcefully than what?) Read the revision and the original aloud several times. Notice how that da-da-dum monotony has vanished? Along with seven prepositional phrases. And we're going with a lard factor of 45% (found by dividing the difference between the number of words in the original and the revision by the number of words in the original—in this case, $31 - 17 = 14 \div 30 = .45$). The sentence puts its action into its verbs.

The drill for this problem stands clear. Circle every form of "to be" ("is," "was," "will be," "seems to be") and every prepositional phrase. Then find out who's kicking who and start rebuilding the sentence with that action. Two prepositional phrases in a row turn on the warning light, three make a problem, and four invite disaster. With a little practice, sentences like "The mood Dickens paints is a bleak one" will turn into "Dickens paints a bleak mood" (LF 38%) almost before you've written them. And you'll just not commit the Normative Undergraduate Sentence, the pure formula:

> Central to our understanding of the character of Lucrece in William Shakespeare's *The Rape of Lucrece* is the long passage toward the end of the poem devoted to a painting of the fall of Troy.

A diagram may help:

> Central to our understanding
>   of the character
>   of Lucrece
>   in William Shakespeare's *The Rape of Lucrece*
> is the long passage
>   towards the end
>   of the poem devoted
>   to a painting
>   of the fall
>   of Troy.

Four prepositional phrases in a row glued to five prepositional phrases in a row by nothing but an epoxy "is" and hope. The catalogue-like monotony shines through the diagram. And how long it takes to get going! The rocket fires, fizzles through "to" da-da-dum, "of" and "in," and then hits "is" and falls back dead onto the launching pad. How to fix it?

Again, where's the action? Here, buried not in a word but in a phrase, "central to our understanding." We need a verb—"reveals," "illuminates," "focuses," "explains," "analyzes." Try "illuminates": the actor, the Troy painting, illuminates Lucrece's character. "The Troy painting, described near the poem's end, illuminates Lucrece's character." Eleven words instead of thirty-five—LF 68%.

The Normative Undergraduate Sentence does not, of course, always come from undergraduates. Look at these "of" strings from a linguist, a literary critic, and a popular gourmet.

> It is the totality *of* the interrelation *of* various components *of* language and the other communication systems which is the basis for referential memory.

> These examples *of* unusual appropriateness *of* the sense *of* adequacy to the situation suggest the primary signification *of* rhyme in the usual run *of* lyric poetry.

> Frozen breads and frozen pastry completed the process *of* depriving the American woman *of* the pleasure *of* boasting *of* her baking.

The "of" strings are the worst of all. They look like a child pulling a gob of bubble gum out into a long string. When you try to revise them, you can feel how fatally easy the "is and of" formulation can be for expository prose. And how fatally confusing, too, since to find an active, transitive verb for "is" means, often, adding a specificity the writer has not provided. So, in the first example, what does "is the basis for" really mean? And does the writer mean that language's components interact with "other communications systems," or is he talking about "components" of "other communication systems" as well? The "of" phrases refer back to those going before in so general a way that you can't keep straight what really modified what. So revision here is partly a guess.

> Referential meaning emerges when the components of language interact with other communication systems.

Or the sentence might mean

> Referential meaning emerges when the components of language interact with components of other communication systems.

Do you see the writer's problem? He has tried to be more specific than he needs to be, to build his sentence on a noun ("totality") which demands a string of "of's" to qualify it. Ask where the action is, build the sentence on a *verb*, and the "totality" follows as an implication. Noun-centeredness like this generates most of our present-day prose sludge.

The second example, out of context, doesn't make much sense. Perhaps "These examples, where adequacy to the situation seems unusually appropriate, suggest how rhyme usually works in lyric poetry." The third is easy to fix. Try it.

In asking who's kicking who, a couple of mechanical tricks come in handy. Besides getting rid of the "is's" and changing every passive voice ("is defended by") to an active voice ("defends"), you can squeeze the compound verbs hard, make every "are able to" into a "can," every "seems to succeed in creating" into "creates," every "cognize the fact that" (no, I didn't make it up) into "think," every "am hopeful that" into "hope," every "provides us with an example of" into "exemplify," every "seeks to reveal" into "shows," every "there is the inclusion of" into "includes."

And you can amputate those mindless introductory phrases, "The fact of the matter is that" and "The nature of the case is that." Start fast and then, as they say in the movies, "cut to the chase" as soon as you can. Instead of "the answer is in the negative," you'll find yourself saying "No."

We now have the beginnings of a Paramedic Method (PM):

1. Circle the prepositions.
2. Circle the "is" forms.
3. Ask "Who is kicking who?"
4. Put this "kicking" action in a simple (not compound) active verb.
5. Start fast—no mindless introductions.

Try out the PM on the following examples. The nonfat versions ought to be half as long and have some zip.

1. The many nouns help you to vividly see numerous things, but there is very little action.

2. I feel *Venus and Adonis* is a satire primarily because of the extreme nature of the mismatch of the two characters.

3. The poem is an allegory of the evolution of the role figures of medieval times to the self-conscious egoist of the Renaissance.

4. The central plot interest of Shakespeare's poem *Venus and Adonis*, Adonis's adamant rejection of Venus's unflagging courtship, is entirely contrary to Ovid's account of the story in *Metamorphoses* and to the original Greek myth.

5. One particularly enticing example of this aspect of water symbolism is the reference to Narcissus kissing himself in the brook.

6. The play is an allegorization of the conception and development of a new concept of justice delivered by the character Angelo and embodied in the character of the Duke.

7. Lost in the rewrite is the intrigue that the reader experienced when wondering what message the author was trying to convey by writing in such an odd fashion. What was gained in the normalized version was a smoother reading and a greater understanding of what was going on.

8. As the churchmen are officially viewed as bastions of virtue in society, the inference that we are expected to draw from this is that it is thus virtuous to squander one's fortune, a proposition logically arrived at but nonetheless false.

9. The techniques proposed here were obtained, in part, by adapting, for qualitative variables, some of the multiple-comparison ideas proposed earlier in the analysis of variance context. This adaptation for the analysis of qualitative variables was carried out in an earlier series of articles by the present author in which simultaneous confidence intervals and multiple test procedures were developed for the simultaneous analysis of a variety of questions pertaining to a given qualitative variable or to a given set of qualitative variables.

10. Dear Faculty Member,
  A program is being developed for implementation in the spring of 1972 that will include the University in the decision-making process which affects all our lives. Special Studies Workshops for Policy Proposal is a new curriculum whose intent it is to discover the needs of the decision-makers, the expertise of the faculty, and the interests of the students, and bring all three together in the workshops.

GEORGE ORWELL
Politics and the English Language

His real name was Eric Blair. He was raised in India, educated in England, and spent time in various capacities (policeman, vagrant, soldier, columnist) in various places (Burma, France, Spain, England).

Most famous for his novels Animal Farm *(1945) and* 1984 *(1949), Orwell was also an essayist who was consistently interested in the relationship of politics and daily life. The following is the best single essay on writing I know. I recommend that you type the questions and rules Orwell lists, tape them to the wall over your desk, and follow them with the devotion of a saint.*

Most people who bother with the matter at all would admit that the English language is in a bad way, but it is generally assumed that we cannot by conscious action do anything about it. Our civilisation is decadent, and our language—so the argument runs—must inevitably share in the general collapse. It follows that any struggle against the abuse of language is a sentimental archaism, like preferring candles to electric light or hansom cabs to aeroplanes. Underneath this lies the half-conscious belief that language is a natural growth and not an instrument which we shape for our own purposes.

Now, it is clear that the decline of a language must ultimately have political and economic causes: it is not due simply to the bad influence of this or that individual writer. But an effect can become a cause, reinforcing the original cause and producing the same effect in an intensified form, and so on indefinitely. A man may take to drink because he feels himself to be a failure, and then fail all the more completely because he drinks. It is rather the same thing that is happening to the English language. It becomes ugly and inaccurate because our thoughts are foolish, but the slovenliness of our language makes it easier for us to have foolish thoughts. The point is that the process is reversible. Modern English, especially written English, is full of bad habits which spread by imitation and which can be avoided if one is willing to take the necessary trouble. If one gets rid of these habits one can think more clearly, and to think clearly is a necessary first step towards political regeneration: so that the fight against bad English is not frivolous and is not the exclusive concern of professional writers. I will come back to this presently, and I hope that by that time the meaning of what I have said here will have become clearer. Meanwhile, here are five specimens of the English language as it is now habitually written.

These five passages have not been picked out because they are especially bad—I could have quoted far worse if I had chosen—but because they illustrate various of the mental vices from which we now suffer. They are a little below the average, but are fairly representative samples. I number them so that I can refer back to them when necessary:

1. I am not, indeed, sure whether it is not true to say that the Milton who once seemed not unlike a seventeenth-century Shelley had not become, out of an experience ever more bitter in each year, more alien (sic) to the founder of that Jesuit sect which nothing could induce him to tolerate.

Professor Harold Laski (Essay in *Freedom of Expression*).

2. Above all, we cannot play ducks and drakes with a native battery of idioms which prescribes such egregious collocations of vocables as the Basic *put up with* for *tolerate* or *put at a loss* for *bewilder*.

Professor Lancelot Hogben (*Interglossa*)

3. On the one side we have the free personality: by definition it is not neurotic, for it has neither conflict nor dream. Its desires, such as they are, are transparent, for they are just what institutional approval keeps in the forefront of consciousness; another institutional pattern would alter their number and intensity; there is little in them that is natural, irreducible, or culturally dangerous. But *on the other side*, the social bond itself is nothing but the mutual reflection of these self-secure integrities. Recall the definition of love. Is not this the very picture of a small academic? Where is there a place in this hall of mirrors for either personality or fraternity?

Essay on psychology in *Politics* (New York).

4. All the "best people" from the gentlemen's clubs, and all the frantic Fascist captains, united in common hatred of Socialism and bestial horror of the rising tide of the mass revolutionary movement, have turned to acts of provocation, to foul incendiarism, to medieval legends of poisoned wells, to legalise their own destruction to proletarian organisations, and rouse the agitated petty-bourgeoisie to chauvinistic fervour on behalf of the fight against the revolutionary way out of the crisis.

Communist pamphlet.

5. If a new spirit *is* to be infused into this old country, there is one thorny and contentious reform which must be tackled, and that is the humanisation and galvanisation of the *BBC*. Timidity here will bespeak canker and atrophy of the soul. The heart of Britain may be sound and of strong beat, for instance, but the British lion's roar at present is like that of Bottom in Shakespeare's *Midsummer Night's Dream*—as gentle as any sucking dove. A virile new Britain cannot continue indefinitely to be traduced in the eyes, or rather ears, of the world by the effete languors of Langham Place, brazenly masquerading as "standard English". When the Voice of Britain is heard at nine o'clock, better far and infinitely less ludicrous to hear aitches honestly dropped than the present priggish, inflated, inhibited, schoolma, amish arch braying of blameless bashful mewing maidens!

Letter in *Tribune*.

Each of these passages has faults of its own, but, quite apart from avoidable ugliness, two qualities are common to all of them. The first is staleness of imagery: the other is lack of precision. The writer either has a meaning and cannot express it, or he inadvertently says something else, or he is almost indifferent as to whether his words mean anything or not. This mixture of vagueness and sheer incompetence is the most marked characteristic of modern English prose, and especially of any kind of political writing. As soon as certain topics are raised, the concrete melts into the abstract and no one seems able to think of turns of speech that are not hackneyed: prose consists less and less of *words* chosen for the sake of their meaning, and more of *phrases* tacked together like the sections of a prefabricated hen-house. I list below, with notes and examples, various of the tricks by means of which the work of prose construction is habitually dodged:

Dying metaphors. A newly invented metaphor assists thought by evoking a visual image, while on the other hand a metaphor which is technically "dead" (e.g. *iron resolution*) has in effect reverted to being an ordinary word and can generally be used without loss of vividness. But in between these two classes there is a huge dump of worn-out metaphors which have lost all evocative power and are merely used because they save people the trouble of inventing phrases for themselves. Examples are: *Ring the changes on, take up the cudgels for, toe the line, ride roughshod over, stand shoulder to shoulder with, play into the hands of, no axe to grind, grist to the mill, fishing in troubled waters, rift within the lute, on the order of the day, Achilles' heel, swan song, hotbed.* Many of these are used without knowledge of their meaning (what is a "rift", for instance?), and incompatible metaphors are frequently mixed, a sure sign that the writer is not interested in what he is saying. Some metaphors now current have been twisted out of their original meaning without those who use them even being aware of the fact. For example, *toe the line* is sometimes written *tow the line*. Another example is *the hammer and the anvil*, now always used with the implication that the anvil gets the worst of it. In real life it is always the anvil that breaks the hammer, never the other way about: a writer who stopped to think what he was saying would be aware of this, and would avoid perverting the original phrase.

Operators, or *verbal false limbs*. These save the trouble of picking out appropriate verbs and nouns, and at the same time pad each sentence with extra syllables which give it an appearance of symmetry. Characteristic phrases are: *render inoperative, militate against, prove unacceptable, make contact with, be subjected to, give rise to, give grounds for, have the effect of, play a leading part (rôle) in, make itself felt, take effect, exhibit a tendency to, serve the purpose of,* etc etc. The keynote is the elimination of simple verbs.

Instead of being a single word, such as *reak, stop, spoil, mend, kill,* a verb becomes a *phrase,* made up of a noun or adjective tacked on to some general-purpose verb such as *prove, serve, form, play, render.* In addition, the passive voice is wherever possible used in preference to the active, and noun constructions are used instead of gerunds (*by examination of* instead of *by examining*) The range of verbs is further cut down by means of the *-ise* and *de-* formations, and banal statements are given an appearance of profundity by means of the *not un-* formation. Simple conjunctions and prepositions are replaced by such phrases as *with respect to, having regard to, the fact that, by dint of, in view of, in the interests of, on the hypothesis that;* and the ends of sentences are saved from anticlimax by such resounding commonplaces as *greatly to be desired, cannot be left out of account, a development to be expected in the near future, deserving of serious consideration, brought to a satisfactory conclusion,* and so on and so forth.

Pretentious diction. Words like *phenomenon, element, individual* (as noun), *objective, categorical, effective, virtual, basic, primary, promote, constitute, exhibit, exploit, utilise, eliminate, liquidate,* are used to dress up simple statements and give an air of scientific impartiality to biassed judgements. Adjectives like *epoch-making, epic, historic, unforgettable, triumphant, age-old, inevitable, inexorable, veritable,* are used to dignify the sordid processes of international politics, while writing that aims at glorifying war usually takes on an archaic colour, its characteristic words being: *realm, throne, chariot, mailed fist, trident, sword, shield, buckler, banner, jackboot, clarion.* Foreign words and expressions such as *cul de sac, ancien régime, deus ex machina, mutatis mutandis, status quo, Gleichschaltung, Weltanschauung,* are used to give an air of culture and elegance. Except for the useful abbreviations *i.e., e.g.,* and *etc.* there is no real need for any of the hundreds of foreign phrases now current in English. Bad writers, and especially scientific, political and sociological writers, are nearly always haunted by the notion that Latin or Greek words are grander than Saxon ones, and unnecessary words like *expedite, ameliorate, predict, extraneous, der-*

acinated, clandestine, sub-aqueous and hundred of others constantly gain ground from their Anglo-Saxon opposite number.[1] The jargon peculiar to Marxist writing (*hyena, hangman, cannibal, petty bourgeois, these gentry, lacquey, flunkey, mad dog, White Guard,* etc) consists largely of words and phrases translated from Russian, German or French; but the normal way of coining a new word is to use a Latin or Greek root with the appropriate affix and, where necessary, the *-ise* formation. It is often easier to make up words of this kind (*deregionalise, impermissible, extramarital, non-fragmentatory* and so forth) than to think up the English words that will cover one's meaning. The result, in general is an increase in slovenliness and vagueness.

Meaningless words. In certain kinds of writing, particularly in art criticism and literary criticism, it is normal to come across long passages which are almost completely lacking in meaning.[2] Words like *romantic, plastic, values, human, dead, sentimental, natural, vitality,* as used in art criticism, are strictly meaningless, in the sense that they not only do not point to any discoverable object, but are hardly even expected to do so by the reader. When one critic writes, "The outstanding features of Mr X's work is its living quality", while another writes, "The immediately striking thing about Mr X's work is its peculiar deadness", the reader accepts this as a simple difference of opinion. If words like *black* and *white* were involved, instead of the jargon words *dead* and *living,* he would see at once that language was being used in an improper way. Many political words are similarly abused. The word *Fascism* has now no meaning except in so far as it signifies "something not desirable". The words *democracy, socialism, freedom, patriotic, realistic, justice,* have each of them several different meanings which cannot be reconciled with one another. In the case of a word like *democracy,* not only is there no agreed definition, but the

---

1. An interesting illustration of this is the way in which the English flower names which were in use till very recently are being ousted by Greek ones, *snapdragon* becoming *antirrhinum, forget-me-not* becoming *myosotis,* etc. It is hard to see any practical reason for this change of fashion: it is probably due to an instinctive turning-away from the more homely word and a vague feeling that the Greek word is scientific.

2. Example: "Comfort's catholicity of perception and image, strangely Whitmanesque in range, almost the exact opposite in aesthetic compulsion, continues to evoke that trembling atmospheric accumulative hinting at a cruel, an inexorably serene timelessness . . . Wrey Gardiner scores by aiming at simple bullseyes with precision. Only they are not so simple, and through this contented sadness runs more than the surface bitter-sweet of resignation." (*Poetry Quarterly.*)

attempt to make one is resisted from all sides. It is almost universally felt that when we call a country democratic we are praising it: consequently the defenders of every kind of régime claim that it is a democracy, and fear that they might have to stop using the word if it were tied down to any one meaning. Words of this kind are often used in a consciously dishonest way. That is, the person who uses them has his own private definition, but allows his hearer to think he means something quite different. Statements like *Marshal Pétain was a true patriot, The Soviet press is the freest in the world, The Catholic Church is opposed to persecution*, are almost always made with intent to deceive. Other words used in variable meanings, in most cases more or less dishonestly, are: *class, totalitarian, science, progressive, reactionary, bourgeois, equality.*

Now that I have made this catalogue of swindles and perversions, let me give another example of the kind of writing that they lead to. This time it must of its nature be an imaginary one. I am going to translate a passage of good English into modern English of the worst sort. Here is a well-known verse from *Ecclesiastes:*

> I returned, and saw under the sun, that the race is not to the swift, nor the battle to the strong, neither yet bread to the wise, nor yet riches to men of understanding, nor yet favour to men of skill; but time and chance happeneth to them all.

Here it is in modern English:

> Objective consideration of contemporary phenomena compels the conclusion that success or failure in competitive activities exhibits no tendency to be commensurate with innate capacity, but that a considerable element of the unpredictable must invariably be taken into account.

This is a parody, but not a very gross one. Exhibit 3, above, for instance, contains several patches of the same kind of English. It will be seen that I have not made a full translation. The beginning and ending of the sentence follow the original meaning fairly closely, but in the middle the concrete illustrations—race, battle, bread—dissolve into the vague phrase "success or failure in competitive activities". This had to be so, because no modern writer of the kind I am discussing—no one capable of using phrases like "objective consideration of contemporary phenomena"—would ever tabulate his thoughts in that precise and detailed way. The whole tendency of modern prose is away from concreteness. Now analyse these two sentences a little more closely. The first contains 49 words but only 60 syllables, and all its words are those of everyday life. The second contains 38 words of 90 syllables: 18 of its words are from Latin roots, and one from Greek. The first sentence contains six vivid images, and only one phrase ("time and chance") that could be called vague. The second contains not a single fresh, arresting phrase, and in spite of its 90 syllables it gives only a shortened version of the meaning contained in the first. Yet without a doubt it is the second kind of sentence that is gaining ground in modern English. I do not want to exaggerate. This kind of writing is not yet universal, and outcrops of simplicity will occur here and there in the worst-written page. Still, if you or I were told to write a few lines on the uncertainty of human fortunes, we should probably come much nearer to my imaginary sentence than to the one from *Ecclesiastes*.

As I have tried to show, modern writing at its worst does not consist of picking out words for the sake of their meaning and inventing images in order to make the meaning clearer. It consists in gumming together long strips of words which have already been set in order by someone else, and making the results presentable by sheer humbug. The attraction of this way of writing is that it is easy. It is easier—even quicker, once you have the habit—to say *In my opinion it is a not unjustifiable assumption that* than to say *I think*. If you use ready-made phrases, you not only don't have to hunt about for words; you also don't have to bother with the rhythms of your sentences, since these phrases are generally so arranged as to be more or less euphonious. When you are composing in a hurry—when you are dictating to a stenographer, for instance, or making a public speech—it is natural to fall into a pretentious, latinised style. Tags like *a consideration which we should do well to bear in mind* or *a conclusion to which all of us would readily assent* will save many a sentence from coming down with a bump. By using stale metaphors, similes and idioms, you save much mental effort, at the cost of leaving your meaning vague, not only for our reader but for yourself. This is the significance of mixed metaphors. The sole aim of metaphor is to call up a visual image. When these images clash—as in *The Fascist octopus has sung its swan song, the jackboot is thrown into the melting-pot*—it can be taken as certain that the writer is not seeing a mental image of the objects he is naming; in other words he is not really thinking. Look again at the examples I gave at the beginning of this essay. Professor Laski (1) uses five negatives in 53 words. One of these is superfluous, making nonsense of the whole passage, and in addition there is the slip *alien* for akin, making futher nonsense, and several avoidable pieces of clumsiness which increase the general vagueness. Professor Hogben (2) plays ducks and drakes with a battery which is able to write prescriptions, and, while disapproving of the everyday phrase *put up with*, is unwilling to look *egregious* up in the dictionary and see what it means. (3), if one takes an uncharitable attitude towards it, is simply meaningless: probably one could work out its intended meaning by reading the whole of the article in which it occurs. In (4) the writer knows more or less what he wants to say, but an accumulation of stale phrases chokes him like tea-leaves blocking a sink. In (5) words and meaning have almost parted company. People who write in this manner usually have a general emotional meaning—they dislike one thing and want to express solidarity with another—but they are not interested in the detail of what they are saying. A scrupulous writer, in every sentence that he writes, will ask himself at least four questions, thus: What am I trying to say? What words will express it? What image or idiom will make it clearer? Is this image fresh enough to have an effect? And he will probably ask himself two more: Could I put it more shortly? Have I said anything that is avoidably ugly? But you are not obliged to go to all this trouble. You can shirk it by simply throwing your mind open and letting the readymade phrases come crowding in. They will construct your sentences for you—even think your thoughts for you, to a certain extent—and at need they will perform the important service of partially concealing your meaning even from yourself. It is at this point that the special connection between politics and the debasement of language becomes clear.

In our time it is broadly true that political writing is bad writing. Where it is not true it will generally be found that the writer is some kind of rebel, expressing his private opinions, and not a "party line". Orthodoxy, of whatever colour, seems to demand a lifeless, imitative style. The political dialects to be found in pamphlets, leading articles, manifestos, White Papers and speeches of Under-Secretaries do, of course, vary from party to party, but they are all alike in that one almost never finds in them a fresh, vivid, home-made turn of speech. When one watches some tired hack on the platform mechanically repeating the familiar phrase—*bestial atrocities, iron heel, bloodstained tyranny, free peoples of the world, stand shoulder to shoulder*—one often has a curious feeling that one is not watching a live human being but some kind of dummy: a feeling which suddenly becomes stronger at moments when the light catches the speaker's spectacles and turns them into blank discs which seem to have no eyes behind them. And this is not altogether fanciful. A speaker who uses that kind of phraseology has gone some distance towards turning himself into a machine. The appropriate noises are coming out of his larynx, but his brain is not involved as it would be if he were choosing his words for himself. If the speech he is making is one that he is accustomed to make over and over again, he may be almost unconscious of what he is saying, as one is when one utters the responses in church. And this reduced state of consciousness, if not indispensable, is at any rate favourable to political conformity.

In our time, political speech and writing are largely the defence of the indefensible. Things like the continuance of British rule in India, the Russian purges and deportations, the dropping of the atom bombs on Japan, can indeed be defended, but only by arguments which are too brutal for most people to face, and which do not square with the professed aims of political parties. Thus political language has to consist largely of euphemism, question-begging and sheer cloudy vagueness. Defenceless villages are bombarded from the air, the inhabitants driven out into the countryside, the cattle machine-gunned, the huts set on fire with incendiary bullets: this is called *pacification*. Millions of peasants are robbed of their farms and sent trudging along the roads with no more than they can carry: this is called *transfer of population* or *rectification of frontiers*. People are imprisoned for years without trial, or shot in the back of the neck or sent to die of scurvy in Arctic lumber camps: this is called *elimination of unreliable elements*. Such phraseology is needed if one wants to name things without calling up mental pictures of them. Consider for instance some comfortable English professor defending Russian totalitarianism. He cannot say outright, "I believe in killing off your opponents when you can get good results by doing so". Probably, therefore, he will say something like this:

> While freely conceding that the Soviet régime exhibits certain features which the humanitarian may be inclined to deplore, we must, I think, agree that a certain curtailment of the right to political opposition is an unavoidable concomitant of transitional periods, and that the rigours which the Russian people have been called upon to undergo have been amply justified in the sphere of concrete achievement.

The inflated style is itself a kind of euphemism. A mass of Latin words falls upon the facts like soft snow, blurring the outlines and covering up all the details. The great enemy of clear language is insincerity. When there is a gap between one's real and one's declared aims, one turns as it were instinctively to long words and exhausted idioms, like a cuttlefish squirting out ink. In our age there is no such thing as "keeping out of politics". All issues are political issues, and politics itself is a mass of lies, evasions, folly, hatred and schizophrenia. When the general atmosphere is bad, language must suffer. I should expect to find—this is a guess which I have not sufficient knowledge to verify—that the German, Russian and Italian languages have all deteriorated in the last ten or fifteen years, as a result of dictatorship.

But if thought corrupts language, language can also corrupt thought. A bad usage can spread by tradition and imitation, even among people who should and do know better. The debased languge that I have been discussing is in some ways very convenient. Phrases like *a not unjustifiable assumption, leaves much to be desired, would serve no good purpose, a consideration which we should do well to bear in mind*, are a continuous temptation, a packet of aspirins always at one's elbow. Look back through this essay, and for certain you will find that I have again and again committed the very faults I am protesting against. By this morning's post I have received a pamphlet dealing with conditions in Germany. The author tells me that he "felt impelled" to write it. I open it at random, and here is almost the first sentence that I see: "(The Allies) have an opportunity not only of achieving a radical transformation of Germany's social and political structure in such a way as to avoid a nationalistic reaction in Germany itself, but at the same time of laying the foundations of a co-operative and unified Europe." You see, he "feels impelled" to write—feels, presumably, that he has something new to say—and yet his words, like cavalry horses answering the bugle, group themselves automatically into the familiar dreary pattern. This invasion of one's mind by ready-made phrases (*lay the foundtions, achieve a radical transformation*) can only be prevented if one is constantly on guard against them, and every such phrase anaesthetises a portion of one's brain.

I said earlier that the decadence of our language is probably curable. Those who deny this would argue, if they produced an argument at all, that language merely reflects existing social conditions, and that we cannot influence its development by any direct tinkering with words and constructions. So far as the general tone or spirit of a language goes, this may be true, but it is not true in detail. Silly words and expressions have often disappeared, not through any evolutionary process but owing to the conscious action of a minority. Two recent examples were *explore every avenue* and *leave no stone unturned*, which were killed by the jeers of a few journalists. There is a long list of fly-blown metaphors which could similarly be got rid of if enough people would interest themselves in the job; and it should also be possible to laugh the *not un-* formation out of existence,[3] to reduce the amount of Latin and Greek in the average sentence, to drive out foreign phrases and strayed scientific words, and, in general, to make pretentiousness unfashionable. But all these are minor points. The defence of the English language implies more than this, and perhaps it is best to start by saying what it does *not* imply.

To begin with, it has nothing to do with archaism, with the salvaging of obsolete words and turns of speech, or with the setting-up of a "standard English" which must never be departed from. On the contrary, it is especially concerned with the scrapping of every word or idiom which has outworn its usefulness. It has nothing to do with correct grammar and syntax, which are of no importance so long as one makes one's meaning clear, or with the avoidance of Americanisms, or with having what is called a "good prose style". On the other hand it is not concerned with fake simplicity and the attempt to make written English colloquial. Nor does it even imply in every case preferring the Saxon word to the Latin one, though it does imply using the fewest and shortest words that will cover one's meaning. What is above all needed is to let the meaning choose the word, and not the other way about. In prose, the worst thing one can do with words is to surrender to them. When you think of a concrete object, you think wordlessly, and then, if you want to describe the thing you have been visualising, you probably hunt about till you find the exact words that seem to fit it. When you think of something abstract you are more inclined to use words from the start, and unless you make a conscious effort to prevent it, the existing dialect will come rushing in and do the job for you, at the expense of blurring or even changing your meaning. Probably it is better to put off using words as long as possible and get one's meaning as clear as one can through pictures or sensations. Afterwards one can choose—not simply *accept*—the phrases that will best cover the meaning, and then switch round and decide what impression one's words are likely to make on another person.

---

3. One can cure oneself of the *not un-* formation by memorising this sentence: *A not unblack dog was chasing a not unsmall rabbit across a not ungreen field.*

This last effort of the mind cuts out all stale or mixed images, all prefabricated phrases, needless repetitions, and humbug and vagueness generally. But one can often be in doubt about the effect of a word or a phrase, and one needs rules that one can rely on when instinct fails. I think the following rules will cover most cases:

    i. Never use a metaphor, simile or other figure of speech which you are used to seeing in print.

    ii. Never use a long word where a short one will do.

    iii. If it is possible to cut a word out, always cut it out.

    iv. Never use the passive where you can use the active.

    v. Never use a foreign phrase, a scientific work or a jargon word if you can think of an everyday English equivalent.

    vi. Break any of these rules sooner than say anything outright barbarous.

These rules sound elementary, and so they are, but they demand a deep change of attitude in anyone who has grown used to writing in the style now fashionable. One could keep all of them and still write bad English, but one could not write the kind of stuff that I quoted in those five specimens at the beginning of this article.

I have not here been considering the literary use of language, but merely language as an instrument for expressing and not for concealing or preventing thought. Stuart Chase and others have come near to claiming that all abstract words are meaningless, and have used this as a pretext for advocating a kind of political quietism. Since you don't know what Facism is, how can you struggle against Fascism? One need not swallow such absurdities as this, but one ought to recognize that the present political chaos is connected with the decay of language, and that one can probably bring about some improvement by starting at the verbal end. If you simplify your English, you are freed from the worst follies of orthodoxy. You cannot speak any of the necessary dialects, and when you make a stupid remark its stupidity will be obvious, even to yourself. Political language—and with variations this is true of all political parties, from Conservatives to Anarchists—is designed to make lies sound truthful and murder respectable, and to give an appearance of solidity to pure wind. One cannot change this all in a moment, but one can at least change one's own habits, and from time to time one can even, if one jeers loudly enough, send some worn-out and useless phrase—some *jackboot, Achilles' heel, hotbed, melting pot, acid test, veritable inferno* or other lump of verbal refuse— into the dustbin where it belongs.

5
Editing

Having written your paper, you must groom it—make it presentable. Let me show you why.

> Forscore and 7 yeirs ago our fourfathers brung forth on this continent a new nation concieved in liberty and, dedicated to the purposal that all men was created the same, we are engaged in a huge civil war testing weather that nation, or any place so concieved and purposed can last very long.
>
> were meeting on a big battlefield of this war weve come to, dedicate a piece of it for them who give there lifes here that there nation could live. It is, alltogether fit and proper, that we should do this thing but in a big way we ca'nt dedicate, consecrate or even get to hollow this ground.

Some linguists say grammar, punctuation, and spelling constitute the mere *surface* of a text. But who wants a new car with no paint, no trim, no wheel covers? Surface is important. Mistakes, however mechanical, are distracting and irritating. They drive readers away in disgust and label the writer illiterate. When the mistakes go deeper—as a good many do in the hash I've made of The Gettysburg Address—readers react even more negatively.

I consider correctness to be relative. Constructions are correct or incorrect relative to current conventions and specific occasions. The issue is one of manners, really, not of law. At a formal dinner we use utensils to eat chicken; at a picnic we use our fingers. Should we eat with our fingers at a formal dinner, we commit a breach of etiquette—not of contract. But breaches of etiquette can be as serious as breaches of contract. To be effective, we need to know how to dress and behave.

In this chapter I define the major conventions of standard edited English—of prose intended for some public or other. I have divided the conventions into three major categories: Grammar, Punctuation, and a catchall I term Usage. Use the Table of Contents in conjunction with this chapter as a quick reference to resolve the most common mechanical problems.

I. GRAMMAR

A. Make Your Parts Agree

Although it is difficult to confuse nouns with verbs, prepositions with adjectives, and adverbs with pronouns, beginning writers often have trouble getting different parts of speech to *agree*. They combine the wrong things, causing discord in the sentence and disgust in the reader. Grammatical agreement is *not* optional. If your parts do not agree, the reader will dismiss you as illiterate, ignorant, even deviant.

1. Subject and Verb

Singular subjects take singular verbs; plural subjects take plural verbs.

> I *am* going.

> He, she, it *is* going.

> We, you, they *are* going.

> I, she, he, it *was* going.

> We, you, they *were* going.

A compound subject is plural.

> She and her friend *are* going.

Or and *nor* do not make a compound subject. The number of the last noun determines the number of the verb.

> Neither Jim nor his friends *are* going.

> Either his friends or Jim *is* going.

Sometimes the subject has company, introduced by phrases like *as well as* and *along with*.

> The President, along with his advisors, is stonewalling.

However close to the subject, such company is never part of the subject. Determine the number of the subject and you determine the number of the verb. Combine them with a conjunction—the President *and* his advisors—and they *are* stonewalling.

Sometimes (not often, please!) you may, for variety and emphasis, invert the usual order of subject/verb to verb/subject. Inversions are tricky, so watch them closely. Be sure the subject and verb agree.

> Not only *has* the nation grown, so *have* its citizens prospered.

Nation is the singular subject of the first clause—therefore *has*. *Citizens* is the plural subject of the second clause—therefore *have*. Using the *there is/are* construction involves the same principle:

> There *are* (or *were*) many citizens, however, who are (or were) still out of the money. There isn't enough money to go around.

Citizens is the subject—thus the plural verb; *money* is the subject—thus the singular verb.

When using *each*, *either*, *neither*, *everyone*, *everybody*, and the like as the subject, the verb is always singular:

> Now hear this: Each of you must give the noun *each* a singular verb.

On the other hand, *collective nouns* are optional. If used as a *unit*, the verb is singular.

> My herd *has* vanished, though my family *is* still here.

If used as components or members, the verb is plural.

> The majority of my herd *have* vanished, though a good number of my family *are* still here.

Then there are nouns plural in form but singular in meaning such as *news*, *economics*, *physics*, *measles*, and *sports*. Match the verb to the meaning.

> Many say physics *is* a hard science, while some say economics *is* the dismal science.

A title involving plural words takes a singular verb.

> *The Sound and the Fury* is a complex book.

Some *-ics* words—*politics*, *athletics*, *statistics*—are used in singular or plural form.

> Statistics *is* an increasingly popular study. The statistics on the increasing popularity of statistics *are* impressive.

Make sure you know the context of the words; then get the verb form to agree.

2. Verb Tense

From a student paper:

> If you are just feeling down, going out and buying something could
> pick you up a bit. You may feel good after buying something but the
> feeling won't always last. The newness wears off and you will no
> longer feel good. So you constantly have to buy something to feel
> good. You could use buying as a medicine, or therapy. If you wanted
> that wicker chair for a long time but thought you couldn't afford it,
> then when you had a bad day you decide to buy it, it really can pick
> up your spirits.

This sort of confusion, primarily one of *tense*, is not unusual. Avoid
committing it. Use the tense (the time of the verb) that is appropriate.

What is *appropriate?* When dealing with past events, use the past
tense—especially in narration. Be consistent—don't mix up tenses—
and avoid the colloquial narrative present tense.

> So I went to him, and I said, "Shut up!"
> And he replies, "Shut up yourself!"
> So I clench my fist and belt him a good one, thus disposing of his
> objections.

In print, narrating in the present tense comes across as Popeye talk,
and you (usually) don't want to sound like a cartoon character. Mixing
tenses comes across as disorientation, and you don't want to appear
addlepated.

When dealing with the present, use the present tense; when dealing
with the future, use the future tense.

> I worked on this book yesterday. I am working on it today, and I will
> work on it tomorrow.

There are, in a manner of speaking, *two* present tenses.

> What do you do for a living?
> I work.

> What are you doing?
> I'm working.

The first, the straight present, implies "habitually"; the second, the
present progressive, implies "going on right now." We use the present
progressive for most true present meaning.

When dealing with more than one tense, put them in logical order.
Compare:

> *Wrong:* When I arrive, I saw he is already there.

> *Right:* When I arrived, I saw he was already there.

Because the two events are simultaneous, put all the verbs in the same tense. When actions precede one another, however, put them in the tenses that express the sequence:

> After I had been there for 45 minutes, he finally arrived. And to think that he had said, "When you arrive, I will have been there for half an hour"!

Do everything possible to keep tense sequences as simple as possible. As Thoreau said, "Simplify, simplify, simplify."

Two problems with tense occur again and again. One concerns written documents. Jefferson (with a little help from his friends) wrote The Declaration of Independence, but it still exists—a continuing record of Jefferson's thought. Because the record exists, the thought also exists—even though conceived in the past. There is a difference, in other words, between art and artifact. As art, The Declaration exists now, in the present; as artifact, it is a historical document, a thing of the past. To speak of it, which tense should you use: past or present?

> In 1776 Thomas Jefferson wrote The Declaration of Independence. In it he (declared? declares?), "We hold these truths to be self-evident. . . ."

Note that the problem occurs only with the document. You cannot say, "In 1776 Thomas Jefferson writes The Declaration of Independence."

I have seen both tenses used. Consistency is the most important factor: Choose one and stick with it. The past tense seems awkward: "Hamlet said, 'To be or not to be. . . .' " To me, Hamlet *says* the lines because he lives now, in the present tense—like Cassandra in Homer's *Iliad* and Luther in his *Ninety-five Theses* and Lincoln in his Gettysburg Address. So I use the present and adjust to avoid inconsistency.

> In The Declaration of Independence, written in 1776, Thomas Jefferson declares certain truths to be self-evident.

The other problem concerns those editors and teachers who *require* the past tense whether it is appropriate or not. It is difficult to discuss a diagram in the past tense when it's on the same page. Such a requirement is demonstrably foolish and genuinely affected. But if it's imposed, submit—however awkward the results—or you won't receive a sympathetic reading. Simply be aware of the divergence of opinion on this issue and modify the style accordingly.

3. Verb Mood

Don't misunderstand. In grammar *mood* doesn't mean happy and sad and so forth. Agreement in mood doesn't mean that if you say *cry* you can't say *laugh*. (*Mood* has been spelled *mode*, meaning "form, variety, or manner.")

In a rather technical sense, mood means the basic disposition toward the subject as reflected by the arrangement of words. The *indicative mood*, for instance, declares matters of fact.

> Jack Sprat could eat no fat.
> His wife could eat no lean.

Such sentences are often termed *declarative*. (If framed as questions— Could Jack eat no fat? Could his wife eat no lean?—they would be termed *interrogative*.)

Use the *imperative mood* to issue orders or make requests.

> Put out that cigarette right now!

> Do not mix singular subjects with plural verbs.

> Please don't tell me what to do.

Use the imperative mood judiciously, especially when issuing orders. Don't put yourself in the position of the gunfighter whose last words are legend.

> Don't you pull that gun on me.

So far, simple. Now for the hard part: the *subjunctive mood*. The subjunctive mood expresses a contrary-to-fact condition. The expression may be in the form of a statement.

> If I were you, I would buy that gold mine.

Or a wish:

> It would be nice if it were a gold mine.

Or a recommendation:

> We recommend that she dig a gold mine.

Or a demand:

> I insist that he buy that gold mine.

Do not arbitrarily change moods. As long as the contrary-to-fact condition exists, stick to the subjunctive. If the condition shifts in the middle, shift the mood.

> If I were your mama, I would go. But I'm not, so I won't.

Use tense and mood to express the precise sense of the sentences.

4. Pronouns

> Just between you and I, everyone wore their finest threads, and I'll say so to whomever asks about it. If it had been me who made the decision, I would have given the responsibility to whoever the delegates elected.

Don't try to make sense of the passage. Just look at the pronouns and count the errors of their ways. I count five.

First: "Between you and I"—a common error based upon ignorance and an abject desire to be correct. *Between* is a preposition. Prepositions take pronouns in the objective case: between you and me. You never say: "give the book to I." "Show the picture to she." When you have *and* or *or* between the two items, the items are reversible. So reverse them: "Between I and you." Now you cannot help but know which form is correct.

The same is true when pronouns are the objects of the verb.

> *Wrong:* Please give George and I a drink.

> *Right:* Please give George and me a drink.

Use the same test we use for prepositions: You never say, "Please give I a drink." So don't say, "Give George and I a drink."

Second: The next error is based upon a strong tendency of the language, a tendency I believe will be accepted practice within half a century. When speaking, most of us do it all the time without being aware of it. It *sounds* correct. However, in writing it is still generally regarded as an error. So be aware of it and limit it to the spoken word.

> Everyone wore their finest threads.

One is singular, *their* is plural—there is no agreement. This disagreement is strictly technical, to be sure. When we say "everyone, everybody, anyone, anybody," we usually *mean* the word as plural—all the people in the group. But the *form* of the word is singular—we say "Everybody is (*not* are) going"—so the possessive pronoun must be singular: his or her. And it's awkward:

> Everyone wore his or her finest threads.

> Everyone wore her and his finest threads.

Until several years ago, *his* was the generic possessive pronoun. However, we now recognize a sexist presumption in that practice. Consequently, we say "his or her," or (occasionally) "her or his," or "his" one time and "her" another.

Although it's awkward and untidy, it is necessary. Consistent use of "his or her" is usually acceptable. Of course, when the intended meaning is plural, use a plural.

All the people wore their finest threads.

Pronouns must agree in number with their antecedents, the words they refer to and fill in for.

pronouns . . . their . . . they

people . . . their

everyone . . . his or her

Number is a formal principle. If the antecedent is singular in form, it requires singular pronouns—period. When the intended meaning is plural, use the plural as soon as possible:

Wrong: The committee was in session. They bickered and fussed. They snickered and gabbed.

Right: The committee was in session. Its members bickered and fussed. They snickered and gabbed.

Third: The next mistake is subtle: "I'll say so to whomever asks about it." *To* is a preposition; therefore, you might think *whomever* is called for. Not so. When you use *who* to introduce a clause, it is a *relative pronoun* and the clause is a *noun clause:* The entire clause serves the grammatical function of a single word—a noun. The clause is the object of the preposition. The case of the relative pronoun (sounds like the title of a dull mystery) is determined by its function in the dependent clause it introduces. In the clause "to whomever asks about it," the verb is *asks;* therefore, the relative pronoun is the subject.

I'll say so to whoever asks about it.

If the relative pronoun is the object of the verb in the clause it introduces, use the objective case.

I'll say so to whomever he brings.

Brings is the verb, *he* the subject, *whomever* the object. (A reminder: He is bringing *her* and *him,* not *she* and *he.*)

Fourth: The next error in the passage involves a problem with word order. In English, objects ordinarily follow verbs. Therefore, when pronouns follow verbs we ordinarily use the objective case: "She bit me!" Along that same line, we have a tendency to say:

If it had been me. . . .

That's her.

But *had been* and *is* are linking, not transitive, verbs. In standard edited English, linking verbs do not take objects (although in ordinary conversation they take objects all the time). Therefore, write:

If it had been I. . . .

That's she.

Likewise:

This is he.

It is I.

It was she who did it.

In such construction, the nominative case (those pronouns serving as subjects: I, he, she, we, they) sound extremely formal—a white-tie affair. However, in standard edited English such is the convention universally practiced. So don your formal attire and enjoy the party.

Fifth: The last error:

I would have given the responsibility to whoever the delegates selected.

I have already discussed this principle; you're on your own.

5. Person

In formal grammar there are only three persons: first (I, we), second (you, you), and third (she, he, one, it, they). When writing, you must use one person or another as the focus—illustrated in this sentence by "you." I could just as well have said:

When writing, we must use one person or another as the focus.

Or:

When writing, one must use one person or another as the focus.

One is quite formal and soon becomes intrusively repetitious. *You* works nicely. Yet many teachers, editors, and disciplines forbid its use as too casual. That prohibition always includes another: Don't use *I* either. I consider such a general prohibition entirely regrettable, mistaken, and shortsighted. However, that's of little help to you. When you encounter it—and you don't want to solve the problems by using the passive voice—use *one*.

Whatever you use, be consistent. Make sure all references to person agree. Keep the focus uniform.

Wrong: If one does not wear his hat, you will get our head wet.

Right: You fill in the blanks.

Alternatives: If a woman does not wear a hat, she will get her head wet.

Or: If a man does not wear a hat, he will get his head wet.

B. Common Mistakes

Certain mistakes are committed over and over again—often by the same persons. These persons ignore pleas and disregard correction. Frustrated, some teachers yearn for the good old days of the lash but settle instead for a drink.

Some of these mistakes are grammatically significant and can make a difference in meaning. All of them are socially significant. Commit them and you are regarded as an ignoramus—well-intentioned perhaps but crude, very crude. Much as if you sip wine with a straw. It's in your best interests, then, to avoid these mistakes.

1. Dangling and Ambiguous Modifiers

A modifier is a word (or group of words) that limits the meaning of another word (or group of words). If grass, for instance, is *short* it cannot be *long*; if it is *brown* it cannot be *green*; if it is *growing an inch a day* it cannot be *dying by the minute*.

However, modifiers tend to cling to the nouns or pronouns nearest them. If that noun or pronoun is not the one modified, confusion may result—and often comedy as well.

Nibbling the grass, I found my horse in the field.

The meaning, of course, is clear; the sentence, however, is ludicrous. Besides, readers should not have to do the writer's work. Say exactly what you mean—just who or what is doing the nibbling.

I found my horse nibbling grass in the field.

In the ludicrous sentence, the modifier is said to be *dangling,* floating in space—far removed from the word it belongs to. Dangling modifiers can be serious. Imagine this police report:

Having the weapon in hand, the officer pursued the suspect into an abandoned building.

Who had the weapon in hand? The answer might make a great difference in a court of law. Suppose you are the officer and meant to report the suspect had the weapon. Now imagine the suspect's lawyer working you over in cross examination.

Modifiers are *ambiguous* when located in compromising positions—between two terms each of which they could modify, but not both.

We decided *when the game was over* to have a party.

What does "when the game was over" modify, "decided" or "to have a party"? We cannot tune in tomorrow to find out. The party may be over.

Ambiguous modifiers are often consequential. Imagine this conspiracy case:

We agreed when the deal was closed to turn him in.

Did you turn him in as a result of the deal? Or did you close the deal in order to turn him in? The difference could be all-important to a judge or jury.

You may dangle your feet but not your modifiers. You may not put them in ambiguous positions, either. What is modified must be clear: this or that—not both.

2. Misused Adjectives and Adverbs

Adjectives and adverbs are modifiers. *Adjectives*—green, broad, slow—modify nouns and pronouns. *Adverbs*—quickly, happily, very—modify verbs, adjectives, and other adverbs. Generally, adjectives and adverbs pose no problems—you use them continuously throughout the day—but in certain applications they are dumbfounding.

She played good. I played poor. I felt terribly about it. She felt pretty well, of course.

What is wrong here? In the first sentences, the verbs are modified—thus use *adverbs*.

She played well. I played poorly.

Many people *say* "She played good," but in standard edited English their knuckles are rapped in reply. In the second sentence, the error is revealed: "I played poor" literally means "I played broke" or "I played without funds." You must say "I played poorly" to make the meaning clear.

In the last two sentences of the passage, the subjects are modified—therefore, use *adjectives*.

I felt terrible about it. She felt pretty good, of course.

"Felt terribly" literally describes the efficiency of touch—not an emotional reaction. "Felt well" describes a state of health—not a state of emotion.

I was sick, but I am well now.

You must know what is to be modified by the modifiers. If you have the slightest hesitation which form is proper—adjective or adverb—look up the words in the dictionary and choose accordingly.

3. Comparatives and Absolutes

When comparing two persons or things, use only the comparative: *better, worse, more complex,* and the like. To use the absolute—the *best,* the *worst,* the *most complex*—there must be at least three items.

Also, in the comparative make the comparison complete. Always include the *than what*—unless the preceding sentence makes the comparison clear.

Wrong: I can do anything better.

Right: I can do anything better than you.

Further, when attributes are by definition absolute—perfect, unique, whole, nothing—there is no comparative.

Wrong: Julius Erving has a more perfect jump shot than Erving Johnson.

Wrong: Olivia Newton-John is a very unique person.

Wrong: *Lear* is more whole than *Hamlet.*

Perfect, unique, whole, and the like have no degrees. Something is either perfect or it is imperfect, unique or not unique, whole or less than whole. And if it *is* either/or, it can't be between. It's one or the other—not both.

You may, however, use such constructions as "almost perfect" and "nearly whole," because they describe approaches to absolute conditions—not percentages.

4. Like and As

Years ago a famous advertisement ran:

> Winston tastes good like a cigarette should.

Criticized by the media, the same advertiser ran companion ads featuring a professor-type correcting the mistake.

> Winston tastes good *as* a cigarette should.

Why *as*? Because the line introduced contains a verb. If there's a verb, use *as*, *as if*, or *as though*.

> I felt as if I had been run over.

> She looked limp, as though she had been steamed.

If there's no verb, use *like*.

> He looked like a swamp.

> She felt like hell.

The rule for *like* and *as* is subtle and thus difficult to deal with when speaking. There is little time to figure it out. When writing, however, there is time enough. Observe the distinction.

5. Who, That, and Which

All three are relative pronouns—pronouns that introduce a subordinate clause and at the same time refer to an antecedent—and the question always arises: which to use?

Use *who* for persons, singular or plural. When speaking, we often use *that* for persons—"She's the kind of girl that will drive you to the airport"—primarily because we are thinking of what we have to say and not of which relative pronoun to pronounce. When writing, use *who*.

> Those people who were here yesterday left their cameras.

> Those representatives who voted *no* should be recalled.

> The guy who belched will be excused.

We are left with *that* and *which*. Use both when referring to antecedents that are not persons.

> The particular marathon that broke my spirit was the one I lost by a mile.

> The marathon, which dates back to ancient Greece, separates the diehards from the milquetoasts.

Notice that like *who, that* and *which* introduce dependent clauses modifying their antecedent (the marathon). The rule for choosing *that* or *which* is complex and not strict. I'll make it simple and strict so you won't have to wonder and can't go wrong. Use *that* when the clause is essential to the meaning of the sentence—remove the clause and the sentence becomes meaningless.

> The particular marathon was the one I lost by a mile.

Use *which* when the clause is *not* essential to the meaning of the sentence—remove the clause and the sentence remains meaningful.

> The marathon separates the diehards from the milquetoasts.

Technically, dependent clauses essential to the sentence are *restrictive*, while dependent clauses not essential are *nonrestrictive*. For ease of reference, here's a package deal:

> *Who*   (or whom, whoever, whomever); all dependent modifying clauses concerning persons.
>
> *That:*   all dependent modifying clauses not concerning persons but essential to the meaning of the sentence (restrictive clauses).
>
> *Which:* all dependent modifying clauses not concerning persons and not essential to the meaning of the sentence (nonrestrictive clauses).

One other thing: In many situations involving dependent clauses, *that* may be understood and thus omitted. In other situations, it must be included. Sometimes both situations occur in the same sentence—in this one, for instance, by Didion:

> One reason I stole it was that I like the sound of the words: *Why I Write.*

Didion could have written, "One reason that I stole it," but she would have had two *thats* quite close to each other—too close for comfort. The sentence would sound jammed. She had to state the second for the same reason: to keep the two clauses from being jammed against each other requiring the reader to separate them with an awkward pause. The convention for including or omitting *that* is not hard and fast. The more formal the occasion, the greater the reason for including *that.* If in doubt, *don't* leave it out.

6. Lie and Lay

In conversation we confuse these two because they have a form in common—lay.

Lie: I am going to lie down.
I lay down all day yesterday.
I have lain here for three hours.

Lay: I am going to lay my troubles down.
I laid my troubles down last week.
I have laid my troubles down for three years.

Lie is intransitive—requires no object. *Lay* is transitive—requires an object.

7. Farther and Further

Farther refers to space, *further* to logic. *Farther* is measurable, *further* isn't.

Sue can throw the ball farther than Jim.

George went further with the problem than Judy.

To remember the distinction, think of this: You don't say *far*thermore, you say *fur*thermore.

8. There, Their, They're

These items are involved in another recurring confusion designed to drive English teachers to thoughts of early retirement.

There—adverb of place; I will be there at six.

There—expletive construction: There are three of them.

Their—possessive pronoun: Are these their hats?

They're—contraction of *they are:* They're leaving now.

If you experience trouble learning to use these, memorize the following limerick:

There are forty grammarians in Clare,
And a few angry students itching to get *there;*
They're spoiling for trouble,
Their tempers bent double
From distinguishing all these *there's* in thin air!

Misusing these gives readers the impression of incompetence in general and illiteracy in particular.

9. It's, Its

It's raining.

The dog lost its bone.

It's = contraction. *Its* = possessive, *without* the apostrophe. On the bases of consistency and reason, *its* is wrong. It's not even fair. But in practice it's right.

10. To, Too, Two

To—preposition: I am going to town.

To—auxiliary of the infinitive verb: I am going to play.

Too—adverb meaning *also:* I want to play, too.

Too—adverb meaning *very:* You play too rough.

Two—2: Two heads are better than one.

If you must make mistakes, find more sophisticated ones than these. And if you confuse *no* and *know*—I know of no hope.

II. PUNCTUATION

Let us consider the ins and outs of punctuation one mark at a time.

A. Period

This is the dot used to end sentences unless they are puzzled (?) or excited (!). The period is used in many abbreviations (e.g., i.e., etc.) but generally not in governmental ones (FBI, SEC, GNP). It's also used to denote numerical percentages and decimals: He hit .047 and made $9.82.

B. Comma

This little curl that hangs on the line like an elbow macaroni is the most popular mark in western literature. It indicates the subtle but essential pauses with which you punctuate statements to ensure coherence, emphasis, and clarity.

Use commas following most introductory phrases and clauses.

According to a recent study by the Carnegie Commission, American education is a mess.

After we had considered the study and our own school system, we agreed.

If introductory phrases and clauses are short, the comma is unnecessary. "Short" is often fixed at three-four words or less.

Before breakfast I ran a mile.

After I ran I took a shower.

Exception: If there is confusion or ambiguity without a comma, fill the gap—however short the phrase or clause.

In writing, it behooves you to be careful.

Without the comma the reader would first think *it* is the object of *writing*, and would have to reread in order to make sense of the sentence. Read your sentences aloud. Listen for the pause you naturally make after longer introductions and introductions that might be ambiguous. Consider also where you don't pause. With a few exceptions, which I will clarify, punctuate accordingly.

Use commas to introduce dialogue.

Jim asked, "How are you?"
"Don't ask," she replied.

Use commas to separate independent clauses joined by conjunctions in compound sentences.

I was going to run in the Boston Marathon, but I was out late the night before and overslept.

We went to the concert in Central Park last night, and we ran into the Smiths.

If the clauses are short—three-four words or less—you may dispense with the commas.

I went downtown and I saw Judy.

Once again, by reading aloud you'll hear the presence or absence of the pause that requires a comma.

A common error among beginning writers is the *comma splice:* separating two independent clauses with only a comma in the absence of a conjunction—as this student did:

> My right leg was all bloody and my right elbow felt shattered, at the time these were the least of my worries, trying to explain how a brand new Ford landed in a lake was uppermost in my mind.

Once in a while a comma splice works, as we see in a sentence from the same essay:

> I was out for a while, I have no idea how long.

This is sometimes termed a borderline comma—useful when each independent clause is short and a quick pause is just right. Generally, however, avoid the comma splice. And *never* commit a run-on.

> I was out for a while I have no idea how long.

Here the independent clauses are not separated at all, and they're far too close for the readers' comfort. The run-on is as serious an offense in our culture as the double negative, as subject-verb disagreement, as cheating on taxes. Don't do it.

Use commas to separate items in a series.

> I have the basket, the icechest, the umbrella, the volleyball, the net, a jug of wine, a loaf of bread, and thou.

Note the comma between the last and next-to-last items. In England and in newspapers, that comma is omitted. If you want to dispense with it, wait until you live in England or write for newspapers. For now, use a comma between the last and next-to-last items in a series.

Punctuate parallel adjectives in a series the same way.

> It was a hot, steamy, lazy afternoon.

No commas are required for a series of adjectives that *aren't* parallel.

> The little red wagon needed wheels.

A dependent modifying phrase or clause not essential to the meaning of the sentence (nonrestrictive) should *always* be set off with commas.

> Old Jeremiah Jones, who even remembers the James boys and the Dalton gang, celebrated his 101st birthday last night.

> Truffaut's last film, which received high praise from the critics, disappointed me.

> The last game, perhaps the best of the series, lasted almost four hours.

Note the commas at the *beginning and end* of such modifiers. Both are essential when the modifier neither begins nor ends the sentence. If the modifier occurs at the beginning or end of the sentence, only one comma is necessary.

I fell madly in love with Carmen, a passionate Gypsy femme fatale.

Reading such sentences aloud helps determine whether or not they need a comma. When the modifiers are essential to the meaning of the sentence (restrictive), there is no pause and thus no need of a comma.

The guy who laughed had better be quiet.

Remember the admonition to begin dependent modifying clauses that are not essential and that do not refer to persons with *which*, not *that*? Another way to remember the rule is to use *which* for all non-personal modifying clauses set off with commas, and to use *that* for all non-personal modifying clauses not set off with commas.

Nonessential: which and commas
This ceiling fan, which was installed only yesterday, doesn't work.

Essential: that and no commas
The fan that you gave me doesn't work.

Places and dates. Watch:

I was born in a trunk in the Princess Theater in Pocatello, Idaho, on July 22, 1947, between the first and second acts.

For places and dates do *not* use the read-aloud test. Pause or no pause, always use a comma after city and state, after day of month and year—but *not* between state and zip code.

Beginning writers often use commas in places they don't belong.

What was bothering me at the time, was whether the old man, (who celebrated his 101st birthday last week) could remember anything.

Never use only one comma between subject and verb. The subject in the preceding sentence is the entire noun clause *What was bothering me at the time* and the verb is *was*. Also, never use a comma in front of a parenthesis.

Transitional expressions—*finally, in fact, furthermore, besides*—are set off by a comma. Such an expression within a sentence, *moreover*, must be set off by commas.

C. Semicolon

The mark is stronger than the comma but weaker than the period. A compromise of sorts, the semicolon is one part period and one part comma—(;).

It has several uses. Its most common use occurs in compound sentences that work better without a conjunction.

> It was raining hard; I put on my hat and coat.

> Jane is a peach; Jim, however, is a nerd.

When the ideas are close enough to belong *in* the same sentence but not quite close enough to be joined by a conjunction—yet require the breathing room of a definite pause—use the semicolon.

In a complicated series of items involving commas within one or more of the items, use semicolons to separate the items and avoid confusion.

> His room was a mess: The floor was not only littered, it was dirty; the bed was not only unmade, it was dirty; the drawers were not only messy, they were crammed with clothes that were dirty.

The items in a series need not be clauses but they must be grammatical equals.

> In his drawers we found old T-shirts, ragged and gray; old underwear, tattered and torn; old shirts frayed at collar and cuff; and old toothless combs, stiff mustache scissors, and rusted fingernail clippers.

If commas were used instead of semicolons, the readers would confront a puzzle instead of a passage.

D. Colon

This mark announces that one thing leads to another.

> His act was an absolute mess: I told him to clean it up.

The nature of the relationship is cause-and-effect. If cause-and-effect is the point, announce it with a colon; if cause-and-effect is not the point, use the semicolon.

> Sam is a wonderful, an absolutely superb fellow: He lent me the money.

The colon is also an announcement of items following in a series, particularly when the series is long and a pause is appropriate before launching into it.

> In his pockets we found the following: an ounce of marijuana, two grams of cocaine, a twelve-inch switchblade, a set of brass knuckles, a blackjack, and a Saturday night special; he said he had no idea how they got there.

We use the colon to tell time: At the sound of the tone the time will be 8:32. We use the colon to address a correspondent in a formal letter: Dear Ms. Jones:. We use the colon to distinguish chapter and verse in the Bible: *Genesis* 3:7. And we use the colon to introduce quoted material, especially quoted material set off from the main text:

> Consider this a passage written by another, identical to the many quoted throughout this text.

E. Quotation Marks

When using another's words verbatim, announce the fact by placing quotation marks around them: "To be or not to be," Hamlet declares, "that is the question." Quoting a verbatim quotation is often called *direct discourse. Indirect discourse* is a paraphrase; no quotation marks are required.

> Hamlet states that the question is whether we want to be or not.

When quoting five lines or more, set them off from the main text by indentation—using no quotation marks—as seen often in this text.

> Consider again that this is a passage by another. Notice there are no quotation marks. The idention alone tells the readers that this is quoted material—not paraphrasing.

I have often set off quoted material of fewer than five lines to ensure that it's read and not passed over. As a rule, however, if the quoted material is fewer than five lines, incorporate it in the main text and announce it with quotation marks.

Many beginning writers (and alas too many experienced writers) surround slang and old expressions and cliches with quotation marks, sparing themselves the trouble of fashioning the right phrase or choosing the right word, and alerting the reader that the quoted material is not original or not standard usage. Such quotation marks are like a wink and nudge between intimates—the old inside joke. This practice is a mark of mediocrity. Avoid it. Yet if you can breathe new life into these corpses and the occasion justifies their use—have the courage of your cliches, your old expressions, your slang. Put them out there in the light of day without apology, wink and nudge, or quote unquote.

Also use quotation marks for titles of works less than book length: essays, articles, short stories, poems and the like. (But not the title at the top of your essay!)

We now come to punctuating quotation marks. Beginning writers throw fits over this. Spare yourself. Memorize these practices.

Place periods and commas inside quotation marks.

> He said, "Yes."

> "No," she replied.

Place exclamation points and question marks inside quotation marks if part of the quoted material.

> "Yes?" he asked.

> "No!" she replied.

If not part of the quoted material, place them outside the marks.

> Did she say "No"?

> Not only that, she also said "Huh uh"!

When question marks and exclamation points are part of the quoted material, no further punctuation is required.

> *Wrong:* "Yes?," he asked.
> *Wrong:* She replied, "No!."
> *Wrong:* "Yes?", he asked.
> *Wrong:* She replied, "No!".

> *Right:* "Yes?" he asked.
> *Right:* She replied, "No!"

Place semicolons, colons, and dashes outside quotation marks.

> She said, "Sit"; I sat. She said, "Stay"; I wagged my tail. Then, when she uttered her next words—"Good boy!"—I jumped up and fawned.

For dialogue, paragraph each time a speaker takes a turn.

> "Yes?" he asked.
> "No!" she replied.
> "Why not?"
> "Because you are repugnant to me. Your values are minimal, your taste is questionable, and your breath is bad."
> "I see," he said.

If quoted material contains other quoted material, use a single mark (the apostrophe on a typewriter) for the quote within the quote.

"I see," he said. "Well, in the words of the bard, 'Bad breath is better than no breath at all.' "

If the quote within the quote also contains quoted material, return to quotation marks: "... '... "Yes." ...' ..." However, resist backing yourself and the readers into such a Chinese box.

F. Italics

The word *itself* is in italics, the script-like type that resembles hand-writing more than printing. In manuscripts—written or typed—indicate italics by underlining.

Use italics for: titles of books, movies, plays, works of art, periodicals, ships, aircraft. Many writers use italics instead of quotation marks.

The expression *to beat a dead horse* has lost all life and most meaning.

When I say *dead*, I mean dead.

For definitions, use italics *and* quotation marks: *Verbatim* means "exactly like the original text."

Use italics for foreign words and phrases unless they have been adopted by the English language.

She had an acute case of *Weltschmerz*, philosophical heartburn—so we bid her *auf Wiedersehen* and bon voyage.

Finally, use italics for emphasis.

When I say *dead*, I mean *dead*.

No, it's *your* turn.

It's quite easy to be promiscuous with italics, to underline all manner and description of words. Avoid the temptation. Use word order and rhythm for emphasis. They're most effective most of the time. When they aren't, however, and emphasis is necessary for clarity—use italics.

G. Dash

I'm not speaking of the 100 meter dash or a pinch of this and a dash of that—but of the lines inserted between words to set off, highlight, or emphasize.

All three of them—Papa Bear, Mama Bear, and Baby Bear—noticed that things were amiss.

Or to summarize:

> Laziness, stupidity, and a big appetite—those are the traits that characterized Big Charlie.

Sometimes writers use the dash instead of the colon—to introduce what follows. It's more emphatic and dramatic than the colon. This practice is informal and somewhat eccentric—do it sparingly and carefully, only when it *clearly* enhances meaning.

(On a typewriter or computer, two hyphens make a dash. There is no space—none—on either side of the dash.)

H. Parentheses

With parentheses—those marks that look like a sliver of moon or a fingernail clipping—you murmur asides (confidential or otherwise) to the readers. With parentheses, nonrestrictive modifiers are about as nonessential as can be. Parentheses are also useful places for additional information, such as the preceding advice on how to make dashes on a typewriter or computer.

Parentheses may occur within sentences or may enclose sentences. If within sentences, they never begin with a capital or end with a period.

> *Wrong:* The old woman (She was Methuselah's wife) lived in a shoe.

> *Right:* The old woman (she was Methuselah's wife) lived in a shoe.

> *Wrong:* She was an old woman (183, to be exact.)
> *Wrong:* She was an old woman (183, to be exact.).

> *Right:* She was an old woman (183, to be exact).

Never precede a parenthesis with a comma. (See *Commas.*)

(Punctuate sentences within parentheses the same as without: capitals, periods, and all. There may be more than one sentence within parentheses. Just don't get carried away, as I've come close to doing.)

I. Brackets

Brackets [hello] serve two purposes. One is to insert your own two cents worth into quoted material.

> Consider this a quote contaneing [sic] a misspelling. The *sic* within brackets lets the reader know the misspelling appears in the original quoted material.

The other purpose (should necessity arise [it probably never will], God forbid) is to insert parentheses within parentheses. Theoretically you may insert parentheses within parentheses for a lifetime, alternating the parenthesis mark and the bracket the same as you can alternate single and double quotation marks. Again, avoid the temptation.

J. Question Mark

A polite request framed as a question does not end with a question mark: Will you please open the door. However, interrogatory sentences do end with question marks: See what I mean?

K. Exclamation Point

The vertical dash hovering over a period is the most frequently abused mark of punctuation! Especially among beginning writers! Some— too many!—use it in virtually every sentence! To emphasize a statement beyond their usual volume and pitch, they use two or three!!! Or even four!!!! Have you ever noticed that such practitioners of this pop art frequently combine them with question marks?! Don't do as I am doing! Do as I say! Use the exclamation point only when there is something actually worth shouting about! (Gag me with a spoon!)

L. Apostrophes

Suspended in midair, these commas are used to spell the possessive case for nouns.

John's hat

Rachel's shoe

In certain instances, primarily abbreviations, use them to spell the plural:

The ABC's

Use them to spell contractions; place them where the letter is omitted:

John's going home.

We're going, too (not *were*).

You're invited yourself (not *your*).

M. Ellipses

As brackets are used to insert material into a quote, the ellipsis (three spaced dots) is used to omit words from a quote:

> To be or . . . to be: *that* is the question [italics added].

If you omit material that includes a period, use four dots instead of three and in this manner:

> To be or not. . . . 'tis nobler in the mind to suffer the slings and arrows of outrageous fortune. . . .

Note: When omitting words from the end of quoted material, use four spaced dots—the three of the ellipsis plus the period. When eliminating words from quoted material, be careful not to distort the sense of the original—as I just did, grossly. Beginning writers often use an ellipsis at the beginning of a quote to indicate it does not begin the piece from which it is taken.

> . . . To be or not to be: that is the question.

Or this:

> As Hamlet says, " . . . that is the question."

Neither ellipsis is necessary. Almost every quote is extracted from a work: it's a given and requires no indication.

Ellipses are also useful to express a tailing off into conjecture.

> I may go, but then again . . .

> Oh, he's honest enough, but . . .

Often it expresses a silence lounder than words—much like Jack Benny's classic response to the mugger's demand, "Your money or your life!"

> . . .

N. Slash

When faced with alternative propostions, we often frame combinations such as either/or, and/or, he/she, and the like. However, either/or situations are unbecoming, and slashes make for bumpy reading—like contracts and treaties. Use them only when there is no other effective choice.

O. Hyphen

A hyphen is the waist-high blip used to join words into a single modifier—like *waist-high*. More than two words may be joined— even clauses—to form a single modifier: The I-can-do-anything-better-than-you complex. Such constructions usually display an air of good humor in their gait. Consequently, use them sparingly and only where such a jaunty gait is suitable.

As a rule, do not use the hyphen for compound nouns. Write icebox, not ice-box, blackbird, not black-bird. To be sure, check the dictionary. Use the hyphen only when the words are normally separate and when they now constitute a single modifier preceding the noun: computer-based language, twentieth-century technology.

Also use the hyphen to mark a syllabic division at the end of a line: hap-pen, coin-cidence, supe-rior. Never divide a word in mid-syllable: happ-en, coi-ncidence, super-ior. Incorrect division implies not only ignorance but laziness—too lazy even to open a book. When dividing a word at the end of a line, look up the syllabic structure in the dictionary.

III. USAGE

Usage is a matter of policy, not grammatical correctness. Textbook writers disagree on certain of these matters. I base the following recommendations on the common editorial standards and practices of publications such as *Harper's*, *The Atlantic Monthly*, and *The Yale Review*. When choices exist, I examine them.

A. There Is, There Are, It Is

Formally termed the *expletive construction*, it is banned in many texbooks. Here is why:

> There is a guy down the street who just got a new car. It is a Corvette. There are not many options available for Corvettes. It is a car that comes with most everything standard.

The expletives are filler: unnecessary syllables, wasted breath.

Still, to ban a practice because it *can* be abused goes beyond the call of wisdom. At times the expletive construction works better than any other.

There was an old woman who lived in a shoe.

There's a tavern in the town.

It's a long way to Tipperary.

'Twas the night before Christmas . . .

Consider these:

There is some s. I will not eat.

> —*cummings*, "*I Sing of Olaf, Glad and Big*"

But here there is no light.

> —*Keats*, "*Ode to a Nightingale*"

Sometimes I think there's naught beyond.

> —*Melville*, Moby Dick

It is a truth universally acknowledged that a single man in possession of a good fortune must be in want of a wife.

> —*Austen*, Pride and Prejudice

And this:

There are several new students in our class.

You may find successful writers who don't use the expletive, but you'll have to do some looking. You will not, however, find successful writers who use the expletive all the time. It's a shy delicate structure and cannot withstand much exposure.

The expletive is useful as a pointer—a guide. Use it sparingly and only when pointing helps clarify the meaning.

B. Beginning with a Conjunction

You have been warned—I know—*never* to begin a sentence with a conjunction. This rule is another example of a taboo resulting from an abuse. You must find it doubly trying. Sometimes, if not often, you consciously *desire* to begin a sentence with a conjunction. Furthermore, when examining the assigned reading—and the reading you do on your own—you not only see it done, but sometimes with regularity. In his autobiography *The Big Sea*, for instance, Langston Hughes describes a childhood experience at a revival meeting.

> And he held out his arms to all us young sinners there on the mourners' bench. And the little girls cried. And some of them jumped up and went to Jesus right away. But most of us just sat there.

Beginning sentences with a conjunction is a common practice. But like the expletive, the structure is delicate and grows tiresome quickly—like a child trying to tell a long, complicated story.

> And she said there was not a Santa Claus. And I said there was, too. And she said I was a dumb Virginia for thinking so. And I said my mommy and daddy told me so, and my mommy and daddy know. And she said my mommy and daddy are liars. And I said they are not. And she said they are too. And I said if my mommy and daddy are liars then her mommy and daddy are not Americans. And she said they are too.

Avoid singsong in speech and prose.

You should note that Hughes begins several sentences in a row with a conjunction precisely to sound childlike, to suggest his actual experience when a child. He does it *not* thoughtlessly but deliberately—for that specific, definable reason.

By beginning with a conjunction, you emphasize that sentence's relationship with the preceding sentence. If such emphasis is meaningful, begin with a conjunction. If such emphasis is meaningless, begin with something else.

C. Ending with a Preposition

This rule was initially predicated on ignorance of the origin of English. Late seventeenth-century grammarians observed that Latin sentences never end with a preposition. Under the mistaken belief that English is derived from Latin, they declared that English sentences must follow suit. Much as it disturbs the cadence and gait of English, the rule survives. It insists on hanging around. I'm sure you've been introduced to it.

English is not Latinate; it is Germanic. It's impossible to end a Latin sentence in a preposition. The language has no such option. Ending a Latin sentence with a preposition is akin to saying, "red wagon little the." In German many sentences end with prepositions, although words so used are termed *postpositions*—because they come after. Life would be much easier if the English-speaking peoples could also call them postpositions and be done with it—but we can't. The rule hangs on, in spite of Winston Churchill's tribute to its absurdity:

> This is the sort of English up with which I will not put.

Currently the rule is not absolute. Even in formal writing a sentence may end with a preposition if the alternative is as awkward as Churchill's barb. Berton Braley puts it best:

> The grammar has a rule absurd
> Which I would call an outworn myth:
> "A preposition is a word
> You mustn't end a sentence with."

This is how the "postposition" improves awkwardness:

> He is a person I would not trade places with.
> (As opposed to: He is a person with whom I would not trade places.)
>
> Cancer is something I can do without.
> (As opposed to: You write it out.)

If the alternative is not embarrassingly clumsy, avoid ending with prepositions. In less formal writing, end with prepositions when by doing so you fashion a more graceful sentence.

A word of caution: Although the rule is stupid, don't you be stupid by refusing to obey and violating it at every chance. This is not the place to lay your principles on the line. Accord it about the same measure of respect as speed limits: compliance according to circumstances. You don't speed every time you drive; you don't go a hundred in a parking lot.

D. Intensifiers

Undoubtedly you notice that I *certainly* subscribe to the *indisputable* truth that not all sentences are created equal. *Indubitably*, sentences that contain words like *indubitably* are *unquestionably* inferior. Me thinks they doth protest too much.

When *certainly* appears in a text, it is reasonably certain the point being made is anything but certain. Likewise *undoubtedly, indubitably,* and their ilk. If the point being made is certain beyond a reasonable doubt, intensifiers are superfluous. And if it's not so certain, it shouldn't be insisted on.

Save intensifiers for your next garage sale.

E. Humble Hedgers

At the opposite end of rhetoric from intensifiers lie the humble hedgers, modifiers that, *in my opinion*, *sort of* serve to hedge my bets
somewhat, so that I do not stick my neck out *more or less* in a statement
that may *perhaps* be contradicted or *possibly* viewed as controversial.

Humble hedgers have a pedantic, namby-pamby, timid air about
them that costs prose considerable power. Unless such a qualification
is essential to meaning and integrity, be positive. Write in a forthright
manner—without apology or limitation:

> *Wrong:*   Ceasar was in all likelihood more or less right. Thin people,
>   relatively speaking, need watching, as it were.

> *Right:*   Caesar was right. Thin people need watching.

> *—Jordan, "That Lean and Hungry Look"*

When you make a statement, the readers know that it is your opinion—that it defines what you think. Unless necessary for clarification,
saying so goes without saying.

> Many people think that income-tax evasion is justified. In my opin-
> ion, it is not.

Or: I think not. Or: I disagree. In this situation you must specify it is
your opinion to distinguish it from others. On occasion, you may need
a qualifier for clarity.

> Thin people are somewhat heavier than skinny people.

Far more often than not, however, your assertions need no distinguishing or qualifying. And if you insist on doing it anyway, you are hedging—and oh so 'umbly, me lord, with a tug o' the forelock and a
scrape o' the knee. Such behavior is not becoming in the republic of
letters.

F. Adverbial Shorthand

> *Fortunately*, we will be going where *thankfully* we can compete and
> *luckily* we will win. *Unfortunately* we must pay our own way but
> *hopefully* a benefactor will come through and *gratefully* our expenses
> will be paid.

By crowding several of these into a small space, I hope you see the
shortcoming of adverbial shorthand: It is semantically sloppy and

often occurs at the expense of verbs. It is common because it is easy to do. Consequently, it's difficult to avoid. If it's a habit, it's worth breaking.

> We are thankful to be going where we can compete. With a little luck we will win. We wish that we did not have to pay our way, but a benefactor may still come through and cover our expenses. We would appreciate the help.

G. Transitional Words and Phrases

Moreover, furthermore, therefore, thus, then, the fact that, by and large, all in all are bridges. You may often feel a tendency—sometimes so strong it's an urge—to bridge the space from one sentence to the next with some transition. I suffer this urge myself, and all too often fail to resist it.

Transitions are necessary only infrequently. Remove all but those that refuse to go, that are necessary for the sentence to make sense. The fewer the better. Apply the same rule to transitions as for adjectives and adverbs: If in doubt, leave them out.

H. Fillers

Fillers are the equivalent of *uh*. They actually are *uh* in costume. They come in two guises, naive and sophisticated. Naive:

> *Okay*, so then we go down to this dance, *man, you know, like* where the guys and chicks, *you know, for sure, kind of* get it on, *if you know what I mean*—*well, you know, man*, make out.

Sophisticated:

> We went to the *so-called* dance where the guys and gals, *so to speak*, get it on, *as it were*, and make out, *in a manner of speaking*.

In speech fillers give us time to think. In writing—because there is time to think—they are unnecessary. There are, of course, exceptions:

> In *Genesis* God creates the heavens and the earth in a manner of speaking. [For God creates *by* pronouncement.]

When meaningful, they are not filler. When not meaningful—when merely loitering, which is most of the time—throw the rascals out.

I. Due To

Often misused in place of *because* or *because of*—usually with a long tail.

> Due to the fact that we arrived late, we missed the first act.

Due to the fact that means *because*. However, *because* is quicker and more precise. *Due to* does not mean *because*. Check the dictionary to learn its meaning, and use it accordingly.

J. Since

Another word often substituted for *because* or *because of*:

> Since we missed the first act, we didn't stick around for the second.

Since is even quicker than *because*, and in casual conversation it's used in place of *because* with no misunderstanding. In standard edited English, however, it is *not* accepted. In formal circumstances, it may only indicate time.

> Since World War II, we have fought two major conflicts.

When expressing a cause-and-effect relationship, say so. Say *because* or *because of*.

K. -ize

This suffix tops the charts among addicts of bureaucratic mumbo jumbo. They get high forming ugly verbs with it: *finalize, politicize, dichotomize, verbalize, accessorize, officialize*, to name a few, including the most grotesque of all—*prioritize*—meaning "to rank."

A good many *-ize* verbs are sound: *legalize, realize, materialize, harmonize, organize, patronize*. To say the same thing otherwise would require several words. Use *-ize* verbs only to save words; never *novelize* or *originalize* a verb by adding this suffix.

L. -wise

Another popular suffix is *-wise*. It generates adverbs about as prolifically as rodents breed: *time-wise, space-wise, weather-wise, morality-wise, comfort-wise, strategy-wise, wisdom-wise*. A few *-wise* words are sound: *Likewise* and *lengthwise* come to mind. Most of them, though, reflect an unwillingness to select the right word for the occasion. *Usage-wise*, they're cop-outs.

M. Contractions

The more formal the writing, the less you should use 'em. Some, like *'em*, are more informal than others, like *aren't*. Even in informal writing—don't use contractions indiscriminately. In "He isn't," the *is* is emphasized; in "He's not," the *not* is emphasized; and "He is not" is not only more formal than the other two constructions but *generally* more emphatic, depending on the context. *Couldn't've* is not acceptable in writing—even though we say it—because in print it looks like a smashup and tends to cross the reader's eyes. (*Should've*, incidentally, is a contraction of "should have" and *not* "should of." That applies to all such contractions.)

Use contractions not just to be informal—the readers' pal in prose—but to enhance the rhythm and sound of a sentence. For example:

> To make the rhythm and sound of this sentence better'n they otherwise'd be, we must remove these contractions.

By contracting *than* and *would*, you sacrifice some alliteration and make the rhythm a bit uneven. Whenever you consider using a contraction—stop, look, and listen. Decide according to what you see and hear.

In highly formal writing—the prose of diplomacy, scientific papers, honors theses, legal documents—use no contractions.

N. Colloquial Language

The words and phrases of informal conversation are termed colloquial. Formally speaking, *nuisance* is a substantial interference with the right to the use and enjoyment of property. Informally speaking, nuisance is *a pain in the neck*.

Just among friends, I like my language in loafers and jeans. But on more formal occasions—where my language mixes with colleagues and strangers—I dress it up. The more formal the occasion, the less informal the diction—according to commonsense.

O. Slang

Hey man, some chick, a real fox. What a hunk! Hubba hubba!

Cheese it, the cops! Twenty-three skiddoo!

Oh groaty, how gay, how bomb!

Notice that the older an expression is, the less sense it makes and the cornier it sounds. Slang, like faddish clothing, is here today and gone tomorrow. Except in letters to friends, avoid it.

P. Vulgar Language

In formal writing, unless it is the subject of the composition, avoid swearing. In any writing, even the most informal, use it sparingly if at all.

Dirty words are extremely weak in print; they have no stamina. They're good for one punch—usually a sucker punch—and then lose all force. Save them for those rare moments when *no* other words will do. And when using them, never hedge them with quotes.

Q. Euphemisms

When people pass away, often a mortician arranges for their interment in a cemetery. In other words, when people die, often an undertaker arranges for their burial in a graveyard.

For unpleasant things and events, we devise less-unpleasant expressions—sometimes going to ridiculous extremes. Victorians were uncomfortable with *legs* and called them *limbs*—even on furniture. Don't smile too smugly at the squeamish Victorians. Even today, when male strippers show their stuff on *The Phil Donahue Show*, we use *private parts* for genitalia, *making love* for sexual intercourse *and* fornication, and *sleeping together* when sleep is the last thing on our minds.

We routinely resort to euphemisms for sex and death. We use them to avoid facing any disquieting truth head-on. In wars, bombing, burning, and killing are *pacification*. The old War Department became the *Department of Defense*. In mental hospitals we *administer aversion therapy*—electric shock. Auto dealerships buy and sell *pre-owned* rather than used cars.

Generally, avoid using euphemisms. They imply a reluctance to face facts because of squeamishness or dishonesty—or both. Euphemisms make readers suspicious.

However, some occasions are delicate and euphemisms may be called for—depending on the intended reader. If a friend's mother dies, you might express sympathy for her death or her passing. If your friend is squeamish about death, express sympathy for his or her loss. Do not, in the name of honesty, say you're sorry to hear the old lady croaked. That's not honest—it's brutal.

R. Sexist Language

Always consider the sensibilities of the readers. We have become aware, thanks to the women's movement, of the sexism implicit in numerous words and expressions. It is presumptuous to use *he* as the sole generic unisex pronoun for everyone. Say *he or she* (and vice versa).

When someone dies, she or he is often buried in a graveyard.

If possible, use the plural to avoid the awkwardness of *he or she*.

When people die, they are often buried in a graveyard.

Man as the abstraction for everyone is presumptuous: *Humankind* or *humanity* says the same thing gracefully *and* impartially. However, don't indulge in such awkward constructions as *personkind*, *police-person*, *waitperson*, *freshperson*, *seamperson*, and the like. Such language is self-conscious and distracting. When in doubt, use *The Handbook of Nonsexist Writing* by Casey Miller and Kate Swift.

S. Numbers

For any number over twelve, use numerals: 13, 14, 15, and so on. For numbers one through twelve, use words. However, when numbers are in a series, use numerals: I have 3 cats, 2 dogs, 14 horses, and 187 head of cattle. When numbers begin a sentence, *always* use words: Three cats were there, and 2 dogs, 14 horses. . . . Use numbers for percentages 100 percent of the time. Inclusive numbers may be complete (pages 327–582) or incomplete (1985–87).

T. Dates

Oscar Wilde's play, *A Woman of No Importance*, ran at His Majesty's Theatre from May 22, 1907, to July 5, 1907. (If you don't include the days, do it this way: The play ran from May to July 1907. Yet another way: The play had a brief run, May 1907–July 1907.) It's a fine example of early twentieth-century satire.

One of the most popular plays of the 1950s (or of the fifties) was *The Death of a Salesman*. It's a splendid example of 20th-century tragedy.

Some of the earliest Western European plays in writing were composed around 400–450 B.C.. Virtually vanishing after the fall of Rome (circa 400 A.D.), drama reemerged in the Church around A.D. 900.

This is an irrelevant but useful observation: In the United States, plays usually begin at 8:00 P.M.

U. Capitals

They are the uppercase (capital) letters with which you begin the first word of each sentence—complete or not; into which you put yourself, *I*—deserving or not; and with which you begin various kinds of words— willing or not.

Academic degrees, spelled out or abbreviated: Bachelor of Science, M.A., Ph.D., M.D., J.D.

Geographical names: England, the Middle East, Asia, Antarctica, the Pacific Ocean

Historical eras, events, and documents: the Victorian Age, the Battle of Bull Run, The Gettysburg Address

Holidays: Christmas, Thanksgiving, Memorial Day

Human groupings (ethnic, tribal, racial): Serbo-Croatian, Arab, Cherokee, Oriental

Personified abstractions: At times Justice is blind.

Political and governmental institutions: the Republican Party, the Senate, the U.S. Navy, the Department of Commerce

Proper names and adjectives: Jane Doe, French, Homeric

Religious names and terms: Christian, Jewish, Islam, God, the Pope, the Nicene Creed

Titles preceding a name: General Grant (without a proper name such titles get only lower case treatment: the general)

Trademarks: Izod, Stroh's, Frederick's of Hollywood, Adidas, Sony, BMW

V. Spelling

A student of mine wrote a good essay about being lost in the woods—but he made an unfortunate error. At one point he heard a trampling of undergrowth and froze, terrified he was about to be attacked by "a pack of wild bores."

A pack of wild bores!

What would happen if you turned to the title page of a large, important-looking novel and read *Moby Duck*? Or *War and Piece*? Or a description of a house with a laundry shoot? Or a cute appendicitis?

Check the spelling before submitting the paper. Use a dictionary. Save yourself embarrassment and grief.

W. Format

When you have written and rewritten and edited, prepare a clean manuscript—preferably typewritten. If you can't type, find someone who does. If you can't type and your social life is on the skids, write the manuscript neatly and in ink. Typewritten or written, it must be double-spaced. Leave a 1 to 1 and 1/2 inch margin along the left and 1 inch margins at the top, along the right, and at the bottom. Paginate either at the top right-hand corner or at the bottom midway between the left and right margins. Proofread carefully. Correct mistakes neatly. If your teacher or supervisor requires a different format, learn it and follow it religiously.

IV. A MATTER OF PERSONAL STANDARDS

To write well you must want to write well. You must use extreme care. Accordingly, adopt the standards of good public writing as your standards. Make the most of what you have for your own advantage, your own satisfaction, your own integrity, your own pleasure. Take pride in your craftsmanship so you can look back and say, "I did my best." But writing is not generally a private affair, something for your eyes only. Except for momentos, diaries, journals, and such, you write for publication—for public consumption. Consequently, at issue is not merely self-respect but the respect of others. My point, an old one, is simple: Always make writing a matter of personal standards and your work will earn the respect of others.

A. The Importance of Impressions

If you submit a careless manuscript, riddled with errors, the readers will infer that you care neither about the work nor about them. And if you don't care, neither will they.

Incidentally, when I say *readers* I don't mean just teachers, but anyone who reads your work—including classmates. As a matter of fact, your classmates are often more irritated by a messy error-ridden manuscript than teachers. They take it personally. They are offended, and with good reason. You are telling them in effect that not only does the work not matter—neither do they.

B. Exhortation

You owe it to yourself to spell correctly and to follow the rules of punctuation and grammar. You owe it to yourself to paragraph precisely, to write sentences that get the message across, and to choose the right word for the right occasion. You owe it to yourself to settle for nothing less than your best. You owe it to yourself to be as smart, as witty, and as able as you can—and to enjoy thereby a rich relationship with readers who are glad, really glad, to have made your acquaintance.

PAUL HORGAN
The Importance of Finish

> *Novelist, biographer, historian, and painter Horgan has published numerous books on many different subjects for a wide variety of readers. But he is known primarily as a novelist and historian of the Southwest.* Great River: The Rio Grande in North American History *(1954) and* Lamy of Sante Fe: His Life and Times *(1975) both won*

Pulitzers for history and represent the qualities that make Horgan a Book-of-the-Month-Club writer who also satisfies the demands of scholars. In this essay Horgan explains why it is important to finish, down to the last comma and letter, the piece you are writing.

Any writer who undertakes to make his living by writing—and most writers hope to do so—must depend first of all on discipline in the simplest details as well as in the most exalted intentions of his task. This discipline he must earn for himself, for it is he, himself, and no one else, who will have to maintain it throughout all his professional life.

The first act of the writer's discipline is to serve an apprenticeship with humility and willingness to learn. I have taught certain aspects of my craft in various universities and I have never ceased being amazed at the almost unanimous expectation of students (graduate and undergraduate alike) who look to the publication and the success of the very first works they commit to paper. You cannot help being touched at their confidence, for you observe it through the eyes of memory. It is the blithe energy of youth working in their imaginations, rehearsing fame, wealth, and position; and you wish you could let their hopes be fulfilled, you wish this until—again through a backward glance—you recall that acceptance of devoted labor at the humblest details of learning how to write, no matter how long it may have to take, will be the best thing you could wish for them.

For not only will they study the technical details of their craft in this period of apprenticeship—they will learn also the habit of work without which the writer will never be more than an amateur. It is this habit of work which will bring the writer to his work table every day at the same hour, there to do about the same amount of work according to the capacity which experience tells him is naturally his. It is this habit of work which will teach him to learn the hazardous and challenging necessity of keeping alive in his imagination a work of art which may take many months or even years to complete. . . .

My own habit brings me to my work table at about the same time every day—roughly at half-past nine. But actually, the working day starts earlier. It starts on awakening, with a sort of bated breath in the thought, if I may put it so. Preparation for the morning's task gets under way in an induced and protected absent-mindedness, as if to allow the work in progress to come clear gradually, so that its daily rebirth suffers no jarring collisions with immediate reality, but establishes its own inner reality from which it will draw conviction. Absurd as it may appear to those in other vocations, any contact with a serious distraction, or obligation elsewhere, may, at this daily moment, disturb a balance already delicate. A phone call is a minor catastrophe and a knock on the door a potential disaster. Until the day's work can actually begin, a frowning selfishness protects all the ingredients of plan, design, idea, and will; and when it begins, it flows forth, if the day is a good one, or it struggles forth, if it is a poor one; but strangely, later, it is difficult to tell by the evidence which pages come from fluent work and which from halting. It is again a reflection of the discipline we have mentioned. . . .

Experience tells the writer what his proper daily quota of work should be. If he exceeds it at all appreciably, he probably finds that the quality of his work falls off, and that in consequence he must rewrite more than usual to make up for it. If the form of a piece of writing has been solved beforehand, rewriting of great blocks of work does not often follow. But revision word by word and sentence does follow, for me, not once, but many times, each for different values.

These embrace precision in meaning; as between two words of equal precision, choice, then, of that one which calls up image more vividly through color or sound or association; rhythm, the great key to readability, in small units of the text, such as the phrase and the sentence, rhythm in larger developments of the text, such as the paragraph and the chapter, and finally rhythm in the work as a whole. In fiction, revision pursues each character of the story in a separate reading to feel the consistency, the living presence of each. Another complete revision is devoted to an examination to improve atmosphere and background. And so on, paying attention to each of the elements, including the humble mechanics, which combine to make a finished work—such matters as simple correctness in spelling, punctuation, grammar, syntax—the technical fabric by which the rich English language, with all its tributaries, is given its primary power of communication.

The writings of many students would lead us to think such matters too trivial to engage the personal attention of a serious author. It is the rare student, even in the graduate school of letters, who can spell, or even cares about it, or who understands the purposes of punctuation, or dissects the sentence in order to learn its anatomy, or even rereads at least once to correct typographic errors. When I have begged students to spare me their acts of simple carelessness, and have assured them that an editor will pay little attention to a typescript whose early pages reveal a sustained illiteracy, I have been told many times by them that "the editor would put in the spelling, punctuation, et cetera."

And yet such elements as I speak of are the structural fibers of writing, and not to respect them for their own sake, and to love their purposes and their powers, is to have little promise as a writer. What would we think of a music student who disdained to master the C major scale because he preferred to think only about playing whole sonatas even with a thousand wrong notes? The illustration is not too fanciful, as any instructor in advanced writing can testify.

One day a university senior whose work I'd been reading, though he was not in my seminar, assured me when I objected to his generally faulty spelling that he had "no interest in spelling." In a story he gave me a week later, about an ambush in the Vietnam War (he had never been in Vietnam), he described how Vietcong *gorillas*, heavily armed and cleverly camouflaged, broke through the jungle wall to massacre a U.S. unit. I showed him the passage and asked him what was wrong with it. He found nothing wrong with it.

"Do you want to be understood in your writing? Do you want it to say exactly what you mean?" I asked.

"Certainly," he said with patience.

"But you have no interest in spelling?"

"No."

"But you don't think there are occasions when meaning depends on spelling?"

"I don't know how there could be," he sighed, now impatiently.

"Then," I said, unable to resist a cheap luxury, "you want me to believe that a band of large anthropoid apes, wearing helmets camouflaged with leafy branches, and carrying firearms in their hands, the knuckles of which are calloused from their use as aids to self-propulsion, staged the ambush?"

"Of course not," he exclaimed with indignation. "That isn't what I wrote."

I handed him the dictionary.

"Yes, it is. Look it up."

LEWIS THOMAS
Notes on Punctuation

A physician, Thomas has served in various academic posts at the University of Minnesota, New York University-Bellevue Medical Center, and Yale University Medical Center. He has been both president and chancellor of Memorial Sloan-Kettering Cancer Center. His first collection of essays, The Lives of a Cell: Notes of a Biology Watcher *(1974), won the National Book Award. Since then he has published three volumes, including a sequel to the first:* The Medusa and the Snail: More Notes of a Biology Watcher *(1979). In this essay from his second volume, we begin to appreciate the flexibility and power of punctuation as well as the wit and charm of Thomas's style.*

There are no precise rules about punctuation (Fowler lays out some general advice (as best he can under the complex circumstances of English prose (he points out, for example, that we possess only four stops (the comma, the semicolon, the colon and the period (the question mark and exclamation point are not, strictly speaking, stops; they are indicators of tone (oddly enough, the Greeks employed the semicolon for their question mark (it produces a strange sensation to read a Greek sentence which is a straightforward question: Why weepest thou; (instead of Why weepest thou? (and, of course, there are parentheses (which are surely a kind of punctuation making this whole matter much more complicated by having to count up the lefthanded parentheses in order to be sure of closing with the right number (but if the parentheses were left out, with nothing to work with but stops, we would have considerably more flexibility in the deploying of layers of meaning than if we tried to separate all clauses by physical barriers (and in the latter case, while we might have more precision and exactitude for our meaning, we would lose the essential flavor of language, which is its wonderful ambiguity)))))))))))).

The commas are the most useful and usable of all the stops. It is highly important to put them in place as you go along. If you try to come back after doing a paragraph and stick them in the various spots that tempt you you will discover that they tend to swarm like minnows into all sorts of crevices whose existence you hadn't realized and before you know it the whole long sentence becomes immobilized and lashed up squirming in commas. Better to use them sparingly, and with affection, precisely when the need for each one arises, nicely, by itself.

I have grown fond of semicolons in recent years. The semicolon tells you that there is still some question about the preceding full sentence; something needs to be added; it reminds you sometimes of the Greek usage. It is almost always a greater pleasure to come across a semicolon than a period. The period tells you that that is that; if you didn't get all the meaning you wanted or expected, anyway you got all the writer intended to parcel out and now you have to move along. But with a semicolon there you get a pleasant feeling of expectancy; there is more to come; to read on; it will get clearer.

Colons are a lot less attractive, for several reasons: firstly, they give you the feeling of being rather ordered around, or at least having your nose pointed in a direction you might not be inclined to take if left to yourself, and, secondly, you suspect you're in for one of those sentences that will be labeling the points to be made: firstly, secondly and so forth, with the implication that you haven't sense enough to keep track of a sequence of notions without having them numbered. Also, many writers use this system loosely and incompletely, starting out with number one and number two as though counting off on their fingers but then going on and on without the succession of labels you've been led to expect, leaving you floundering about searching for the ninethly or seventeenthly that ought to be there but isn't.

Exclamation points are the most irritating of all. Look! they say, look at what I just said! How amazing is my thought! It is like being forced to watch someone else's small child jumping up and down crazily in the center of the living room shouting to attract attention. If a sentence really has something of importance to say, something quite remarkable, it doesn't need a mark to point it out. And if it is really, after all, a banal sentence needing more zing, the exclamation point simply emphasizes its banality!

Quotation marks should be used honestly and sparingly, when there is a genuine quotation at hand, and it is necessary to be very rigorous about the words enclosed by the marks. If something is to be quoted, the *exact* words must be used. If part of it must be left out because of space limitations, it is good manners to insert three dots to indicate omission, but it is unethical to do this if it means connecting two thoughts which the original author did not intend to have tied together. Above all, quotation marks should not be used for ideas that you'd like to disown, things in the air so to speak. Nor should they be put in place around clichés; if you want to use a cliché you must take full responsibility for it yourself and not try to fob it off on anon., or on society. The most objectionable misuse of quotation marks, but one which illustrates the dangers of misuse in ordinary prose, is seen in advertising, especially in advertisements for small restaurants, for example "just around the corner," or "a good place to eat." No single, identifiable, citable person ever really said, for the record, "just around the corner," much less "a good place to eat," least likely of all for restaurants of the type that use this type of prose.

The dash is a handy device, informal and essentially playful, telling you that you're about to take off on a different tack but still in some way connected with the present course—only you have to remember that the dash is there, and either put a second dash at the end of the notion to let the reader know that he's back on course, or else end the sentence, as here, with a period.

The greatest danger in punctuation is for poetry. Here it is necessary to be as economical and parsimonious with commas and periods as with the words themselves, and any marks that seem to carry their own subtle meanings, like dashes and little rows of periods, even semicolons and question marks, should be left out altogether rather than inserted to clog up the thing with ambiguity. A single exclamation point in a poem, no matter what else the poem has to say, is enought to destroy the whole work.

The things I like best in T. S. Eliot's poetry, expecially in the *Four Quartets*, are the semicolons. You cannot hear them, but they are there, laying out the connections between the images and the ideas. Sometimes you get a glimpse of a semicolon coming, a few lines farther on, and it is like climbing a steep path through woods and seeing a wooden bench just at a bend in the road ahead, a place where you can expect to sit for a moment, catching your breath.

Commas can't do this sort of thing; they can only tell you how the different parts of a complicated thought are to be fitted together, but you can't sit, not even take a breath, just because of a comma,

JOHN R. TRIMBLE
Punctuation

An associate professor at the University of Texas at Austin, Trimble was born and raised in Nigara Falls, Ontario, Canada, earned a Ph.D. in English from the University of California at Berkeley, and published Writing With Style: Conversations on the Art of Writing *(1975)—from which this selection is taken. Although he devotes most of his time to the classroom teaching of composition and professional lectures on teaching writing, Trimble finds time to author an occasional newspaper article and scholarly paper. Here he makes a forceful argument for the necessity of correct and thoughtful punctuation.*

Don't expect your reader to accept a piece of writing that you wouldn't accept yourself.

DONALD H. ROSS

Proofreading is like the quality-control stage at the end of an assembly line. Think of it in these terms and you'll see why you shouldn't consider a paper finished until you have proofread it with finicky thoroughness. Proofreading is your responsibility, not the reader's. But even beyond the question of responsibility is the crucial matter of basic reader psychology. Your object is to court your reader, not alienate him. If you give him a carelessly proofread paper, you hazard his concluding at least one of these opinions about you: (a) you are an undisciplined, lazy individual; (b) you will probably be found to be as grubbyminded a thinker as you are a proofreader; and (c) you are the kind of writer whom it's going to be pure drudgery to read. It may be unjust, I agree, but it's reality.

Proofreading involves two things: spotting your errors and then correcting them in a way that is instantly intelligible to your reader. Correcting them intelligibly, though, requires that you be familiar with the conventional proofreaders' marks. This takes but a few minutes' study. A complete list of the symbols can be found at the back of most good dictionaries. (*The American Heritage Dictionary* prints its list, though, alongside the entry for *proofread*. This list, incidentally, provides the clearest explanation of proofreaders' marks I have seen.) Some dictionaries, such as *Webster's New Collegiate*, even supply a sample of an error-ridden text that has been properly corrected so that you can see how the various marks are applied.

Below are suggestions on how to correct some of the most common errors:

1   If you have left out a word or phrase, put a caret (∧) just below the line at the place where the omission occurred and then write in the word or phrase directly above the caret. Example:

Write in the ∧ phrase.   *word or*

2   If you have omitted an entire sentence, put a caret where the omission occurred, write "See over for insert" in the adjacent margin, and write the sentence on the back of the page. If the omission exceeds one or two sentences, it may be best to retype the whole page.

3   If you have used the wrong word or badly misspelled a word, draw a line through it and write the correction directly *above* it. However, if the misspelling involves the mistyping or omission of merely a single letter, put a caret just below the line at the place where the error occurred, cross out the error, and then write in the letter directly above it.

4   If you wish to delete a period or comma, simply circle it. (Note: this procedure will suffice except when submitting a manuscript for typesetting—i.e., publication. At such a time, you can delete a period or comma only by running the delete sign (⅘) through the mark, since a circle around a comma changes it to a period.)

5   If your typewriter has skipped a space in the typing of a word, close up that space with a *pair* of horizontal parentheses, not just one. Example:

Close up that sp͡ace.

6   If letters or words need transposing, proceed thus:

Jack ⌣Jill ⌢and went up ten⌢ hill.

7   If you wish to designate a sentence as the beginning of a new paragraph, put the paragraph sign (¶) just before it and well above the line where it will be clearly visible.

It frequently happens that, during either the writing or the proof-reading of a paper, you are uncertain as to the correctness of an idiom, a punctuation mark, an assertion, or whatever. At such times, I recommend that you put a circled number in the adjacent margin and then, at the end of your essay, write a corresponding number followed by a note explaining your confusion. Example:

①   Is "alternative" correct here, or should I have said "alternate" instead?

You will want to leave a space, of course, below each question for your teacher to write in his answer. Students who have used this procedure report that it is very helpful to them. Among other advantages, it gives them courage to try out the new and the strange. Its chief advantage, though, is that it gives them quick feedback on questions which they might not otherwise receive answers to.

II

Readings

I
Memories of Childhood

ANNIE DILLARD
God in the Doorway

> *Dillard, a native of Pittsburgh, has lived (and written about living) in Virginia and Washington and now resides in Connecticut. She won the Pulitzer Prize for* Pilgrim at Tinker Creek *(1974) and since then has published several books of several sorts: poetry, meditation, literary criticism, and essays. Among her many gifts is Dillard's ability to tie disparate strands together into a single, simple, thought-provoking knot.*

One cold Christmas Eve I was up unnaturally late because we had all gone out to dinner—my parents, my baby sister, and I. We had come home to a warm living room, and Christmas Eve. Our stockings dropped from the mantel; beside them, a special table bore a bottle of ginger ale and a plate of cookies.

I had taken off my fancy winter coat and was standing on the heat register to bake my shoe soles and warm my bare legs. There was a commotion at the front door; it opened, and cold wind blew around my dress.

Everyone was calling me. "Look who's here! Look who's here!" I looked. It was Santa Claus. Whom I never—ever—wanted to meet. Santa Claus was looming in the doorway and looking around for me. My mother's voice was thrilled: "Look who's here!" I ran upstairs.

Like everyone in his right mind, I feared Santa Claus, thinking he was God. I was still thoughtless and brute, reactive. I knew right from wrong, but had barely tested the possibility of shaping my own behavior, and then only from fear, and not yet from love. Santa Claus was an old man whom you never saw, but who nevertheless saw you; he

277

knew when you'd been bad or good. He knew when you'd been bad or good! And I had been bad.

My mother called and called, enthusiastic, pleading; I wouldn't come down. My father encouraged me; my sister howled. I wouldn't come down, but I could bend over the stairwell and see: Santa Claus stood in the doorway with night over his shoulder, letting in all the cold air of the sky; Santa Claus stood in the doorway monstrous and bright, powerless, ringing a loud bell and repeating Merry Christmas, Merry Christmas. I never came down. I don't know who ate the cookies.

For so many years now I have known that this Santa Claus was actually a rigged-up Miss White, who lived across the street, that I confuse the *dramatic personae* in my mind, making of Santa Claus, God, and Miss White an awesome, vulnerable trinity. This is really a story about Miss White.

Miss White was old; she lived alone in the big house across the street. She liked having me around; she plied me with cookies, taught me things about the world, and tried to interest me in finger painting, in which she herself took great pleasure. She would set up easels in her kitchen, tack enormous slick soaking papers to their frames, and paint undulating undersea scenes: horizontal smears of color sparked by occasional vertical streaks which were understood to be fixed kelp. I liked her. She meant no harm on earth, and yet half a year after her failed visit as Santa Claus, I ran from her again.

That day, a day of the following summer, Miss White and I knelt in her yard while she showed me a magnifying glass. It was a large, strong hand lens. She lifted my hand and, holding it very still, focused a dab of sunshine on my palm. The glowing crescent wobbled, spread, and finally contracted to a point. It burned; I was burned; I ripped my hand away and ran home crying. Miss White called after me, sorry, explaining, but I didn't look back.

Even now I wonder: if I meet God, will he take and hold my bare hand in his, and focus his eye on my palm, and kindle that spot and let me burn?

But no. It is I who misunderstood everything and let everybody down. Miss White, God, I am sorry I ran from you. I am still running, running from that knowledge, that eye, that love from which there is no refuge. For you meant only love, and love, and I felt only fear, and pain. So once in Israel love came to us incarnate, stood in the doorway between two worlds, and we were all afraid.

QUESTIONS

1. Writing is a process of selection, of inclusion and exclusion. In the second paragraph, when the front door opens, Dillard includes only one detail: "cold wind blew around my dress." What else *might* she have included? Does this inclusion tell us all we need to know? What does it tell us?

2. Why does Dillard repeat the refrain from "Santa Claus Is Coming to Town"?

3. How is this essay "really a story about Miss White"?

4. In the Rhetoric I emphasize the importance of having an upshot— defining *the* point of the entire essay. What is the point of this essay? How does the point complete the essay? (To answer, consider what the essay would be without it.)

SUGGESTED ACTIVITIES

1. Write of an event in your childhood that involved misunderstanding adult motives and intentions.

2. Write of something in your childhood that you were supposed to love but actually feared.

POSTSCRIPT

Writing *God in the Doorway*

Ten years ago, a magazine editor asked me to describe Christmas memories. At first I refused, thinking I couldn't come up with anything more original than the usual "we-all-sat-around-the-big-table-at-Grandma's," with its usual overwritten descriptions of platters of food. Writing is tough. I don't like to take pains to come up with the usual. I told the editor I was sorry.

But I no sooner got off the phone than I recalled this scene, this old, sore business of Miss White's playing Santa Claus. I'd run from Miss White because, when I was small, I was afraid of the wrathful, omnipotent God: who wants to meet the God who'll make you fry in hell for your sins? (My parents didn't give me these notions; I must have picked them up from the world at large.) Now, when I was thirty, I saw I was still afraid of the forgiving God: who wants to be on the receiving end of undeserved love? I was still running from the vulnerable God whose love I'd refused, the God people hurt as I'd hurt Miss White. Miss White forgave me, I believe, just as Santa Claus forgives bad children by bringing them presents anyway, and just as God, I'd heard, forgives people. The trouble was, I hadn't forgiven myself. I was still brooding over it all when I was thirty.

I began roughing out a draft of the incidents. First I'd tell the Santa Claus story, then the magnifying glass story; at the end I'd swiftly make the point, that we are still running from God's love, God's "eye." As I write this now, at forty, it's still hard to see which is worse: God's eye which sees your sins (all the times you've hurt people), or God's eye which seeks you out with its forgiveness, when you haven't forgiven yourself.

The first draft started abstractly: "Like everyone in his right mind, I feared Santa Claus. Maybe this is the beginning of every child's wisdom. Of course I thought he was God. He was unseen but real and somehow omnipresent." . . .

Reading this over I saw how appallingly boring it was. Who would want to read something that practically begins with the word "omnipresent"? Who would want to read something so vague and drippy it uses the word "somehow"? Where are we, anyhow? What, if anything, is happening? So I chucked all this and began with the scene: it's Christmas eve, some time ago, in a living room.

Even so, my description of this scene wandered off the point right away. In the second draft there was extraneous speculation about what restaurant the family might have gone to that night. There was extraneous description of how my lined coat felt on my bare arms on the drive home from the restaurant. That's the trouble with writing about your life: you keep babbling because you're so marvelously interested. You're always tempted to indulge yourself. The babbling does no real harm if you have sense enough to drag yourself back on course from time to time, and, more important, if you have sense enough to recognize and cut out all the babble before you let anyone read the thing.

In the course of the second or third draft I'd gotten interested not only in my own irrelevant memories, but also in an abstract side issue: how a child shapes behavior. I went on for a page about this. Again I saw how boring readers would find it; it had little to do with the matter at hand, which was an image: Santa Claus in the doorway. I tossed this page and later used the ideas in another essay.

Almost everything I cut from the early drafts was too abstract. You don't say, I was eagerly awaiting Santa Claus. You say, We'd set out ginger ale and cookies. When you're telling any kind of story, every sentence should be full of things to see, hear, smell, or touch.

It's important to cut out weak parts; it's even more important to strengthen strong parts. I revised to strengthen the central image. Images are more powerful than ideas. They stick in the imagination. If they are good symbolic images, they carry ideas with them; they embody and vivify ideas.

The essay describes Santa Claus in the doorway twice. First it gives the setting and lays out the picture plainly: Santa Claus was looming in the doorway and looking around for me. Then it explains why I was afraid of Santa Claus. Then it describes Santa Claus again (once more with feeling), hoping that the second time the same image would resound with multiple meanings: Santa Claus is like the omnipotent God we fear as we fear the cold abyss of eternal night, etc. To make an occasion for describing it twice, I had the narrator take another look at Santa Claus from upstairs.

This business of describing something more than once is effective. I learned it from Faulkner. You give the picture, stop the action and fill in some background which invests the picture with a wealth of feeling and meaning, and then give the picture again. If I were writing this piece now, I'd go over it a third time, bringing out the contrast between the two worlds—the cold eternal night, and the warm bright room (like a stable with a manger) here on earth where loving people love imperfectly and Christmases are not always merry. There's a lot of meaning packed too tightly here; I didn't really develop it all.

The details of the second description suggest various aspects of the idea: Santa Claus stood in the doorway with night over his shoulder, letting in all the cold air of the sky; Santa Claus monstrous and bright, powerless, ringing a loud bell and repeating Merry Christmas, Merry Christmas. I wanted the image to be paradoxical, nagging unresolved in the mind. "Bright" is usually a positive word, and ringing bells are usually cheerful things; together they set up a weird tension (a *frisson*) with "monstrous"—which in turn usually doesn't go with "powerless." Good description doesn't moronically insist on one simple mood—the lyric flowery meadow, the terrifying avalanche. Interesting feelings are complex and contradictory; I try to evoke complex feelings by shading things with their opposites. (And of course good writing doesn't *describe* feelings at all; it evokes them in the reader by describing the observable world with vivid language.)

Miss White is an innocent. She gives cookies to a neighbor child; she enjoys fingerpainting. We hurt innocent people (or gods) because we are wrongly afraid they'll hurt us. I ran from Miss White as Santa Claus; I ran from her again when I fancied she'd burned me with her magnifying glass. In both cases the essay likens her to the omnipotent, angry God. But in both cases, it turns out, she is more like the innocent, vulnerable, forgiving God whose love we refuse—by crucifying Christ, you could say, or by hurting our innocent neighbor.

The essay draws parallels between Santa Claus and the omnipotent God through logic: He's an old man who knows when you've been bad or good. It draws parallels between Miss White and the omnipotent God through language: After describing the magnifying glass incident (with as many active verbs as I could muster), I skipped a few lines and used the same imagery to imagine God's burning me in hell. At its very end, the essay draws parallels between Miss White and the vulnerable God (of whom the familiar symbol is Christ) through the inner logic of imagery: So Santa Claus powerless in the doorway with night over his shoulder invokes (at least subconsciously) two other images: the infant Jesus in Bethlehem, and Christ crucified. Both are standard representations of love's vulnerability and ultimate triumph.

Note how remarkably less interesting all this is than the anecdotal essay itself. This is why no one reads literary criticism. This is also why writers are well advised to keep mum about what they've written. If they can please us with vivid little bits of story, who cares what weird ideas drove them to their typewriters in the first place?

The essay's last paragraph is crucial. It brings it all together nicely: So once in Israel love came to us incarnate, stood in the doorway between two worlds, and we were all afraid. The omnipotent God/Santa Claus becomes the vulnerable Christ/Miss White, the neighbor whom I failed to love. The fearful little girl on Christmas eve becomes by implication the loud crowd on Good Friday crying "crucify him." And the adult who's writing the essay converges on past themes and writes in the present: I am still running.

But its tone is worrisome. It suddenly sounds too solemn; it sounds preachy and pious. It still bothers me. It sounds like an evangelist making a pitch: "You ever feel this way? You need Jesus Christ."

I thought a little intellectual Christianity wouldn't hurt a magazine's Christmas issue—but that's no excuse. More profoundly I hoped that the phrase "stood in the doorway between two worlds" would bring it all down to earth, and back to the essay's narrative surface. Right then, I fondly hoped, the reader would see in a flash how well the essay works; the metaphor holds. The reader would be so pleased, so positively stunned, he'd forgive the pompous tone of "So once in Israel love came to us incarnate." I hoped he'd forgive it—but now, ten years later, I don't really think it's forgiveable.

Annie Dillard, Easter Week, 1984

EDWARD RIVERA
First Communion

> *Rivera was born in Puerto Rico and raised in Spanish Harlem. He published his autobiographical* Family Installments; Memories of Growing Up Hispanic *in 1982. As this excerpt shows, he has a marvelous sense of incongruity in detail and in dialogue. He also manages to convey a child's-eye view of events without sacrificing an adult perspective.*

I made it up to the Communion railing without tripping over myself. It was a long slow walk, halting half-steps all the way, as if we'd sprained our ankles to qualify for the You-carry-this-blanket. I hit a bump when I got to where the central aisle of the nave ran into another aisle called the "crossing" (all these symbols of what this House was all about didn't help out my nerves). This happened a few feet from the railing, but it wasn't all my fault; I knew a loose floorboard when I stepped on one, even if it was hidden by a Catholic rug with symbolic designs all over it. A couple of other first-time receivers ahead of me had also stepped on it and had given a start as if the rug had teeth in it. It was like a trap set there to catch daydreamers, or anyone who'd cursed before receiving, or held back a couple of "grievous" sins at Confession, cold-feet types who'd go through life lying to Fathers Confessor about how many pennies they'd really stolen from their mothers, while the poor woman was tied up in the kitchen, tending the pot of this and that with hacked codfish and oregano, unaware that she had given birth to a crook who was depleting the family's tight budget and stealing confiscated magnets from Sister's desk during lunch period: giving our people a bad name.

But I was doing it again, daydreaming. I had stopped when I got to the first line of pews at the crossing and waited there, inches from the trap, trying to make myself as stiff as possible so I wouldn't pee in my pants (we had rehearsed all this: "I don't want anyone passing water in his or her pants, whichever applies," Sister had told us during run-throughs), waiting for Sister to give me the go-ahead for the Host. You couldn't just walk up to the railing and kneel there with the others;

W

you had to wait until you were told. Sister had been very strict about that for weeks. "Remember," she had told us, "you're not going up to a cafeteria for a frankfurter. Our church is not a luncheonette and the Host is not a hot dog. So just watch your *deportment.*" (I wrote that new one down in my spelling notebook first chance I got, but I misspelled it as "department," and misused it for a long time.)

While I was waiting there, turning to stone, or salt, or liquid, someone grabbed my arm, the same spot where Sister had pinched it. It was still sore. "Don't move." It was her voice again, down low. It sounded like something out of a cowboy movie I'd seen with Papi. "Okay, Malánguezzz, don't move. This is a chodown."

She was only getting me ready for the walk to the railing. She held me there in a tight grip for about ten seconds, and as soon as one of the kneeling receivers, looking no better than before, had made a stiff about-face and started solemnly back to his pew with the Host in his mouth, Sister pointed a finger at the opening and told me to go get It, before one of Sister Haughney's girls beat me to It. Then she let go my arm, and it was as if she had pressed a button or released a spring I·didn't know I had: I took off for that railing like a hungry dog tearing ass for a bowl of chow. But there was a lot of "chow" for everyone. Father Rooney's ciborium was stacked, and there was plenty more Host back in the tabernacle. One of the assisting priests, Father Mooney, had already replaced Father Rooney's empty ciborium with a fresh ciborium, and was standing by in front of the altar, waiting for another nod from the railing.

"Walk, Ssantoss Malánguezzz, don't run!" Sister hizzed behind me. Too late. I was already kneeling at the railing, hands joined under my chin. She'd get me tomorrow morning. Maybe in the auditorium. Special assembly for the execution. Organ music and chorus.

And then Father Rooney and his other assistant were on top of me with the ciborium. The assistant stuck a golden plate with a handle under my chin—a paten, it was called, a metallic bib just in case. Father Rooney was holding the Host between thumb and index and wagging It in front of my mouth, which suddenly wouldn't open. Lockjaw from fright. My punishment for cursing in church.

"Open your mouth, young man," Father Rooney suggested. We hadn't rehearsed this part.

I used both hands to do it: one hand under my nose, the other pushing down on my chin. But then my tongue wouldn't come out for the presence. The spit in my mouth had thickened and turned to glue, and my tongue was stuck to my palate.

"Stick out your tongue," the priest with the paten said.

I stuck two fingers in my mouth and unstuck my tongue.

"What's he doing, Matt?" Father Rooney asked his assistant.

"You got me, Mark. What are you doing, kid?"

"I am sorry, Father," I said. "The tongue got stuck to the—"

"Shh! You're not supposed to talk in here during Mass," the pastor said. He wasn't looking too happy.

"I am sorry, Father," I said automatically, trying to get the spit going again.

"Out with the tongue, son," Father Matt repeated. "Or leave the railing."

I closed my eyes and did as he said. Then Father Rooney delivered his Latin lines: "*Corpus Domini nostri Jesu Christi custodiat animam tuam,* etcetera. Amen." Father Matt had his paten under my chin—cold metal—and I felt a familiar warm dribble working its way down my thigh, spoiling my fresh pair of First Communion shorts. The whole place was looking on, except possibly Papi and Mami, who must have been staring down at their hands in embarrassment. Then the worst of all possible things happened: the Host broke in half on my nose. I still had my eyes shut, so I didn't see just how Father Rooney managed to do it but I could figure it out. I must have made him nervous, and instead of slapping It down on the tip of my tongue, he caught the tip of my nose, and the presence broke in two. One half stayed in Father Rooney's fingers, and the other floated past my tongue, bounced off the railing, missing Father Matt's paten altogether, and came to a stop on the symbol-crowded rug on their side of the railing, between Father Matt's shoes, which were barely visible under his alb, as Sister Felicia had called that fancy undergarment.

Both priests gasped at the same time and crossed themselves. Everyone in church, except for the sleeping winos in the back, must have done the same thing. Padilla's organ began playing *"En mi viejo San Juan,"* a golden oldie, probably to distract everyone from the horrible accident I'd just caused at the railing. And my bladder was having itself a time with my new shorts. Father Matt stooped quickly, with his paten held tight to his heart, and started looking for the half-Host. I remembered what Sister had said about "His body broken in pieces" is why something-something, and felt horrible. The people who had nailed Him to the Cross couldn't have felt worse afterwards than I did just then.

Father Matt was still down on his knees looking for It. He was getting warm. I could have told him, but I was afraid to open my mouth. He was saying something under his breath, and Father Rooney, all out of patience, said, "Just pick It up, Matt. We'll be here all day at this rate."

"Sorry, Mark," said Father Matt. "Here It is." He used his paten as a dust pan to scoop It up, nudging It with his index finger. It broke again during this delicate recovery, but that didn't matter. You could split It up into a couple of hundred pieces, and It was still one. That was part of the mystery behind It. The "accidents" were one thing, Sister had told us; the "essence" was something else. You couldn't violate *that*. She had told us about an egg named Humpty Dumpty to illustrate the difference between a "material" object, in this case a talking egg, and the mysterious "indivisible Host." Just the same I was having my doubts. One piece was in Father Rooney's chalice (he had slipped it back inside when no one was looking), and the other half was down there, getting scooped up by Father Matt; and I was having trouble understanding how both pieces were one and the same. Sister Felicia would tell me all about it first thing tomorrow morning, in front of everyone. I wanted to go back home. I wanted no part of this business; I was unfit, unworthy, un-everything, but I was frozen there on my knees, terrified.

Father Matt finally got back to his feet, the paten with the two extra pieces held against his chest, and the thumb and index finger of his other hand pinning Them down to prevent another accident. Then Father Rooney held out his ciborium, which looked like a fancy trophy to me—it had jewels in the middle and was made of gold, or something that resembled gold—and Father Matt nudged the two pieces into it. I thought Father Rooney was going to slap a fresh sample on my tongue, but he had nothing like that in mind. I didn't even get the three broken pieces. I had my tongue out again, but all I got was a piece of advice. "Go back to your pew, kid," he told me. "You're not ready to receive."

And Father Matt said, "Grow up, son. You're seven already." I was eight, already one year behind, and no end in sight. And then he turned to Father Rooney and said, in a whisper, "This whole neighborhood's going to the—"

But Father Rooney cut him short: "Not here, Matt. Later, in the rectory."

"You're the boss, Mark." And off they went to plant an intact presence on Grippe's tongue. The worst disgrace in my life to date; and once you started in with the disgraces, it was hard to stop. Some types couldn't do a thing right. They talked in church when they should have been praying in silence, they cursed before receiving, they didn't know their own neck size, or the size of their feet, and they conned their parents into paying for half their First Communion outfits, just to insult Sister. And now this. In public, too. Hundreds had seen it. Maybe a thousand. And my own parents sitting in the back, next to Saint Anthony and his lilies, pretending they didn't know who I was. At least I thought they were pretending. I wanted them to.

Sister Felicia helped me up to my feet and turned me around toward the pews. She walked back there with me, slowly, because my knees seemed to have run out of the oil that makes knees work and my shoes felt like something poured from cement. Heavy construction. She led me back to my pew by the arm she'd pinched, and as she was sitting me down she put her mouth to my ear and said, "Ssantoss Malánguezzz, you are a disgrace to our school," bearing down on "disgrace." "You are not fit for First Communion, and maybe never will be. We have a lot to discuss tomorrow morning."

I nodded; but did she think I was going to show up at school next morning? Even as I sat there in my wet shorts, my mind was out in Central Park playing hooky next day. They were going to get me anyway, day after next, no way out of it; but in the meantime I thought I was entitled to a day of rest and I was going to take it. Maybe they'd send me to P.S. Genghis Khan, where I'd have no trouble blending in with the "barbarians," which might not be a bad idea.

Papi and Mami didn't bring it up on the way home—we left in a hurry—or in the house, where they insisted I sit down to eat after I changed out of my outfit, washed the pee off my thighs, and changed into normal clothes and sneakers.

Menu: Fricasseed chicken (boneless), saffron rice, a hot loaf of unconsecrated garlic bread, a bottle of grape juice (full strength), and Humpty Dumpty egg custard. Not exactly my first post-Communion meal, but no reason to throw it out, either. Mami reminded me that in the world at large a lot of people were going hungry right now. I knew she'd say that.

"You was nervous, Santos," Papi said in English while we were living it up in the dining room. I'd been expecting that one too. But he wasn't going to preach at me. "Next time," he added in Spanish, "no more accidents, okay?"

"Okay, Papi." But didn't he know it wasn't up to me?

QUESTIONS

1. How many sentence fragments can you find in this piece? Are they justified? (That is, do they work?) If not, why not? If so, how so?

2. How would you characterize the dialogue between the priests? What does this dialogue contribute to this essay?

3. Diction. Word choice. Why does Rivera say "the *Host* broke in half on my nose" and "the *presence* broke in two"? What other words could he have used? Do they work as well?

4. Rivera points out that the ciborium looked to him like a fancy trophy. How is this simile both inappropriate and appropriate?

SUGGESTED ACTIVITIES

1. Write of a childhood episode that proved particularly embarrassing to you.

2. Write of a childhood accomplishment—a success story.

3. Read the two to a group of classmates. Listen to their two stories. You probably find the stories of failure and catastrophe more interesting than the stories of success. Discuss the reasons for this. If there are exceptions, analyze them.

MAXINE HONG KINGSTON

Going to the Drugstore

A Chinese-American from California, Kingston has taught English and math in high school and creative writing in college. Her first book, The Woman Warrior: Memories of a Girlhood Among Ghosts *(1975) won the National Book Critics Circle Award. Her second book,* Chinese Men *(1980), was also well received. The following excerpt from her first book, shows how some divides are impassable and how we can sympathize with persons on both sides, even as they are opposed to each other.*

We were working at the laundry when a delivery boy came from the Rexall drugstore around the corner. He had a pale blue box of pills, but nobody was sick. Reading the label we saw that it belonged to another Chinese family, Crazy Mary's family. "Not ours," said my father. He pointed out the name to the Delivery Ghost, who took the pills back. My mother muttered for an hour, and then her anger boiled over. "That ghost! That dead ghost! How dare he come to the wrong house?" She could not concentrate on her marking and pressing. "A mistake! Huh!" I was getting angry myself. She fumed. She made her press crash and hiss. "Revenge. We've got to avenge this wrong on our future, on our health, and on our lives. Nobody's going to sicken my children and get away with it." We brothers and sisters did not look at one another. She would do something awful, something embarrassing. She'd already been hinting that during the next eclipse we slam pot lids together to scare the frog from swallowing the moon. (The word for "eclipse" is *frog-swallowing-the-moon*). When we had not banged lids at the last eclipse and the shadow kept receding anyway, she'd said, "The villagers must be banging and clanging very loudly back home in China."

("On the other side of the world, they aren't having an eclipse, Mama. That's just a shadow the earth makes when it comes between the moon and the sun."

"You're always believing what those Ghost Teachers tell you. Look at the size of the jaws!")

"Aha!" she yelled. "You! The biggest." She was pointing at me. "You go to the drugstore."

"What do you want me to buy, Mother?" I said.

"Buy nothing. Don't bring one cent. Go and make them stop the curse."

"I don't want to go. I don't know how to do that. There are no such things as curses. They'll think I'm crazy."

"If you don't go, I'm holding you responsible for bringing a plague on this family."

"What am I supposed to do when I get there?" I said, sullen, trapped. "Do I say, 'Your delivery boy made a wrong delivery'?"

"They know he made a wrong delivery. I want you to make them rectify their crime."

I felt sick already. She'd make me swing stinky censers around the counter, at the druggist, at the customers. Throw dog blood on the druggist. I couldn't stand her plans.

"You get reparation candy," she said. "You say, 'You have tainted my house with sick medicine and must remove the curse with sweetness.' He'll understand."

"He didn't do it on purpose. And no, he won't, Mother. They don't understand stuff like that. I won't be able to say it right. He'll call us beggars."

"You just translate." She searched me to make sure I wasn't hiding any money. I was sneaky and bad enough to buy the candy and come back pretending it was a free gift.

"Mymotherseztagimmesomecandy," I said to the druggist. Be cute and small. No one hurts the cute and small.

"What? Speak up. Speak English," he said, big in his white druggist coat.

"Tatatagimme somecandy."

The druggist leaned way over the counter and frowned. "Some free candy," I said. "Sample candy."

"We don't give sample candy, young lady," he said.

"My mother said you have to give us candy. She said that is the way the Chinese do it."

"What?"

"That is the way the Chinese do it."

"Do what?"

"Do things." I felt the weight and immensity of things impossible to explain to the druggist.

"Can I give you some money?" he asked.

"No, we want candy."

He reached into a jar and gave me a handful of lollipops. He gave us candy all year round, year after year, every time we went into the drugstore. When different druggists or clerks waited on us, they also gave us candy. They had talked us over. They gave us Halloween candy in December, Christmas candy around Valentine's day, candy hearts at Easter, and Easter eggs at Halloween. "See?" said our mother. "They understand. You kids just aren't very brave." But I knew they did not understand. They thought we were beggars without a home who lived in back of the laundry. They felt sorry for us. I did not eat their candy. I did not go inside the drugstore or walk past it unless my parents forced me to. Whenever we had a prescription filled, the druggist put candy in the medicine bag. This is what Chinese druggists normally do, except they give raisins. My mother thought she taught the Druggist Ghosts a lesson in good manners (which is the same word as "traditions").

QUESTIONS

1. The paragraph beginning "Mymotherseztagimmesomecandy" has no transition from the preceding paragraph. Why does Kingston provide no transition? Does the absence hurt or help? How? Why?

2. Why didn't Kingston demand the candy as her mother ordered? Should she have? Why? Why not?

3. How do you respond to Kingston's mother?

SUGGESTED ACTIVITIES

1. Write about a time when one or both of your parents embarrassed you.

2. To be fair, write about a time when you embarrassed your parents.

CURTIS K. STADTFELD

Trapping Days

Stadtfeld grew up on a family farm in central Michigan, a childhood he memorialized in From the Land and Back *(1973). He has published a book on the white-tailed deer and written numerous magazine articles, one of which, "Cheap Chemicals and Dumb Luck," won the National Magazine Award for excellence in reporting. He has also been a reporter for the St. Louis Post-Dispatch, has single-handedly run a small-town weekly newspaper and has taught journalism at the college level. In the following essay Stadtfeld shows how honest, unapologetic confession wins the readers' immediate sympathy.*

Muskrat pelts were worth three or four dollars in the late 1940s, a practical fortune for a farmboy—enough money to set him multiplying it and dreaming. There simply was no real money. Even in the relative prosperity of the war years, income had not reached past three or four thousand dollars a year for us, and there was a long list of hungry needs lingering from the depression, snapping away every scrap of cash to repay an ancient debt, replace an old piece of furniture or machinery, or buy a bracelet for one of the girls who had never had one.

There was no money yet for a speedometer for a boy's bike, or a Gene Autry shirt, or a compass or telescope or any of the other useless things that a boy needs with such desperation when he is twelve or so.

Thus, the lure of the muskrat skins. A neighbor trapped. Each morning, in that part of the winter that represented trapping season, he would be up before dawn to run his trapline. Later in the day, or on a Saturday when I saw him, he would have a skin or two or three, and he would sell them—I have forgotten precisely how he marketed them—and there was money in his pocket.

So I coaxed from him the loan of several traps—half a dozen or so of his oldest ones, borrowed against the hope of a few catches so that I could buy new ones or those old ones from him. He promised to lend me skin-stretchers for anything I caught. I was in business.

They were small, single-spring traps. Set, the jaws made a little round opening five or six inches across, the size of a small plate or a saucer. The spring was a strap of steel in a V-shape, and the trap was set by squeezing the spring until the jaws lay flat and then fixing it open with a little trigger in the middle, with a flat trigger pad the size of a dog's paw.

They were not, by trappers' standards, very big traps or very strong ones. Yet they had that cold lethal strength inherent in every trap; that impersonal strength born of its function, which is to intrude death into the circle of nature.

Each trap had a length of chain to hold it to a stake so that if an animal sprung it he could not flee with the trap, but would be there when the trapper came.

My friend showed me all about the traps—how to set them so that I did not catch my hand, how to drive the stake to keep them fast, and he reminded me to carry a .22 rifle along, so that I could kill anything I found in the trap before taking it out.

What he did not tell me, for some reason that does not come down through the years, is that there was not the slightest chance that I would ever catch a muskrat, for there were simply none on our farm. He had a stream that wandered across his place; there was a lake at the back of his farm, and a big swamp, and I think he cut through to a neighbor's farm where another small river swung through the woods. It was not rich trapping but it brought him a regular catch, if a small one.

I had none of those things, and not the knowledge to know it. So I took my pitiful little string of traps out, and set some at the edge of a swamp which never saw a muskrat, others in the edge of the woods where I knew there were deer, and took to reading the Sears, Roebuck catalog for ways to spend the money that would soon be pouring in.

It meant getting up even earlier, walking back the half-mile to the swamp and the edge of the wood in the earliest half-light of winter dawn, running the line before it was time to do the milking and get to school. Days went by without a catch.

Then one morning, snug in long white underwear that doubtless smelled a little of several days' wearing, feet firm in the Wolverine work shoes that were the standard uniform of farmboys in that region, warm in some kind of plaid coat, toting the .22, I jogged back the lane to check the trapline, still too silly or too stubborn to know that there would never be a marketable pelt in any of those traps.

It was in the second trap. In the part light, I could see at first only that there was something. Beaver? Mink? Otter? I was reading James

Oliver Curwood and Zane Grey and Jack London in those days. As I approached the trap, reality approached me and I thought for a moment it was a skunk.

It was my big black-and-white tomcat, fixed there with one back foot forever in the trap, and he stood rigid as he recognized me. We had thought we were friends, but an eon separated us suddenly, for he had been caught in the middle of his other life.

He was not locked in the house at night, but came in if he chose or spent the night in the barn among the warm hay and the cattle, or about his own business. As long as he kept the mice from the mow, we did not bother him about his private life.

This night, he had slipped back the lane in the dark, seeking bigger game than the harried bits of fur that skulked around the granary. Perhaps he had a rabbit in mind, or a pheasant. Or simply other company.

Even, as a thoughtful cat, he may have gone back into the woods at night to sit by a brush and remember the world as it was a few thousand years ago when his ancestors were young, and their teeth were longer and the patches of ice were still nearby and the animals they hunted had longer fur. Perhaps the past came to him, alone in the woods, and gave him dreams to last the day by the wood stove in the living room where he twitched a little as he napped. Who knows, after all, what a cat remembers?

Whatever his mission, I had caught him at it, and had snapped the bonds that held us together. No longer friend with a warm hand and milk, I was hunter, and I had caught him, and he stood there glaring at me across several thousand years.

He could not bridge the gap of those years, and I could not forget them. Each time I tried to reach out and press the spring to free him, he tried to attack me. This was not the playful cuff that he offered in the living room; he understood that the game was over. So I could not set him free from his trap.

Nor could I set him free from his torment; each time I raised the rifle to aim, I remembered the nights he had slept on the foot of my bed, or dozed on my lap, played with a tag of string or begged for milk. I could not bring myself to shoot him.

When it became clear that there was nothing I could do, I quit my trap run for the day, hurried back to the barn for the milking, breakfasted, and caught the school bus. But all day, that black-and-white face, expressionless, leering across the ages, hung between me and the classroom.

It was not a problem that seemed sharable. I was sure that either of my elder brothers would simply shoot the cat—they seemed more direct than I in things like that. I feared my father's rage if he discovered my mistake. So I could not free the cat, could not kill him, could not even seek help.

I went back that night before chore time and gathered up my traps. I strung them all on a hook, hanging them from the rings at the end of the chains where the stakes had held them to the ground. I took them back to the friend, thanked him for the use of them, and told him that I guessed we didn't have any muskrats on our farm.

He asked me about the missing trap and I said I simply couldn't find it. Somehow, in the foolishness of my youth, I had forgotten where I had put it. He laughed and said that sometimes happened, a man would forget where he put a trap. It wasn't worth much anyway, he said, and I could pay him for it when I got the money.

I never went back to the other trap. I never mentioned it to anyone. The cat came up missing, and we got another one from somewhere, and everyone else forgot the old black-and-white tom. I do not know what finally released him. But I have never set another steel trap for a living thing.

QUESTIONS

1. Why does Stadtfeld mention that he has forgotten how his neighbor marketed his skins? (Review *anticipation* in the Rhetoric.)

2. Why does Stadtfeld mention the authors he had been reading at the time he was trapping?

3. How could Stadtfeld's cat glare at him "across several thousand years"? (Review *metaphor*).

4. How do you feel about what Stadtfeld did and didn't do? How do you feel about Stadtfeld the twelve-year-old? How do you feel about Stadtfeld the writer? What kind of relationship do you find between disapproval and sympathy?

SUGGESTED ACTIVITIES

1. Write about something you once did or didn't do (or both) that you now disapprove of. Try to justify your behavior.

2. Write about it again, condemning your behavior.

3. Write about it again, only this time focus on *explaining* your behavior without apology or blame.

4. Review *honesty* in Chapter IV.

POSTSCRIPT

Commentary on *Trapping Days*

The thing that strikes me most about "Trapping Days" some years after writing it is that it illustrates the most important thing I know about writing: Writing is not a game played with words; writing is having interesting thoughts or observations, and finding ways to present them with force and clarity.

I couldn't have written "Trapping Days" at the time of the experience, not because I didn't have the words—there isn't a word in the story that I didn't know at that age—but because I didn't understand the experience. I was moved by it at the time—ashamed and saddened—but most of my reaction came from emotions arising from causes I did not understand.

Later, reading, studying, thinking, I saw some of the differences between men and animals, especially partly domesticated animals like cats. The center of this essay deals with that difference, with how the game of domesticity had been revealed as a fraud, how we were separated, in the end, that soft fierce old cat and I, by forces of nature neither of us could control. I was surely not precocious enough to understand that at 12 or 14.

All good writing comes from good thinking. In my case, good thinking follows hard study and long reflection; intuition is the result of hard work. The prose follows, and is fairly easy by comparison.

Curtis K. Stadtfeld

RUSHWORTH M. KIDDER

Depths on the Surface

*A former professor of English in Kansas and now a feature editor of
The Christian Science Monitor, Kidder has written critical books on
the poets Dylan Thomas and e. e. cummings. As a columnist he
writes about the Boston area and current issues. As the following
essay demonstrates, with attention to detail and diction—and with
persistent questioning—it is possible to define a deep beauty in the
commonplace.*

Ice. It hung in spikes from the eaves. It gathered in great cobbled
chunks in the downspouts. It grew in frosted thickets inside the storm
windows, and rattled like broken bottles along the sidewalks, and lay
in shattered panes over the places where puddles used to be. In the
rural Massachusetts winters of my youth, it was everywhere.

But most of all, it turned an otherwise indifferent pond in the local
woods into a hockey rink. Many a Saturday I gathered up my thickest
socks, scrounged among mittens and caps for a puck, and took my
tape-wrapped stick from the garage where it leaned incongruously
among a summer stack of rakes and spades. Then I would set off for
the mile-long trudge through the woods, the black skates with toes
like baseballs strung over my shoulder.

I was never very good at hockey. Nor were my friends. Frankly, we
never had much chance to practice: we spent most of our time shov-
elling snow off the make-shift rink. After that, we were too tired to
play. So we'd sit on the mounds we'd made and talk, our thick seaters
warm from exertion and the wan winter sun.

That of course, is the problem with New England ice: a lot of the
time there's snow. So the skates, exuding an air of hurt rebuke like
dogs you have forgotten to feed, hang in a thousand woodsheds and
chimney corners for weeks on end, awaiting that rare season when
the freeze comes smoothly across a still night and the cold stands
snowless for days.

When that happened, of course, we looked to greater things than
our two-bit makeshift rink. I had friends who lived in a village north
of town near a mile-long pond. They kept close watch on it. When
enough below-zero days had passed, and enough fishermen had been
seen strolling across its surface, and enough fathers had looked down
the fishing-holes and nodded approvingly at the thickness of the ice,
the word went around: there would be a party on Saturday night,
down by the church where the road swings close to the shore.

And so we would gather in the cracking cold, with the moon hung like a great lemon ice over the trees, so close you wanted to eat it. Someone would build a fire far out from the shore, dragging out tree trunks to circle it. There we would bend into agonizing shapes, tugging our rebellious laces to tightness—until at last we stumbled into motion, spreading ourselves outwards from the fire into our own individual worlds while the ice, like a gruff old patriarch proud of his grandchildren, grumbled beneath us. It was entirely exhilarating. And yet it was somehow so wholly commonplace. I remember thinking, even then, how much I delighted in the experience, yet how little I knew why.

I had occasion to think on these things again recently when, as though flung back twenty winters, I found myself once more on skates. The lake—this time in Maine—was frozen under a snowless afternoon. Again we spread out, putting a quarter of a mile between us with a few minute's effort. Again the ice grumbled, and the great ragged cracks gaped harmlessly beneath our blades. And again, by an entirely natural *legerdemain*, the impassable depth became an easily-charted land.

And as we skated that day, I began to grasp what it was that for so many years had appealed to me. It was not just that, like the skaters in a Breugel painting or a Currier and Ives print, we were carrying forward a tradition of almost classic purity, one that had changed hardly at all over the years. Nor was it simply that we were conquering the winter, turning to our advantage the dragon that defends New England from those who care only for warmth. It was more. We were, however accidently, exploring the unknown.

For a frozen lake is always, in some ways, unknown. Map it though we might, it will never again be the same. This black patch of ice over here, that rough and rippled section over there—under the different winds of another year, they will not set up that way again. A tract of unaccustomed territory, it is the creation of a particular year. Like the various people on it—the skaters, the few fishermen, the occasional walker with dogs—its various years have common features of islands and shorelines. Yet each year, like faces and fingerprints, the details are wholly unique.

How does that great uniqueness shape itself? Why does it happen that one year the ice is smooth just by the shore and rippled farther out, when the next year reverses the pattern? Why should it be that, far away from any obstacles to bend the wind, a mirror-smooth mid-lake patch sits right beside a swirled and rippled washboard surface? Why does ice shade so variously from deep black to opaque white?

I haven't any answers. Nor do I mean to sound mystical, delighting in ignorance for its own sake. I find it, instead, rather humbling. I'm sure there is a science governing these effects, and that if we knew it we could explain—perhaps even predict—the entire topography of each winter's lake. But the fact is that, as in more things than we care to admit, we don't know the underlying laws.

And therein, perhaps, lies a message for those of us who mistakenly imagine that man has got his vision of nature all tidy and under control. We need not look upon the baffled rings of Saturn or the undersea mysteries of the Cayman Trench to sense the limits of our comprehension. Even the ice throws up its constant queries. It reminds us that we are not as profound as we think, that our so-called laws have hardly touched the depth of nature's grain, that we are skating on the surface of our ignorance.

To realize that is to sense the promise of a still-uncaptured world. It is to delight in the recollection of our own meekness, refreshed by the still-unfathomed grandeur of the commonplace.

QUESTIONS

1. Kidder begins the second paragraph with the phrase, "But most of all." What does he mean by that?

2. What does Kidder mean by saying that skating on a pond "was entirely exhilarating"?

3. How does the eighth paragraph move the essay forward?

4. What basic question does Kidder's essay answer? In fact, does Kidder's essay answer it? If so, how? If not, why?

SUGGESTED ACTIVITIES

1. Locate the different ways and places that Kidder combines the known and the unknown.

2. Write an essay involving a time you revisited a scene or activity of your childhood. Compare and contrast the experiences. Like Kidder, try to explain the significance of the scene or activity in retrospect.

POSTSCRIPT

Commentary on *Depths on the Surface*

It's become commonplace, these days, to say that writing is a process of discovery. I'd love to think of some clever way to deny that assertion, to set myself apart from the crowd by some breathtaking feat of logic. But the fact is that it's true. With apologies to Miss Halpin (who taught us in ninth grade, very wisely, how to make outlines before we wrote anything), I confess that I've never been sure where I was headed when I sat down to write.

So I've usually been suspicious (and occasionally envious) of those who attach prepositions to the verb *to write*—who assert that they're going to write something *up*, or *out*, or *down*, as though the thing to be written had a life of its own prior to the writing, and as though one had only to copy out the verbal equivalent of some mental construction. I think of writing, instead, largely as revelation: it reveals its essence in its practice. Philosophically, perhaps, an essay contains its end in its beginning and is all of a piece before it ever gets written. But I've never been smart enough to think it all out ahead of time, nor prescient enough to foreknow the revelation. So I've always had to wait and see what would happen as the words begin forming themselves on the page.

That's what happened in "Depths on the Surface." Not that it happened blindly—far from it. Before I ever sat down I had assembled a battery of ideas in my head, had turned them over this way and that to find their best sides, had mixed and matched them to get their proper order. I knew that I wanted to begin, imagistically, with the ice: it's a fascinating symbol, and it seemed best to let the word stand alone in the first sentence. I knew, too, that I wanted to build, thematically, upon a boyhood experience: all of us were young once, and somehow the universality and unpretentiousness of that common experience both engages the reader and fends off the demons of pedantry. And I wanted to link image and theme together in the narration of a recent experience on the lake in Maine one winter afternoon.

Formula writing? Sure, to some extent. A lot of my essays intertwine a dominant image with a childhood recollection updated by a recent experience. But there is an element of the formulaic in all good writing. And there's a vast body of literary criticism devoted to discovering the formulae that allowed Shakespeare, Keats, Hopkins, Yeats, or

Cummings to produce their finest works. All of them depended, again and again, on literary structures, syntactical habits, and patterns of logic that they knew were successful. And all of them must have discovered, in writing each work, things they never foresaw. That's what the formula does: it keeps the piece going until the writer discovers what the work is *really* about.

So I launch out into an essay according to some rough guidelines that, having worked in the past, might help again. For some two-thirds of the piece, they stay in place. Then I find myself having to ask larger and larger questions, probing for the deep significance of the piece. That confluence of image and theme has become its own river, bearing the essay toward its own logical conclusion. The landscape along the shore takes on a new look—familiar in general characteristics but utterly novel in detail, like villages you've never visited in a countryside you've grown up in. And that's when the third element—the genuine substance of the piece—comes into view.

"Depths on the Surface," for example, began as an explanation of the unfamiliarity of a frozen lake. Only in the writing did the more substantial meaning appear. Only then did it become clear that the entire experience was itself a metaphor for our lack of deep understanding and our need for intellectual humility. Only then did I see that I was writing *about the art of writing*. And only then did I find the phrase that ends the essay and see that we can actually be *refreshed*—as all discoveries are refreshing—by "the still-unfathomed grandeur of the commonplace."

That last phrase, to me, remains the essence of this essay. I'm afraid I didn't realize it until it appeared on the page; but having written it, I felt at once how right it was. For if the personal essay has a defining characteristic, it is that it probes the commonplace—showing the vast significance that ordinary events and details have when we bother to think about them.

Which, in the end, is why I don't mind accepting the commonplace that writing is a process of discovery. Were it otherwise, which of us could ever shoulder the responsibility of inventing meaningful things to say?

Rushworth M. Kidder

II

Reflections on Nature

HENRY BESTON
The Headlong Wave

An editor of The Living Age, *Beston lived a good deal of his life at Cape Cod and Maine where he wrote fairy tales and such nature books as* The Outermost House *(1928),* Herbs and the Earth *(1935), and* White Pine and Blue Water *(1950). In this essay Beston proves that the best way to show that you love something is not to insist that you do but to describe it in careful (care-full) loving detail.*

This morning I am going to try my hand at something that I do not recall ever having encountered either in a periodical or in a book, namely, a chapter on the ways, the forms, and the sounds of ocean near a beach. Friends are forever asking me about the surf on the great beach and if I am not sometimes troubled or haunted by its sound. To this I reply that I have grown unconscious of the roar, and though it sounds all day long in my waking ears, and all night long in my sleeping ones, my ears seldom send on the long tumult to the mind. I hear the roar the instant I wake in the morning and return to consciousness, I listen to it a while consciously, and then accept it and forget it; I hear it during the day only when I stop again to listen, or when some change in the nature of the sound breaks through my acceptance of it to my curiosity.

They say here that great waves reach this coast in threes. Three great waves, then an indeterminate run of lesser rhythms, then three great waves again. On Celtic coasts it is the seventh wave that is seen

coming like a king out of the grey, cold sea. The Cape tradition, however, is no half-real, half-mystical fancy, but the truth itself. Great
waves do indeed approach this beach by threes. Again and again have
I watched three giants roll in one after the other out of the Atlantic,
cross the outer bar, break, form again, and follow each other in to
fulfilment and destruction on this solitary beach. Coast guard crews
are all well aware of this triple rhythm and take advantage of the lull
that follows the last wave to launch their boats.

It is true that there are single giants as well. I have been roused by
them in the night. Waked by their tremendous and unexpected crash,
I have sometimes heard the last of the heavy overspill, sometimes only
the loud, withdrawing roar. After the roar came a briefest pause, and
after the pause the return of ocean to the night's long cadences. Such
solitary titans, flinging their green tons down upon a quiet world,
shake beach and dune. Late one September night, as I sat reading,
the very father of all waves must have flung himself down before the
house, for the quiet of the night was suddenly overturned by a gigantic,
tumbling crash and an earthquake rumbling; the beach trembled
beneath the avalanche, the dune shook, and my house so shook in its
dune that the flame of a lamp quivered and pictures jarred on the
wall.

The three great elemental sounds in nature are the sound of rain,
the sound of wind in a primeval wood, and the sound of outer ocean
on a beach. I have heard them all, and of the three elemental voices,
that of ocean is the most awesome, beautiful, and varied. For it is a
mistake to talk of the monotone of ocean or of the monotonous nature
of its sound. The sea has many voices. Listen to the surf, really lend
it your ears, and you will hear in it a world of sounds: hollow boomings
and heavy roarings, great watery tumblings and tramplings, long hissing seethes, sharp, rifle-shot reports, splashes, whispers, the grinding
undertone of stones, and sometimes vocal sounds that might be the
half-heard talk of people in the sea. And not only is the great sound
varied in the manner of its making, it is also constantly changing its
tempo, its pitch, its accent, and its rhythm, being now loud and thundering, now almost placid, now furious, now grave and solemn-slow,
now a simple measure, now a rhythm monstrous with a sense of
purpose and elemental will.

Every mood of the wind, every change in the day's weather, every
phase of the tide—all these have subtle sea musics all their own. Surf
of the ebb, for instance, is one music, surf of the flood another, the
change in the two musics being most clearly marked during the first

hour of a rising tide. With the renewal of the tidal energy, the sound of the surf grows louder, the fury of battle returns to it as it turns again on the land, and beat and sound change with the renewal of the war.

Sound of surf in these autumnal dunes—the continuousness of it, sound of endless charging, endless incoming and gathering, endless fulfilment and dissolution, endless fecundity, and endless death. I have been trying to study out the mechanics of that mighty resonance. The dominant note is the great spilling crash made by each arriving wave. It may be hollow and booming, it may be heavy and churning, it may be a tumbling roar. The second fundamental sound is the wild seething cataract roar of the wave's dissolution and the rush of its foaming waters up the beach—this second sound *diminuendo*. The third fundamental sound is the endless dissolving hiss of the inmost slides of foam. The first two sounds reach the ear as a unisonance— the booming impact of the tons of water and the wild roar of the up-rush blending—and this mingled sound dissolves into the foam-bub-ble hissing of the third. Above the tumult, like birds, fly wisps of watery noise, splashes and counter splashes, whispers, seethings, slaps, and chucklings. An overtone sound of other breakers, mingled with a general rumbling, fells earth and sea and air.

Here do I pause to warn my reader that although I have recounted the history of a breaker—an ideal breaker—the surf process must be understood as mingled and continuous, waves hurrying after waves, overwhelming waves. Moreover, I have described the sound of a high surf in fair weather. A storm surf is mechanically the same thing, but it *grinds*, and this same long, sepulchral grinding—sound of utter terror to all mariners—is a development of the second fundamental sound; it is the cry of the breaker water roaring its way ashore and dragging at the sand. A strange underbody of sound when heard through the high, wild screaming of a gale.

Breaking waves that have to run up a steep tilt of the beach are often followed by a dragging, grinding sound—the note of the baffled water running downhill again to the sea. It is loudest when the tide is low and breakers are rolling beach stones up and down a slope of the lower beach.

I am, perhaps, most conscious of the sound of surf just after I have gone to bed. Even here I read myself to drowsiness, and, reading, I hear the cadenced trampling roar filling all the dark. So close is the Fo'castle to the ocean's edge that the rhythm of sound I hear oftenest in fair weather is not so much a general tumult as an endless arrival, overspill, and dissolution of separate great seas. Through the dark, mathematic square of the screened half window, I listen to the rushes and the bursts, the tramplings, and the long, intermingled thunderings, never wearying of the sonorous and universal sound.

Away from the beach, the various sounds of the surf melt into one great thundering symphonic roar. Autumnal nights in Eastham village are full of this ocean sound. The "summer people" have gone, the village rests and prepares for winter, lamps shine from kitchen windows, and from across the moors, the great levels of the marsh, and the bulwark of the dunes resounds the long wintry roaring of the sea. Listen to it a while, and it will seem but one remote and formidable sound; listen still longer and you will discern in it a symphony of breaker thunderings, an endless, distant, elemental cannonade. There is beauty in it, and ancient terror. I heard it last as I walked through the village on a starry October night; there was no wind, the leafless trees were still, all the village was abed, and the whole sombre world was awesome with the sound.

QUESTIONS

1. Why does Beston set upon the task he defines? What's the point? Why bother?

2. According to Beston, what are the three elemental sounds in nature? Do you agree? Do you think he is omitting any? Are there sounds not in nature that you regard as "elemental"? What is an "elemental" sound, anyway? Of what significance are such sounds? (To answer, imagine what life would be like without them.)

SUGGESTED ACTIVITIES

1. Think about the sounds that mean a lot—and I mean a lot—to you, that you would hate to live without or that you would give almost anything to live without. Write an essay about them, exploring and explaining their significance.

2. Try to *describe* some of those sounds, as Beston tries to describe the sound of the surf.

JOSEPH WOOD KRUTCH

What Are Flowers For?

Krutch came from Tennessee, taught drama and literature at Colum-bia University in New York City, then moved to Arizona where he became a naturalist and conservationist. He wrote many articles and books on literature, theater, nature, and values. He is best-known, perhaps, for The Modern Temper: A Study and a Confession *(1929) and* If You Don't Mind My Saying So: Essays on Man and Nature *(1964). In the following essay, Krutch not only explores the function of flowers but distinguishes between the concerns of naturalists and scientists.*

"Nature," said Sir Thomas Browne, "is the Art of God." And of all nature's works the most delicately perfect, as well as the most uni-versally admired, is the flower.

There are those who are indifferent to the sea or oppressed by the mountains, who find forests gloomy and animals repulsive. There are even those who say that they hate the country. But no one ever hated flowers, and no other beauty—not even woman—has been more often celebrated.

There is nothing to which poets have referred more frequently, and the poetry of everyday speech pays its own tribute in a score of familiar phrases: the flower of youth; the flower of chivalry; the flower of civ-ilization. Nothing else, either natural or manmade, seems to embody so completely or to symbolize so adequately that perfect beauty which, if the expression be permissible, flowers in the flower.

Grass and leaves are grateful to the eye. No other color is so restful as green. But how monotonous the earth would be if this green were not shattered again and again by the joyous exclamation of the flower! It seems to add just that touch of something more than the merely utilitarian which human beings need if they are to find life fully sat-isfactory. Flowers seem like a luxury that Nature has grown prosper-ous enough to afford.

The stern scientist will, of course, dismiss this last statement as an absurd fantasy. Flowers, he will insist, are strictly utilitarian—except, of course, in the case of those which man himself has perverted in cultivation. Flowers are the plants' organs of generation and their purpose is not to be beautiful, but to produce seeds with a maximum of efficiency. Yet, even the stern scientist will admit that Nature invented many remarkable devices before she hit upon anything at once so useful and so pleasing to the human eye.

It was—so he will tell us—a mere hundred million or so years ago that the very first flower opened its petals to the sun. And though that was a long time ago as we measure time, though ninety-nine million of those years were to pass before the first member of our own species was there to see a flower and to begin, no one knows how soon, his long love affair with it, still it was not long ago in the history of living things. Primitive green plants had already been thriving in the water for perhaps a billion years or even more. They had come out upon dry land many millions of years later, and the great forests that laid down the coal beds flourished at a time which antedates the first flowers by a longer stretch than that which separates the first flowers from us. Then, quite suddenly as such things go (so suddenly indeed that evolutionists are still puzzled by the phenomenon) the earth burst into bloom. Moreover, some of the earliest blossoms of which a record has been preserved in stone were already quite spectacular, and the late dinosaurs may have looked with dull eyes on the dogwood and the magnolia that their sluggish brains were no doubt incapable of admiring.

Having granted that much and instructed us thus far, the scientist will go on to say that the poets have, as usual, preferred their own silly fantasies to the truth and preferred them so persistently that it was not until about the time of the American Revolution, when mankind was already half a million years old at the very least, that he cared enough about facts to discover that the flower, like everything else in nature, is merely part of the struggle for survival. Thomas Gray could just possibly be forgiven for babbling about the flower that "wastes its fragrance on the desert air," because most of his contemporaries did not know that this fragrance was not wasted if it enticed the insects it was secreted to attract. But Wordsworth was only deceiving himself when he found in the meanest flower that blows "a thought too deep for tears," and as for Tennyson, who lived in one of the great ages of science, he ought to have been ashamed of himself to write anything so foolish as his apostrophe to the "Flower in the Crannied Wall":

> . . . if I could understand
> What you are, root and all, and all and all,
> I should know what God and man is.

The flower, the scientist will go on, was not invented (or rather did not mechanically invent itself) to please us. It flaunted its petals and spread its perfumes because the pollen wasted when distributed at random by the winds could be conserved if an insect could be tricked into carrying it directly from flower to flower. What we call a flower's beauty is merely, so he would conclude, a by-product and a human invention. The perfume isn't there to please us; it pleases us because it is there and we have been conditioned to it. A few flowers pollinated by flesh-eating flies have the odor of rotten meat. If that were usual, rather than unusual, we would by now love the stink.

In some of these contentions the scientist is right, or at least partly right, if you grant him his premise that man is a mere accident in nature, a freak to whose desires and needs Nature is serenely indifferent. But there are other ways of looking at the matter. Nature did create man and did create his unique qualities, among which is the ability to believe that beauty, even if useful, is also its own excuse for being. That conviction is, therefore, as natural as anything else—as natural, for instance, as the struggle for survival. Man is quite properly proud of the fact that he sometimes succeeds in transforming the sex impulse into something beautiful, and he finds some of what the anatomists call "secondary sex characteristics" very appealing in themselves. But the plants were millions of years ahead of him, and if flowers are merely the organs of reproduction, they are the most attractive of such in all animate nature.

In fact, it was in this light that the eighteenth century tended to see its new realization that plants also could "love." Aristotle, the master of those who knew, had proved by logic absolute and to his own satisfaction that the vegetable kingdom was sexless; in spite of the fact that the people of the Near East had known since Babylonian times that their female date palms would bear no fruit unless they were married to the male blossoms from another tree. But even Linnaeus, the prince of botanists, saw this as a reason for, not an argument against, the poetic interpretation of the flowers he so much loved. And he described them in quaintly rapturous terms: "The petals of the flower contribute nothing to generation but serve only as bridal beds, gloriously arranged by the great Creator, who has adorned with such noble bed curtains and perfumed them with so many sweet perfumes that the bridegroom may celebrate his nuptials with all the greater solemnity." The grandfather of Charles Darwin wrote an enormously popular poem called "The Loves of the Flowers" in which he included such lines as these (which, incidentally, seemed very embarrassing to his famous descendant):

With honey'd lips the enamoured woodbines meet,
Clasped with fond arms, and mix their kisses sweet.

If that is extravagant, it is hardly more so than the sternly scientific view which sees nothing but mechanics in the evolution of the flower.

Is it wholly fantastic to admit the possibility that Nature herself strove toward what we call beauty? Face to face with any one of the elaborate flowers which man's cultivation has had nothing to do with, it does not seem fantastic to me. We put survival first. But when we have a margin of safety left over, we expend it in the search for the beautiful. Who can say that Nature does not do the same?

To that botanist who said that "the purpose of a flower is to produce seeds" John Ruskin replied in high indignation that it was the other way around. The purpose of the seed is to produce a flower. To be able to see the way in which Ruskin was as right as the botanist is itself one of the flowers of human sensibility and perhaps man's greatest creative act. If Nature once interested herself in nothing but survival (and who knows that she did not care for anything else?) she at least created in time a creature who cared for many other things. There may still be something to learn from one of the first English naturalists who defended his science by insisting on man's duty to admire what he called The Works of God because "no creature in this sublunary world is capable of doing so, save man." Even if Nature was blind until man made his appearance, it is surely his duty not to blind himself in the interest of what he calls "sober fact." It will be a great pity if science in its search for one kind of knowledge should forget to exercise a peculiarly human capacity. Gardeners who believe the purpose of seed is to produce the flower should keep that capacity alive.

QUESTIONS

1. What is Krutch's thesis? Does he prove it to your satisfaction? If not, why not? Is he trying to prove it conclusively? What is the primary purpose of this essay—to explore, explain, or persuade? How can you tell?

2. If flowers are not intended for our pleasure—and Krutch does not think they are—how does he justify the poets he cites who say they are? What is his argument, his logic?

3. Is Krutch against science? If you think so, why do you think so? If you think not, why not?

SUGGESTED ACTIVITIES

1. Write an essay about what difference it makes, if any, whether flowers are utilitarian or aesthetic in value. That is, write about the dispute Krutch is concerned with, but in your own terms.

2. Write an essay on the utility (usefulness, value) of beauty. Focus on something that means much to you—music, art, drama (including television)—whatever you enjoy for the sake of enjoyment.

LEWIS THOMAS
The Medusa and the Snail

In this essay—the namesake for his second book—Thomas demonstrates his skill in defining the connections between large human concerns (such as the nature of self) with various organisms and processes in the natural world (such as the medusa and the snail).

We've never been so self-conscious about our selves as we seem to be these days. The popular magazines are filled with advice on things to do with a self: how to find it, identify it, nurture it, protect it, even, for special occasions, weekends, how to lose it transiently. There are instructive books, best sellers on self-realization, self-help, self-development. Groups of self-respecting people pay large fees for three-day sessions together, learning self-awareness. Self-enlightenment can be taught in college electives.

You'd think, to read about it, that we'd only just now discovered selves. Having long suspected that there was *something alive* in there, running the place, separate from everything else, absolutely individual and independent, we've celebrated by giving it a real name. My self.

It is an interesting word, formed long ago in much more social ambiguity than you'd expect. The original root was *se* or *seu*, simply the pronoun of the third person, and most of the descendant words, except "self" itself, were constructed to allude to other, somehow connected people; "sibs" and "gossips," relatives and close acquaintances, came from *seu*. *Se* was also used to indicate something outside or apart, hence words like "separate," "secret," and "segregate." From an extended root *swedh* it moved into Greek as *ethnos*, meaning people of one's own sort, and *ethos*, meaning the customs of such people. "Ethics" means the behavior of people like one's self, one's own ethnics.

We tend to think of our selves as the only wholly unique creations in nature, but it is not so. Uniqueness is so commonplace a property of living things that there is really nothing at all unique about it. A phenomenon can't be unique and universal at the same time. Even individual, free-swimming bacteria can be viewed as unique entities, distinguishable from each other even when they are the progeny of a single clone. Spudich and Koshland have recently reported that motile microorganisms of the same species are like solitary eccentrics in their swimming behavior. When they are searching for food, some tumble in one direction for precisely so many seconds before quitting, while others tumble differently and for different, but characteristic, periods of time. If you watch them closely, tethered by their flagellae to the surface of an antibody-coated slide, you can tell them from each other by the way they twirl, as accurately as though they had different names.

Beans carry self-labels, and are marked by these as distinctly as a mouse by his special smell. The labels are glycoproteins, the lectins, and may have something to do with negotiating the intimate and essential attachment between the bean and the nitrogen-fixing bacteria which live as part of the plant's flesh, embedded in root nodules. The lectin from one line of legume has a special affinity for the surfaces of the particular bacteria which colonize that line, but not for bacteria from other types of bean. The system seems designed for the maintenance of exclusive partnerships. Nature is pieced together by little snobberies like this.

Coral polyps are biologically self-conscious. If you place polyps of the same genetic line together, touching each other, they will fuse and become a single polyp, but if the lines are different, one will reject the other.

Fish can tell each other apart as individuals, by the smell of self. So can mice, and here the olfactory discrimination is governed by the Same H2 locus which contains the genes for immunologic self-marking.

The only living units that seem to have no sense of privacy at all are the nucleated cells that have been detached from the parent organism and isolated in a laboratory dish. Given the opportunity, under the right conditions, two cells from wildly different sources, a yeast cell, say, and a chicken erythrocyte, will touch, fuse, and the two nuclei will then fuse as well, and the new hybrid cell will now divide into monstrous progeny. Naked cells, lacking self-respect, do not seem to have any sense of self.

The markers of self, and the sensing mechanisms responsible for detecting such markers, are conventionally regarded as mechanisms for maintaining individuality for its own sake, enabling one kind of creature to defend and protect itself against all the rest. Selfness, seen thus, is for self-preservation.

In real life, though, it doesn't seem to work this way. The self-marking of invertebrate animals in the sea, who must have perfected the business long before evolution got around to us, was set up in order to permit creatures of one kind to locate others, not for predation but to set up symbiotic households. The anemones who live on the shells of crabs are precisely finicky; so are the crabs. Only a single species of anemone will find its way to only a single species of crab. They sense each other exquisitely, and live together as though made for each other.

Sometimes there is such a mix-up about selfness that two creatures, each attracted by the molecular configuration of the other, incorporate the two selves to make a single organism. The best story I've ever heard about this is the tale told of the nudibranch and medusa living in the Bay of Naples. When first observed, the nudibranch, a common sea slug, was found to have a tiny vestigial parasite, in the form of a jellyfish, permanently affixed to the ventral surface near the mouth. In curiosity to learn how the medusa got there, some marine biologists began searching the local waters for earlier developmental forms, and discovered something amazing. The attached parasite, although apparently so specialized as to have given up living for itself, can still produce offspring, for they are found in abundance at certain seasons of the year. They drift through the upper waters, grow up nicely and astonishingly, and finally become full-grown, handsome, normal jellyfish. Meanwhile, the snail produces snail larvae, and these too begin to grow normally, but not for long. While still extremely small, they become entrapped in the tentacles of the medusa and then engulfed within the umbrella-shaped body. At first glance, you'd believe the medusae are now the predators, paying back for earlier humiliations, and the snails the prey. But no. Soon the snails, undigested and insatiable, begin to eat, browsing away first at the radial canals, then the borders of the rim, finally the tentacles, until the jellyfish becomes reduced in substance by being eaten while the snail grows correspondingly in size. At the end, the arranement is back to the first scene, with the full-grown nudibranch basking, and nothing left of the jellyfish except the round, sucessfully edited parasite, safely affixed to the skin near the mouth.

It is a confusing tale to sort out, and even more confusing to think about. Both creatures are designed for this encounter, marked as selves so that they can find each other in the waters of the Bay of Naples. The collaboration, if you want to call it that, is entirely specific; it is only this species of medusa and only this kind of nudibranch that can come together and live this way. And, more surprising, they cannot live in any other way; they depend for their survival on each other. They are not really selves, they are specific *others*.

The thought of these creatures gives me an odd feeling. They do not remind me of anything, really. I've never heard of such a cycle before. They are bizarre, that's it, unique. And at the same time, like a vaguely remembered dream, they remind me of the whole earth at once. I cannot get my mind to stay still and think it through.

QUESTIONS

1. What does "uniqueness" mean to Thomas? Does his consideration of it make you reconsider yours? How so?

2. According to Thomas, what is the relation between uniqueness and self?

3. Does Thomas ever define self? If so, what is it? If not, should he have? Likewise, does Thomas ever define the biological function and basis of self? If so, what are they? If not, should he have?

4. I have said that every essay needs an upshot, a point to it that answers the question "So what?" What is Thomas's upshot in this essay? Does his essay conform to my rule or is it an exception?

SUGGESTED ACTIVITIES

1. Write an essay comparing and contrasting Thomas's essay and Jean George's. Consider their respective purposes. If you prefer one, explain your preference.

2. Write an essay exploring what the story of the medusa and the snail means to you.

3. Write an essay on the strangest thing you know of. See if you can figure out what it means. Then see if it means the same thing to a group of classmates.

JEAN GEORGE

That Astounding Creator— Nature

A roving reporter for Reader's Digest, *George has published numerous essays in such magazines as* Audubon, National Geographic, *and* National Wildlife. *She has written numerous books as well, among them* My Side of the Mountain *(1967),* Julie of the Wolves *(1972), and* The American Walk Book *(1979). The following essay demonstrates the value of detail and the rewards of research.*

A bird that eats feathers, a mammal that never drinks, a fish that grows a fishing line and worm on its head to catch other fish. Creatures in a nightmare? No, they are very much with us as co-inhabitants of this earth.

Nature has fashioned most animals to fit the many faces of the land—moose to marshes, squirrels to trees, camels to deserts, frogs to lily pads. Give nature an environment or situation and she will evolve a creature, adapting a toe here, an eye there, until the being fits the niche. As a result of this hammering and fitting, however, some really unbelievable creatures circle the sun with us.

One summer in Maine I saw a sleek mother horned grebe herding her three bobbing young to supper among the green pickerelweed. Suddenly I noticed through my binoculars that she was feeding her babies quantities of feathers from a deserted duck's nest. As she stuffed the dry feathers into the gaping mouths, she made two or three pokes to get each one down. Finally she worked a dozen or so down her own throat; then, sailing low on the water, she vanished contentedly among the plants.

I later learned that 60 percent of the grebe's diet is feathers. When I asked why, a biologist from the U.S. Fish and Wildlife Service answered, "Because nature finds a use for everything. Feathers seem to act as a strainer to prevent fishbones from entering and damaging the intestines."

Australia has many strange beasts, one of the oddest of which is the koala. Perfectly adapted to one specific tree, the eucalyptus, this living teddy bear does not need anything else, not even a drink! The moisture in the leaves is just right for the koala, making it the only land animal that doesn't need water to supplement its food.

The creature with the fishing line on its head was created for the dark canyons of the sea. Here food is so scarce that the deep-sea fish, which preys on smaller fish, grew a line, and an appendage on the end that wiggles like a worm. This catches the attention of the occasional passerby. A fish approaches the bait, and the toothy angler swirls up and swallows him.

The gigantic ocean bottom creates other problems. A male angler fish could swim for years without meeting a female of his own species. Nature's solution to this problem is for the female to carry a dwarfed husband tightly fused to her body. Marine biologists believe that this nuptial begins when the eggs first hatch and there are many fry of both sexes. A male then grabs hold of a female with his mouth and hangs on until he has literally become a part of her. His mouth becomes fused to her stomach, and for the rest of his life the male remains attached to his mate, marking the most amazing union on earth.

Sound has shaped the bodies of many beasts. Noise tapped away at the bullfrog until his ears became bigger than his eyes. Now he hears so well that at the slightest sound of danger he quickly plops to safety under a sunken leaf. The rabbit has long ears to hear the quiet "whoosh" of the owl's wings, while the grasshopper's ears are on the base of his abdomen, the lowest point of his body, where he can detect the tread of a crow's foot or the stealthy approach of a shrew.

Sometimes food will determine an animal's appearance. Earthworms have shaped the woodcock, a snipe-like bird of the forest floor. This creature has a long narrow bill that looks like a pencil and fits neatly into the burrows of the worms. But the bill has its disadvantages; with it buried deep in a worm hole the woodcock is vulnerable to attack from above. To counteract this danger the woodcock has eyes near the top of his head. This singular device permits him to scan the trees for danger even when his beak is buried. A successful arrangement for longevity—but it certainly creates an odd-looking creature.

The need to catch elusive prey has evolved some staggering biological tricks. The sea anemone, a flower-like animal of the tidemark, is usually riveted to one spot, yet it feeds on darting fish. A diabolically clever trap was necessary to catch them, so the anemone developed tentacles with bombs in the end of each. When a fish forages into these tentacles the ends shoot a thin thread into the fish's body. The thread in turn explodes a paralyzing poison. The stunned fish is hauled in by the tentacles and shoved into the anemone's gullet.

Nature seems to have gone all out in creating preposterous gadgets for self-defense. The jacana, a bird of the American tropics, for instance, is endowed with spurs which unfold like a switchblade at the bend of the bird's wings and with which he can slash his enemies to shreds.

Lizards are professionals in the art of warding off attack. The two-headed skink, whose tail is shaped like his head, confuses his enemy. A hawk, upon attacking this fellow, anticipates that he will run in the direction of the lifted head and makes allowance for the movement. However, the bird usually strikes nothing, for he is aiming at the tail. The real head took off the other way.

In order to travel in a hostile world, the Portuguese man-of-war first mastered the art of floating. To do this it evolved a purple bag and inflated it with gas from a special gland. As a crowning idea it also grew a sail! Launched, the man-of-war can blow away from enemies or approach food by putting its sail up and down. When severely threatened, it forces the gas out of the float and submerges.

There is hardly any environment, however hostile, that some creature has not mastered. Land is, of course, the nemesis of the fish. If they flop out on it they die. If their ponds dry up, they are helpless. Given this situation, it was almost certain that some fish would evolve a way to beat it; and so there is a lungfish. It is an air breather and must come to the surface every 20 minutes or so; otherwise it drowns. When the ponds of Africa dry up in the arid season, the lungfish wrap themselves in mud and wait it out, sometimes for years. When the rains finally return, they resume their water life.

Just as nature adds things on creatures that need them, so she occasionally takes things away from those that don't. The adult Mayfly, for example, has no mouth or stomach. Last year, by a northern New York lake, I found myself amid hundreds of thousands of these insects. I told the conservation officer whom I was with that I was glad they didn't bite. He replied that they have no mouths to bite with. "An adult Mayfly lives but one day," he explained, "and that day is devoted entirely to pleasure. They do nothing but dance and mate all their short life, and so they do not need a mouth."

With all this elaborate evolution, it is not surprising that some of nature's inventions got out of hand. Into this category falls the speedometer of reindeer. A tendon snaps back and forth over a bone in the reindeer's foot, noisily tapping out the speed of his gait. Useless. And so is the nose on the stomach of the scorpion and the feather-like tongue of the toucan, a bird of Africa.

But probably the most dumbfounding of nature's extraordinary creations is the horned toad of our Southwest. A herpetologist once invited me to observe one of these lizards right after it had molted. In a sand-filled glass cage I saw a large male. Beside him lay his old skin. The herpetologist began to annoy the beast with mock attacks, and the old man of the desert with his vulnerable new suit became frightened. Suddenly his eyeballs reddened. A final fast lunge from my friend at the beast and I froze in astonishment—a fine spray of blood shot from the lizard's eye, like fire from a dragon! The beast had struck back with a weapon so shocking that it terrifies even the fiercest enemy.

Later I walked home, pondering the bizarre methods for survival with which evolution has endowed earth's creatures, sometimes comical, sometimes pathetic. I knew the biologists were right: If any adaptation is possible, nature has tried it.

QUESTIONS

1. George says "some really unbelievable creatures circle the sun with us." What does she mean by "unbelievable"? Why does she use the image of circling the sun.?

2. George quotes a biologist who says that "use" accounts for all of nature's adaptations. Do all of George's examples illustrate this principle? Are any other principles involved?

3. Occasionally George uses mechanistic metaphors: invention, gadget, speedometer. How many does she use? Are they effective? *How* are they effective?

SUGGESTED ACTIVITIES

1. List the 15 strangest human acts you personally know of. Find a common theme for 10 of them and write an essay.

2. Define a subject—anything that interests you. Go to the library and research 25 strange facts about it, the stranger the better. Write an essay using 15 of them.

JOAN DIDION

The Santa Ana

In this essay Didion combines many different orders of information to provide a complete definition and an unforgettable impression of the subject.

There is something uneasy in the Los Angeles air this afternoon, some unnatural stillness, some tension. What it means is that tonight a Santa Ana will begin to blow, a hot wind from the northeast whining down through the Cajon Pass, blowing up sandstorms out along Route 66, drying the hills and the nerves to the flash point. For a few days now we will see smoke back in the canyons, and hear sirens in the night. I have neither heard nor read that a Santa Ana is due, but I know it, and almost everyone I have seen today knows it too. We know it because we feel it. The baby frets. The maid sulks. I rekindle a waning argument with the telephone company, then cut my losses and lie down, given over to whatever it is in the air. To live with the Santa Ana is to accept, consciously or unconsciously, a deeply mechanistic view of human behavior.

I recall being told, when I first moved to Los Angeles and was living on an isolated beach, that the Indians would throw themselves into the sea when the bad wind blew. I could see why. The Pacific turned ominouly glassy during a Santa Ana period, and one woke in the night, troubled not only by the peacocks screaming in the olive trees but by the eerie absence of surf. The heat was surreal. The sky had a yellow cast, the kind of light sometimes called "earthquake weather." My only neighbor would not come out of her house for days, and there were no lights at night, and her husband roamed the place with a machete. One day he would tell me that he had heard a trespasser, the next a rattlesnake.

"On nights like that," Raymond Chandler once wrote about the Santa Ana, "every booze party ends in a fight. Meek little wives feel the edge of the carving knife and study their husbands' necks. Anything can happen." That was the kind of wind it was. I did not know then that there was any basis for the effect it had on all of us, but it turns out to be another of those cases in which science bears out folk wisdom. The Santa Ana, which is named for one of the canyons it rushes through, is a *foehn* wind, like the *foehn* of Austria and Switzerland and the *hamsin* of Israel. There are a number of persistent, malevolent winds, perhaps the best known of which are the mistral of France and the Mediterranean sirocco, but a *foehn* wind has distinct characteristics: It occurs on the leeward slope of a mountain range and, although the air begins as a cold mass, it is warmed as it comes down the mountain and appears finally as a hot dry wind. Whenever and wherever a *foehn* blows, doctors hear about headaches and nausea and allergies, about "nervousness," about "depression." In Los Angeles some teachers do not attempt to conduct formal classes during a Santa Ana, because the children become unmanageable. In Switzerland the suicide rate goes up during the *foehn*, and in the courts of some Swiss cantons the wind is considered a mitigating circumstance for crime. Surgeons are said to watch the wind, because blood does not clot normally during a *foehn*. A few years ago an Israeli physicist discovered that not only during such winds, but for the 10 or 12 hours that precede them, the air carries an unusually high ratio of positive to negative ions. No one seems to know exactly why that should be; some talk about friction and others suggest solar disturbances. In any case the positive ions are there, and what an excess of positive ions does, in the simplest terms, is to make people unhappy. One cannot get much more mechanistic than that.

Easterners commonly complain that there is no "weather" at all in Southern California, that the days and seasons slip by relentlessly, numbingly bland. That is quite misleading. In fact, the climate is characterized by infrequent but violent extremes: two periods of torrential subtropical rains which continue for weeks and wash out the hills and send subdivisions sliding toward the sea; about 20 scattered days a year of the Santa Ana, which, with its incendiary dryness, invariably means fire. At the first prediction of a Santa Ana, the Forest Service flies men and equipment from northern California into the southern forests, and the Los Angeles Fire Department braces for disaster. The Santa Ana caused Malibu to burn the way it did in 1956, and Bel Air in 1961, and Santa Barbara in 1964. Last winter 11 men were killed fighting a Santa Ana fire that spread through the San Gabriel Mountains.

Just to watch the front-page news out of Los Angeles during a Santa Ana is to get very close to what it is about the place. The longest single Santa Ana period in recent years was in 1957, and it lasted not the usual three or four days but fourteen days, from November 21 until December 4. On the first day 25,000 acres of the San Gabriel Mountains were burning, with gusts reaching 100 miles an hour. In town, the wind reached Force 12, or hurricane force, on the Beaufort Scale; oil derricks were toppled and people were ordered off the downtown streets to avoid injury from flying objects. On November 22 the fire in the San Gabriels was out of control. On November 24 six people were killed in automobile accidents, and by the end of the week the Los Angeles *Times* was keeping a box score of traffic deaths. On November 26 a prominent Pasadena attorney, depressed about money, shot and killed his wife, their two sons and himself. On November 27 a South Gate divorcée, 22, was murdered and thrown from a moving car. On November 30 the San Gabriel fire was still out of control, and the wind in town was blowing 80 miles an hour. On the first day of December four people died violently, and on the third the wind began to break.

It is hard for people who have not lived in Los Angeles to realize how radically the Santa Ana figures in the local imagination. The city burning is Los Angeles's deepest image of itself: Nathanael West perceived that, in *The Day of the Locust*; and at the time of the Watts riots two summers ago what struck the local imagination most indelibly were the fires. For days one could drive along the Harbor Freeway and see the city on fire, just as we had always known it would be in the end. Los Angeles weather is the weather of catastrophe, of apocalypse, and, just as the reliably long and bitter winters of New England determine the way life is lived there, so the violence and the unpredictability of the Santa Ana affect the entire quality of life in Los Angeles, accentuate its impermanence, its unreliability. The wind shows us how close to the edge we are.

QUESTIONS

1. This is the thesis of Didion's essay: "To live with the Santa Ana is to accept, consciously or unconsciously, a deeply mechanistic view of human behavior." What does she mean by that? Does the essay support that thesis? If so, how so? If not, how not?

2. How is this essay organized?

3. What kinds of detail and fact does Didion use in defining the Santa Ana?

4. This is the upshot of Didion's essay: "The wind shows us how close to the edge we are." What does she mean?

SUGGESTED ACTIVITIES

1. Write an essay examining the effect of weather (or of certain kinds of weather) on you.

2. Try to frame an argument against the mechanistic interpretation of human behavior that Didion offers.

3. Using some of the reference works cited in Chapter II, research several articles on the effects of the moon on human behavior. Write an essay accounting for those effects. Write an essay refuting those so-called effects. (See my discussion of cause and effect, and always be alert for the confusion of *sequence* with cause and effect.)

4. Compare the arguments concerning the effects of weather with the arguments concerning the effects of the moon. See if one case is the more convincing.

III

Life in the City

GAY TALESE /
New York

A reporter for the New York Times *and a contributing editor to* Esquire *magazine, Talese is well-known for a number of books that reflect his journalistic skills, among them* The Kingdom and the Power *(1969),* Honor Thy Father *(1971), and* Thy Neighbor's Wife *(1980). In the following essay we see the investigative reporter at work on the curiosities of his city.*

New York is a city of things unnoticed. It is a city with cats sleeping under parked cars, two stone armadillos crawling up St. Patrick's Cathedral, and thousands of ants creeping on top of the Empire State Building. The ants probably were carried up there by wind or birds, but nobody is sure; nobody in New York knows any more about the ants than they do about the panhandler who takes taxis to the Bowery; or the dapper man who picks trash out of Sixth Avenue trash cans; or the medium in the West Seventies who claims, "I am clairvoyant, clairaudient and clairsensuous."

New York is a city for eccentrics and a center for odd bits of information. New Yorkers blink twenty-eight times a minute, but forty when tense. Most popcorn chewers at Yankee Stadium stop chewing momentarily just before the pitch. Gum chewers on Macy's escalators stop chewing momentarily before they get off—to concentrate on the last step. Coins, paper clips, ballpoint pens, and little girls' pocketbooks are found by workmen when they clean the sea lion's pool at the Bronx Zoo.

A Park Avenue doorman has parts of three bullets in his head—there since World War I. Several young gypsy daughters, influenced by television and literacy, are running away from home because they don't want to grow up and become fortunetellers. Each month a hundred pounds of hair is delivered to Louis Feder on 545 Fifth Avenue, where blond hairpieces are made from German women's hair; brunette hairpieces from Italian women's hair; but no hairpieces from American women's hair which, says Mr. Feder, is weak from too-frequent rinses and permanents.

Some of New York's best-informed men are elevator operators, who rarely talk, but always listen—like doormen. Sardi's doormen listen to the comments made by Broadway's first-nighters walking by after the last act. They listen closely. They listen carefully. Within ten minutes they can tell you which shows will flop and which will be hits.

On Broadway each evening a big, dark, 1948 Rolls-Royce pulls into Forty-Sixth Street—and out hop two little ladies armed with Bibles and signs reading, "The Damned Shall Perish." These ladies proceed to stand on the corner screaming at the multitudes of Broadway sinners, sometimes until 3 A.M., when their chauffeur in the Rolls picks them up, and drives them back to Westchester.

By this time Fifth Avenue is deserted by all but a few strolling insomniacs, some cruising cab drivers, and a group of sophisticated females who stand in store windows all night and day wearing cold, perfect smiles. Like sentries they line Fifth Avenue—these window mannequins who gaze onto the quiet street with tilted heads and pointed toes and long rubber fingers reaching for cigarettes that aren't there.

At 5 A.M. the Broadway regulars either have gone home or to all-night coffee shops where, under the glaring light, you see their whiskers and wear. And on Fifty-First Street a radio press car is parked at the curb with a photograper who has nothing to do. So he just sits there for a few nights, looks through the windshield, and soon becomes a keen observer of life after midnight.

"At 1 A.M.," he says, "Broadway is filled with wise guys and with kids coming out of the Astor Hotel in white dinner jackets—kids who drive to dances in their fathers' cars. You also see cleaning ladies going home, always wearing kerchiefs. By 2 A.M. some of the drinkers are getting out of hand, and this is the hour for bar fights. At 3 A.M. the last show is over in the night clubs, and most of the tourists and out-of-town buyers are back in hotels. And small-time comedians are criticizing big-time comedians in Hanson's Drugstore. At 4 A.M. after the bars close, you see the drunks come out—and also the pimps and prostitutes who take advantage of drunks. At 5 A.M., though, it is mostly quiet. New York is an entirely different city at 5 A.M." At 6 A.M. the early workers begin to push up from the subways. The traffic begins to move down Broadway like a river. And Mrs. Mary Woody jumps out of bed, dashes to her office and phones dozens of sleepy New Yorkers to say in a cheerful voice, rarely appreciated: "Good morning. Time to get up." For twenty years, as an operator of Western Union's Wake-Up Service, Mrs. Woody has gotten millions out of bed.

By 7 A.M. a floridly robust little man, looking very Parisian in a blue beret and turtle-neck sweater, moves in a harried step along Park Avenue visiting his wealthy lady friends—making certain that each is given a brisk, before-breakfast rubdown. The uniformed doormen greet him warmly and call him either "Biz" or "Mac" because he is Biz Mackey, a ladies' masseur *extraordinaire*. He never reveals the names of his customers, but most of them are middle-aged and rich. He visits each of them in their apartments, and has special keys to their bedrooms; he is often the first man they see in the morning, and they lie in bed waiting for him.

The doormen that Biz passes each morning are generally an obliging, endlessly articulate group of sidewalk diplomats who list among their friends some of Manhattan's most powerful men, most beautiful women and snootiest poodles. More often than not, the doormen are big, slightly Gothic in design, and the possessors of eyes sharp enough to spot big tippers a block away in the year's thickest fog. Some East Side doormen are as proud as grandees, and their uniforms, heavily festooned, seem to come from the same tailor who outfitted Marshal Tito.

Shortly after 7:30 each morning hundreds of people are lined along Forty-Second Street waiting for the 8 A.M. opening of the ten movie houses that stand almost shoulder-to-shoulder between Times Square and Eighth Avenue. Who are these people who go to the movies at 8 A.M.? They are the city's insomniacs, night watchmen, and people who can't go home, do not want to go home, or have no home. They are derelicts, homosexuals, cops, hacks, truck drivers, cleaning ladies and restaurant men who have worked all night. They are also alcoholics who are waiting at 8 A.M. to pay forty cents for a soft seat and to sleep in the dark, smoky theatre. And yet, aside from being smoky, each of Times Square's theatres has a special quality, or lack of quality, about it. At the Victory Theatre one finds horror films, while at the Times

Square Theatre they feature only cowboy films. There are first-run films for forty cents at the Lyric, while at the Selwyn there are always second-run films for thirty cents. But if you go to the Apollo Theatre you will see, in addition to foreign films, people in the lobby talking with their hands. These are deaf-and-dumb movie fans who patronize the Apollo because they read the subtitles. The Apollo probably has the biggest deaf-and-dumb movie audience in the world.

New York is a city of 38,000 cab drivers, 10,000 bus drivers, but only one chauffeur who has a chauffeur. The wealthy chauffeur can be seen driving up Fifth Avenue each morning, and his name is Roosevelt Zanders. He earns $100,000 a year, is a gentleman of impeccable taste and, although he owns a $23,000 Rolls-Royce, does not scorn his friends who own Bentleys. For $150 a day, Mr. Zanders will drive anyone anywhere in his big, silver Rolls. Diplomats patronize him, models pose next to him, and each day he receives cables from around the world urging that he be waiting at Idlewild, on the docks, or outside the Plaza Hotel. Sometimes at night, however, he is too tired to drive any more. So Bob Clarke, his chauffeur, takes over and Mr. Zanders relaxes in the back.

New York is a town of 3,000 bootblacks whose brushes and rhythmic rag-snaps can be heard up and down Manhattan from midmorning to midnight. They dodge cops, survive rainstorms, and thrive in the Empire State Building as well as on the Staten Island Ferry. They usually wear dirty shoes.

New York is a city of headless men who sit obscurely in subway booths all day and night selling tokens to people in a hurry. Each weekday more than 4,500,000 riders pass these money-changers who seem to have neither heads, faces, nor personalities—only fingers. Except when giving directions, their vocabulary consists largely of three words: "How many, please?"

In New York there are 200 chestnut venders, and they average $25 on a good day peddling soft, warm chestnuts. Like many venders, the chestnut men do not own their own rigs—they borrow or rent them from pushcart makers such as David Amerman.

Mr. Amerman, with offices opposite a defunct public bathhouse on the Lower East Side, is New York's master builder of pushcarts. His father and grandfather before him were pushcart makers, and the family has long been a household word among the city's most discriminating junk men, fruit venders and hot-dog peddlers.

In New York there are 500 mediums, ranging from semi-trance to trance to deep-trance types. Most of them live in New York's West

Seventies and Eighties, and on Sundays some of these blocks are communicating with the dead, vibrating to trumpets, and solving all problems.

The Manhattan Telephone Directory has 776,300 names, of which 3,316 are Smith, 2,835 are Brown, 2,444 are Williams, 2,070 are Cohen—and one is Mike Krasilovsky. Anyone who doubts this last fact has only to look at the top of page 876 where, in large black letters, is this sign: "There is only one Mike Krasilovsky. Sterling 3-1990."

In New York the Fifth Avenue Lingerie shop is on Madison Avenue; The Madison Pet Shop is on Lexington Avenue; the Park Avenue Florist is on Madison Avenue, and the Lexington Hand Laundry is on Third Avenue. New York is the home of 120 pawnbrokers and it is where Bishop Sheen's brother, Dr. Sheen, shares an office with one Dr. Bishop.

New York is a town of thirty tattooists where interest in mankind is skin-deep, but whose impressions usually last a lifetime. Each day the tattooists go pecking away over acres of anatomy. And in downtown Manhattan, Stanley Moskowitz, a scion of a distinguished family of Bowery skin-peckers, does a grand business.

When it rains in Manhattan, automobile traffic is slow, dates are broken and, in hotel lobbies, people slump behind newspapers or walk aimlessly about with no place to sit, nobody to talk to, nothing to do. Taxis are harder to get; department stores do between fifteen and twenty-five per cent less business, and the monkeys in the Bronx Zoo, having no audience, slouch grumpily in their cages looking more bored than the lobby-loungers.

While some New Yorkers become morose with rain, others prefer it, like to walk in it, and say that on rainy days the city's buildings seem somehow cleaner—washed in an opalescence, like a Monet painting. There are fewer suicides in New York when it rains. But when the sun is shining, and New Yorkers seem happy, the depressed person sinks deeper into depression, and Bellevue Hospital gets more suicide calls.

New York is a town of 8,485 telephone operators, 1,364 Western Union messenger boys, and 112 newspaper copy boys. An average baseball crowd at Yankee Stadium uses over ten gallons of liquid soap per game—an unofficial high mark for cleanliness in the major leagues; the stadium also has the league's top number of ushers (360), sweepers (72), and men's rooms (34). New York is a town in which the brotherhood of Russian Bath Rubbers, the only union advocating sweat shops, appears to be heading for its last rubdown. The union has been going in New York City for years, but now most of the rubbers are pushing seventy and are deaf—from all the water and the hot temperatures.

Each afternoon in New York a rather seedy saxophone player, his cheeks blown out like a spinnaker, stands on the sidewalk playing *Danny Boy* in such a sad, sensitive way that he soon has half the neighborhood peeking out of windows tossing nickels, dimes and quarters at his feet. Some of the coins roll under parked cars, but most of them are caught in his outstretched hand. The saxophone player is a street musician named Joe Gabler; for the past thirty years he has serenaded every block in New York and has sometimes been tossed as much as $100 a day in coins. He is also hit with buckets of water, empty beer cans and eggs, and chased by wild dogs. He is believed to be the last of New York's ancient street musicians.

New York is a town of nineteen midget wrestlers. They all can squeeze into the Hotel Holland's elevator, six can sleep in one bed, eight can be comfortably transported to Madison Square Garden in the chauffeur-driven Cadillac reserved for the midget wrestlers.

In New York from dawn to dusk to dawn, day after day, you can hear the steady rumble of tires against the concrete span of George Washington Bridge. The bridge is never completely still. It trembles with traffic. It moves in the wind. Its great veins of steel swell when hot and contract when cold; its span often is ten feet closer to the Hudson River in summer than in winter. It is an almost restless structure of graceful beauty which, like an irresistible seductress, withholds secrets from the romantics who gaze upon it, the escapists who jump off it, the chubby girl who lumbers across its 3,500-foot span trying to reduce, and the 100,000 motorists who each day cross it, smash into it, shortchange it, get jammed up on it.

When street traffic dwindles and most people are sleeping in New York, some neighborhoods begin to crawl with cats. They move quickly through the shadows of buildings; night watchmen, policemen, garbage collectors and other nocturnal wanderers see them—but never for very long. There are 200,000 stray cats in New York. A majority of them hang around the fish market, or in Greenwich Village, and in the East and West Side neighborhoods where garbage cans abound. No part of the city is without its strays, however, and all-night garage attendants in such busy neighborhoods as Fifty-Fourth Street have counted as many as twenty of them around the Ziegfeld Theatre early in the morning. Troops of cats patrol the water-front piers at night searching for rats. Subway trackwalkers have discovered cats living in the darkness. They seem never to get hit by trains, though some are occasionally liquidated by the third rail. About twenty-five cats live seventy-five feet below the west end of Grand Central Terminal, are fed by the underground workers, and never wander up into the daylight.

New York is a city in which large, cliff-dwelling hawks cling to skyscrapers and occasionally zoom to snatch a pigeon over Central Park, or Wall Street, or the Hudson River. Bird-watchers have seen these peregrine falcons circling lazily over the city. They have seen them perched atop tall buildings, even around Times Square. About twelve of these hawks patrol the city, sometimes with a wingspan of thirty-five inches. They have buzzed women on the roof of the St. Regis Hotel, have attacked repairmen on smokestacks, and, in August, 1947, two hawks jumped women residents in the recreation yard of the Home of the New York Guild for the Jewish Blind. Maintenance men at the Riverside Church have seen hawks dining on pigeons in the bell tower. The hawks remain there for only a little while. And then they fly out to the river, leaving pigeons' heads for the Riverside maintenance men to clean up. When the hawks return, they fly in quietly— *unnoticed*, like the cats, the headless men, the ants, the ladies' masseur, the doorman with three bullets in his head, and most of the other offbeat wonders in this town without time.

QUESTIONS

1. How many of the odd things are peculiar to New York? How many could be found in any city? Why does Talese combine them in an essay specifically about New York? Should he have been more exclusive?

2. How many names does Talese use? How many instances does he not use names when he could have? How many instances, if any, *should* he have used names when he doesn't. Why does he use names at all? (Review the discussion in the Rhetoric on being specific.)

3. How many paragraphs begin with a transition? How many don't? How many of them, if any, should? How many of those that do should not? Why?

SUGGESTED ACTIVITIES

1. Use an afternoon to examine a congested area—your college campus, your downtown area (or part of it). Look for and note everything that's odd.

2. Use another afternoon to examine a bit of countryside in the same way.

3. Fashion the two sets of notes into a comparison and contrast essay to determine which (if either) is the stranger: country or city.

GEORGE F. WILL

On Her Own in the City

Will has professed political science, served as an aide to a senator, served as an editor of the National Review, *and written a political column for* Newsweek *magazine and* The Washington Post—*earning a Pulitzer Prize for his efforts. Will writes consistently with notable succinctness and wit, and he quotes more effectively than any writer I've read. In this essay he proves the power and (perhaps) the futility of compassion.*

When police, responding to her call, arrived at her East Harlem tenement, she was hysterical: "The dog ate my baby." The baby girl had been four days old, twelve hours "home" from the hospital. Home was two rooms and a kitchen on the sixth floor, furnished with a rug, a folding chair, and nothing else, no bed, no crib.

"Is the baby dead?" asked an officer. "Yes," the mother said, "I saw the baby's insides." Her dog, a German shepherd, had not been fed for five days. She explained: "I left the baby on the floor with the dog to protect it." She had bought the dog in July for protection from human menaces.

She is twenty-four. She went to New York three years ago from a small Ohio community. She wanted to be on her own. She got that wish.

She was employed intermittently, until the fifth month of her pregnancy, which she says was the result of a rape she did not report to the police. She wanted the baby. She bought child-care books, and had seven prenatal checkups at Bellevue Hospital. Although she rarely called home or asked for money, she called when the baby was born. Her mother mailed twenty-five dollars for a crib. It arrived too late.

When labor began she fed the dog with the last food in the apartment and went alone to the hospital. The baby was born on Wednesday. When she left Bellevue Sunday evening, the hospital office holding her welfare payment was closed. With six dollars in her pocket and a baby in her arms, she took a cab home. The meter said four dollars and the driver demanded a dollar tip. When she asked his assistance in getting upstairs, he drove off.

The hospital had given her enough formula for three feedings for the baby. Rather than spend her remaining dollar that night on food for herself and the dog, she saved it for the bus ride back to Bellevue to get her welfare money. Having slept with the baby on a doubled-up rug, she left the baby and dog at 7 A.M. It was 53 degrees, too cold she thought to take the baby. She had no warm baby clothes and she thought the hospital had said the baby was ailing. She got back at 8:30 A.M. Then she called the police.

Today the forces of law and order and succor are struggling to assign "blame" in order to escape it. Her attorney and Bellevue are arguing about how she was released, or expelled, on Sunday evening. Welfare officials are contending with charges that they are somehow culpable for her failure to receive a crib before giving birth, and for her living conditions. (She was receiving payment of $270 a month; her rent was $120.) She has been arraigned on a charge of negligent homicide, but no one seems anxious to prosecute.

Late in New York's U.S. Senate primary, Daniel P. Moynihan, talking like a senator prematurely, said that this case dramatizes weaknesses of the welfare system, and indicated that it also dramatizes the need for him in Washington. Perhaps.

But because cities are collections of strangers, they are, inevitably, bad places to be poor. Not that there are good places, but cities, being kingdoms of the strong, are especially hellish for the poor.

Cities have their indispensable purposes, and their charms, not the least of which is that you can be alone in a crowd. But that kind of living alone is an acquired taste, and not for the weak or unfortunate. They are apt to learn that no city's institutions can provide protective supports like those of an extended family or real community. No metropolis can provide a floor of support solid enough to prevent the bewildered—like the woman from Ohio—from falling through the cracks.

Through those cracks you get an occasional glimpse of what George Eliot meant: "If we had a keen vision and feeling of all ordinary human life, it would be like hearing the grass grow and the squirrel's heart-beat, and we should die of that roar which lies on the other side of silence."

QUESTIONS

1. What is the common point—the unifying principle—of the facts Will cites concerning the mother's story?

2. According to Will, what is wrong with Moynihan's observation?

3. What is the problem the mother's story illustrates? What is the solution?

4. What is the point of the quotation at the end?

SUGGESTED ACTIVITIES

1. Rewrite Will's piece as a police report (or as you imagine a police report).

2. Rewrite Will's piece as a social agency's report—as if you were a social worker.

3. Rewrite Will's piece as a case study in a sociology text.

IMAMU AMIRI BARAKA (Leroi Jones)
Streets of Despair ✓

A native of Newark, New Jersey, Baraka is a social activist who has turned his pen to every literary form—poetry, fiction, drama, essay, and criticism. His best-known works are a play, Dutchman *(1967); a novel,* The System of Dante's Hell *(1965); and* Home: Social Essays *(1966), of which the following essay is a part. It exhibits Baraka's keen sense of the vicious paradoxes that reduce the ghetto to hell on earth.*

These streets stretch from one end of America to the other and connect like a maze from which very few can fully escape. Despair sits on this country in most places like a charm, but there is a special gray death that loiters in the streets of an urban Negro slum. And the men who walk those streets, tracing and retracing their steps to some hopeless job or a pitiful rooming house or apartment or furnished room, sometimes stagger under the weight of that gray, humiliated because it is not even "real."

Sometimes walking along among the ruined shacks and lives of the worst Harlem slum, there is a feeling that just around the next corner you'll find yourself in south Chicago or South Philadelphia, maybe even Newark's Third Ward. In these places life, and its possibility, has been distorted almost identically. And the distortion is as old as its sources: the fear, frustration, and hatred that Negroes have always been heir to in America. It is just that in the cities, which were once the black man's twentieth century "Jordan," *promise* is a dying bitch with rotting eyes. And the stink of her dying is a deadly killing fume. The blues singers know all this. They knew before they got to the cities. "I'd rather drink muddy water, sleep in a hollow log, than be in New York City treated like a dirty dog." And when they arrived, in those various cities, it was much worse than even they had imagined. The city blues singers are still running all that down. Specifically, it's what a man once named for me unnatural adversity. It is social, it is economic, it is cultural and historical. Some of its products are emotional and psychological; some are even artistic, as if Negroes suffered better than anyone else. But it's hard enough to be a human being under any circumstances, but when there is an entire civilization determined to stop you from being one, things get a little more desperately complicated. What do you do then?

You can stand in doorways late nights and hit people in the head. You can go to church Saturday nights and Sundays and three or four times during the week. You can stick a needle in your arm four or five times a day, and bolster the economy. You can buy charms and herbs and roots, or wear your hat backwards to keep things from getting worse. You can drink till screaming is not loud enough, and the coldest night is all right to sleep outside in. You can buy a big car . . . if the deal goes down. There's so much, then, you can do, to yourself, or to somebody else. Another man sings, "I'm drinkin' t.n.t., I'm smokin' dynamite, I hope some screwball starts a fight."

One can never talk about Harlem in purely social terms, though there are ghetto facts that make any honest man shudder. It is the tone, the quality of suffering each man knows as his own that finally must be important, but this is the most difficult thing to get to. (There are about twenty young people from one small Southern town, all friends, all living within the same few blocks of the black city, all of whom are junkies, communally hooked. What kind of statistic is *that*? And what can you say when you read it?)

The old folks kept singing, there will be a better day . . . or, the sun's gonna shine in my back door some day . . . or, I've had my fun if I don't get well no more. What did they want? What would that sun turn out to be?

Hope is a delicate suffering. Its waste products vary, but most of them are meaningful. And as a cat named Mean William once said, can you be glad, if you've never been sad?

QUESTIONS

1. What kind of detail does Baraka use? Is it the same as or different from the sort of detail that Talese and Will use? How so?

2. How does sticking a needle in your arm bolster the economy? What is Baraka's point?

3. "Hope is a delicate suffering. Its waste products vary, but most of them are meaningful." What do those sentences mean? And how does the statement by Mean William help explain them?

SUGGESTED ACTIVITIES

1. Describe despair as you have known it. (Look up the word, so you know its precise definition.)

2. Describe despair you think you have seen in others.

3. Describe your experience with hope as a delicate (or not so delicate) suffering.

CHRISTOPHER MORLEY

Chestnut Street from a Fire Escape

A prolific and amusing man of letters—poet, novelist, essayist, critic, and author of travel books—Morely is well-known for such works as The Haunted Bookshop *(1919),* Inward Ho! *(1923),* Parnassus on Wheels *(1925),* Internal Revenue *(1933), and* The Ironing Board *(1949). In this piece, a chapter from* Travels in Philadelphia *(1920), Morley shows that by listening as well as looking we can find charm in something as ordinary as a street.*

Just outside our office window is a fire-escape with a little iron balcony. On warm days, when the tall windows are wide open, that rather slender platform is our favorite vantage ground for watching Chestnut street. We have often thought how pleasant it would be to have a pallet spread out there, so that we could do our work in that reclining posture that is so inspiring. But we can tell a good deal of what is going on along Chestnut street without leaving our desk. Chestnut street sings a music of its own. Its genial human symphony could never be mistaken for that of any other highway. The various strands of sound that compose its harmony gradually sink into our mind without our paying conscious heed to them. For instance, there is the light sliding swish of the trolley poles along the wire, accompanied by the deep rocking rumble of the car, and the crash as it pounds over the crosstracks at Sixth street. There is the clear mellow clang of the trolley gongs, the musical trill of fast wagon wheels running along the trolley rails, and the rattle of hoofs on the cobbled strip between the metals. Particularly easy to identify is the sound every citizen knows, the rasping, sliding clatter of a wagon turning off the car track so that a trolley can pass it. The front wheels have left the track, but the back pair are scraping along against the setts before mounting over the rim.

Every street has its own distinctive noises and the attentive ear accustoms itself to them until they become almost a part of the day's enjoyment. The deep-toned bell of Independence Hall bronzing the hours is part of our harmony here, and no less familiar is the vigorous tap-tap of Blind Al's stick. Al is the well-known newsdealer at the corner of Chestnut and Fifth. Several times a day he passes along under our windows, and the tinkle of his staff is a well-known and pleasant note in our ears. We like to imagine, too, that we can recognize the peculiarly soft and easy-going rumble of a wagon of watermelons.

But what we started to talk about was the balcony, from which we can get a long view of Chestnut street all the way from Broad street almost to the river. It is a pleasant prospect. There is something very individual about Chestnut street. It could not possibly be in New York. The solid, placid dignity of most of the buildings, the absence of skyscrapers, the plain stone fronts with the arched windows of the sixties, all these bespeak a city where it is still a little bit bad form for a building to be too garishly new. I may be wrong, but I do not remember in New York any such criss-cross of wires above the streets. Along Chestnut street they run at will from roof to roof over the way.

Gazing from our little balcony the eye travels down along the uneven profile of the northern flank of Chestnut street. From the Wanamaker wireless past the pale, graceful minaret of the Federal Reserve Bank, the skyline drops down to the Federal Building which, standing back from the street, leaves a gap in the view. Then the slant of roofs draws the eye upward again, over the cluster of little conical spires on Green's Hotel (like a French château) to the sharp ridges and heavy pyramid roof of the Merchants' Union Trust Company. This, with its two attendant banks on either side, is undoubtedly the most extraordinary architectural curiosity Chestnut street can boast. The façade, with its appalling quirks and twists of stone and iron grillwork, its sculptured Huns and Medusa faces, is something to contemplate with alarm.

After reaching Seventh street, Chestnut becomes less adventurous. Perhaps awed by the simple and stately beauty of Independence Hall and its neighbors, it restrains itself from any further originality until Fourth street, where the ornate Gothic of the Provident claims the eye. From our balcony we can see only a part of Independence Hall, but we look down on the faded elms along the pavement in front and the long line of iron posts beloved of small boys for leapfrog. Then the eye climbs to the tall and graceful staff above the Drexel Building, where the flag ripples cleanly against the blue. And our view is bounded, far away to the east, by the massive tower of the Victor factory in Camden.

It is great fun to watch Chestnut street from the little balcony. On hot days, when the white sunlight fills the street with a dazzle of brightness and bands of dark shadow, it is amusing to see how all pedestrians keep to the shady southern pavements. When a driving shower comes up and the slants and rods of rain lash against the dingy brownstone fronts, one may look out and see passers-by huddled under the awnings and the mounted policemen's horses sleek as satin in the wet. The pavement under our balcony is notable for its slipperiness: it has been chipped into ribs by stonemasons to make it less so. In the rain it shines like a mirror. And our corner has its excitements, too. Once every few months the gas mains take it into their pipes to explode and toss manholes and paving sixty feet in air.

The part of Chestnut street that is surveyed by our balcony is a delightful highway: friendly, pleasantly dignified, with just a touch of oldfashioned manners and homeliness. It is rather akin to a London street. And best of all, almost underneath our balcony is a little lunch room where you can get custard ice cream with honey poured over it, and we think it is the best thing in the world.

QUESTIONS

1. "But what we started to talk about was the balcony," Morley says, as if his discussion of sounds were an inadvertent digression. Why

does he construe that discussion in those terms? Is it a digression? Should it be omitted? Or is it integral? If so, how? If not, how not?

2. Why does Morley say "what we started to talk about"? What else could he have said? If said in other ways, what difference would it make to the meaning and the effect of his statement?

3. What does he like about Chestnut Street? Is there anything he dislikes? If so, what and why? If he mentions or infers no dislikes, should he have? Would a more balanced view have made a better essay?

SUGGESTED ACTIVITIES

1. Close your eyes and listen carefully for a time to the sounds outside a window. Distinguish between the usual and the unusual. Note the responses they evoke in you—the images, the memories, the feelings—and write them down.

2. Now go look out a window. See everything you can see. In addition, note the differences (if any) between the two experiences. Does the street look the same as it sounds? Write an essay comparing and contrasting the two experiences.

IV

Personal Relations

MAEVE BRENNAN
On the A Train

Born in Ireland, Brennan lives in and writes about New York City,
publishing most of her stories and essays, appropriately enough, in
The New Yorker. *She has collected her stories in two volumes,* In
and Out of Never-Never Land *(1964) and* Christmas Eve *(1974), and*
has published a number of her essays in The Long-Winded Lady
(1969). The long-winded breathless style of this essay dramatizes
how we think and feel—and don't—in a pinch.

There were no seats to be had on the A train last night, but I had a
good grip on the pole at the end of one of the seats and I was reading
the beauty column of the *Journal-American*, which the man next to
me was holding up in front of him. All of a sudden I felt a tap on my
arm, and I looked down and there was a man beginning to stand up
from the seat where he was sitting. "Would you like to sit down?" he
said. Well, I said the first thing that came into my head, I was so
surprised and pleased to be offered a seat in the subway. "Oh, thank
you very much," I said, "but I am getting out at the next station." He
sat back and that was that, but I felt all set up and I thought what a
nice man he must be and I wondered what his wife was like and I
thought how lucky she was to have such a polite husband, and then
all of a sudden I realized that I wasn't getting out at the next station
at all but the one after that, and I felt perfectly terrible. I decided to
get out at the next station anyway, but then I thought, If I get out at

the next station and wait around for the next train I'll miss my bus and they only go every hour and that will be silly. So I decided to brazen it out as best I could, and when the train was slowing up at the next station I stared at the man until I caught his eye and then I said, "I just remembered this isn't my station after all." Then I thought he would think I was asking him to stand up and give me his seat, so I said, "But I still don't want to sit down, because I'm getting off at the next station." I showed him by my expression that I thought it was all rather funny, and he smiled, more or less, and nodded, and lifted his hat and put it back on his head again and looked away. He was one of those small, rather glum or sad men who always look off into the distance after they have finished what they are saying, when they speak. I felt quite proud of my strong-mindedness at not getting off the train and missing my bus simply because of the fear of a little embarrassment, but just as the train was shutting its doors I peered out and there it was 168th Street. "Oh, dear!" I said. "That was my station and now I have missed the bus!" I was fit to be tied, and I had spoken quite loudly, and I felt extremely foolish, and I looked down, and the man who had offered me his seat was partly looking at me, and I said, "Now, isn't that silly? That was my station. A Hundred and Sixty-eighth Street is where I'm supposed to get off." I couldn't help laughing, it was all so awful, and he looked away, and the train fidgeted along to the next station, and I got off as quickly as I possibly could and tore over to the downtown platform and got a local to 168th, but of course I had missed my bus by a minute, or maybe two minutes. I felt very much at a loose end wandering around 168th Street, and I finally went into a rudely appointed but friendly bar and had a Martini, warm but very soothing, which only cost me fifty cents. While I was sipping it, trying to make it last to exactly the moment that would get me a good place in the bus queue without having to stand too long in the cold, I wondered what I should have done about that man in the subway. After all, if I had taken his seat I probably would have got out at 168th Street, which would have meant that I would hardly have been sitting down before I would have been getting up again, and that would have seemed odd. And rather grasping of me. And he wouldn't have got his seat back, because some other grasping person would have slipped into it ahead of him when I got up. He seemed a retiring sort of man, not pushy at all. I hesitate to think of how he must have regretted offering me his seat. Sometimes it is very hard to know the right thing to do.

QUESTIONS

1. Why does Brennan make this essay one paragraph only?

2. Why does Brennan write so many long compound sentences featuring *and?* Why doesn't she use a comma with the conjunction more often?

3. "I showed him by my expression that I thought it was all rather funny, and he smiled, more or less, and nodded, and lifted his hat and put it back on his head again and looked away." How do you explain Brennan's punctuation?

SUGGESTED ACTIVITIES

1. Write an essay about a time when you had difficulty figuring out "the right thing to do" with a stranger.

2. Write an essay on such a difficulty with an acquaintance (family or friend).

3. Write a long-winded breathless sentence about feeling flustered. Write some short choppy sentences about feeling agitated. Write a long easy going sentence about feeling relaxed. Write some short sentences about feeling in charge of a situation.

ANNE TAYLOR FLEMING
In Defense of Flirting

> *Fleming lives where she was born and raised, in Los Angeles, and is a free-lance journalist. With her husband she wrote* The First Time *(1975), and she has written numerous essays for many magazines. In the essay below Fleming shows how important it is—in arguing for a position—to consider the opposition, to define reasonable limits, and to be perfectly honest.*

There was, I think, only a brief period in my life when I actually turned heads. It was the summer of my seventeenth year when, newly graduated from a private girls' school, I was in that transition stage between being an old child and a young woman, a state of half and half that men of all ages apparently find disarmingly erotic. I guess each one looking at such a wobbly almost-woman fancies that he shall be the first. It was that summer that I learned to flirt with the opposite sex. I learned a whole host of new smiles with which to invite, or fend off, the attentions of my sudden suitors: the shy smile, the half-smile, the serious smile, the come-on smile, the go-away smile. I learned when to use each one and when not to. I understood for the first time that if I wore white against my summer skin I was much more appealing than if I wore red or green or any other color. So I wore white.

It was as if I had suddenly caught on to some very complicated and subtle dance steps. From then on those steps were part of my act. From then on flirting was just something I did when I bumped into someone who was male; it seemed to soften the edges of our collision. It made things easier, nicer, gentler, and certainly more fun.

Touchless Touching

Right from the beginning I understood that flirting had its own rules and its own chivalry. I knew I should not flirt a serious favor out of someone; a small favor was OK. I knew that I must not as a woman abuse my privilege to flirt, that I should not flirt to inflame the jealousy of a present love or to tease the passion of a prospective one. Then flirting became a weapon and to my mind just wasn't flirting any more. To me flirting was the delicate eye-play, talk-play, touchless touching by which I could show affection or approval for someone else, tell him he was pleasing to me, without promising anything or hurting anyone.

Those days of delicate flirtation are apparently over. Flirting is a casualty of the two great revolutions of our times: the women's liberation movement and the so-called sexual revolution. Women seeking their liberation cast a cold eye on flirting and found it to be sexist, divisive, demeaning, role-playing and otherwise ugly and useless. With men they would be straight, demanding, fair, nonfrivolous—no games, no lowered lids, no blushing cheeks, no sleight of hand or eye. They would get their jobs, and their sex, on merit.

A friend of mine once told me that before she finished college she intended as a matter of course to sleep with all of her friends. She wasn't talking about just the friends she loved or lusted for; she was talking about all those chums one studied with past many midnights, those steady, stolid friends with whom one debated through endless hours over endless cups of weak cafeteria coffee the fate or state of the world. These, one after the other, like taking required courses for her major, she would sleep with.

Matter-of-Fact Sex

I remember feeling slightly sick when she told me. It all sounded so
cold-blooded, so listless, so lustless, so totally without flirtation. I had
a deep fear of ending up in bed with someone for whom I felt no
passion or desire. That to me was really dirty. And flirting, it seemed,
was a way of protecting myself from that kind of nonpassionate sex,
a way of trying out my lust before bedding—like trying out a play in
Boston before opening on Broadway.

I understand that for my college girlfriend, as for many other women,
bedding with friends was a safe starting place, a way of stretching
one's limbs after a long winter. And, of course, by the time I was in
college in the late '60s, the sexual revolution was in full swing and
bed-hopping was *de rigueur*. If flirting was offensive to the fledgling
feminists among us, to the free lovers and flower children it was child's
play. Bed was for the asking anytime anywhere. I remember a typical
college party where there was a lot of drink and a lot of dope, then a
lot of sex and a boy I knew ended up in the arms of a woman with
whom he had shared a house for more than a year, a woman he said
he regarded as a sister, not as a sex partner. Why, I asked him the next
day, had they finally shared a bed? "Well," he said simply, "someone
had to sleep with her."

Clearly this was a different world from the one into which I awak-
ened that summer when I was 17, when shy smiles and tentative
touches were the limits to sex. This new world was a world of matter-
of-fact, purposeful sex where flirting was no more than frivolous and
unnecessary foreplay.

Goo-Goo Eyes

Perhaps flirting is only possible in a society of definite limits and
thwarted lusts, the kind of society, for example, that nurtured the
Southern belle. Obviously, I don't want to have all the limitations back.
I'm as grateful as any woman for my new freedoms. But now that my
body is somewhat unbuckled and my consciousness reasonably raised
I would very much like to be able to flirt with immunity again. Flirting
is evocative of tenderer times in all of our lives and of tenderer times
in the lives of our marriages. I miss those times. I still think making
goo-goo eyes (there is no dignified way to say it) at someone and having
them made back at me is nicely sexy—and safe.

I've discovered that I really don't want to talk to, let alone touch,
most people, and flirting is a way of being affable, even affectionate,

even slightly wicked without having to do either. It's a way of saying maybe, and I've always been a sucker for the romance of the near miss.

QUESTIONS

1. After explaining her discovery that white made her more appealing than any other color, Fleming writes, "So I wore white." Why does she say that? Isn't it sufficiently clear from the preceding sentence?

2. Where does Fleming anticipate objections to her defense? What are the objections she anticipates? Does she answer them to your satisfaction? If not, why not? Are there any objections she fails to anticipate?

3. What does Fleming mean when she says she would "very much like to be able to flirt with immunity again"?

SUGGESTED ACTIVITIES

1. Write an essay attacking flirting *as Fleming defines and defends it.*

2. Write an essay describing the sort of romance you're likely to fall victim to.

3. Describe a way you enjoy being slightly wicked and safe.

JUDITH VIORST

Friends, Good Friends—and Such Good Friends

Born in New Jersey and residing in Washington, D.C., Viorst is a poet, a journalist, and an award-winning writer of many children's books. Her publications for grownups include It's Hard to Be Hip over Thirty and Other Tragedies of Married Life *(1968),* Yes, Married: A Saga of Love and Complaint *(1972), and* Love and Guilt and the Meaning of Life, Etc. *(1979). Viorst is a contributing editor and columnist for* Redbook *magazine. Her essay on friends demonstrates the rhetorical value of personal testimony. It also shows how ordinary experience and common knowledge—we all have friends—are good sources of material.*

Women are friends, I once would have said, when they totally love and support and trust each other, and bare to each other the secrets of their souls, and run—no questions asked—to help each other, and tell harsh truths to each other (no, you can't wear that dress unless you lose ten pounds first) when harsh truths must be told.

Women are friends, I once would have said, when they share the same affection for Ingmar Bergman, plus train rides, cats, warm rain, charades, Camus, and hate with equal ardor Newark and Brussels sprouts and Lawrence Welk and camping.

In other words, I once would have said that a friend is a friend all the way, but now I believe that's a narrow point of view. For the friendships I have and the friendships I see are conducted at many levels of intensity, serve many different functions, meet different needs and range from those as all-the-way as the friendship of the soul sisters mentioned above to that of the most nonchalant and casual playmates.

Consider these varieties of friendship:

1. Convenience friends. These are the women with whom, if our paths weren't crossing all the time, we'd have no particular reason to be friends: a next-door neighbor, a woman in our car pool, the mother of one of our children's closest friends or maybe some mommy with whom we serve juice and cookies each week at the Glenwood co-op Nursery.

Convenience friends are convenient indeed. They'll lend us their cups and silverware for a party. They'll drive our kids to soccer when we're sick. They'll take us to pick up our car when we need a lift to the garage. They'll even take our cats when we go on vacation. As we will for them.

But we don't, with convenience friends, ever come too close or tell too much; we maintain our public face and emotional distance. "Which means," says Elaine, "that I'll talk about being overweight but not about being depressed. Which means I'll admit being mad but not blind with rage. Which means I might say that we're pinched this month but never that I'm worried sick over money."

But which doesn't mean that there isn't sufficient value to be found in these friendships of mutual aid, in convenience friends.

2. Special-interest friends. These friendships aren't intimate, and they needn't involve kids or silverware or cats. Their value lies in some interest jointly shared. And so we may have an office friend or a yoga friend or a tennis friend or a friend from the Women's Democratic Club.

"I've got one woman friend," says Joyce, "who likes, as I do, to take psychology courses. Which makes it nice for me—and nice for her. It's fun to go with someone you know and it's fun to discuss what you've learned, driving back from the classes." And for the most part, she says, that's all they discuss.

"I'd say that what we're doing is *doing* together, not being together," Suzanne says of her Tuesday-doubles friends. "It's mainly a tennis relationship, but we play together well. And I guess we all need to have a couple of playmates."

I agree.

My playmate is a shopping friend, a woman of marvelous taste, a woman who knows exactly *where* to buy *what*, and furthermore is a woman who always knows beyond a doubt what one ought to be buying. I don't have the time to keep up with what's new in eyeshadow, hemlines and shoes and whether the smock look is in or finished already. But since (oh, shame!) I care a lot about eyeshadow, hemlines and shoes, and since I don't *want* to wear smocks if the smock look is finished, I'm very glad to have a shopping friend.

3. Historical friends. We all have a friend who knew us when . . . maybe way back in Miss Meltzer's second grade, when our family lived in that three-room flat in Brooklyn, when our dad was out of work for seven months, when our brother Allie got in that fight where they had to call the police, when our sister married the endodontist from Yonkers and when, the morning after we lost our virginity, she was the first, the only friend we told.

The years have gone by and we've gone separate ways and we've little in common now, but we're still an intimate part of each other's past. And so whenever we go to Detroit we always go to visit this friend of our girlhood. Who knows how we looked before our teeth were straightened. Who knows how we talked before our voice got un-Brooklyned. Who knows what we ate before we learned about artichokes. And who, by her presence, puts us in touch with an earlier part of ourself, a part of ourself it's important never to lose.

"What this friend means to me and what I mean to her," says Grace, "is having a sister without sibling rivalry. We know the texture of each other's lives. She remembers my grandmother's cabbage soup. I remember the way her uncle played the piano. There's simply no other friend who remembers those things."

4. Crossroads friends. Like historical friends, our crossroads friends are important for *what was*—for the friendship we shared at a crucial, now past, time of life. A time, perhaps, when we roomed in college together; or worked as eager young singles in the Big City together; or

went together, as my friend Elizabeth and I did, through pregnancy, birth and that scary first year of new motherhood.

Crossroads friends forge powerful links, links strong enough to endure with not much more contact than once-a-year letters at Christmas. And out of respect for those crossroads years, for those dramas and dreams we once shared, we will always be friends.

5. Cross-generational friends. Historical friends and crossroads friends seem to maintain a special kind of intimacy—dormant but always ready to be revived and though we may rarely meet, whenever we do connect, it's personal and intense. Another kind of intimacy exists in the friendships that form across generations in what one woman calls her daughter-mother and her mother-daughter relationships.

Evelyn's friend is her mother's age—"but I share so much more than I ever could with my mother"—a woman she talks to of music, of books and of life. "What I get from her is the benefit of her experience. What she gets—and enjoys—from me is a youthful perspective. It's a pleasure for both of us."

I have in my own life a precious friend, a woman of 65 who has lived very hard, who is wise, who listens well; who has been where I am and can help me understand it; and who represents not only an ultimate ideal mother to me but also the person I'd like to be when I grow up.

In our daughter role we tend to do more than our share of self-revelation; in our mother role we tend to receive what's revealed. It's another kind of pleasure—playing wise mother to a questing younger person. It's another very lovely kind of friendship.

6. Part-of-a-couple friends. Some of the women we call our friends we never see alone—we see them as part of a couple at couples' parties. And though we share interests in many things and respect each other's views, we aren't moved to deepen the relationship. Whatever the reason, a lack of time or—and this is more likely—a lack of chemistry, our friendship remains in the context of a group. But the fact that our feeling on seeing each other is always, "I'm *so* glad she's here" and the fact that we spend half the evening talking together says that this too, in its own way, counts as a friendship.

(Other part-of-a-couple friends are the friends that came with the marriage, and some of these are friends we could live without. But sometimes, alas, she married our husband's best friend, and sometimes, alas, she is our husband's best friend. And so we find ourself dealing with her, somewhat against our will, in a spirit of what I'll call *reluctant* friendship.)

7. Men who are friends. I wanted to write just of women friends, but the women I've talked to won't let me—they say I must mention man-woman friendships too. For these friendships can be just as close and as dear as those that we form with women. Listen to Lucy's description of one such friendship:

"We've found we have things to talk about that are different from what he talks about with my husband and different from what I talk about with his wife. So sometimes we call on the phone or meet for lunch. There are similar intellectual interests—we always pass on to each other the books that we love—but there's also something tender and caring too."

In a couple of crises, Lucy says, "he offered himself, for talking and for helping. And when someone died in his family he wanted me there. The sexual, flirty part of our friendship is very small, but *some*—just enough to make it fun and different." She thinks—and I agree—that the sexual part, though small is always *some*, is always there when a man and a woman are friends.

It's only in the past few years that I've made friends with men, in the sense of a friendship that's *mine*, not just part of two couples. And achieving with them the ease and the trust I've found with women friends has value indeed. Under the dryer at home last week, putting on mascara and rouge, I comfortably sat and talked with a fellow named Peter. Peter, I finally decided, could handle the shock of me minus mascara under the dryer. Because we care for each other. Because we're friends.

8. There are medium friends, and pretty good friends, and very good friends indeed, and these friendships are defined by their level of intimacy. And what we'll reveal at each of these levels of intimacy is calibrated with care. We might tell a medium friend, for example, that yesterday we had a fight with our husband. And we might tell a pretty good friend that this fight with our husband made us so mad that we slept on the couch. And we might tell a very good friend that the reason we got so mad in that fight that we slept on the couch had something to do with that girl who works in his office. But it's only to our very best friends that we're willing to tell all, to tell what's going on with that girl in his office.

The best of friends, I still believe, totally love and support and trust each other, and bare to each other the secrets of their souls, and run— no questions asked—to help each other, and tell harsh truths to each other when they must be told.

But we needn't agree about everything (only 12-year-old girl friends agree about *everything*) to tolerate each other's point of view. To accept, without judgment. To give and to take without ever keeping score. And to *be* there, as I am for them and as they are for me, to comfort our sorrows, to celebrate our joys.

QUESTIONS

1. Why does Viorst begin her essay with a notion she no longer believes in?

2. Who is Elaine? Who are Joyce, Suzanne, Grace? Why does Viorst include *them* in her essay?

3. Can you think of a category of friends that Viorst has overlooked? Or do you think she has too many, and stretches the word *friend* until it is out of shape?

4. Has this essay affected your understanding of friendship? If so, how?

SUGGESTED ACTIVITIES

1. Write an essay answering question four above.

2. Write an essay on the troubles of friendship.

3. President Warren G. Harding said, "With such friends, who needs enemies?" Create circumstances for such a statement and write an essay explaining Harding's point.

4. Write an essay on the finest friendship (not friend, but friendship) you have ever enjoyed.

5. Write an essay on the relationship between sex and friendship.

6. Write an essay describing the kind of best friend you would like to be. Be specific.

SUSAN ALLEN TOTH

Cinematypes

Raised in Iowa—a childhood she examined in her first book, Blooming: A Small Town Girlhood *(1981)—Toth now lives in Minnesota where she teaches writing at Macalester College. She has published widely in scholarly journals and in such magazines as* Harper's, Redbook, Ms., Cosmopolitan, *and* McCall's. *The essay below is notable for, among other things, making two classifications at the same time.*

Aaron takes me only to art films. That's what I call them, anyway: strange movies with vague poetic images I don't always understand, long dreamy movies about a distant Technicolor past, even longer black-and-white movies about the general meaninglessness of life. We do not go unless at least one reputable critic has found the cinematography superb. We went to *The Devil's Eye,* and Aaron turned to me in the middle and said, "My God, this is *funny.*" I do not think he was pleased.

When Aaron and I go to the movies, we drive our cars separately and meet by the box office. Inside the theater he sits tentatively in his seat, ready to move if he can't see well, poised to leave if the film is disappointing. He leans away from me, careful not to touch the bare flesh of his arm against the bare flesh of mine. Sometimes he leans so far I am afraid he may be touching the woman on his other side. If the movie is very good, he leans forward, too, peering between the heads of the couple in front of us. The light from the screen bounces off his glasses; he gleams with intensity, sitting there on the edge of his seat, watching the screen. Once I tapped him on the arm so I could whisper a comment in his ear. He jumped.

After *Belle de Jour* Aaron said he wanted to ask me if he could stay overnight. "But I can't," he shook his head mournfully before I had a chance to answer, "because I know I never sleep well in strange beds." Then he apologized for asking. "It's just that after a film like that," he said, "I feel the need to assert myself."

Pete takes me only to movies that he thinks have redeeming social value. He doesn't call them "films." They tend to be about poverty, war, injustice, political corruption, struggling unions in the 1930s, and the military-industrial complex. Pete doesn't like propaganda movies, though, and he doesn't like to be too depressed, either. We stayed away from *The Sorrow and the Pity*; it would be, he said, just too much. Beside, he assured me, things are never that hopeless. So most of the movies we see are made in Hollywood. Because they are always topical, these movies offer what Pete calls "food for thought." When we saw *Coming Home*, Pete's jaw set so firmly with the first half-hour that I knew we would end up at Poppin' Fresh Pies afterward.

When Pete and I go to the movies, we take turns driving so no one owes anyone else anything. We leave the car far from the theater so we don't have to pay for a parking space. If it's raining or snowing, Pete offers to let me off at the door, but I can tell he'll feel better if I go with him while he finds a spot, so we share the walk too. Inside the theater Pete will hold my hand when I get scared if I ask him. He puts my hand firmly on his knee and covers it completely with his own hand. His knee never twitches. After a while, when the scary part is past, he loosens his hand slightly and I know that is a signal to take mine away. He sits companionably close, letting his jacket just touch my sweater, but he does not infringe. He thinks I ought to know he is there if I need him.

One night, after *The China Syndrome*, I asked Pete if he wouldn't like to stay for a second drink, even though it was past midnight. He thought a while about that, considering my offer from all possible angles, but finally he said no. Relationships today, he said, have a tendency to move too quickly.

Sam likes movies that are entertaining. By that he means movies that Will Jones in the *Minneapolis Tribune* loved and either *Time* or *Newsweek* rather liked; also movies that do not have sappy love stories, are not musicals, do not have subtitles, and will not force him to think. He does not go to movies to think. He liked *California Suite* and *The Seduction of Joe Tynan*, though the plots, he said, could have been zippier. He saw it all coming too far in advance, and that took the fun out. He doesn't like to know what is going to happen. "I just want my brain to be tickled," he says. It is very hard for me to pick out movies for Sam.

When Sam takes me to the movies, he pays for everything. He thinks that's what a man ought to do. But I buy my own popcorn, because he doesn't approve of it; the grease might smear his flannel slacks. Inside the theater, Sam makes himself comfortable. He takes off his jacket, puts one arm around me, and all during the movie he plays with my hand, stroking my palm, beating a small tattoo on my wrist. Although he watches the movie intently, his body operates on instinct.

Once I inclined my head and kissed him lightly just behind his ear. He beat a fast tattoo on my wrist, quick and musical, but he didn't look away from the screen.

When Sam takes me home from the movies, he stands outside my door and kisses me long and hard. He would like to come in, he says regretfully, but his steady girlfriend in Duluth wouldn't like it. When the *Tribune* gives a movie four stars, he has to save it to see with her. Otherwise her feelings might be hurt.

I go to some movies by myself. On rainy Sunday afternoons I often sneak into a revival house or a college auditorium for old Technicolor musicals, *Kiss Me Kate, Seven Brides for Seven Brothers, Calamity Jane*, even, once, *The Sound of Music*. Wearing saggy jeans so I can prop my feet on the seat in front, I sit toward the rear where no one will see me. I eat large handfuls of popcorn with double butter. Once the movie starts, I feel completely at home. Howard Keel and I are old friends; I grin back at him on the screen. I know the sound tracks by heart. Sometimes when I get really carried away I hum along with Kathryn Grayson, remembering how I once thought I would fill out a formal like that. I am rather glad now I never did. Skirts whirl, feet tap, acrobatic young men perform impossible feats, and then the camera dissolves into a dream sequence I know I can comfortably follow. It is not, thank God, Bergman.

If I can't find an old musical, I settle for Hepburn and Tracy, vintage Grant or Gable, on adventurous days Claudette Colbert or James Stewart. Before I buy my ticket I make sure it will all end happily. If necessary, I ask the girl at the box office. I have never seen *Stella Dallas* or *Intermezzo*. Over the years I have developed other peccadilloes: I will, for example, see anything that is redeemed by Thelma Ritter. At the end of *Daddy Long Legs* I wait happily for the scene when Fred Clark, no longer angry, at last pours Thelma a convivial drink. They smile at each other, I smile at them, I feel they are smiling at me. In the movies I go to by myself, the men and women always like each other.

QUESTIONS

1. Why wasn't Aaron pleased that the film was funny? Why doesn't Toth *explain* why? (Or does she—in a way—explain why, a way better than overt explanation?)

2. Why doesn't Pete call movies "films"? Why doesn't Toth explain why?

3. Sam likes movies that tickle his brain but do not force him to think. What's the difference?

4. Why is it so pleasing to Toth that the men and women in her films like each other?

SUGGESTED ACTIVITIES

1. Structure your own classification of movies.

2. Explain the differences (according to your experience) between watching a movie, a TV drama, and a play.

3. Describe the way you enjoy going to a movie—the sort of theater, the time, the company—and explain why.

POSTSCRIPT

Commentary on *Cinematypes*

The main change from Draft #1 to #2 followed the advice of my editor at *Harper's*, which was to heighten the point of the essay by describing the movies I like to see when I go to them alone. The first draft of section IV, with its one-sentence ending ("Most of the time, I go to movies by myself"), was indeed somewhat bleak—though I'd meant it to be ironic as well. I'm not sure the more muted pessimism of the new ending is a great change in terms of cheerfulness, but the effect is more wistful, less flat. (Watching old movies alone says more about loneliness than the other sections do, I think.)

My characters were based on real people, and I wrote about these incidents with a mixture of frustration, laughter, and pleasure at saying to myself what I couldn't say out loud to the real-life prototypes. I changed enough detail so that one of the "characters" read this piece, enjoyed it, and had no idea that he had played a part in its background.

Susan Allen Toth

I don't always understand

Going To The Movies

I.

Aaron only takes me ~~s~~ to art films. That's what I call them, anyway:
strange ~~about~~ movies whose *vague* poetic images are *further* blurred by a hand-held camera,
long dreamy movies about ~~the~~ distant *a* past, ~~in a Technicolor haze~~, *Technicolor* even
longer black-and-white movies about the general hopelessness and meaining-
lessness of life. We do not go unless at least one reputable critic has
found the cinematography superb. We went to "Manhattan," and Aaron
turned ~~to me~~ to me in the middle and said, "My God, this is _funny_."
I do not think he was pleased.

When Aaron and I go to the movies, we drive our cars separately and
meet by the box ~~f~~ffice. Inside the theatre he sits tentataively in his
seat, ready to move if he can't see well, poised to leave if the film
is disappointing. He leans away from me, careful not to touch the bare
flesh of his arm against the bare flesh of mine. Sometimes he leans so
far I am afraid he may be touching the woman on his other side instead.
If the movie is very good, he leans forward too, peering between the
heads of the couple in front of me. The light from the screen bounces
off his glasses; he gleams with intensity, sitting there on the edge of
his chair, watching the screen. Once I tapped him on the arm so I could
whisper a comment in his ear. He jumped.

After ~~the movie~~ "The Discreet Charm of the Bourgeoisie" Aaron
said he wanted to ask *me* if he could~~x~~ stay overnight. "But I can,t" he
shook his head mournfully before I had a chance to answer, ~~"You see,~~ I *because I know*
~~don't~~ *never* sleep well in strange beds." *Then he apologized for asking.*
" is just that after a film like that," he said, "I feel the need
to ~~prove a statement~~ *assort* ~~do something~~ *myself. "*

II.

Bob only takes me to movies that have a redeeming social conscience.
He doesn't call them "films." They tend to be about poverty, war, in-
                                political corruption,
justice, ~~politics~~, struggling unions, ~~greedy corporations~~, and the military-industrial complex. They are usually shorter than the art films.
Because they are always highly relevant, they offer what Bob calls
"food for thought." When we saw "Coming Home," Bob's jaw set so firmly
                                        ~~have to~~ ~~and we just~~ end up at
in the first half hour that I knew we would ~~go~~ to Poppin' Fresh Pies
afterwards, ~~so we could really talk about it.~~

When Bob and I go to the movies, we take turns driving so no one
                    anything
owes anyone else. We park far away from the theatre so we don't have
to pay for a lot. If it's raining, ~~sleeting~~ or snowing, Bob offers
to let me off at the door, but I can tell he'd feel better if I went
with him while he parked, so we share the walk too. Inside the theatre
Bob will hold my hand ~~if I want~~ when [I] get scared, if I ask him. He
puts my hand firmly on his ~~the~~ knee and ~~ever~~ covers it completely with
his ~~own~~ own hand. His knee never twitches. After a while, when the
scary part is past, he loosens his hand slightly and I know that is a
signal to take mine away. He sits companionably close, letting his
jacket just touch my sweater, but he does ~~it~~ not infringe. He thinks
I ought to know he is there if I need him.

One night after "The China Syndrome" I asked Bob ~~if he~~ if he wouldn't
like to stay for a second drink, even though it was past midnight. He
thought a while about that, considering my offer from all possible angles,
but finally he said no. Relationships today, he said, have a tendency
     move
to ~~progress~~ too ~~fast.~~ quickly.

III.

Sam likes movies that are entertaining. By that he means movies that
Will Jones in the Minneapolis _Tribune_ and at least one New York critic
rather liked; also movies that do not have sappy stories, are not musicals, and
will not force him to think. He does not go to movies to think. When
we saw "California Suite," he thought it was not too
bad. So far we have not seen what he calls a really good movie.

When Sam takes me to the movies, he pays for everything. He thinks
that's what a man ought to do. But I buy my own popcorn, because he
doesn't approve of it; the grease might smear his flannel slacks.
Inside the theatre, Sam makes himself comfortable. He takes off his
jacket, puts one arm around me, and takes my hand if I am usually careful to wipe it dry
from the popcorn. All during the movie he plays with my
finger
hand, running his finger up my arm, stroking my palm, beating a small
tattoo on my wrist. Although he watches the movie intently, his body
operates on instinct near a female body. Once I
inclined my head and kissed him lightly just behind his ear.
He didn't look away from the screen but he beat a faster tattoo
quick and musical,
on my wrist, but
When Sam takes me home from the movies, he stands outside my door
and kisses me long and hard. He would like to come in, he says regretfully, but his steady girlfirend in Duluth wouldn't like it. He
only sees her on weekends, so he has plenty of time to go to the movies
has to
during the week. When the _Tribune_ gives a movie four stars, he saves it
to see with her. Otherwise her feelings might be hurt.

IV.

Most of the time I go to movies by myself.

IV.

I go to some movies by myself. ~~Mostly~~ On/ rainy unday aftrnooons I, sneak after ~~mx college auditorium~~ or a college auditorium
into a revival house for old Technicolor musicals, "Kiss Me ^Kate," "Seven
"Calamity Jane,"
Brides for Seven Brothers," even, once, "The Sound of Music." I sit
towards the ~~back~~ her where no one will recognize me ~~and I wear old baggy~~ wearing saggy

jeans so I can propr my feet up ~~inxfrxn~~ on the seat in front. Once the

movie starts, I feel comple tely at home. Howard Keel and I are old

freinds; I grin back at him on the screen, admiring all his teeth.
I know the sound tracks by heart.
Sometimes when I get really carried away I hum along with Kathryn

Grayson, remembering how I once thought I would fil l out a formal

like that. I ~~rxt~~ am rather glad now I never did. Skirts whirl,
~~bx drxxx of shiny men in tuxedos perfom~~
feet tap, ∧impossible ~~aerobatic~~ feats and then the camera dissolves
                                        comfortably It is
into a dream sequence I ~~xxx~~ know I can/follow. ~~Itxs~~ not, thank God,

Bergman.
                  IE
~~Because I know everything will end happily, I~~ rela x completely.

[~~If I'm in a theatre,~~ I eat popcorn with double the amount of butter]
                                                      or selected
If I can't find an old musical, I settle for Hepburn and Tracy, vintage
    or ~~Clark Gable, Claudette Colbert, Jimmy Stewart.~~ Almost any maybe a adjective don
C~~ary~~ Grant, ~~or any movie which I know the characters men and women~~
~~movie is a redeemed by Thelma Ritter.~~
~~are going to like each other.~~
Before I buy my ticket and it
I ~~make sure~~ that it will all end happily. ~~before I go~~ If necessary, I ask for old
    girl at the box office.   movies
the ticket clerk. I have never seen "Mrs. Miniver" or "Stella Dallas."
Over the years I have developed other ~~peculiarities~~ fear no one else
~~Sometimes I even go to an old movie because of its nonromantic leads;~~
would understand; I will ~~go down~~ for example, see almost
~~almost~~ anything is ~~redeemed~~ redeemed by Thelma Ritter. At the end of "Daddy
            happily
Long Legs" I wait∧for the scene when ~~shudder~~ Fred Wynn, pours ~~les~~ a convivial. Thelma
                                                    at last
drink, ~~and~~ they smile at each other, ~~I love movies where in the end men~~ no longer angry,
~~and women like each other.~~   I smile at them, I feel they are
                                   smiling at me. ~~I feel good~~

In the movies I go to, I make sure that the
men o women always like each other.

Bob takes me only to movies that he thinks have a redeeming social

onscience. He doesn't call them ,films." They tend to be about

poverty, war, injustic, political corruption, struggling unions in the

1930s, and the military-industrial complex. Bob doesn't like propaganda
                                                                  though,
films, ~~hxxxyxy~~ and he doesn't like to be ~~d~~ too depressed, either.
Deffles, he ~~pdxxx~~ assured me,   moves
Things are never that hopeless, ~~he says~~. So most of the ~~films~~ we
                              started every frm.
see are made in Hollywood. [We ~~xxxidxd~~ had to avoid "The Sorrow and
                         just   moves
the Pity"! it would be, he said, too much .) Because these ~~films~~ are
                    very topical,
always highly relevant, they offer what Bob ca ls "food for thougr t."

He liked "California Suite" and "The Séduction of Joe Tynan," though
          plots   He saw it all coming too far in advance, an
the ~~xtxrixx~~, he said, could have been zippier. He doesn't like to   that took
                                                                          run out.
know what is ~~xxxixx~~ going to happen. "I just want my brains to be
~~Xxixxxxixinterviexxxxxxxxxxfrixxdxxixxxdvxxxxwhxxxxxxxxxxxxxxx~~,
tickled," he says. It is very hard for me to pick out movies for

Sam

      k"The 7½5 Solution" would have been fine, but it was too grim.
      do they always have to
Why rub if in? Sam asked me. I didn't answer.

V

Ordinary Life

C. W. SMITH
Pumping Iron

A Texan, Smith has written many stories and essays, a screenplay, and two novels: Thin Man of Haddam *(1974) and* Country Music *(1975). He is at work on a third novel. In this essay, Smith proves that manhood is an attitude, not a role.*

Don't spread it around, but I love to iron. Every Sunday evening when the *60 Minutes* clock starts ticking, I haul my folding board out of the hall closet, mantle it upright about five paces from my television set, get out a week's worth of shirts, trousers, and jeans (ironing jeans is an old cowboy tradition), and press the bejesus out of everything while Ed, Morley, Harry, and Mike yammer away about problems far more serious than wrinkled fabric, and far less easily remedied. Talk's the cheap coin of information there, so it takes only an occasional glance from the board to the screen—say, when I'm flipping a sleeve—to keep up with what's going on.

I'm not the only man who irons. I know a Pulitzered photographer who braved the fire in El Salvador (credentials for machismo seem necessary here), and he gets fifty cents for every blouse of his girl-friend's he irons. (He works too cheap.) One academic dean of my acquaintance does the smoothing, as it once was called, for his wife and son. Three cases may not constitute a trend, but it's obvious that the distaff half of the global population has forsaken this old, joyous craft. Like so much of our work done by hand, it has fallen into disfavor. It's linked with domestic slavery; of all the household chores once designated as women's work, ironing seems to have been the most odious, so it now carries the most trenchant political overtones.

You don't ask a woman to iron a garment for you (even if you've found one who knows how) any more than you might request that she greet you at the door in a rip-off French maid's costume, a martini in hand and your slippers in her teeth.

Naturally I could argue that it was good enough for my mother, but she's given it up, too. In the days before steam irons my mother had to douse her clean wash in a cooked starch solution, dry it on a clothes-line, and sprinkle each piece with water from a huge green Coca-Cola bottle stoppered with a perforated aluminum nozzle shaped like a flower. She'd roll each piece and place it in a plastic bag to let it marinate for a time. Then she'd unfold the items one by one and diligently cook them just short of scorching, until they were stiff as canvas. To get into one of my just-ironed shirts, I'd have to form a wedge with my hand and peel the interior surfaces of the sleeves apart as I stuck my arm through. Now *that* was ironing! (You can still buy the same result by sending shirts to the laundry and ordering "heavy starch" but by the fourth time around the buttons will have disinte-grated from, I'm guessing, harsh chemicals or too much heat.) I remember how she'd put her hair up in a bandanna like Lucy, and the sweat would pop from her brow; she wasn't a soap opera fan, but she always ironed near the radio to hear Don McNeill and the Breakfast Club. ("And now . . . let's march around the breakfast table!") These days, though, she never buys cotton unless it's meant to be worn rumpled or it sneaks into the house as dental floss or on the ends of Q-Tips.

My mother-in-law is a throwback who still irons handkerchiefs, underwear, and sheets. But her daughter (my wife) kept her eyes shut all the years she lived at home, largely because of the sound suspicion that learning a craft might require that it be practiced later in life. So her white double-breasted Calvin Klein blouse of 100 percent cotton with ten pearl snaps up the front goes into my laundry basket. I don't mind; in fact, nothing pleases me more than to square off against an all-cotton garment. It comes out of the dryer as wrinkled as used tinfoil; it requires a lot of ironing, but then, it also takes it well. The metamorphosis is profound and admirable. Nothing is more frus-trating than to try to make a shirt of 65 percent polyester and 35 percent cotton look as if it has been ironed. It resists my efforts in a nightmarish way, retains the wrinkles "permanent press' is not sup-posed to have in the first place, and when I'm finished, I can't tell the difference. These never-press fabrics were supposed to have freed women from the slavery of ironing, but in me they merely produce an exas-perating sense of impotence.

Old female hands at this no doubt snicker to hear a man grumble about these small difficulties. Any man who takes up ironing will hear a lot of *I-told-you-so's* from women who are also encouraging us to cook, wash, and baby-sit, on the theory that if we get a taste of it we'll understand why they want to give it all up for more-glamorous careers in used-car sales and digital-watch assembly. They've been at this switcheroo ever since somebody talked Roosevelt Grier into taking up needlepoint, and they persist in protesting that ironing cripples the spirit. For instance, Erma Bombeck, who recently claimed that she ironed "by appointment only," once told an inveterate ironer who pressed the tongues of her son's tennis shoes that women simply did not do that anymore. "Did you ever see the women on the soap operas iron?" she asked this Mrs. Breck. "No! They're out having abortions, committing murder, blackmailing their boss, undergoing surgery, having fun! If you weren't chained to this ironing board, you, too, could be out doing all sorts of exciting things!"

I could claim that I iron only because I can't find a woman who'll do it for me, but that's not even a half-truth. I don't have to iron; I *get* to iron. It's been that way with me since boot camp, when I was nineteen and first discovered the joy of creasing khaki with a hot aluminum plate. I won my first iron by shooting in the top five in my platoon on the rifle range. That iron's been lost for years, and I now use an ordinary B-flat GE I picked up in a garage sale. Now and then I get a yen for what I think of as the Cadillac of steam irons, a Sunbeam "Deluxe Shot of Steam Iron." (How quaint—"Deluxe"!) You got your watergauge on it, so you don't have to guess by watching the steam languish that it needs refilling. You got your fifty-one big steam vents. (Mine has thirty-eight.) You got your "Extra Steam at the Touch of a Button" for that surge of power you need passing on hills. It's self-cleaning—no starch buildups that make the skating surface gummy and hard to slide. At three pounds of chrome-plated steel, this baby will put a sizable dent in your Adidas if you drop it. A manly tool. It retails for around forty-eight dollars. I'd buy one, except that I'm waiting for my old one to wear out, and that's like keeping your eye peeled for Halley's comet. With only one or two moving parts, irons don't break down. You can gunk one up by using highly mineralized water in it or by not emptying the surplus when you finish ironing, so that the heating elements rust or collect deposits, but it's pretty hard to outlive this machinery.

Over the years manufacturers have added improvements, such as the reversible cord for switch-hitting—this year Sunbeam even came out with a model that shuts itself off if it suspects a scorched shirt or a distracting phone call—but the durable simplicity of the design leaves little room for tampering to make it better. The old rowboat shape, with a bow that bobs easily between buttons and a broad stern that sails trippingly o'er the main, has never been altered, to my knowledge, for hundreds of years, and that motif is carried out in the contours of the board. (Apply a little elementary Freudian symbolism here, and your hand becomes "the little man in the boat," with the iron as the boat; or, in a significantly telling nesting image, the iron itself becomes "the little man" sailing his boat, the board. I could, but I won't, go on with this.) To my mind, the only improvement left to be made in the tools is to have a board that goes up and down with ease. I've never tried to set one up that I didn't feel as if I were wrestling with an angry stork.

Once I've done that, though, the rest is, well, smooth sailing. I take a shirt, spread it on my board and give it a few shots from my can of spray starch (both sides, extra dose on the collar), then set to work. My movements are ritualistic: first the sleeves (both sides), then the collar (first pressed flat, then folded and ironed along the crease), then I fit the shirt over the broad end of the board as if the board were to be wearing it, press one side of the breast (if the pocket has flaps, all the better), then the other, turn the shirt over to do the back in one piece, then tug the hem down to bring the yoke over the end of the board to be pressed. Along about the third item, I can feel my pulse slowing, my breathing leveling out. Something like a trance descends as I smell the clean starch-and-steam aroma drifting up from the iron. My problems seem to dissipate with the steam, and soon I hear a humming in my inner ear; a calm, somnolent voice purrs, "Al-pha, al-pha, al-pha," as all rejection and dejection are pressed into harmless memory like petals between pages.

When I'm finished with the shirt, I can hold it up between my hands and see if I've done a good job or not. Precious few things in life lend themselves to such immediate, definitive judgment. What you've done, good or bad, is undeniable: you've brought order to chaos, and it's either ironed well or it's not. If it's not, you can touch it up in seconds flat. You apply a minimum of energy in an enjoyable fashion, and the payoff far exceeds that small cost. It's not like a customer lost for reasons that must be discerned and then explained to yourself or your superior; it's not one of your children who has done something childish but who is too big to spank; it's not an argument with your spouse over whose career is to take precedence. No sticky, no-win trade-offs. No relativism. I am; therefore, I iron.

"But," objected one woman I know who used to iron, "aren't you frustrated when it just gets wrinkled again?" I said, honestly, no. It makes me feel adult and rather manly, the way my mother and grandmother must have always felt when they stood in the hot kitchen for days making pies and cakes from scratch and stuffing the turkey so that when company came, they'd have a whooping, thirty-minute Thanksgiving orgy. Glad the men enjoyed it, they'd savor with relish their secret—the men had no idea how much work had gone into it.

A chore, by definition, must be done over and over. That's what makes it different from a task. The objection raised by my woman friend suggests to me that women are growing childishly masculine about doing chores, because they have retrained themselves to perceive that tasks—changing a tire, shooting one deer a year—are masculine by tradition and are therefore more attractive.

And sure they are, in a way. They're easier; any fool can do something once, but it takes a mature adult to do something again and again and know that it will never really be finished. Performing this weekly chore is like a little disciplinary *koan*, a humble pleasure-giving mantra that can bring serenity to my hectic life. Well, that's laying it on a bit thick. But at least I've had so much fun doing such a common and mundane thing that as I'm putting the last flourish to my Levi's while *60 Minutes* that goes off I wonder why Andy Rooney hasn't discovered it yet.

QUESTIONS

1. Instead of a question—an assignment: Examine the first sentence and figure out what it does to get Smith's essay off and running.

2. How many parentheses does Smith use? Are all of them necessary? Are there too many? How do they affect the rhythm of the prose? The tone?

3. How often—and in how many ways—does Smith refer to masculinity (or the lack thereof)?

4. How many benefits of ironing does Smith define?

SUGGESTED ACTIVITIES

1. Write an argument against Smith's definition of maturity.

2. Describe a mundane chore you enjoy doing. Like Smith, figure out what it means to you—*why* you enjoy it.

3. Describe a mundane chore you find especially disagreeable. Figure out why you dislike it so much. Specify the ways you cope or refuse to cope with it.

POSTSCRIPT

Commentary on *Pumping Iron*

My essay began when I was ironing one day and thought that I better think of a way to write about this. This is standard practice for me, since about one-third of my income is derived from writing pieces such as this, as well as reviews, short stories and an occasional novel or three. You get accustomed to not letting any motion you make go wasted. I mentioned to my agent that I was thinking about writing such an article, and her eyes widened with delight. "Great!" she said. I can tell when something hits a commercial nerve by listening to her inflection, but I honestly thought it would sell, if at all, to a woman's magazine—I mean, I thought it would be entertaining (or provoking) for women readers to listen to some man yammering on and on about the joys of ironing.

With this kind of piece, if you don't do it with style you don't do it at all. It's not investigative journalism or spot news; nor is it meditative philosophy. It's trivia. When you write about trivia or about the mundane things we all do, your first (and most persistent) challenge is to try to accomplish a triumph of style over substance. Because there's so little substance. A guy is ironing. Big deal. Unfortunately, this kind of style is rarely gained from practicing it, and writing a good many drafts usually doesn't help. It either comes as a package with the subject matter, or it doesn't. (I've had "doesn't" happen more often than "does," too.) You're in a certain frame of mind or mood or mindset, and that chooses your words, your jokes, your structure. Later, you can tinker with it, of course.

I tend to write a lot before I put anything down on paper with these little projects. So a good many weeks went by between the time I decided I should write about ironing and the point where I actually sat down at my keyboard. In the meantime, I was still doing my shirts, and so while I would be ironing, I could talk to myself about the process, knowing that eventually I would be writing about it. What's this like, anyway? What is going on here with the tools, the materials, the worker? What is it similar to? What do I remember about ironing over the ages, so to speak? (The childhood impressions, etc.) What's hard, easy, fun, not fun? What do I feel? Basically I was just gathering information in a casual way, doing a protracted interview with myself. When I did sit down to write the piece, it came out more or less as it appeared in Esquire with a few minor changes. (I think the business about the "man in the boat" was a thought that came after the first draft and I inserted it into the ms. in another position before finally settling on putting it where it is.) This seldom happens to me, this just-as-you-see-it business. It's far more common to have to work and rework things at least a half dozen times, working usually more on the beginning and ending than on the middle. For me, revising sometimes seems to mean discovering the right place to begin more than anything else. This happened to be a case of beginning the essay just the way (or at the point where) I begin ironing, though that is seldom the case: rarely does the beginning of an activity or an experience turn out to be the place to begin a description about it. When you discover why that's so, you will have solved a good many writing problems.

C. W. Smith

JOHN MCPHEE
The Conching Rooms

A native and resident of Princeton, New Jersey, McPhee is a staff writer for The New Yorker *and has written many books on a wide diversity of topics, among them* Oranges *(1967),* The Deltoid Pumpkin Seed *(1973),* The Survival of the Bark Canoe *(1975), and, his best-known—a look at Alaska from several viewpoints—Coming into the Country *(1977). As the following essay illustrates McPhee is tops when it comes to process analysis.*

Pools and pools and pools of chocolate—fifty-thousand-pound, ninety-thousand-pound, Olympic-length pools of chocolate—in the conching rooms in the chocolate factory in Hershey, Pennsylvania. Big, aromatic rooms. Chocolate, far as the eye can see. Viscous, undulating, lukewarm chocolate, viscidized, undulated by the slurping friction of granite rollers rolling through the chocolate over crenellated granite beds at the bottoms of the pools. The chocolate moves. It stands up in brown creamy dunes. Chocolate eddies. Chocolate currents. Gulfs of chocolate. Chocolate deeps. Mares' tails on the deeps. The world record for the fifty-yard free-style would be two hours and ten minutes.

Slip a little spatula in there and see how it tastes. Waxy? Claggy? Gritty? Mild? Taste it soft. That is the way to get the flavor. Conching—

granite on granite, deep in the chocolate—ordinarily continues for seventy-two hours, but if Bill Wagner thinks the flavor is not right he will conch for hours extra, or even an extra day. Milky? Coarse? Astringent? Caramely? For forty-five years, Mr. Wagner has been tasting the chocolate. His taste buds magnified a hundred times would probably look like Hershey's kisses. He is aging now, and is bent slightly forward—a slender man, with gray hair and some white hair. His eyeglasses have metal rims and dark plastic brows. He wears thin white socks and brown shoes, black trousers, a white shirt with the company's name on it in modest letters. Everyone wears a hat near the chocolate. Most are white paper caps. Wagner's hat is dapper, white, visored: a chocolate-making supervisor's linen hat.

A man in a paper hat comes up and asks Wagner, "Are we still running tests on that kiss paste?"

"Yes. You keep testing."

Wagner began in cocoa, in 1924. The dust was too much for him. After a few weeks, he transferred to conching. He has been conching ever since, working out the taste and texture. Conching is the alchemy of the art, the transmutation of brown paste into liquid Hershey bars. Harsh? Smooth? Fine? Bland? There are viscosimeters and other scientific instruments to aid the pursuit of uniformity, but the ultimate instrument is Wagner. "You do it by feel, and by taste," he says. "You taste for flavor and for fineness—whether it's gritty. There's one area of your tongue you're more confident in than others. I use the front end of my tongue and the roof of my mouth." He once ate some Nestlé's; he can't remember when. He lays some chocolate on the tip of his tongue and presses it upward. The statement that sends ninety thousand pounds on its way to be eaten is always the same. Wagner's buds blossom, and he says, "That's Hershey's."

Milton Hershey's native town was originally called Derry Church, and it was surrounded, as it still is, by rolling milkland. Hershey could not have been born in a better place, for milk is twenty per cent of milk chocolate. Bill Wagner grew up on a farm just south of Derry Church. "It was a rented farm. We didn't own a farm until 1915. I lived on the farm through the Second World War. I now live in town." Wagner's father, just after 1900, had helped Milton Hershey excavate the limestone bedrock under Derry Church to establish the foundations of the chocolate plant. Derry Church is Hershey now, and its main street, Chocolate Avenue, has street lamps shaped like Hershey's kisses—tinfoil, tassel, and all. The heart of town is the corner of Chocolate and Cocoa. Other streets (Lagos, Accra, Para) are named for the places the beans come from: quotidian freight trains full of beans that are roasted and, in studied ratios, mixed together—base beans, flavor beans, African beans, American beans—and crushed by granite millstones arranged in cascading tiers, from which flow falls of dark cordovan liquor. This thick chocolate liquor is squeezed mechanically in huge cylindrical accordion compressors. Clear cocoa butter rains down out of the compressors. When the butter has drained off, the compressors open, and out fall dry brown discs the size of manhole covers. These discs are broken into powder. The powder is put into cans and sold. It is Hershey's Cocoa—straight out of the jungle and off to the A. & P., pure as a driven freak, pure as the purest sunflower seed in a whole-earth boutique.

Concentrate fresh milk and make a paste with sugar. To two parts natural chocolate liquor add one part milk-and-sugar paste and one part pure cocoa butter. Conch for three days and three nights. That—more or less—is the recipe for a Hershey bar. (Baking chocolate consists of nothing but pure chocolate liquor allowed to stand and harden in molds. White chocolate is not really chocolate. It is made from milk, sugar, and cocoa butter, but without cocoa.) In the conching rooms, big American flags hang from beams above the chocolate. "Touch this," Mr. Wagner says. The cast-iron walls that hold in the chocolate are a hundred and thirty degrees Fahrenheit. "We have no heat under this. It's only created heat—created by the friction that the granite rollers produce."

"What if the rollers stop?"

"The chocolate will freeze."

When that happens, the result is a brown icecap, a chocolate-coated Nome. Sometimes fittings break or a worker forgets to shut off a valve and thousands of pounds of chocolate spill over, spread out, and solidify on the floor. Workers have to dig their way out, with adzes, crowbars, shovels, picks—chocolate Byrds, chocolate Amundsens.

"The trend today is people want to push buttons," Wagner says. "They'll try to find ways to shortcut. It's a continual struggle to get people to do their share. There's no shortcut to making Hershey's. There have been times when I wished I'd stayed on the farm." Every day, he works from six in the morning until four-thirty in the afternoon, so he can cover parts of all shifts. He walks (twelve minutes) from his home, on Para Avenue. "Para is a bean, I think. It's a bean or a country, I'm not sure which. We have another street called Ceylon. That's not a bean. It's a country." In the conching rooms, Wagner can see subtleties of hue that escape the untrained eye; he can tell where the kiss paste is, and the semisweet, and the chocolate chips, and the bar milk chocolate. Kiss paste has to be a little more dense, so the kisses will sit up. Wagner has grandchildren in Hershey, Colebrook, and Mechanicsburg. When he goes to see them, he slips them kisses.

Within the connoisseurship, there are acknowledgedly superior chocolates, and, God knows, inferior ones, but undeniably there is no chocolate flavor quite like that of a Hershey bar. No one in Hershey can, or will, say exactly why. There is voodoo in the blending of beans, and even more voodoo in the making of the milk-and-sugar paste. There is magic in Bill Wagner when he decides that a batch is done. All this, however, does not seem to add up to a satisfactory explanation of the uniqueness of the product. Mystery lingers on. Notice, though, in the conching rooms, what is happening to the granite rollers rolling under the chocolate on the granite beds. Slowly, geologically, the granite is eroding. The granite beds last about thirty years. The granite rollers go somewhat sooner than that. Rolling back and forth, back and forth, they become flat on one side. Over the days, months, years, this wearing down of the granite is uniform, steady, consistent, a little at a time. There seems to be an ingredient that is not listed on the label. Infinitesimal granitic particles have nowhere to go but into the chocolate. A Hershey bar is part granite.

Ask management where the granite comes from. The official answer is "New England."

"Where in New England?"

"New England. That is all we are saying. Nestle's won't say anything about anything. Mars is the same way. So we don't say anything, either."

QUESTIONS

1. How many fragments does McPhee use in the first paragraph? Are they justified? How so? How not?

2. What does McPhee mean by saying that Hershey's Cocoa is "pure as a driven freak"?

3. "Para is a bean, I think," says Mr. Wagner. "It's a bean or a country, I'm not sure which. We have another street called Ceylon. That's not a bean. It's a country." Why does McPhee include this statement? What does it reveal?

4. Why does McPhee end his essay as he does? What is the point?

SUGGESTED ACTIVITIES

1. List the ways McPhee holds our interest in an industrial process. Compare your list with the lists of a group of classmates.

2. Analyze a process yourself, using as many of McPhee's techniques as the subject allows.

WILLIAM G. WING
Christmas Comes First on the Banks

A veteran correspondent for the defunct New York Herald Tribune, Wing *writes for publications like the* New York Times *and* Audubon Magazine. *This essay shows how it is possible to make profound connections with utter simplicity.*

The Christmas sun rises first, in America, on trawlermen fishing the undersea meadows of Georges Bank.

At the moment before sunrise a hundred miles east of Cape Cod, the scene aboard a trawler is so unchanging it can be imagined. The net has been hauled and streamed again. The skipper is alone in the pilot house, surrounded by the radiotelephone's racket and the green and amber eyes of electronic instruments, instruments that are supposed to tell him not only where he is but where the fish are, too. But this is only hope, not science. Despite the instruments, despite the boat's resemblance to a plow horse, methodically crisscrossing the meadow, her men are not engineers or farmers, but hunters who seek their prey in the wilderness of the sea. The trawlermen are, in fact, the last tribe of nomadic huntsmen left in the East.

The skipper is alone, then, with a huntsman's anxieties: the whereabouts of the prey, the uncertainties of the weather, the chances of hitting a good market. On deck before him the men are processing the catch just brought aboard. They sit in a circle of brilliance, the deck lights reflecting from their yellow and Daybrite-orange oilskins and from the brown curve of the riding sail above. They sit on the edges of the pens, holding the big white and silver fish between their knees, ripping with knives and tearing with hands, heaving the disemboweled bodies into a central basket. Nothing is visible beyond the cone of light but the occasional flash of a whitecap or comber. There is much noise, though—wind and water and seabirds that have gathered in mobs for the feast of haulback.

There is an appropriateness to Christmas in this scene, east of the sleeping mainland, so marked that it seems quaint. The names of the trawlers themselves—*Holy Family Immaculate Conception, St. Mary, St.Joseph*—give the flavor. On the engine room bulkhead of the trawler *Holy Cross*, beyond the ugga-chugging Atlas diesel, is a painting of Christ at Gethsemane. There is an appropriateness, too, among the men. They share alike—equal shares of profit, equal shares of danger. To work together in such small quarters and stern conditions requires a graciousness of spirit that is the essence of Christmas.

The sun is up and the pens are empty. As the deck is hosed down and the trash fish pitchforked overboard, the noise from the birds rises hysterically—barnyard sounds, shrieks, whistles, klaxon horns. Now the birds can be seen flying in a circle around the boat. Each can hold position for only a few moments beside the point where the remains of fish are washing over. Then it falls astern and has to come up to windward on the other side of the boat, cross ahead and fall backward to the critical point. The birds pumping up the windward side look like six-day bicycle riders, earnest and slightly ridiculous, but when they reach the critical point there is a miraculous moment of aerobatics as the birds brake, wheel and drop in the broken air.

Gulls snatch, gannets plunge, but the little kittiwakes balance delicately, their tails spread like carved ivory fans. There is a column of descending, shrieking birds, a scintillating feathered mass. The birds revolving about the boat have made themselves not only guests at the feast but have formed the wreath as well.

Christmas Day has begun, but for the men it is time to sleep. They hose each other off and then disappear through the whaleback for a mug-up below. Boots and oilskins off, they will have a minute or two for a James Bond novel or a crossword puzzle in the bunks, braced against the elevator motions of the hull, not hearing the sounds of Niagara outside. Then the instant unconsciousness that seamen and children know. The skipper alone remains awake, watching Christmas come.

Christmas came first to men on lonely meadows. It will come first again to the men on the lonely meadows offshore, fishing the Bank in boats wreathed by seabirds.

QUESTIONS

1. How many times and in how many ways does Wing compare sea and land? What does the comparison accomplish?

2. How many religious images does Wing use? Do they seem to flow naturally from the subject? Or does he impose them (or some of them) on the material? Is it important that they seem to flow naturally from the material? If so, how so? If not, why not?

SUGGESTED ACTIVITIES

1. List five secular activities that can be depicted in religious terms. Expand one into a 500-word essay.

2. List five religious activities that can be depicted in secular terms. Expand one into a 500-word essay.

JOAN DIDION

In Bed

In this essay Didion incorporates the personal and the medical to make a point of general significance.

Three, four, sometimes five times a month, I spend the day in bed with a migraine headache, insensible to the world around me. Almost every day of every month, between these attacks, I feel the sudden irrational irritation and the flush of blood into the cerebral arteries which tell me that migraine is on its way, and I take certain drugs to avert its arrival. If I did not take the drugs, I would be able to function perhaps one day in four. The physiological error called migraine is, in brief, central to the given of my life. When I was 15, 16, even 25, I used to think that I could rid myself of this error by simply denying it, character over chemistry. "Do you have headaches *sometimes? frequently? never?*" the application forms would demand. "Check one." Wary of the trap, wanting whatever it was that the successful circumnavigation of that particular form could bring (a job, a scholarship, the respect of mankind and the grace of God), I would check one. "*Sometimes*," I would lie. That in fact I spent one or two days a week almost unconscious with pain seemed a shameful secret, evidence not merely of some chemical inferiority but of all my bad attitudes, unpleasant tempers, wrongthink.

For I had no brain tumor, no eyestrain, no high blood pressure, nothing wrong with me at all: I simply had migraine headaches, and migraine headaches were, as everyone who did not have them knew, imaginary. I fought migraine then, ignored the warnings it sent, went to school and later to work in spite of it, sat through lectures in Middle English and presentations to advertisers with involuntary tears running down the right side of my face, threw up in washrooms, stumbled home by instinct, emptied ice trays onto my bed and tried to freeze the pain in my right temple, wished only for a neurosurgeon who would do a lobotomy on house call, and cursed my imagination.

It was a long time before I began thinking mechanistically enough to accept migraine for what it was: something with which I would be living, the way some people live with diabetes. Migraine is something more than the fancy of a neurotic imagination. It is an essentially hereditary complex of symptoms, the most frequently noted but by no means the most unpleasant of which is a vascular headache of blinding severity, suffered by a surprising number of women, a fair number of men (Thomas Jefferson had migraine, and so did Ulysses S. Grant, the day he accepted Lee's surrender), and by some unfortunate children as young as two years old. (I had my first when I was eight. It came on during a fire drill at the Columbia School in Colorado Springs, Colorado. I was taken first home and then to the infirmary at Peterson Field, where my father was stationed. The Air Corps doctor prescribed an enema.) Almost anything can trigger a specific attack of migraine: stress, allergy, fatigue, an abrupt change in barometric pressure, a contretemps over a parking ticket. A flaming light. A fire drill. One inherits, of course, only the predisposition. In other words I spent yesterday in bed with a headache not merely because of my bad attitude, unpleasant tempers and wrongthink, but because both my grandmothers had migraine, my father has migraine and my mother has migraine.

No one knows precisely what it is that is inherited. The chemistry of migraine, however, seems to have some connection with the nerve hormone named serotonin, which is naturally present in the brain. The amount of serotonin in the blood falls sharply at the onset of migraine, and one migraine drug, methysergide, or Sansert, seems to have some effect on serotonin. Methysergide is a derivative of lysergic acid (in fact Sancoz Pharmaceuticals first synthesized LSD-25 while looking for a migraine cure), and its use is hemmed about with so many contraindications and side effects that most doctors prescribe it only in the most incapacitating cases. Methysergide, when it is prescribed, is taken daily, as a preventive; another preventive which works for some people is old-fashioned ergotamine tartrate, which helps to constrict the swelling blood vessels during the "aura," the period which in most cases precedes the actual headache.

Once an attack is under way, however, no drug touches it. Migraine gives some people mild hallucinations, temporarily blinds others, shows up not only as a headache but as a gastrointestinal disturbance, a painful sensitivity to all sensory stimuli, an abrupt overpowering fatigue, a strokelike aphasia, and a crippling inability to make even the most routine connections. When I am in a migraine aura (for some people the aura lasts fifteen minutes, for others several hours), I will drive through red lights, lose the house keys, spill whatever I am holding, lose the ability to focus my eyes or frame coherent sentences, and generally give the appearance of being on drugs, or drunk. The actual headache, when it comes, brings with it chills, sweating, nausea, a debility that seems to stretch the very limits of endurance. That no one dies of migraine seems, to someone deep into an attack, an ambiguous blessing.

My husband also has migraine, which is unfortunate for him but fortunate for me: perhaps nothing so tends to prolong an attack as the accusing eye of someone who has never had a headache. "Why not take a couple of aspirin," the unafflicted will say from the doorway, or "I'd have a headache, too, spending a beautiful day like this inside with all the shades drawn." All of us who have migraine suffer not only from the attacks themselves but from this common conviction that we are perversely refusing to cure ourselves by taking a couple of aspirin, that we are making ourselves sick, that we "bring it on ourselves." And in the most immediate sense, the sense of why we have a headache this Tuesday and not last Thursday, of course we often do. There certainly is what doctors call a "migraine personality," and that personality tends to be ambitious, inward, intolerant of error, rather rigidly organized, perfectionist. "You don't look like a migraine personality," a doctor once said to me. "Your hair's messy, but I suppose you're a compulsive housekeeper." Actually my house is kept even more negligently than my hair, but the doctor was right nonetheless: perfectionism can also take the form of spending most of a week writing and rewriting and not writing a single paragraph.

But not all perfectionists have migraine, and not all migrainous people have migraine personalities. We do not escape heredity. I have tried in most of the available ways to escape my own migrainous heredity (at one point I learned to give myself two daily injections of histamine with a hypodermic needle, even though the needle so frightened me that I had to close my eyes when I did it), but I still have migraine. And I have learned now to live with it, learned when to expect it, how to outwit it, even how to regard it, when it does come, as more friend than lodger. We have reached a certain understanding, my migraine and I. It never comes when I am in real trouble. Tell me that my house is burned down, my husband has left me, that there is gunfighting in the streets and panic in the banks, and I will not respond by getting a headache. It comes instead when I am fighting not an open but a guerrilla war with my own life, during weeks of small household confusions, lost laundry, unhappy help, canceled appointments, on days when the telephone rings too much and I get no work done and the wind is coming up. On days like that my friend comes uninvited.

And once it comes, now that I am wise in its ways, I no longer fight it. I lie down and let it happen. At first every small apprehension is magnified, every anxiety a pounding terror. Then the pain comes, and I concentrate only on that. Right there is the usefulness of migraine, there in that imposed yoga, the concentration on the pain. For when the pain recedes, ten or twelve hours later, everything goes with it, all the hidden resentments, all the vain anxieties. The migraine has acted as a circuit breaker, and the fuses have emerged intact. There is a pleasant convalescent euphoria. I open the windows and feel the air, eat gratefully, sleep well. I notice the particular nature of a flower in a glass on the stair landing. I count my blessings.

QUESTIONS

1. "Wary of the trap, wanting whatever it was that the successful circumnavigation of that particular form could bring (a job, a scholarship, the respect of mankind and the grace of God), I would check one." Why does Didion say "circumnavigation"? And how are we to understand her list of particulars in parentheses? Is it increasingly facetious? Entirely serious? Seriously facetious? Whatever it is, what does it mean?

2. When she went home in pain Didion would, she says, among other things, "curse my imagination." Why? Why doesn't she anymore?

3. In the next-to-last paragraph, Didion personifies migraine. Why? And why call it her *friend*?

4. Compare the case for a mechanistic interpretation of events that Didion makes here with the one she makes in "The Santa Ana." Do you find it stronger? Weaker? About the same? How so?

SUGGESTED ACTIVITIES

1. Write about a time you suffered from a debilitating mental or physical problem. Use the same order of detail as Didion does.

2. Write an essay on the *benefits* of such a problem. Be personal as well as general.

3. Write an essay on pain.

E. B. WHITE
A Report in Spring

Considered by many to be the best American essayist of the twentieth century, for years White divided his life between a farm in Maine and an apartment in New York City while writing for The New Yorker. *He collected his essays in numerous volumes, and in addition wrote two famous children's novels,* Stuart Little *(1945) and* Charlotte's Web *(1952). White's "A Report in Spring" demonstrates his ability to spin gold out of the sort of topic often assigned to students. His trick? No trick: He pays attention to detail.*

Turtle Bay, May 10, 1957

I bought a puppy last week in the outskirts of Boston and drove him to Maine in a rented Ford that looked like a sculpin. There had been talk in our family of getting a "sensible" dog this time, and my wife and I had gone over the list of sensible dogs, and had even ventured once or twice into the company of sensible dogs. A friend had a litter of Labradors, and there were other opportunities. But after a period of uncertainty and waste motion my wife suddenly exclaimed one evening, "Oh, let's just get a dachshund!" She had had a glass of wine, and I could see that the truth was coming out. Her tone was one of exasperation laced with affection. So I engaged a black male without further ado.

For the long ordeal of owning another dachshund we prepared ourselves by putting up for a night at the Boston Ritz in a room overlooking the Public Garden, where from our window we could gaze, perhaps for the last time, on a world of order and peace. I say "for the last time" because it occurred to me early in the proceedings that this was our first adoption case in which there was a strong likelihood that the dog would survive the man. It had always been the other way round. The Garden had never seemed so beautiful. We were both up early the next morning for a final look at the fresh, untroubled scene; then we checked out hastily, sped to the kennel, and claimed our prize, who is the grandson of an animal named Direct Stretch of the Walls. He turned out to be a good traveller, and except for an interruption caused by my wife's falling out of the car in Gardiner, the journey went very well. At present, I am a sojourner in the city again, but here in the green warmth of Turtle Bay I see only the countenance of spring in the country. No matter what changes take place in the world, or in me, nothing ever seems to disturb the face of spring.

The smelts are running in the brooks. We had a mess for Monday lunch, brought to us by our son, who was fishing at two in the morning. At this season, a smelt brook is the night club of the town, and when the tide is a late one, smelting is for the young, who like small hours and late society.

No rain has fallen in several weeks. The gardens are dry, the road to the shore is dusty. The ditches, which in May are usually swollen to bursting, are no more than a summer trickle. Trout fishermen are not allowed on the streams; pond fishing from a boat is still permissible. The landscape is lovely to behold, but the hot, dry wind carries the smell of trouble. The other day we saw the smoke of a fire over in the direction of the mountain.

Mice have eaten the crowns of the Canterbury bells, my white-faced steer has warts on his neck (I'm told it's a virus, like everything else these days), and the dwarf pear has bark trouble. My puppy has no bark trouble. He arises at three, for tennis. The puppy's health, in fact, is exceptionally good. When my wife and I took him from the kennel, a week ago today, his mother kissed all three of us good-bye, and the lady who ran the establishment presented me with complete feeding instructions, which included a mineral supplement called Pervinal and some vitamin drops called Vi-syneral. But I knew that as soon as the puppy reached home and got his sea legs he would switch to the supplement *du jour*—a flake of well-rotted cow manure from my boot, a dead crocus bulb from the lawn, a shingle from the kindling box, a bloody feather from the execution block behind the barn. Time has borne me out; the puppy was not long discovering the delicious supplements of the farm, and he now knows where every vitamin hides, under its stone, under its loose board. I even introduced him to the tonic smell of coon.

On Tuesday, in broad daylight, the coon arrived, heavy with young, to take possession of the hole in the tree, but she found another coon in possession, and there was a grim fight high in the branches. The new tenant won, or so it appeared to me, and our old coon came down the tree in defeat and hustled off into the woods to examine her wounds and make other plans for her confinement. I was sorry for her, as I am for any who are evicted from their haunts by the younger and stronger—always a sad occasion for man or beast.

The stalks of rhubarb show red, the asparagus has broken through. Peas and potatoes are in, but it is not much use putting seeds in the ground the way things are. The bittern spent a day at the pond, creeping slowly around the shores like a little round-shouldered peddler. A setting of goose eggs has arrived by parcel post from Vermont, my goose having been taken by the fox last fall. I carried the package into the barn and sat down to unpack the eggs. They came out of the box in perfect condition, each one wrapped in a page torn from the *New England Homestead*. Clustered around me on the floor, they looked as though I had been hard at it. There is no one to sit on them but me, and I had to return to New York, so I ordered a trio of Muscovies from a man in New Hampshire, in the hope of persuading a Muscovy duck to give me a Toulouse gosling. (The theme of my life is complexity-through-joy.) In reply to my order, the duck-farm man wrote saying there would be a slight delay in the shipment of Muscovies, as he was "in the midst of a forest-fire scare." I did not know from this whether he was too scared to drive to the post office with a duck or too worried to fit a duck into a crate.

By day the goldfinches dip in yellow flight, by night the frogs sing the song that never goes out of favor. We opened the lower sash of the window in the barn loft, and the swallows are already building, but mud for their nests is not so easy to come by as in most springtimes. One afternoon, I found my wife kneeling at the edge of her perennial border on the north side, trying to disengage Achillea-the-Pearl from Coral Bell. "If I could afford it," she said bitterly, "I would take every damn bit of Achillea out of this border." She is a woman in comfortable circumstances, arrived at through her own hard labor, and this sudden burst of poverty, and her inability to indulge herself in a horticultural purge, startled me. I was so moved by her plight and her unhappiness that I went to the barn and returned with an edger, and we spent a fine, peaceable hour in the pretty twilight, rapping Achillea over the knuckles and saving Coral Bell.

One never knows what images one is going to hold in memory, returning to the city after a brief orgy in the country. I find this morning that what I most vividly and longingly recall is the sight of my grandson and his little sunburnt sister returning to their kitchen door from an excursion, with trophies of the meadow clutched in their hands—she with a couple of violets, and smiling, he serious and holding dandelions, strangling them in a responsible grip. Children hold spring so tightly in their brown fists—just as grownups, who are less sure of it, hold it in their hearts.

QUESTIONS

1. "Her tone was one of exasperation laced with affection"—what does that mean? Have you ever been in a similar states?

2. How many kinds of trouble turn up in this essay? What is White's attitude toward these troubles? How do you know? Do you sympathize with his attitude?

3. How many times does White refer explicitly and implicity to his age? Why does he? How is his age relevant to the subject?

SUGGESTED ACTIVITIES

1. In an essay, answer question one in detail and at length.

2. Write about some troubles you have experienced, comparing your views of them at the time with your views of them now.

3. Write a report on any season you prefer.

4. Write an essay on the benefits of the troubles we face in our daily lives.

VI
Common
Attitudes

E. B. WHITE
Democracy

In this piece, White demonstrates the supreme value of the specific in dealing with the abstract.

July 3, 1944

We received a letter from the Writers' War Board the other day, asking for a statement on 'The Meaning of Democracy.' It presumably is our duty to comply with such a request, and it is certainly our pleasure.

Surely the Board knows what democracy is. It is the line that forms on the right. It is the don't in Don't Shove. It is the hole in the stuffed shirt through which the sawdust slowly trickles; it is the dent in the high hat. Democracy is the recurrent suspicion that more than half of the people are right more than half of the time. It is the feeling of privacy in the voting booths, the feeling of communion in the libraries, the feeling of vitality everywhere. Democracy is the score at the beginning of the ninth. It is an idea which hasn't been disproved yet, a song the words of which have not gone bad. It's the mustard on the hot dog and the cream in the rationed coffee. Democracy is a request from a War Board, in the middle of a morning in the middle of a war, wanting to know what democracy is.

QUESTIONS

1. How is democracy "the line that forms on the right"?

2. How is democracy "the don't in Don't Shove"?

3. How is democracy "the score at the beginning of the ninth"?

SUGGESTED ACTIVITIES

1. Explain White's upshot.

2. Write an essay as short as White's explaining what democracy *isn't*.

YI-FU TUAN

American Space, Chinese Place

Raised in China, Tuan is a professor of geography at the University of Minnesota and is the author of a number of books, among them China *(1970),* Man and Nature *(1971),* Topophilia *(1974)—the title means "love of place—and* Landscapes of Fear *(1980). This essay, comparing and contrasting two cultures, is a model of compression in which every word counts and every sentence provokes.*

Americans have a sense of space, not of place. Go to an American home in exurbia, and almost the first thing you do is drift toward the picture window. How curious that the first compliment you pay your host inside his house is to say how lovely it is outside his house! He is pleased that you should admire his vistas. The distant horizon is not merely a line separating earth from sky, it is a symbol of the future. The American is not rooted in his place, however lovely: his eyes are drawn by the expanding space to a point on the horizon, which is his future.

By contrast, consider the traditional Chinese home. Blank walls enclose it. Step behind the spirit wall and you are in a courtyard with perhaps a miniature garden around the corner. Once inside the private compound you are wrapped in an ambiance of calm beauty, an ordered world of buildings, pavement, rock, and decorative vegetation. But you have no distant view: nowhere does space open out before you. Raw nature in such a home is experienced only as weather, and the only open space is the sky above. The Chinese is rooted in his place. When he has to leave, it is not for the promised land on the terrestrial horizon, but for another world altogether along the vertical, religious axis of his imagination.

The Chinese tie to place is deeply felt. Wanderlust is an alien sentiment. The Taoist classic *Tao Te Ching* captures the ideal of rootedness in place with these words: "Though there may be another country in the neighborhood so close that they are within sight of each other and the crowing of cocks and barking of dogs in one place can be heard in the other, yet there is no traffic between them; and throughout their lives the two peoples have nothing to do with each other." In theory if not in practice, farmers have ranked high in Chinese society. The reason is not only that they are engaged in the "root" industry of producing food but that, unlike pecuniary merchants, they are tied to the land and do not abandon their country when it is in danger.

Nostalgia is a recurrent theme in Chinese poetry. An American reader of translated Chinese poems may well be taken aback—even put off—by the frequency, as well as the sentimentality, of the lament for home. To understand the strength of this sentiment, we need to know that the Chinese desire for stability and rootedness in place is prompted by the constant threat of war, exile, and the natural disasters of flood and drought. Forcible removal makes the Chinese keenly aware of their loss. By contrast, Americans move, for the most part, voluntarily. Their nostalgia for hometown is really longing for childhood to which they cannot return: in the meantime the future beckons and the future is "out there," in open space. When we criticize American rootlessness we tend to forget that it is a result of ideals we admire, namely, social mobility and optimism about the future. When we admire Chinese rootedness, we forget that the word "place" means both location in space and position in society: to be tied to place is also to be bound to one's station in life, with little hope of betterment. Space symbolizes hope; place, achievement and stability.

QUESTIONS

1. What does Tuan mean by saying the horizon is the American future? Does that make sense in terms of your own experience?

2. What does Tuan mean by "the vertical religious axis of imagination"?

3. Do you agree with Tuan's interpretation of American nostalgia? How so? Why not?

SUGGESTED ACTIVITIES

1. Write an essay advocating the value of place over space. Among other things, use your own experience to support your case.

2. Write an essay advocating the value of space over place. Among other things, use your own experience to support your case.

E. M. FORSTER
My Wood

One of the most distinguished British novelists of the twentieth century, Forster is best known for his novel A Passage to India *(1924). He was also an exceptional critic—his* Aspects of the Novel *(1927) is a classic—and a superb essayist, as evidenced by* Two Cheers for Democracy *(1951). In "My Wood" Forster does a remarkable job of linking the personal with the general and the mundane with the sublime.*

A few years ago I wrote a book which dealt in part with the difficulties of the English in India. Feeling that they would have had no difficulties in India themselves, the Americans read the book freely. The more they read it the better it made them feel, and a cheque to the author was the result. I bought a wood with the cheque. It is not a large wood—it contains scarcely any trees, and it is intersected, blast it, by a public footpath. Still, it is the first property that I have owned, so it is right that other people should participate in my shame, and should ask themselves, in accents that will vary in horror, this very important question: What is the effect of property upon the character? Don't let's touch economics; the effect of private ownership upon the community as a whole is another question—a more important question, perhaps, but another one. Let's keep to psychology. If you own things, what's their effect on you? What's the effect on me of my wood?

In the first place, it makes me feel heavy. Property does have this effect. Property produces men of weight, and it was a man of weight who failed to get into the Kingdom of Heaven. He was not wicked, that unfortunate millionaire in the parable, he was only stout; he stuck out in front, not to mention behind, and as he wedged himself this way and that in the crystalline entrance and bruised his well-fed flanks, he saw beneath him a comparatively slim camel passing through the eye of a needle and being woven into the robe of God. The Gospels all through couple stoutness and slowness. They point out what is perfectly obvious, yet seldom realized: that if you have a lot of things you cannot move about a lot, that furniture requires dusting, dusters require servants, servants require insurance stamps, and the whole tangle of them makes you think twice before you accept an invitation to dinner or go for a bathe in the Jordan. Sometimes the Gospels proceed further and say with Tolstoy that property is sinful; they approach the difficult ground of asceticism here, where I cannot follow them. But as to the immediate effects of property on people, they just show straightforward logic. It produces men of weight. Men of weight cannot, by definition, move like the lightning from the East unto the West, and the ascent of a fourteen-stone bishop into a pulpit is thus the exact antithesis of the coming of the Son of Man. My wood makes me feel heavy.

In the second place, it makes me feel it ought to be larger.

The other day I heard a twig snap in it. I was annoyed at first, for I thought that someone was blackberrying, and depreciating the value of the undergrowth. On coming nearer, I saw it was not a man who had trodden on the twig and snapped it, but a bird, and I felt pleased. My bird. The bird was not equally pleased. Ignoring the relation between us, it took fright as soon as it saw the shape of my face, and flew straight over the boundary hedge into a field, the property of Mrs. Henessy, where it sat down with a loud squawk. It had become Mrs. Henessy's bird. Something seemed grossly amiss here, something that would not have occurred had the wood been larger. I could not afford to buy Mrs. Henessy out, I dared not murder her, and limitations of this sort beset me on every side. Ahab did not want that vineyard— he only needed it to round off his property, preparatory to plotting a new curve—and all the land around my wood has become necessary to me in order to round off the wood. A boundary protects. But— poor little thing—the boundary ought in its turn to be protected. Noises on the edge of it. Children throw stones. A little more, and then a little more, until we reach the sea. Happy Canute! Happier Alexander! And after all, why should even the world be the limit of possession? A rocket containing a Union Jack, will, it is hoped, be shortly fired at the moon. Mars. Sirius. Beyond which . . . But these immensities ended by saddening me. I could not suppose that my wood was the destined nucleus of universal dominion—it is so very small and contains no mineral wealth beyond the blackberries. Nor was I comforted when Mrs. Hennessy's bird took alarm for the second time and flew clean away from us all, under the belief that it belonged to itself.

In the third place, property makes its owner feel that he ought to do something to it. Yet he isn't sure what. A restlessness comes over him, a vague sense that he has a personality to express—the same sense which, without any vagueness, leads the artist to an act of creation. Sometimes I think I will cut down such trees as remain in the wood, at other times I want to fill up the gaps between them with new trees. Both impulses are pretentious and empty. They are not honest movements towards money-making or beauty. They spring from a foolish desire to express myself and from an inability to enjoy what I have got. Creation, property, enjoyment form a sinister trinity in the human mind. Creation and enjoyment are both very, very good, yet they are often unattainable without a material basis, and at such moments property pushes itself in as a substitute, saying "Accept me instead—I'm good enough for all three." It is not enough. It is, as Shakespeare said of lust, "The expense of spirit in a waste of shame": it is "Before, a joy proposed; behind, a dream." Yet we don't know how to shun it. It is forced on us by our economic system as the alternative to starvation. It is also forced on us by an internal defect in the soul, by the feeling that in property may lie the germs of self-development and of exquisite or heroic deeds. Our life on earth is, and ought to be, material and carnal. But we have not yet learned to manage our materialism and carnality properly; they are still entangled with the desire for ownership, where (in the words of Dante) "Possession is one with loss."

And this brings us to our fourth and final point: the blackberries.

Blackberries are not plentiful in this meagre grove, but they are easily seen from the public footpath which traverses it, and all too easily gathered. Foxgloves, too—people will pull up the foxgloves, and ladies of an educational tendency even grub for toadstools to show them on the Monday in class. Other ladies, less educated, roll down the bracken in the arms of their gentlemen friends. There is paper, there are tins. Pray, does my wood belong to me or doesn't it? And, if it does, should I not own it best by allowing no one else to walk there? There is a wood near Lyme Regis, also cursed by a public footpath, where the owner has not hesitated on this point. He had built high stone walls each side of the path, and has spanned it by bridges, so that the public circulate like termites while he gorges on the blackberries unseen. He really does own his wood, this able chap. Dives in Hell did pretty well, but the gulf dividing him from Lazarus could be traversed by vision, and nothing traverses it here. And perhaps I shall come to this in time. I shall wall in and fence out until I really taste the sweets of property. Enormously stout, endlessly avaricious, pseudo-creative, intensely selfish, I shall weave upon my forehead the quadruple crown of possession until those nasty Bolshies come and take it off again and thrust me aside into the outer darkness.

QUESTIONS

1. Why does Forster begin his essay with an account of his book?
2. Why does he mention shame and horror regarding the possession of property?
3. What is the difference between being wicked and being stout (as Forster defines stout)?
4. Why does Forster say the bird was "*under the belief* that it belonged to itself'" (italics mine)?
5. What do Dante's words mean: "Possession is one with loss"?
6. Why doesn't Forster get rid of his wood?

SUGGESTED ACTIVITIES

1. Write an essay on the sweets of ownership.
2. Write an essay on some way (other than possession) that you consistently behave and yet disapprove of.
3. Define the limits of your desire (ambition, greed, drive) for things. In other words, figure out the *enough* that you think would be enough.

SUZANNE BRITT JORDAN
That Lean and Hungry Look

> *Raised in North Carolina, after a two-year sojourn in St. Louis Jordan has made her home in Raleigh. She has taught high school and college, tended house and children, and written numerous essays which she recently collected in a book,* Show & Tell *(1982). In this essay Jordan uses the facetious to argue for a way of looking at the world and coming to grips with it.*

Caesar was right. Thin people need watching. I've been watching them for most of my adult life, and I don't like what I see. When these narrow fellows spring at me, I'm zero at the bone. Thin people come in all personalities, most of them menacing. You've got your "together" thin person, your mechanical thin person, your condescending thin person, your tsk-tsk thin person and your efficiency-expert thin person. All of them are dangerous.

In the first place, thin people aren't fun. They don't know how to goof off, at least in the best, fat sense of the word. They've always got to be adoing. Give them a coffee break, and they'll jog around the block. Supply them with a quiet evening at home, and they'll fix the screen door or clip coupons. They say things like "there aren't enough hours in the day." Fat people never say that. Fat people think the day is too damn long already.

Thin people make me tired. They've got speedy little metabolisms that cause them to bustle briskly. They're forever rubbing their bony hands together and eying new problems to tackle. I like to surround myself with sluggish, inert, easygoing fat people, the kind who believe that if you clean it up today, it'll just get dirty again tomorrow.

Some people say the business about the jolly fat person is a myth, that all of us chubbies are neurotic, sick, sad people. I disagree. Fat people may not be chortling all the day long, but they're a hell of a lot *nicer* than the wizened and shriveled. Thin people turn surly, mean and hard at a young age because they never learn the value of a hot-fudge sundae for easing tension. Thin people don't like gooey things because they themselves are neither gooey nor soft. They are crunchy and dull, like carrots. They go straight to the jugular of things while fat people let things stay all blurry, hazy and vague, the way life actually is. Thin people want to face the truth. Fat people know there is no truth. One of my thin friends is always staring at complex, unsolvable problems and saying, "The key thing is . . . " Fat people never say that. They know there isn't any such thing as the key thing, and even if they found the key, it would be for the wrong door.

Thin people believe in logic. Fat people see all sides. The sides fat people see are rounded blobs, usually gray, always nebulous and truly not worth worrying about. But the thin person persists: "If you consume more calories than you burn," says one thin friend, "you will gain weight. It's that simple." Fat people always grin when they hear statements like that. They know better. Fat people realize that life is both illogical and unfair. They know very well that God is not in his heaven and all is not right with the world. If God was up there, fat people could have two doughnuts and a big orange drink anytime they wanted to.

Thin people have a long list of logical things they are always spouting off to me. They spout them all day long, largely because their mouths are never full of Sugar Daddies or mashed potatoes. Thin people hold up one finger at a time as they go through the list, so I won't lost track. They speak slowly as if to a young child. The list is long and full of holes. It contains words like "get a grip on yourself," "cigarettes kill," "cholesterol clogs," "fit as a fiddle," "drawer dividers" and "sound fiscal management." Phrases like that.

They think these two-thousand-point plans lead to happiness. Fat people know happiness is elusive and fleeting at best, and even if they could get the kind thin people talk about, they wouldn't want it. Wisely, fat people see that such programs are too dull, too hard, too off the mark. They are never better than a whole cheesecake.

Fat people know all about the mystery of life. They are the ones acquainted with the night, with luck, with fate, with playing it by ear. One thin person I know suggested that we arrange all the parts of a jigsaw puzzle into groups, according to size, shape and color. He figured this method would cut the time needed to assemble the puzzle by at least 50 per cent. I said I wouldn't do it. One, the whole idea turned me off. Two, I like to muddle through. Three, what good would it do to finish early? Four, the jigsaw puzzle wasn't the key thing. The key thing was the fun of four people (one thin person included) sitting around a card table, working a jigsaw puzzle. My thin friend had no use for my list. He stalked outside to mulch the boxwoods. The three remaining fat people finished the puzzle and the bourbon and celebrated with a big pan of doublefudge brownies.

The main problem with thin people is that they oppress. Their good intentions, bony torsos, tight ships, neat corners, cerebral machinations and pat solutions loom darkly over the loose, comfortable, spread-out world of fat people. Long after fat people have removed their coats and shoes and put their feet up on the coffee table, thin people are still sitting on the edge of the sofa, looking neat as a pin, discussing rutabagas. Fat people are heavily into fits of laughter, slapping their thighs and whooping it up, while thin people are still waiting politely for the punch line.

Thin people are downers. They like math and morality and reasoned evaluations of the limitations of human beings. They have their skinny little acts together. They expound, prognose, probe and prick.

Fat people are convivial. They will like you even if you're irregular and have acne. They will come up with a good reason why you never wrote the great American novel. They will cry in your beer with you. They will put your name in the pot. They will let you off the hook. Fat people will gab, giggle, gaffaw, gallumph, gyrate and gossip. They are generous, giving and gallant. They are gluttonous, goodly and great. What you want when you're down is soft and jiggly, not muscled and stable. Fat people know this. Fat people have plenty of room. Fat people will take you in.

QUESTIONS

1. What is wrong with "adoing"?

2. How does Jordan handle the objection that fat people are actually unhappy?

3. "If you consume more calories than you burn, you will gain weight. It's that simple." Why and how isn't it "that simple"?

4. How are "two-thousand-point plans" off the mark?

5. Is Jordan's use of alliteration in the last paragraph effective or not? If so, how so? If not, why not?

6. What is Jordan *really* talking about?

SUGGESTED ACTIVITIES

1. Write an essay advocating thin over fat.

2. Write an essay on the value of stereotypes.

3. Write an essay on the dangers of stereotypes.

4. Write an essay on tall and short.

POSTSCRIPT

Commentary on *That Lean and Hungry Look*

The truth is—I do not agonize well, except about imaginary, inconsequential things—crammed ashtrays, no place to go on Saturday night, the conversation that stops when I enter the room. Real pain sends me flying into corners. I shake my fist at the gods. I was furious over the really remarkable pain of childbirth, and felt it as a betrayal. I cursed the arrogant male doctor, the indifferent nurses, the cruel daughter who would not be born, even after 16 or 17 hours. Can she be worth it? I ranted. Next day, like the good girl my first-born would surely grow up to be, I apologized to the young nurses but never to the male doctor. What did he know about childbirth?

And so I am about writing. I am awed and bewildered by Flannery O'Connor, working "all the time" and, for three hours every morning, sitting at her typewriter, no matter what. I would never do that, and perhaps that is why I will never do much. One of my happiest moments came when I read in William James' "The Religion of Healthy-mindedness" that there were two ways to get things done: trying and not trying. All my life I have been trying not to try. It is not inspiration I seek. It is ease.

So when I begin to write, I have to have my comforts around me: cigarettes, a big ashtray, a glass of something (carbonated and caffeinated in the morning, alcoholic toward afternoon), a comfortable breeze through the office window, a comfortable silence, a comfortable thesis and a comfortable distance between the first sentence and suppertime. Panic and pressure discombobulate me, as does too much time. Three hours will do to produce a zippy, one-sided, arrogant tirade. Four hours will net me a thoughtful, perhaps profound, well-reasoned and tender reflection.

If what I whip out doesn't "work," out it goes. The green letters on my Apple 2 screen vanish, and I begin again, foolishly and superstitiously typing my name, phone number, address at the top of the screen. Fresh starts are bliss for cowardly writers. All I remember from my college sociology course was that if you give a rich kid and a poor kid a choice between a candy bar now and five bucks next week, the poor kid will take the candy bar, the rich kid the five bucks. I am a poor kid, starved for the gratification of the minute I am living in.

I remember writing "That Lean and Hungry Look," which is, in my opinion, a real thigh-slapper and thoroughly offensive to all the right people. I had, as have many women, wasted my twenties on my body. I had done nothing about my body, mind you, being incapable of sustaining deprivation for more than three days. I was thirty-one years old, and what had I done for thirty years? Nothing except scrunch up over how I looked. Actually, I was quite nice-looking, in a rollicking, robust way. I had been kicking around the absurd furniture of vanity and fashion for many years. Suddenly, sitting in the office of a professor friend at NC State, I got mad as hell. I raced upstairs to my office, yanked my rolling typewriter table out from the wall, and let the skinnies have it, right between the clavicles. I was suddenly mad for all the time wasted, for all the women still waiting in the wings of life until they had lost ten pounds, for all the husbands patiently enumerating the ways in which their chubby wives could regain their figgers, for all the industries and publishers raking in fat profits on the miniscule confidence of women convinced, utterly, that they were the "wrong size." Nobody is the "wrong size." I just walked right up to the communion table at the sacred altar and, being Baptist, took three glasses of Welch's grape juice and a whole handful of unleavened bread. And I felt great.

I made lots of other fat folks of varying right sizes feel great as well. They rolled on the floor. They slapped their cellulite until they liked to died with hilarity. And the skinnies ran true to form, calling me dangerous, irresponsible, unnutritious. "Oh, happy day," says the spiritual, "when Jesus washed, when Jesus washed, when Jesus washed, washed my sins away." Ever since I wrote "That Lean and Hungry Look" and the book that followed, *Skinny People Are Dull and Crunchy like Carrots,* I have hated malted-milk balls and felt, for Sara Lee and all her silly temptations, a boredom and indifference amounting to what I feel for Vacation Bible School and dutiful submission.

All essays can not be written in anger, but they'd best be written in passion or grim conviction, otherwise they will hit the stomach like chow mein and leave the reader hungry an hour later. There is no place to lie down in an essay, no place to flit, flirt, hide, mince, strut, preen, pose. Lacking conviction, passion, wit, rage, you will produce thin gruel, not turnip greens and salt pork, full of danger and tasting deliciously of life.

Suzanne Britt Jordan

ZORA NEALE HURSTON

How It Feels to Be Colored Me

After studying anthropology at Howard University, Barnard College, and Columbia University, Hurston became a writer and folklorist whose work celebrated American Black culture. She wrote plays, novels—the best of which is considered to be Their Eyes Were Watching God *(1937)—anthropological studies such as* Voodoo Gods: An Inquiry Into Native Myths and Magic in Jamaica and Haiti *(1939), and the autobiography* Tracks on a Road *(1939). As this essay vividly demonstrates, Hurston forged a powerful voice that transcended color and like considerations even as she talked about them.*

I am colored but I offer nothing in the way of extenuating circumstances except the fact that I am the only Negro in the United States whose grandfather on the mother's side was *not* an Indian chief.

I remember the very day that I became colored. Up to my thirteenth year I lived in the little Negro town of Eatonville, Florida. It is exclusively a colored town. The only white people I knew passed through the town going to or coming from Orlando. The native whites rode dusty horses, the Northern tourists chugged down the sandy village

road in automobiles. The town knew the Southerners and never stopped
cane chewing when they passed. But the Northerners were something
else again. They were peered at cautiously from behind curtains by
the timid. The more venturesome would come out on the porch to
watch them go past and got just as much pleasure out of the tourists
as the tourists got out of the village.

The front porch might seem a daring place for the rest of the town,
but it was a gallery seat for me. My favorite place was atop the gate-
post. Proscenium box for a born first-nighter. Not only did I enjoy the
show, but I didn't mind the actors knowing that I liked it. I usually
spoke to them in passing. I'd wave at them and when they returned
my salute, I would say something like this: "Howdy-do-well-I-thank-
you-where-you-going'?" Usually automobile or the horse paused at
this, and after a queer exchange of compliments, I would probably
"go a piece of the way" with them, as we say in farthest Florida. If
one of my family happened to come to the front in time to see me, of
course negotiations would be rudely broken off. But even so, it is clear
that I was the first "welcome-to-our-state" Floridian, and I hope the
Miami Chamber of Commerce will please take notice.

During this period, white people differed from colored to me only
in that they rode through town and never lived there. They liked to
hear me "speak pieces" and sing and wanted to see me dance the
parse-me-la, and gave me generously of their small silver for doing
these things, which seemed strange to me for I wanted to do them so
much that I needed bribing to stop. Only they didn't know it. The
colored people gave no dimes. They deplored any joyful tendencies in
me, but I was their Zora nevertheless. I belonged to them, to the
nearby hotels, to the county—everybody's Zora.

But changes came in the family when I was thirteen, and I was sent
to school in Jacksonville. I left Eatonville, the town of the oleanders,
as Zora. When I disembarked from the river-boat at Jacksonville, she
was no more. It seemed that I had suffered a sea change. I was not
Zora of Orange County any more, I was now a little colored girl. I
found it out in certain ways. In my heart as well as in the mirror, I
became a fast brown—warranted not to rub nor run.

But I am not tragically colored. There is no great sorrow dammed
up in my soul, nor lurking behind my eyes. I do not mind at all. I do
not belong to the sobbing school of Negrohood who hold that nature
somehow has given them a lowdown dirty deal and whose feelings
are all hurt about it. Even in the helter-skelter skirmish that is my

life, I have seen that the world is to the strong regardless of a little pigmentation more or less. No, I do not weep at the world—I am too busy sharpening my oyster knife.

Someone is always at my elbow reminding me that I am the grand-daughter of slaves. It fails to register depression with me. Slavery is sixty years in the past. The operation was successful and the patient is doing well, thank you. The terrible struggle that made me an American out of a potential slave said "On the line!" The Reconstruction said "Get set!"; and the generation before said "Go!" I am off to a flying start and I must not halt in the stretch to look behind and weep. Slavery is the price I paid for civilization, and the choice was not with me. It is a bully adventure and worth all that I have paid through my ancestors for it. No one on earth ever had a greater chance for glory. The world to be won and nothing to be lost. It is thrilling to think— to know that for any act of mine, I shall get twice as much praise or twice as much blame. It is quite exciting to hold the center of the national stage, with the spectators not knowing whether to laugh or to weep.

The position of my white neighbor is much more difficult. No brown specter pulls up a chair beside me when I sit down to eat. No dark ghost thrusts its leg against mine in bed. The game of keeping what one has is never so exciting as the game of getting.

I do not always feel colored. Even now I often achieve the unconscious Zora of Eatonville before the Hegira. I feel most colored when I am thrown against a sharp white background.

For instance at Barnard. "Beside the waters of the Hudson" I feel my race. Among the thousand white persons, I am a dark rock surged upon, and overswept, but through it all, I remain myself. When covered by the waters, I am; and the ebb but reveals me again.

Sometimes it is the other way around. A white person is set down in our midst, but the contrast is just as sharp for me. For instance, when I sit in the drafty basement that is The New World Cabaret with a white person, my color comes. We enter chatting about any little nothing that we have in common and are seated by the jazz waiters. In the abrupt way that jazz orchestras have, this one plunges into a number. It loses no time in circumlocutions, but gets right down to business. It constricts the thorax and splits the heart with its tempo and narcotic harmonies. This orchestra grows rambunctious, rears on its hind legs and attacks the tonal veil with primitive fury, rending it, clawing it until it breaks through to the jungle beyond. I follow those heathen—follow them exultingly. I dance wildly inside myself; I yell within, I whoop; I shake my assegai above my head, I hurl it true to the mark *yeeeeooww!* I am in the jungle and living in the jungle way. My face is painted red and yellow and my body is painted blue. My pulse is throbbing like a war drum. I want to slaughter something— give pain, give death to what, I do not know. But the piece ends. The men of the orchestra wipe their lips and rest their fingers. I creep back slowly to the veneer we call civilization with the last tone and find the white friend sitting motionless in his seat, smoking calmly.

"Good music they have here," he remarks, drumming the table with his fingertips.

Music. The great blobs of purple and red emotion have not touched him. He has only heard what I felt. He is far away and I see him but dimly across the ocean and the continent that have fallen between us. He is so pale with his whiteness then and I am *so* colored.

At certain times I have no race, I am *me*. When I set my hat at a certain angle and saunter down Seventh Avenue, Harlem City, feeling as snooty as the lions in front of the Forty-Second Street Library, for instance. So far as my feelings are concerned, Peggy Hopkins Joyce on the Boule Mich with her gorgeous raiment, stately carriage, knees knocking together in a most aristocratic manner, has nothing on me. The cosmic Zora emerges. I belong to no race nor time. I am the eternal feminine with its string of beads.

I have no separate feeling about being an American citizen and colored. I am merely a fragment of the Great Soul that surges within the boundaries. My country, right or wrong.

Sometimes, I feel discriminated against, but it does not make me angry. It merely astonishes me. How *can* any deny themselves the pleasure of my company? It's beyond me.

But in the main, I feel like a brown bag of miscellany propped against a wall. Against a wall in company with other bags, white, red and yellow. Pour out the contents, and there is discovered a jumble of small things priceless and worthless. A first-water diamond, an empty spool, bits of broken glass, lengths of string, a key to a door long since crumbled away, a rusty knife-blade, old shoes saved for a road that never was and never will be, a nail bent under the weight of things too heavy for any nail, a dried flower or two still a little fragrant. In your hand is the brown bag. On the ground before you is the jumble it held—so much like the jumble in the bags, could they be emptied, that all might be dumped in a single heap and the bags refilled without altering the content of any greatly. A bit of colored glass more or less would not matter. Perhaps that is how the Great Stuffer of Bags filled them in the first place—who knows?

QUESTIONS

1. Why does Hurston open with the crack about not being kin to an Indian chief?

2. How has Hurston organized her essay? How does the organization fit the meaning?

3. "The operation was successful and the patient is doing well, thank you." Does this metaphor work? If so, how? If not, why not? Is the statement it makes true—in any sense? If so, how? If not, why not?

4. What does Hurston mean by the line, "My country, right or wrong"? Does she give it new meaning? Or is she content with the old?

SUGGESTED ACTIVITIES

1. Write an essay describing what you think it would be like to meet Hurston.

2. Write an essay on how it feels to be you.

3. Describe yourself as neatly coherent, and include the principle and the particulars of your makeup.

4. Describe yourself as an incoherent mess, and cite the miscellany that makes you whatever it is you are.

VII
Life Beyond the Usual

ANNIE DILLARD
The Death of a Moth

*In this essay we see not only Dillard's ability to relate odd things but
also her ability to describe things in remarkable detail and amazing
metaphor that together—detail and metaphor—make meaning as
well as music.*

I live alone with two cats, who sleep on my legs. There is a yellow
one, and a black one whose name is Small. In the morning I joke to
the black one, Do you remember last night? Do you remember? I throw
them both out before breakfast, so I can eat.

There is a spider, too, in the bathroom, of uncertain lineage, bulbous
at the abdomen and drab, whose six-inch mess of web works, works
somehow, works miraculously, to keep her alive and me amazed. The
web is in a corner behind the toilet, connecting tile wall to tile wall.
The house is new, the bathroom immaculate, save for the spider, her
web, and the sixteen or so corpses she's tossed to the floor.

The corpses appear to be mostly sow bugs, those little armadillo
creatures who live to travel flat out in houses, and die round. In addition to sow-bug husks, hollow and sipped empty of color, there are
what seem to be two or three wingless moth bodies, one new flake of
earwig, and three spider carcasses crinkled and clenched.

I wonder on what fool's errand an earwig, or a moth, or a sow bug,
would visit that clean corner of the house behind the toilet; I have not
noticed any blind parades of sow bugs blundering into corners. Yet

393

they do hazard there, at a rate of more than one a week, and the spider thrives. Yesterday she was working on the earwig, mouth on gut; today he's on the floor. It must take a certain genius to throw things away from there, to find a straight line through that sticky tangle to the floor.

Today the earwig shines darkly, and gleams, what there is of him: a dorsal curve of thorax and abdomen, and a smooth pair of pincers by which I knew his name. Next week, if the other bodies are any indication, he'll be shrunk and gray, webbed to the floor with dust. The sow bugs beside him are curled and empty, fragile, a breath away from brittle fluff. The spiders lie on their sides, translucent and ragged, their legs drying in knots. The moths stagger against each other, headless, in a confusion of arcing strips of chitin like peeling varnish, like a jumble of buttresses for cathedral vaults, like nothing resembling moths, so that I would hesitate to call them moths, except that I have had some experience with the figure Moth reduced to a nub.

Two summers ago I was camped alone in the Blue Ridge Mountains of Virginia. I had hauled myself and gear up there to read, among other things, *The Day on Fire*, by James Ullman, a novel about Rimbaud that had made me want to be a writer when I was sixteen; I was hoping it would do it again. So I read every day sitting under a tree by my tent, while warblers sang in the leaves overhead and bristle worms trailed their inches over the twiggy dirt at my feet; and I read every night by candlelight, while barred owls called in the forest and pale moths seeking mates massed round my head in the clearing, where my light made a ring.

Moths kept flying into the candle. They would hiss and recoil, reeling upside down in the shadows among my cooking pans. Or they would singe their wings and fall, and their hot wings, as if melted, would stick to the first thing they touched—a pan, a lid, a spoon—so that the snagged moths could struggle only in tiny arcs, unable to flutter free. These I could release by a quick flip with a stick; in the morning I would find my cooking stuff decorated with torn flecks of moth wings, ghostly triangles of shiny dust here and there on the aluminum. So I read, and boiled water, and replenished candles, and read on.

One night a moth flew into the candle, was caught, burnt dry, and held. I must have been staring at the candle, or maybe I looked up when a shadow crossed my page; at any rate, I saw it all. A golden female moth, a biggish one with a two-inch wingspread, flapped into the fire, dropped abdomen into the wet wax, stuck, flamed, and frazzled in a second. Her moving wings ignited like tissue paper, like angels' wings, enlarging the circle of light in the clearing and creating out of the darkness the sudden blue sleeves of my sweater, the green leaves of jewelweed by my side, the ragged red trunk of a pine; at once the light contracted again and the moth's wings vanished in a fine, foul smoke. At the same time, her six legs clawed, curled, blackened, and ceased, disappearing utterly. And her head jerked in spasms, making a spattering noise; her antennae crisped and burnt away and her heaving mouthparts cracked like pistol fire. When it was all over, her head was, so far as I could determine, gone, gone the long way of her wings and legs. Her head was a hole lost to time. All that was left was the glowing horn shell of her abdomen and thorax—a fraying, partially collapsed gold tube jammed upright in the candle's round pool.

And then this moth-essence, this spectacular skeleton, began to act as a wick. She kept burning. The wax rose in the moth's body from her soaking abdomen to her thorax to the shattered hole where her head should have been, and widened into flame, a saffron-yellow flame that robed her to the ground like an immolating monk. That candle had two wicks, two winding flames of identical light, side by side. The moth's head was fire. She burned for two hours, until I blew her out.

She burned for two hours without changing, without swaying or kneeling—only glowing within, like a building fire glimpsed through silhouetted walls, like a hollow saint, like a flame-faced virgin gone to God, while I read by her light, kindled, while Rimbaud in Paris burnt out his brain in a thousand poems, while night pooled wetly at my feet.

So that is why I think those hollow shreds on the bathroom floor are moths. I believe I know what moths look like, in any state.

I have three candles here on the table which I disentagle from the plants and light when visitors come. The cats avoid them, although Small's tail caught fire once; I rubbed it out before she noticed. I don't mind living alone. I like eating alone and reading. I don't mind sleeping alone. The only time I mind being alone is when something is funny; then, when I am laughing at something funny, I wish someone were around. Sometimes I think it is pretty funny that I sleep alone.

QUESTIONS

1. Why does Dillard begin an essay on the death of a moth by talking about her cats?

2. What does Dillard mean by the statement, "I have had some experience with the figure Moth reduced to a nub"?

3. How does Dillard tie the novel she was reading into the subject of the essay?

4. How many religious images can you find in the essay? What do you think of them?

5. The ending of this essay returns to the beginning. What does it add to the beginning? How does it define the point of the essay? What *is* the point of this essay?

SUGGESTED ACTIVITIES

1. Describe an actual death—any death—that you have witnessed.

2. Describe a metaphorical death that you have witnessed. (For example, the death of a hope, of an expectation, of a friendship, of a love affair.)

3. Death means loss, of course. But discuss a time when, in your own experience, death involved a gain as well as a loss.

E. B. WHITE
The Ring of Time

This essay is a description of and a meditation on transcendence.

Fiddler Bayou, March 22, 1956

After the lions had returned to their cages, creeping angrily through the chutes, a little bunch of us drifted away and into an open doorway nearby, where we stood for a while in semidarkness, watching a big brown circus horse go harumphing around the practice ring. His trainer was a woman of about forty, and the two of them, horse and woman, seemed caught up in one of those desultory treadmills of afternoon from which there is no apparent escape. The day was hot, and we kibitzers were grateful to be briefly out of the sun's glare. The long rein, or tape, by which the woman guided her charge counterclockwise in his dull career formed the radius of their private circle, of which she was the revolving center; and she, too, stepped a tiny circumfer-

ence of her own, in order to accommodate the horse and allow him
his maximum scope. She had on a short-skirted costume and a conical
straw hat. Her legs were bare and she wore high heels, which probed
deep into the loose tanbark and kept her ankles in a state of constant
turmoil. The great size and meekness of the horse, the repetitious
exercise, the heat of the afternoon, all exerted a hypnotic charm that
invited boredom; we spectators were experiencing a languor—we neither expected relief nor felt entitled to any. We had paid a dollar to
get into the grounds, to be sure, but we had got our dollar's worth a
few minutes before, when the lion trainer's whiplash had got caught
around a toe of one of the lions. What more did we want for a dollar?

Behind me I heard someone say, "Excuse me, please," in a low voice.
She was halfway into the building when I turned and saw her—a girl
of sixteen or seventeen, politely threading her way through us onlook-
ers who blocked the entrance. As she emerged in front of us, I saw
that she was barefoot, her dirty little feet fighting the uneven ground.
In most respects she was like any of two or three dozen showgirls you
encounter if you wander about the winter quarters of Mr. John Ringling
North's circus, in Sarasota—cleverly proportioned, deeply browned by
the sun, dusty, eager, and almost naked. But her grave face and the
naturalness of her manner gaver her a sort of quick distinction and
brought a new note into the gloomy octagonal building where we had
all cast our lot for a few moments. As soon as she had squeezed
through the crowd, she spoke a word or two to the older woman,
whom I took to be her mother, stepped to the ring, and waited while
the horse coasted to a stop in front of her. She gave the animal a couple
of affectionate swipes on his enormous neck and then swung herself
aboard. The horse immediately resumed his rocking canter, the woman
goading him on, chanting something that sounded like "Hop! Hop!"

In attempting to recapture this mild spectacle, I am merely acting
as recording secretary for one of the oldest of societies—the society of
those who, at one time or another, have surrendered, without even a
show of resistance, to the bedazzlement of a circus rider. As a writing
man, or secretary, I have always felt charged with the safekeeping of
all unexpected items of worldly or unworldly enchantment, as though
I might be held personally responsible if even a small one were to be
lost. But it is not easy to communicate anything of this nature. The
circus comes as close to being the world in microcosm as anything I
know; in a way, it puts all the rest of show business in the shade. Its
magic is universal and complex. Out of its wild disorder comes order;
from its rank smell rises the aroma of courage and daring; out of its

preliminary shabbiness comes the final splendor. And buried in the familiar boasts of its advance agents lies the modesty of most of its people. For me the circus is at its best before it has been put together. It is at its best at certain moments when it comes to a point, as through a burning glass, in the activity and destiny of a single performer out of so many. One ring is always bigger than three. One rider, one aerialist, is always greater than six. In short, a man has to catch the circus unawares to experience its full impact and share its gaudy dream.

The ten-minute ride the girl took achieved—as far as I was concerned, who wasn't looking for it, and quite unbeknownst to her, who wasn't even striving for it—the thing that is sought by performers everywhere, on whatever stage, whether struggling in the tidal currents of Shakespeare or bucking the difficult motion of a horse. I somehow got the idea she was just cadging a ride, improving a shining ten minutes in the diligent way all serious artists seize free moments to hone the blade of their talent and keep themselves in trim. Her brief tour included only elementary postures and tricks, perhaps because they were all she was capable of, perhaps because her warmup at this hour was unscheduled and the ring was not rigged for a real practice session. She swung herself off and on the horse several times, gripping his mane. She did a few knee-stands—or whatever they are called—dropping to her knees and quickly bouncing back up on her feet again. Most of the time she simply rode in a standing position, well aft on the beast, her hands handing easily at her sides, her head erect, her straw-colored ponytail lightly brushing her shoulders, the blood of exertion showing faintly through the tan of her skin. Twice she managed a one-foot stance—a sort of ballet pose, with arms outstretched. At one point the neck strap of her bathing suit broke and she went twice around the ring in the classic attitude of a woman making minor repairs to a garment. The fact that she was standing on the back of a moving horse while doing this invested the matter with a clownish significance that perfectly fitted the spirit of the circus—jocund, yet charming. She just rolled the strap into a neat ball and stowed it inside her bodice while the horse rocked and rolled beneath her in dutiful innocence. The bathing suit proved as self-reliant as its owner and stood up well enough without benefit of strap.

The richness of the scene was in its plainness, its natural condition—of horse, of ring, of girl, even to the girl's bare feet that gripped the bare back of her proud and ridiculous mount. The enchantment grew not out of anything that happened or was performed but out of something that seemed to go round and around and around with the girl, attending her, a steady gleam in the shape of a circle—a ring of ambition, of happiness, of youth. (And the positive pleasure of equilibrium under difficulties.) In a week or two, all would be changed, all (or almost all) lost: the girl would wear makeup, the horse would wear gold, the ring would be painted, the bark would be clean for the feet of the horse, the girl's feet would be clean for the slippers that she'd wear. All, all would be lost.

As I watched with the others, our jaws adroop, our eyes alight, I became painfully conscious of the element of time. Everything in the hideous old building seemed to take the shape of a circle, conforming to the course of the horse. The rider's gaze, as she peered straight ahead, seemed to be circular, as though bent by force of circumstance; then time itself began running in circles, and so the beginning was where the end was, and the two were the same, and one thing ran into the next and time went round and around and got nowhere. The girl wasn't so young that she did not know the delicious satisfaction of having a perfectly behaved body and the fun of using it to do a trick most people can't do, but she was too young to know that time does not really move in a circle at all. I thought: "She will never be as beautiful as this again"—a thought that made me acutely unhappy— and in a flash my mind (which is too much of a busybody to suit me) had projected her twenty-five years ahead, and she was now in the center of the ring, on foot, wearing a conical hat and highheeled shoes, the image of the older woman, holding the long rein, caught in the treadmill of an afternoon long in the future. "She is at that enviable moment in life [I thought] when she believes she can go once around the ring, make one complete circuit, and at the end be exactly the same age as at the start." Everything in her movements, her expression, told you that for her the ring of time was perfectly formed, changeless, predictable, without beginning or end, like the ring in which she was travelling at this moment with the horse that wallowed under her. And then I slipped back into my trance, and time was circular again—time, pausing quietly with the rest of us, so as not to disturb the balance of a performer.

Her ride ended as casually as it had begun. The older woman stopped the horse, and the girl slid to the ground. As she walked toward us to leave, there was a quick, small burst of applause. She smiled broadly, in surprise and pleasure; then her face suddenly regained its gravity and she disappeared through the door.

It has been ambitious and plucky of me to attempt to describe what is indescribable, and I have failed, as I knew I would. But I have discharged my duty to my society; and besides, a writer, like an acrobat, must occasionally try a stunt that is too much for him. At any rate, it is worth reporting that long before the circus comes to town, its most notable performances have already been given. Under the bright lights of the finished show, a performer need only reflect the electric candle power that is directed upon him; but in the dark and dirty old training rings and in the makeshift cages, whatever light is generated, whatever excitement, whatever beauty, must come from original sources—from internal fires of professional hunger and delight, from the exuberance and gravity of youth. It is the difference between planetary light and the combustion of stars.

QUESTIONS

1. Is "harumphing" a good verb for a horse going around a ring? How so? Why not?

2. How is the phrase "dull career" precise?

3. Why does White describe the girl as "cleverly proportioned"?

4. How is the dream of the circus "gaudy"? What *is* the dream of the circus? Is it like any other dream?

5. How is the girl's mount both proud and ridiculous?

6. Why does White describe the girl's body as "perfectly behaved"?

7. How does the last line define the upshot of the essay?

8. How many images of rings can you find in the essay?

SUGGESTED ACTIVITIES

1. Write about an event that made you acutely conscious of the passing of time.

2. Write about an event in which you lost all awareness of time.

3. Write an essay defining—in personal, specific terms—what time means to you.

4. Write an essay defining what you think time will mean to you 25 years from now.

GLORIA EMERSON
Take the Plunge . . .

*Although in the following essay Emerson implies that she doesn't
have much in the courage department, the fact is that from 1965 to
1972 she was a foreign correspondent for the New York Times covering Northern Ireland, the Nigerian Civil War, and Vietnam. In
1978 she won the National Book Award for her work on the war in
Vietnam, Winners and Losers. This essay demonstrates the value of
close attention: Note how meticulously Emerson records not only how
she felt but how she displaced feeling as well.*

It was usually men who asked me why I did it. Some were amused,
others puzzled. I didn't mind the jokes in the newspaper office where
I worked about whether I left the building by window, roof or in the
elevator. The truth is that I was an unlikely person to jump out of an
airplane, being neither graceful, daring nor self-possessed. I had a bad
back, uncertain ankles and could not drive with competence because
of deficient depth perception and a fear of all buses coming toward
me. A friend joked that if I broke any bones I would have to be shot
because I would never mend.

I never knew why I did it. It was in May, a bright and dull May, the
last May that made me want to feel reckless. But there was nothing
to do then at the beginning of a decade that changed almost everything. I could not wait that May for the Sixties to unroll. I worked in
women's news; my stories came out like little cookies. I wanted to be
brave about something, not just about love, or a root canal, or writing
that the shoes at Arnold Constable looked strangely sad.

Once I read of men who had to run so far it burned their chests to
breathe. But I could not run very far. Jumping from a plane, which
required no talent or endurance, seemed perfect. I wanted to feel the
big, puzzling lump on my back that they promised was a parachute,
to take serious strides in the absurd black boots that I believed all
generals wore.

I wanted all of it: the rising of a tiny plane with the door off, the
earth rushing away, the plunge, the slap of the wind, my hands on
the back straps, the huge curve of white silk above me, the drift
through the space we call sky.

It looked pale green that morning I fell into it, not the baby blue I
expected. I must have been crying; my cheeks were wet. Only the

thumps of a wild heart made noise; I did not know how to keep it quiet.

That May, that May my mind was as clear as clay. I did not have the imagination to perceive the risks, to understand that if the wind grew nasty I might be electrocuted on high-tension wires, smashed on a roof, drowned in water, hanged in a tree. I was sure nothing would happen, because my intentions were so good, just as young soldiers start out certain of their safety because they know nothing.

Friends drove me to Orange, Massachusetts, seventy miles west of Boston, for the opening of the first U.S. sports parachuting center, where I was to perform. It was the creation, the passion, of a Princetonian and ex-Marine named Jacques Istel, who organized the first U.S. jumping team in 1956. Parachuting was "as safe as swimming," he kept saying, calling it the "world's most stimulating and soul-satisfying sport." His center was for competitions and the teaching of skydiving. Instead of hurtling toward the earth, sky divers maintain a swan-dive position, using the air as a cushion to support them while they maneuver with leg and arm movements until the rip cord must be pulled.

None of that stuff was expected from any of us in the little beginners class. We were only to jump, after brief but intense instruction, with Istel's newly designed parachute, to show that any dope could do it. It was a parachute with a thirty-two-foot canopy; a large cutout hole funneled escaping air. You steered with two wooden knobs instead of having to pull hard on the back straps, or risers. The new parachute increased lateral speed, slowed down the rate of descent, reduced oscillation. We were told we could even land standing up but that we should bend our knees and lean to one side. The beginners jumped at eight A.M., The expert sky divers performed their dazzling tricks later when a crowd came.

Two of us boarded a Cessna 180 that lovely morning, the wind no more than a tickle. I was not myself, no longer thin and no longer fast. The jump suit, the equipment, the helmet, the boots, had made me into someone thick and clumsy, moving as strangely as if they had put me underwater and said I must walk. It was hard to bend, to sit, to stand up. I did not like the man with me; he was eager and composed. I wanted to smoke, to go the bathroom, but there were many straps around me that I did not understand. At twenty-three hundred feet, the hateful, happy man went out, making a dumb thumbs-up sign.

When my turn came, I suddenly felt a stab of pain for all the for-

gotten soldiers who balked and were kicked out, perhaps shot, for
their panic and for delaying the troops. I was hooked to a static line,
an automatic opening device, which made it impossible to lie down
or tie myself to something. The drillmaster could not hear all that I
shouted at him. But he knew the signs of mutiny and removed my
arms from his neck. He took me to the doorway, sat me down, and
yelled "Go!" or "Now!" or "Out!" There was nothing to do but be
punched by the wind, which knocked the spit from my mouth, reach
for the wing strut, hold on hard, kick back the feet so weighted and
helpless in those boots, and let go. The parachute opened with a plop,
as Istel had sworn to me that it would. When my eyelids opened as
well, I saw the white gloves on my hands were old ones from Saks
Fifth Avenue, gloves I wore with summer dresses. There was dribble
on my chin; my eyes and nose were leaking. I wiped everything with
the gloves.

There was no noise; the racket of the plane and wind had gone
away. The cold and sweet stillness seemed an astonishing, undreamed-
of gift. Then I saw what I had never seen before, will never see again:
endless sky and earth in colors and textures no one had ever described.
Only then did the parachute become a most lovable and docile toy:
this wooden knob to go left, this wooden knob to go right. The pleasure
of being there, the drifting and the calm, rose to a fever; I wanted to
stay pinned in the air and stop the ground from coming closer. The
target was a huge arrow in a sandpit. I was cross to see it, afraid of
nothing now, for even the wind was kind and the trees looked soft. I
landed on my feet in the pit with a bump, then sat down for a bit.
Later that day I was taken over to meet General James Gavin, who
had led the 82nd Airborne in the D-day landing at Normandy. Perhaps
it was to prove to him that the least promising pupil, the gawkiest,
could jump. It did not matter that I stumbled and fell before him in
those boots, which walked with a will of their own. Later, Mr. Istel's
mother wrote me a charming note of congratulations. Everyone at the
center was pleased; in fact, I am sure they were surprised. Perhaps
this is what I had in mind all the time.

QUESTIONS

1. Why do you suppose it was usually men who asked Emerson why
   she took the plunge? Why do you suppose Emerson herself doesn't
   speculate about the observation with which she starts her essay?

2. Emerson says she never understood why she did it. Does she not

understand at all? Does she make any effort to understand? What is it about her feat that she doesn't understand?

3. Why does Emerson repeat "that May"?

4. Why does Emerson include the detail about her gloves?

5. Why do *you* think Emerson did it?

SUGGESTED ACTIVITIES

1. Describe a time when you took a plunge.

2. Write an essay about something you did for reasons you still don't understand. Try to understand now.

3. Write about something you would like to do if you had the nerve. Figure out why you would like to do it.

DON ETHAN MILLER
A State of Grace: Understanding the Martial Arts

> *Miller has taught t'ai chi and related disciplines at The Joy of Movement Center in Boston, various hospitals, Dartmouth, Emerson College, and Clark University. Miller is a frequent contributor to* The Atlantic, The Village Voice, *and* Vogue. *He has published two books,* Body Mind: The Whole Person Health Book (1974) *and* The Book of Jargon: An Essential Guide to the Inside Languages of Today (1982). *In this essay Miller explains the true meaning of the Oriental martial arts: knowledge of one's self.*

In the summer of 1967, I was enrolled as an exchange student from Dartmouth at the University of Leningrad, USSR. One evening, at a talent show presented by the foreign students, I gave a karate demonstration to a large audience of Russian students, professors, and invited friends. I had been studying karate in the States for several years and was fairly proficient at it, though some distance from the black belt level I was to attain three years later. After demonstrating the classic *kata*, or choreographed forms, and delivering a brief dissertation on the art, the climax of my act was to break a brick with my bare hand—a skill I had acquired a year before, and had repeated dozens of times.

My Russian friends proudly produced a construction brick easily twice the size and three times the weight of the baked red bricks I was accustomed to splitting back home. Undaunted, I set it precisely to bridge the space between a pair of similar bricks laid parallel on the stage floor. I knelt, and held one end of the brick slightly off the base with my left hand. Rising slightly from my kneeling position, I inhaled, raised my right hand in a short arc up to shoulder level, and then, yelling sharply, brought my clenched fist down with the full force of my body behind it, tightening all my muscles just at the moment of impact to transmit the force into the stone. Nothing happened. I felt a dull pain in the base of my hand, and the shock wave of the blow traveled back up my arm and shoulder. No matter; this sometimes happens if the blow is not exactly right. I immediately reset the oversize brick and struck down again, quickly, absolutely as hard as I could. But again, it merely smacked into the base brick and stopped.

I struck again and again, ten or fifteen violent, staccato blows with my right hand, until the flesh broke and the blood spurted out into the audience. Then I switched to my uninjured left hand, hammering down with every particle of strength I possessed: the brick remained indestructible. I was angry, charged, determined; my adrenaline was flowing; I was hitting the thing hard enough, it seemed, to go through steel. But the Russian brick could not be broken.

After a long time, and only when both my hands were smashed and bloody, and my friends in the wings urged me to let the rest of the show continue, did I finally give up. I said something by way of apology to the audience, walked off stage, changed out of my karate uniform into my street clothes, and walked alone and sullen into the Leningrad night air.

Across the street from the university hall was a construction site, and there, barely visible in the half-light from a distant streetlamp, lay a large pile of the very same bricks. I crossed the street and picked one up. Slowly I turned it over in my battered hands and the angrily hurled it to the ground—where it broke on the edge of another brick! I knelt down, grabbed another brick, and half hit, half threw it against two others from close range; this one broke as well. I gathered up an armful of fresh bricks and hurried back inside the auditorium. Over the objections of several performers, I strode onstage and briskly set up the bricks. "Watch this," I said to the audience, in English. I inhaled, raised my fist, and struck downward with a confident yell. The brick didn't break!

I immediately hit it again: nothing. Two or three more shots in as many seconds, and I realized that to break the brick in this manner was truly impossible. Bewildered and humiliated after this new defeat, I sat back on my heels and closed my eyes—more to avoid looking out at the audience than anything else. I took a deep breath and relaxed my muscles. I forgot about the brick. I forgot the pain in my hands. White clouds drifted across a purple sky within my mental field of vision. I was aware of the wind of my own breathing. In a few seconds I had almost completely forgotten where I was and what I was "supposed" to be doing.

Just at that moment I opened my eyes, gently cradled the brick with my left hand, and—without tension, without haste, without any real effort—came down smoothly with my right hand, which *passed right through the brick*, without any sensation of impact.

I had, in fact, broken the brick with my hand, but the feeling was much more that it had "parted" in response to the completely new kind of action I had generated. I held up the two halves of the severed brick for the audience to see, but they had already seen and were on their feet, clapping and cheering wildly. The Russians are a people who know a lot about suffering and transcendence, and though I'm sure they had no idea of the particulars of my breakthrough, they recognized a victory of the spirit over insensate matter. I felt sure it was this victory, rather that the feat itself, that they were applauding.

I began studying the Oriental martial arts twenty years ago, a short, overweight smart kid with glasses on the Upper West Side of Manhattan. I hated being unable to defend myself from the gangs of tough kids around whom I had to thread the most circuitous of routes to reach Junior High School 44 unscathed. Though I was motivated originally by self-defense, something else grabbed hold of me from the very first time I walked into the Downtown Dojo, a school of judo, in 1960. I was taken by the aesthetic of the place: the huge, open, mat-covered practice hall, the shoes lined up outside the door, the neatly displayed wooden membership plaques on the stark white walls. I didn't understand it then, but in the architecture of the place there was a single-mindedness, a focusing of the attention, an austere, negative beauty that moved me strangely, like déjà vu. There was a mystery there beyond the mere exoticisms of a foreign culture. After two decades, I can at least name the mystery: the martial arts have been for me a doorway into terrains of experience beyond the normal "limits," into other realms where the common assumptions about conflict and fear, effort and energy, and even the nature of physical reality may be overturned and completely reordered.

I studied Kodokan judo for three years, becoming the most avid and devoted junior member of the school. In 1963 I discovered karate (more properly Tae Kwon Do, or Korean karate), and plunged into that discipline with equal fervor. I studied Tae Kwon Do for eight years, under three different teachers, receiving my black belt in the summer of 1970. Earlier that same year, I had begun my study of T'ai Chi Ch'uan, a Chinese art of meditation-in-motion that is also a remarkable fighting style. Although I did not see the conflict between them at the time, karate and T'ai Chi eventually proved to be antagonistic disciplines, and I chose the latter. I have studied and taught both meditative T'ai Chi and practical self-defense for the past ten years. During this period I also studied aikido and ki development, Western boxing, a smattering of kung fu, sword work, wrestling, and so on. I am recounting this list solely to indicate that, if I tend to wax a little philosophical, it is philosophy that I have not dreamed up but have sweated for.

For the most part, the "external" arts, such as judo and karate, emphasize the acquisition of physical skills—speed, balance, accuracy, coordination, power. They are, especially in the first few years of training, basically athletic disciplines that develop that student's facility in punching, kicking, blocking, throwing, grappling, and so forth. Unfortunately, most students never reach the higher levels of these arts, where physical technique assumes less importance than psychological transformation. Fewer than one out of every hundred students of the martial arts persist to the black-belt level—which, it must be understood, confers not mastery but only the beginning of serious study.

One of the major differences between the external arts and those that are termed "internal" (T'ai Chi, aikido, Pa Kua, and a few others) is that the internal schools work on one's state of mind—or rather, *with* one's state of mind—from the very beginning. The acquisition of physical skills is but a secondary outgrowth of one's psychological or spiritual development. Fighting is, in fact, not the real subject of these arts; rather, they deal with the quality of one's energy.

I first encountered the magic of the internal schools in the persona of Master T. T. Liang. It was 1970, and I had brought a group of my karate students to a growth center in southern New Hampshire called Cumbres, where Liang was ensconced as T'ai Chi teacher-in-residence. He was an elderly Chinese man, slightly stooped, it seemed, but with a rich, dramatic voice and shining brown eyes. After demonstrating some of the slow, majestically flowing movements of the long form, Liang lectured briefly on the principles of the art. He listed its ancient tenets: "Sink the ch'i (vital energy). Relax. All movements should be directed by the mind, rather than the external muscular force. Meditation in action; action in meditation."

These were words I had been waiting to hear—a deliberate method that unified the mind and the body, that dealt with the inner and outer dimensions simultaneously. I was elated. Liang called me to the center of the floor with him, to show the practical application of the T'ai Chi philosophy. He raised one arm slightly in front of his body and invited me to push him. At the moment that my hand touched his wrist, he started to laugh, and I started to laugh with him. I wasn't sure why we were laughing; the situation seemed both silly and sublime—here we were, the young karate man and the old T'ai Chi master, our arms touching, our spirits meeting—at what felt to be the center of the whole universe.

"Push," he said. I pushed, expecting his resistance; instead, he turned his body easily to the side, in perfect coordination with my movement, but without severing the connection of my hands to his forearm, so that I had the illusion of pushing something solid when in fact his body had "disappeared" from my line of force. I stumbled forward into the vacuum that his turn created, nearly falling. And we laughed again. Liang was showing the T'ai Chi principle of "neutralization" or yielding. I didn't mind being made to look clumsy at all; he liked that. It was the beginning of a beautiful friendship.

One evening, after more instruction than we could handle, and a fresh array of stories, someone discreetly asked him to show a bit of the double sword form—a complex sequence using two double-edged swords. Seeming to begin causally, while still talking, Liang was soon immersed in the form—spinning, leaping, twirling the steel blades and the long colored tassels that trailed from their handles. At the climactic section both swords were a blur, whirring around his body in an intricate series of interwoven figure-eights, faster than the eye could follow. He appeared to be surrounded by a field of flashing metal, yet inside, as one looked at his face, there was no trace of strain, or even of effort: he was in a kind of trance, eyes half-closed, moving with the utmost serenity and gentleness. For a timeless, luminous ten or fifteen seconds he was as close to perfection as anyone that I have ever seen.

The class applauded him soundly when he finished the form, and he returned to being our friendly, funny old teacher again; but what we had seen was something beyond applause and beyond skill. The Chinese call it *wei wu wei*, "to do without doing," the condition of effortless accomplishment that comes from attunement with Tao, the greater order of Nature. In the West we might call it a state of grace.

In 1975, and again in 1976 and 1977, I had the good fortune to study directly with Koichi Tohei, grandmaster of aikido and arguably the world's foremost living martial artist. At sixty, Tohei moves with the power of an NFL lineman combined with the weightless grace of a ballet dancer. He is the embodiment of the most serious traditions of Oriental *budo*, or martial ways—but is genuinely nonviolent, compassionate, earthy, and human. The majority of his teaching effort is concerned not with the formal art of aikido but with the system he has evolved for ki development—the cultivation and utilization of each person's own life force.

Using the power of ki, Tohei performs astounding feats: at five foot three and 150 pounds, he can make himself so "heavy" that four young men cannot lift him off the ground. He can resist three six-footers lined up to push him backward—using only the little finger on one hand to stop them. He can inhale and exhale loudly enough to be heard across an open gymnasium floor—yet make a single breath cycle last as long as three minutes. When he performs the characteristic whirling throws of traditional aikido, there is no effort involved: his compact, soft-edged body in the black *hakama* skirts of the samurai spins, twirls, drops, rises like a tornado or a whirlpool, revolving and spiraling around a steady, calm center of power in the lower abdomen, which he calls *seika itten*, "the One-point."

In one of the first seminars I attended, he invited me to hold his wrists, as forcefully as I could, and keep him from bringing his hands together. My arms are strong, from decades of calisthenics, weight lifting, karate, wood chopping; he tenses against them, but cannot move. He smiles; "Ve-rry strong," he pronounces, in a lilting Japanese basso. "Once again, please." Again I grasp him tightly, but this time he does not tense against my force: he opens his hands, stretching the fingers, his body relaxed. Something fundamental about the nature of the encounter changes; I suddenly feel that I am holding, or trying to hold, two powerful streams of rushing water—not the constellation of skin, muscle, and bone I had gripped a few seconds earlier. Gently, deliberately, he turns his fingers inward and with the utmost ease moves his hands slowly toward each other. The movement, like a river turning, is impossible to resist. His hands come together softly; when I look to his face, the eyes are shining and kind. We are both smiling. "This," he says, "is coordination of mind and body."

But Tohei is adamant about one thing: that his abilities are nothing special, that they are powers accessible to everyone who trains in the coordination of the mental with the physical. "I am at the center of the universe," he declares, "but universe is infinite. So you can also be at center of universe. Anything I can do, everybody can do." Later, I will learn to perform some of the same "tricks" he has demonstrated—which are not really tricks, but manifestations of the greater power one has easily available when the body is relaxed, the attention directed, the emotions confident and positive, the mind perfectly calm. This is the state called being *centered*, and it is the basis of Tohei's art and power.

There *are* ways to make the magic work, with some consistency. I have learned, over the course of my twenty-year odyssey through the martial arts, that the capacity of the human mind to coordinate and focus physiological energy is infinitely greater than the standard assumptions of biology and physics would lead us to believe. I have become convinced that there is something, a spirit or vital force, which the Japanese call *ki* and the Chinese *ch'i*, which is universal in origin yet manifest uniquely in every living creature; which can be cultivated and increased through certain types of practice. And, since that first night in Leningrad, I have acquired a reliable method for entering that particular state of effortless accomplishment.

Thus, when I now approach a stack of three two-inch cinder blocks to attempt a breaking feat, I do not set myself to "try hard," or to summon up all my strength. Instead I relax, sinking my awareness into my belly and legs, feeling my connection with the ground. I breathe deeply, mentally directing the breath through my torso, legs, and arms. I imagine a line of force coming up from the ground through my legs, down one arm, and out through an acupuncture point at the base of my palm, through the stone slabs, and down again into the ground, penetrating to the center of the earth. I do not focus any attention on the objects to be broken. Although when I am lifting or holding them in a normal state of consciousness the blocks seem tremendously dense, heavy, and hard, in the course of my one- or two-minute preparation their reality seems to change, as indeed the reality of the whole situation changes. I am no longer a thirty-two-year-old American writer in basketball sneakers doing strange breathing exercises in his suburban back yard in front of a pile of red patio blocks: I am a spiritual traveler, making the necessary preparations for a journey to a different world.

I know that I am in the other "zone" by certain signs: my breathing takes on a deep, raspy, unearthly tone; my vision changes, such that tiny pebbles on the ground appear huge, like asteroids; my body feels denser, yet at the same time light and free of tension. I feel that what I am doing is extremely important, that the attention of the entire universe is focused upon me. When I make my final approach to the bricks, if I regard them at all they seem light, airy, and friendly; they do not have the insistent inner drive in them that I do.

I do not hit the bricks; I do not break them. Rather, I take a deep breath, hold it for half a second, then *release* suddenly but smoothly, focusing on the energy line and allowing my arm to express it. My palm passes right through the place where the blocks were, but they have apparently parted just before I get there, and there is no sensation of impact, no shock wave, no pain. Whoever is watching usually applauds and congratulates me, but in the zone there is nothing to be congratulated for and it seems silly. One is merely surprised to realize how easy such things are if one is in the correct body-mind state. Gradually, one comes out of it, one tries to explain, but the essence of it is beyond the reach of words. Hours later, what remains is not the sense of destructive power but the feeling of atunement with universal forces, of identification with the mysterious but very real power of life itself. Passing through the bricks is only a way of entering another realm.

The real value of martial arts study, in other words, has nothing to do with physical feats such as brickbreaking; in fact, it is not even primarily concerned with fighting. In our modern technologized society, it would be easier to buy a gun or carry a can of mace. Their real value lies in what the martial arts tell us about ourselves: that we can be much more than we are now; that we have no need of fear; and that our capacities for energy, awareness, courage, and compassion are far greater than we have been led to believe. They tell us that all our personal limits—and by extension, our destructive social and historical patterns—can be transcended. Beginning with the next breath, drawn deeply.

QUESTIONS

1. What is the relationship between suffering and transcendence that Miller seems to take for granted?

2. What does Miller mean by "negative beauty"?

3. What is the difference between working "on one's state of mind" and working "*with* one's state of mind"?

4. What is a "timeless, luminous 10 or 15 seconds"? And what is a feat that "was something beyond applause and beyond skill"? And why that order? Why not skill and applause?

5. How has Miller organized the exposition? Does the organization make sense? What kind of sense?

SUGGESTED ACTIVITIES

1. Using Miller's essay, your religious knowledge, and the dictionary— define "a state of grace."

2. Write a consideration of how grace can occur in secular as well as in religious events.

3. Describe a secular or religious event when you experienced, however slightly, a state of grace.

ROGER ROSENBLATT
The Man in the Water

> Rosenblatt taught English at Harvard, served as Director of Education for the National Endowment for the Humanities, and was literary editor of the New Republic. A columnist for TIME Magazine, he has written essays for many magazines and published a critical book, Black Fiction (1974). In this essay Rosenblatt shows how rigorous meditation on an event can guide one to its profound significance.

As disasters go, this one was terrible, but not unique, certainly not among the worst on the roster of U.S. air crashes. There was the unusual element of the bridge, of course, and the fact that the plane clipped it at a moment of high traffic, one routine thus intersecting another and disrupting both. Then, too, there was the location of the event. Washington, the city of form and regulations, turned chaotic, deregulated, by a blast of real winter and a single slap of metal on metal. The jets from Washington National Airport that normally swoop around the presidential monuments like famished gulls are, for the moment, emblemized by the one that fell; so there is that detail. And there was the aesthetic clash as well—blue-and-green Air Florida, the name a flying garden, sunk down among gray chunks in a black river. All that was worth noticing, to be sure. Still, there was nothing very special in any of it, except death, which, while always special, does not necessarily bring millions to tears or to attention. Why, then, the shock here?

Perhaps because the nation saw in this disaster something more than a mechanical failure. Perhaps because people saw in it no failure at all, but rather something successful about their makeup. Here, after all, were two forms of nature in collision: the elements and human character. Last Wednesday, the elements, indifferent as ever, brought down Flight 90. And on that same afternoon, human nature—groping and flailing in mysteries of its own—rose to the occasion.

Of the four acknowledged heroes of the event, three are able to account for their behavior. Donald Usher and Eugene Windsor, a park police helicopter team, risked their lives every time they dipped the skids into the water to pick up survivors. On television, side by side in bright blue jumpsuits, they described their courage as all in the line of duty. Lenny Skutnik, a 28-year-old employee of the Congressional Budget Office, said: "It's something I never thought I would do"— referring to his jumping into the water to drag an injured woman to shore. Skutnik added that "somebody had to go in the water," delivering every hero's line that is no less admirable for its repetitions. In fact, nobody had to go into the water. That somebody actually did so is part of the reason this particular tragedy sticks in the mind.

But the person most responsible for the emotional impact of the disaster is the one known at first simply as "the man in the water." (Balding, probably in his 50s, an extravagant mustache.) He was seen clinging with five other survivors to the tail section of the airplane. This man was described by Usher and Windsor as appearing alert and in control. Every time they lowered a lifeline and flotation ring to him, he passed it on to another of the passengers. "In a mass casualty, you'll find people like him," said Windsor. "But I've never seen one with that commitment." When the helicopter came back for him, the man had gone under. His selflessness was one reason the story held national attention; his anonymity another. The fact that he went unidentified invested him with a universal character. For a while he was Everyman, and thus proof (as if one needed it) that no man is ordinary.

Still, he could never have imagined such a capacity in himself. Only minutes before his character was tested, he was sitting in the ordinary plane among the ordinary passengers, dutifully listening to the stewardess telling him to fasten his seat belt and saying something about the "no smoking sign." So our man relaxed with the others, some of whom would owe their lives to him. Perhaps he started to read, or to doze, or to regret some harsh remark made in the office that morning. Then suddenly he knew that the trip would not be ordinary. Like every other person on that flight, he was desperate to live, which makes his final act so stunning.

For at some moment in the water he must have realized that he would not live if he continued to hand over the rope and ring to others. He *had* to know it, no matter how gradual the effect of the cold. In his judgment he had no choice. When the helicopter took off with what was to be the last survivor, he watched everything in the world move away from him, and he deliberately let it happen.

Yet there was something else about the man that kept our thoughts on him, and which keeps our thoughts on him still. He was *there*, in the essential, classic circumstance. Man in nature. The man in the water. For its part, nature cared nothing about the five passengers. Our man, on the other hand, cared totally. So the timeless battle commenced in the Potomac. For as long as that man could last, they went at each other, nature and man; the one making no distinctions of good and evil, acting on no principles, offering no lifelines; the other acting wholly on distinctions, principles and, one supposes, on faith.

Since it was he who lost the fight, we ought to come again to the conclusion that people are powerless in the world. In reality, we believe the reverse, and it takes the act of the man in the water to remind us of our true feelings in this matter. It is not to say that everyone would have acted as he did, or as Usher, Windsor and Skutnik. Yet whatever moved these men to challenge death on behalf of their fellows is not peculiar to them. Everyone feels the possibility in himself. That is the abiding wonder of the story. That is why we would not let go of it. If the man in the water gave a lifeline to the people gasping for survival, he was likewise giving a lifeline to those who observed him.

The odd thing is that we do not even really believe that the man in the water lost his fight. "Everything in Nature contains all the powers of Nature," said Emerson. Exactly. So the man in the water had his own natural powers. He could not make ice storms, or freeze the water until it froze the blood. But he could hand life over to a stranger, and that is a power of nature too. The man in the water pitted himself against an implacable, impersonal enemy; he fought it with charity; and he held it to a standoff. He was the best we can do.

QUESTIONS

1. What is Rosenblatt doing in the first paragraph? Why does he include so many considerations? Why not get right to the subject—the man in the water?

2. Why does Rosenblatt include Usher's and Windsor's observations that the man appeared "alert and in control"?

3. On what basis (bases) does Rosenblatt feel entitled to assert, "Still, he could never have imagined such a capacity in himself"? On what basis (or bases) can he say, "In his judgment he had no choice"?

4. What does Rosenblatt mean when he says the man fought nature "with charity" and "held it to a standoff"?

SUGGESTED ACTIVITIES

1. Describe an act of heroism that you personally witnessed.

2. Describe a personal act of heroism. If heroism is too strong a word— if you find it embarrassing—substitute *courage*. Keep in mind that acts of courage come in all shapes and sizes.

3. It has been argued that if heroism is selfless, there is no such thing as heroism because there is no such thing as selflessness. If for no other reason, we act courageously for the sake of our good opinion of ourselves. Write an essay attacking that position.

VIII
Values and Society

GILBERT HIGHET
Diogenes and Alexander

A native of Scotland, Highet was a classicist who lived and taught in the United States for many years. His books include The Classical Tradition *(1949),* The Art of Teaching *(1950), and* The Anatomy of Satire *(1962). The following essay exhibits Highet's gift for explaining ideas in commonsense terms and for using anecdote as telling detail.*

Lying on the bare earth, shoeless, bearded, half-naked, he looked like a beggar or a lunatic. He was one, but not the other. He had opened his eyes with the sun at dawn, scratched, done his business like a dog at the roadside, washed at the public fountain, begged a piece of breakfast bread and a few olives, eaten them squatting on the ground, and washed them down with a few handfuls of water scooped from the spring. (Long ago he had owned a rough wooden cup, but he threw it away when he saw a boy drinking out of his hollowed hands.) Having no work to go to and no family to provide for, he was free. As the market place filled up with shoppers and merchants and gossipers and sharpers and slaves and foreigners, he had strolled through it for an hour or two. Everybody knew him, or knew of him. They would throw sharp questions at him, and get sharper answers. Sometimes they threw jeers, and got jibes; sometimes bits of food, and got scant thanks; sometimes a mischievous pebble, and got a shower of stones and abuse. They were not quite sure whether he was mad or not. He knew they were mad, all mad, each in a different way; they amused him. Now he was back at his home.

It was not a house, not even a squatter's hut. He thought everybody lived far too elaborately, expensively, anxiously. What good is a house? No one needs privacy: natural acts are not shameful; we all do the same things, and need not hide them. No one needs beds and chairs and such furniture: the animals live healthy lives and sleep on the ground. All we require, since nature did not dress us properly, is one garment to keep us warm, and some shelter from rain and wind. So he had one blanket—to dress him in the daytime and cover him at night—and he slept in a cask. His name was Diogenes. He was the founder of the creed called Cynicism (the word means "doggishness"); he spent much of his life in the rich, lazy, corrupt Greek city of Corinth, mocking and satirizing its people, and occasionally converting one of them.

His home was not a barrel made of wood: too expensive. It was a storage jar made of earthenware, something like a modern fuel tank— no doubt discarded because a break had made it useless. He was not the first to inhabit such a thing: the refugees driven into Athens by the Spartan invasion had been forced to sleep in casks. But he was the first who ever did so by choice, out of principle.

Diogenes was not a degenerate or a maniac. He was a philosopher who wrote plays and poems and essays expounding his doctrine; he talked to those who cared to listen; he had pupils who admired him. But he taught chiefly by example. All should live naturally, he said, for what is natural is normal and cannot possibly be evil or shameful. Live without conventions, which are artificial and false; escape complexities and superfluities and extravagances: only so can you live a free life. The rich man believes he possesses his big house with its many rooms and its elaborate furniture, his pictures and his expensive clothes, his horse and his servants and his bank accounts. He does not. He depends on them, he worries about them, he spends most of his life's energy looking after them; the thought of losing them makes him sick with anxiety. They possess him. He is their slave. In order to procure a quantity of false, perishable goods he has sold the only true, last good, his own independence.

There have been many men who grew tired of human society with its complications, and went away to live simply—on a small farm, in a quiet village, in a hermit's cave, or in the darkness of anonymity. Not so Diogenes. He was not a recluse, or a stylite, or a beatnik. He was a missionary. His life's aim was clear to him: it was "to restamp the currency." (He and his father had once been convicted for counterfeiting, long before he turned to philosophy, and this phrase was Diogenes' bold, unembarrassed joke on the subject.) To restamp the currency: to take the clean metal of human life, to erase the old false conventional markings, and to imprint it with its true values.

The other great philosophers of the fourth century before Christ taught mainly their own private pupils. In the shady groves and cool sanctuaries of the Academy, Plato discoursed to a chosen few on the unreality of this contingent existence. Aristotle, among the books and instruments and specimens and archives and research-workers of his Lyceum, pursued investigations and gave lectures that were rightly named *esoteric*, "for those within the walls." But for Diogenes, laboratory and specimens and lecture halls and pupils were all to be found in a crowd of ordinary people. Therefore he chose to live in Athens or in the rich city of Corinth, where travelers from all over the Mediterranean world constantly came and went. And, by design, he publicly behaved in such ways as to show people what real life was. He would constantly take up their spiritual coin, ring it on a stone, and laugh at its false superscription.

He thought most people were only half-alive, most men only half-men. At bright noonday he walked through the market place carrying a lighted lamp and inspecting the face of everyone he met. They asked him why. Diogenes answered, "I am trying to find a *man*."

To a gentleman whose servant was putting on his shoes for him, Diogenes said, "You won't be really happy until he wipes your nose for you: that will come after you lose the use of your hands."

Once there was a war scare so serious that it stirred even the lazy, profit-happy Corinthians. They began to drill, clean their weapons, and rebuild their neglected fortifications. Diogenes took his old cask and began to roll it up and down, back and forward. "When you are all so busy," he said, "I felt I ought to do *something*!"

And so he lived—like a dog, some said, because he cared nothing for privacy and other human conventions, and because he showed his teeth and barked at those whom he disliked. Now he was lying in the sunlight, as contented as a dog on the warm ground, happier (he himself used to boast) than the Shah of Persia. Although he knew he was going to have an important visitor, he would not move.

The little square began to fill with people. Page boys elegantly dressed, spearmen speaking a rough foreign dialect, discreet secretaries, hard-browed officers, suave diplomats, they all gradually formed a circle centered on Diogenes. He looked them over, as a sober man looks at a crowd of tottering drunks, and shook his head. He knew who they were. They were the attendants of the conqueror of Greece, the servants of Alexander, the Macedonian king, who was visiting his newly subdued realm.

Only twenty, Alexander was far older and wiser than his years. Like all Macedonians he loved drinking, but he could usually handle it; and toward women he was nobly restrained and chivalrous. Like all Macedonians he loved fighting; he was a magnificent commander, but he was not merely a military automaton. He could think. At thirteen he had become a pupil of the greatest mind in Greece, Aristotle. No exact record of his schooling survives. It is clear, though, that Aristotle took the passionate, half-barbarous boy and gave him the best of Greek culture. He taught Alexander poetry: the young prince slept with the *Iliad* under his pillow and longed to emulate Achilles, who brought the mighty power of Asia to ruin. He taught him philosophy, in particular the shapes and uses of political power: a few years later Alexander was to create a supranational empire that was not merely a power system but a vehicle for the exchange of Greek and Middle Eastern cultures.

Aristotle taught him the principles of scientific research: during his invasion of the Persian domains Alexander took with him a large corps of scientists, and shipped hundreds of zoological specimens back to Greece for study. Indeed, it was from Aristotle that Alexander learned to seek out everything strange which might be instructive. Jugglers and stunt artists and virtuosos of the absurd he dismissed with a shrug; but on reaching India he was to spend hours discussing the problems of life and death with naked Hindu mystics, and later to see one demonstrate Yoga self-command by burning himself impassively to death.

Now, Alexander was in Corinth to take command of the League of Greek States which, after conquering them, his father Philip had created as a disguise for the New Macedonian Order. He was welcomed and honored and flattered. He was the man of the hour, of the century: he was unanimously appointed commander-in-chief of a new expedition against old, rich, corrupt Asia. Nearly everyone crowded to Corinth in order to congratulate him, to seek employment with him, even simply to see him: soldiers and statesmen, artists and merchants, poets and philosophers. He received their compliments graciously. Only Diogenes, although he lived in Corinth, did not visit the new monarch. With that generosity which Aristotle had taught him was a quality of the truly magnanimous man, Alexander determined to call upon Diogenes. Surely Dio-genes, the God-born, would acknowledge the conqueror's power by some gift of hoarded wisdom.

With his handsome face, his fiery glance, his strong supple body, his purple and gold cloak, and his air of destiny, he moved through the parting crowd, toward the Dog's kennel. When a king approaches, all rise in respect. Diogenes did not rise, he merely sat up on one elbow. When a monarch enters a precinct, all greet him with a bow or an acclamation. Diogenes said nothing.

There was a silence. Some years later Alexander speared his best friend to the wall, for objecting to the exaggerated honors paid to His Majesty; but now he was still young and civil. He spoke first, with a kindly greeting. Looking at the poor broken cask, the single ragged garment, and the rough figure lying on the ground, he said, "Is there anything I can do for you, Diogenes?"

"Yes," said the Dog. "Stand to one side. You're blocking the sunlight."

There was silence, not the ominous silence preceding a burst of fury, but a hush of amazement. Slowly, Alexander turned away. A titter broke out from the elegant Greeks, who were already beginning to make jokes about the Cur that looked at the King. The Macedonian officers, after deciding that Diogenes was not worth the trouble of kicking, were starting to guffaw and nudge one another. Alexander was still silent. To those nearest him he said quietly, "If I were not Alexander, I should be Diogenes." They took it as a paradox, designed to close the awkward little scene with a polite curtain line. But Alexander meant it. He understood Cynicism as the others could not. Later he took one of Diogenes' pupils with him to India as a philosophical interpreter (it was he who spoke to the naked *saddhus*). He was what Diogenes called himself, a *cosmopolitēs*, "citizen of the world." Like Diogenes, he admired the heroic figure of Hercules, the mighty conqueror who labors to help mankind while all others toil and sweat only for themselves. He knew that of all men then alive in the world only Alexander the conqueror and Diogenes the beggar were truly free.

QUESTIONS

1. How could Diogenes justifiably consider everyone else mad in some way or other?

2. Why was Diogenes unembarrassed by his counterfeiting (ar͏ his conviction of it as well)?

3. What did Diogenes mean by "a *man*"?

4. "Some years later Alexander speared his best friend to the wall, for objecting to the exaggerated honors paid to His Majesty; but now he was still young and civil." How does this point conform to Diogenes' view of ordinary life?

5. How was Alexander free?

SUGGESTED ACTIVITIES

1. Try to refute Diogenes' views.

2. Write an essay on the value of not being free, in defense of what Diogenes considered to be corruption.

3. Write an essay on the value of being free as Diogenes views freedom.

GEORGE ORWELL
A Hanging

Here Orwell shows us, time and again, how detail can speak with greater eloquence and force than abstraction can against the brutalizing effects of capital punishment.

It was in Burma, a sodden morning of the rains. A sickly light, like yellow tinfoil, was slanting over the high walls into the jail yard. We were waiting outside the condemned cells, a row of sheds fronted with double bars, like small animal cages. Each cell measured about ten feet by ten and was quite bare within except for a plank bed and a pot for drinking water. In some of them brown, silent men were squatting at the inner bars, with their blankets draped round them. These were the condemned men, due to be hanged within the next week or two.

One prisoner had been brought out of his cell. He was a Hindu, a puny wisp of a man, with a shaven head and vague liquid eyes. He had a thick, sprouting moustache, absurdly too big for his body, rather like the moustache of a comic man on the films. Six tall Indian warders were guarding him and getting him ready for the gallows. Two of them stood by with rifles and fixed bayonets, while the others handcuffed him, passed a chain through his handcuffs and fixed it to their belts, and lashed his arms tight to his sides. They crowded very close about him, with their hands always on him in a careful, caressing grip, as though all the while feeling him to make sure he was there. It was like men handling a fish which is still alive and may jump back into the water. But he stood quite unresisting, yielding his arms limply to the ropes, as though he hardly noticed what was happening.

Eight o'clock struck and a bugle call, desolately thin in the wet air, floated from the distant barracks. The superintendent of the jail, who was standing apart from the rest of us, moodily prodding the gravel with his stick, raised his head at the sound. He was an army doctor, with a grey toothbrush moustache and a gruff voice. "For God's sake hurry up, Francis," he said irritably. "The man ought to have been dead by this time. Aren't you ready yet?"

Francis, the head jailer, a fat Dravidian in a white drill suit and gold spectacles, waved his black hand. "Yes sir, yes sir," he bubbled. "All iss satisfactorily prepared. The hangman iss waiting. We shall proceed."

"Well, quick march, then. The prisoners can't get their breakfast till this job's over."

We set out for the gallows. Two warders marched on either side of the prisoner, with their rifles at the slope; two others marched close against him, gripping him by arm and shoulder, as though at once pushing and supporting him. The rest of us, magistrates and the like followed behind. Suddenly, when we had gone ten yards, the procession stopped short without any order or warning. A dreadful thing had happened—a dog, come goodness knows whence, had appeared in the yard. It came bounding among us with a loud volley of barks, and leapt round us wagging its whole body, wild with glee at finding so many human beings together. It was a large woolly dog, half Airedale, half pariah. For a moment it pranced round us, and then, before anyone could stop it, it had made a dash for the prisoner and jumping up tried to lick his face. Everyone stood aghast, too taken aback even to grab at the dog.

"Who let that bloody brute in here?" said the superintendent angrily. "Catch it, someone!"

A warder detached from the escort, charged clumsily after the dog, but it danced and gambolled just out of his reach, taking everything as part of the game. A young Eurasian jailer picked up a handful of gravel and tried to stone the dog away, but it dodged the stones and came after us again. Its yaps echoed from the jail walls. The prisoner, in the grasp of the two warders, looked on incuriously, as though this was another formality of the hanging. It was several minutes before someone managed to catch the dog. Then we put my handkerchief through its collar and moved off once more, with the dog still straining and whimpering.

It was about forty yards to the gallows. I watched the bare brown back of the prisoner marching in front of me. He walked clumsily with his bound arms, but quite steadily, with that bobbing gait of the Indian who never straightens his knees. At each step his muscles slid neatly into place, the lock of hair on his scalp danced up and down, his feet printed themselves on the wet gravel. And once, in spite of the men who gripped him by each shoulder, he stepped slightly aside to avoid a puddle on the path.

It is curious, but till that moment I had never realized what it means to destroy a healthy, conscious man. When I saw the prisoner step aside to avoid the puddle I saw the mystery, the unspeakable wrongness, of cutting a life short when it is in full tide. This man was not dying, he was alive just as we are alive. All the organs of his body were working—bowels digesting food, skin renewing itself, nails growing, tissues forming—all toiling away in solemn foolery. His nails would still be growing when he stood on the drop, when he was falling through the air with a tenth-of-a-second to live. His eyes saw the yellow gravel and the grey walls, and his brain still remembered, foresaw, reasoned—reasoned even about puddles. He and we were a party of men walking together, seeing, hearing, feeling, understanding the same world; and in two minutes, with a sudden snap, one of us would be gone—one mind less, one world less.

The gallows stood in a small yard, separate from the main grounds of the prison, and overgrown with tall prickly weeds. It was a brick erection like three sides of a shed, with planking on top, and above that two beams and a crossbar with the rope dangling. The hangman, a grey-haired convict in the white uniform of the prison, was waiting beside his machine. He greeted us with a servile crouch as we entered. At a word from Francis the two warders, gripping the prisoner more closely than ever, half led half pushed him to the gallows and helped him clumsily up the ladder. Then the hangman climbed up and fixed the rope round the prisoner's neck.

We stood waiting, five yards away. The warders had formed in a rough circle round the gallows. And then, when the noose was fixed, the prisoner began crying out to his god. It was a high, reiterated cry of "Ram! Ram! Ram! Ram!" not urgent and fearful like a prayer or cry for help, but steady, rhythmical, almost like the tolling of a bell. The dog answered the sound with a whine. The hangman, still standing on the gallows, produced a small cotton bag like a flour bag and drew it down over the prisoner's face. But the sound, muffled by the cloth, still persisted, over and over again: "Ram! Ram! Ram! Ram! Ram!"

The hangman climbed down and stood ready, holding the lever. Minutes seemed to pass. The steady, muffled crying from the prisoner went on and on, "Ram! Ram! Ram!" never faltering for an instant. The superintendent, his head on his chest, was slowly poking the ground with his stick; perhaps he was counting the cries, allowing the prisoner a fixed number—fifty, perhaps, or a hundred. Everyone had changed colour. The Indians had gone grey like bad coffee, and one or two of the bayonets were wavering. We looked at the lashed, hooded man on the drop, and listened to his cries—each cry another second of life; the same thought was in all our minds: oh, kill him quickly, get it over, stop that abominable noise!

Suddenly the superintendent made up his mind. Throwing up his head he made a swift motion with his stick. "Chalo!" he shouted almost fiercely.

There was a clanking noise, and then dead silence. The prisoner had vanished, and the rope was twisting on itself. I let go of the dog, and it galloped immediately to the back of the gallows; but when it got there it stopped short, barked, and then retreated into a corner of the yard, where it stood among the weeds, looking timorously out at us. We went round the gallows to inspect the prisoner's body. He was dangling with his toes printed straight downwards, very slowly revolving, as dead as a stone.

The superintendent reached out with his stick and poked the bare brown body; it oscillated slightly. "*He's* all right," said the superintendent. He backed out from under the gallows, and blew out a deep breath. The moody look had gone out of his face quite suddenly. He glanced at his wrist-watch. "Eight minutes past eight. Well, that's all for this morning, thank God."

The warders unfixed bayonets and marched away. The dog, sobered and conscious of having misbehaved itself, slipped after them. We walked out of the gallows yard, past the condemned cells with their waiting prisoners, into the big central yard of the prison. The convicts, under the command of warders armed with lathis, were already receiving their breakfast. They squatted in long rows, each man holding a tin pannikin, while two warders with buckets marched round ladling out rice; it seemed quite a homely, jolly scene, after the hanging. An enormous relief had come upon us now that the job was done.

One felt an impulse to sing, to break into a run, to snigger. All at once everyone began chattering gaily.

The Eurasian boy walking beside me nodded towards the way we had come, with a knowing smile: "Do you know, sir, our friend (he meant the dead man) when he heard his appeal had been dismissed, he pissed on the floor of his cell. From fright. Kindly take one of my cigarettes, sir. Do you not admire my new silver case, sir? From the boxwallah, two ruppes eight annas. Classy European style."

Several people laughed—at what, nobody seemed certain.

Francis was walking by the superintendent, talking garrulously: "Well, sir, all hass passed off with the utmost satisfactoriness. It was all finished—flick! like that. It iss not always so—oah, no! I have known cases where the doctor wass obliged to go beneath the gallows and pull the prissoner's legs to ensure decease. Most disagreeable!"

"Wriggling about, eh? That's bad," said the superintendent.

"Ach, sir, it iss worse when they become refractory! One man, I recall, clung to the bars of hiss cage when we went to take him out. You will scarcely credit, sir, that it took six warders to dislodge him, three pulling at each leg. We reasoned with him. 'My dear fellow,' we said, 'think of all the pain and trouble you are causing to us!' But no, he would not listen! Ach, he was very troublesome!"

I found that I was laughing quite loudly. Everyone was laughing. Even the superintendent grinned in a tolerant way. "You'd better all come out and have a drink," he said quite genially. "I've got a bottle of whisky in the car. We could do with it."

We went through the big double gates of the prison into the road. "Pulling at his legs!" exclaimed a Burmese magistrate suddenly, and burst into a loud chuckling. We all began laughing again. At that moment Francis' anecdote seemed extraordinarily funny. We all had a drink together, native and European alike, quite amicably. The dead man was a hundred yards away.

QUESTIONS

1. "It was like men handling a fish which is still alive and may jump back into the water"—is this image effective? How so? How not?

2. Why is the superintendent impatient?

3. Why is everyone aghast at the dog?

4. What does Orwell mean by "one mind less, one world less"?

5. What does the inspector mean when he says, "*He's* all right"?
   What does his statement mean to you?

6. Why does Francis's anecdote strike them all as extraordinarily funny?
   And why does Orwell include this episode in his essay? How does
   it help make his case?

SUGGESTED ACTIVITIES

1. Describe the cruelest event you ever witnessed.

2. Describe the cruelest thing you ever did.

3. Discuss why laughter often accompanies cruelty.

4. In Orwell's essay, a mere puddle provides a major means of insight.
   Discuss a time when something inherently insignificant became
   somehow important to you.

JACQUES BARZUN
In Favor of Capital Punishment

*While Orwell demonstrates the value of detail, Barzun proves the
value and necessity of thought in considering any public policy. He
also demonstrates the role of refutation in proving one's own point
of view.*

A passing remark of mine in the Mid-Century magazine has brought
me a number of letters and a sheaf of pamphlets against capital punishment. The letters, sad and reproachful, offer me the choice of pleading
ignorance or being proved insensitive. I am asked whether I know that
there exists a worldwide movement for the abolition of capital punishment which has everywhere enlisted able men of every profession,
including the law. I am told that the death penalty is not only inhuman
but also unscientific, for rapists and murderers are really sick people
who should be cured, not killed. I am invited to use my imagination
and acknowledge the unbearable horror of every form of execution.

I am indeed aware that the movement for abolition is widespread
and articulate, especially in England. It is headed there by my old
friend and publisher, Mr. Victor Gollancz, and it numbers such well-
known writers as Arthur Koestler, C. H. Rolph, James Avery Joyce and
Sir John Barry. Abroad as at home the profession of psychiatry tends

to support the cure principle, and many liberal newspapers, such as the *Observer*, are committed to abolition. In the United States there are at least twenty-five state leagues working to the same end, plus a national league and several church councils, notably the Quaker and the Episcopal.

The assemblage of so much talent and enlightened goodwill behind a single proposal must give pause to anyone who supports the other side, and in the attempt to make clear my views, which are now close to unpopular, I start out by granting that my conclusion is arguable; that is, I am still open to conviction, *provided* some fallacies and frivolities in the abolitionist argument are first disposed of and the difficulties not ignored but overcome. I should be glad to see this happen, not only because there is pleasure in the spectacle of an airtight case, but also because I am not more sanguinary than my neighbor and I should welcome the discovery of safeguards—for society *and* the criminal—other than killing. But I say it again, these safeguards must really meet, not evade or postpone, the difficulties I am about to describe. Let me add before I begin that I shall probably not answer any more letters on this arousing subject. If this printed exposition does not do justice to my cause, it is not likely that I can do better in the hurry of private correspondence.

I readily concede at the outset that present ways of dealing out capital punishment are as revolting as Mr. Koestler says in his harrowing volume, *Hanged by the Neck*. Like many of our prisons, our modes of execution should change. But this objection to barbarity does not mean that capital punishment—or rather, judicial homicide—should not go on. The illicit jump we find here, on the threshold of the inquiry, is characteristic of the abolitionist and must be disallowed at every point. Let us bear in mind the possibility of devising a painless, sudden and dignified death, and see whether its administration is justifiable.

The four main arguments advanced against the death penalty are: 1. punishment for crime is a primitive idea rooted in revenge; 2. capital punishment does not deter; 3. judicial error being possible, taking life is an appalling risk; 4. a civilized state, to deserve its name, must uphold, not violate, the sanctity of human life.

I entirely agree with the first pair of propositions, which is why, a moment ago, I replaced the term capital punishment with "judicial homicide." The uncontrollable brute whom I want put out of the way is not to be punished for his misdeeds, nor used as an example or a warning; he is to be killed for the protection of others, like the wolf that escaped not long ago in a Connecticut suburb. No anger, vindictiveness or moral conceit need preside over the removal of such dangers. But a man's inability to control his violent impulses or to imagine the fatal consequences of his acts should be a presumptive reason for his elimination from society. This generality covers drunken driving and teen-age racing on public highways, as well as incurable obsessive violence; it might be extended (as I shall suggest later) to other acts that destroy, precisely, the moral basis of civilization.

But why kill? I am ready to believe the statistics tending to show that the prospect of his own death does not stop the murderer. For one thing he is often a blind egotist, who cannot conceive the possibility of his own death. For another, detection would have to be infallible to deter the more imaginative who, although afraid, think they can escape discovery. Lastly, as Shaw long ago pointed out, hanging the wrong man will deter as effectively as hanging the right one. So, once again, why kill? If I agree that moral progress means an increasing respect for human life, how can I oppose abolition?

I do so because on this subject of human life, which is to me the heart of the controversy, I find the abolitionist inconsistent, narrow or blind. The propaganda for abolition speaks in hushed tones of the sanctity of human life, as if the mere statement of it as an absolute should silence all opponents who have any moral sense. But most of the abolitionists belong to nations that spend half their annual income on weapons of war and that honor research to perfect means of killing. These good people vote without a qualm for the political parties that quite sensibly arm their country to the teeth. The West today does not seem to be the time or place to invoke the absolute sanctity of human life. As for the clergymen in the movement, we may be sure from the experience of two previous world wars that they will bless our arms and pray for victory when called upon, the sixth commandment notwithstanding.

"Oh, but we mean the sanctity of life *within* the nation!" Very well: is the movement then campaigning also against the principle of self-defense? Absolute sanctity means letting the cutthroat have his sweet will of you, even if you have a poker handy to bash him with, for you might kill. And again, do we hear any protest against the police firing at criminals on the street—mere bank robbers usually—and doing this, often enough, with an excited marksmanship that misses the artist and hits the bystander? The absolute sanctity of human life is, for the abolitionist, a slogan rather than a considered proposition.

Yet it deserves examination, for upon our acceptance or rejection of it depend such other highly civilized possibilities as euthanasia and seemly suicide. The inquiring mind also wants to know, why the sanctity of *human* life alone? My tastes do not run to household pets, but I find something less than admirable in the uses to which we put animals—in zoos, laboratories and space machines—without the excuse of the ancient law, "Eat or be eaten."

It should moreover be borne in mind that this argument about sanctity applies—or would apply—to about ten persons a year in Great Britain and to between fifty and seventy-five in the United States. These are the average numbers of those executed in recent years. The count by itself should not, of course, affect our judgment of the principle: one life spared or forfeited is as important, morally, as a hundred thousand. But it should inspire a comparative judgment: there are hundreds and indeed thousands whom, in our concern with the horrors of execution, we forget: on the one hand, the victims of violence; on the other, the prisoners in our jails.

The victims are easy to forget. Social science tends steadily to mark a preference for the troubled, the abnormal, the problem case. Whether it is poverty, mental disorder, delinquency or crime, the "patient material" monopolizes the interest of increasing groups of people among the most generous and learned. Psychiatry and moral liberalism go together; the application of law as we have known it is thus coming to be regarded as an historic prelude to social work, which may replace it entirely. Modern literature makes the most of this same outlook, caring only for the disturbed spirit, scorning as bourgeois those who pay their way and do *not* stab their friends. All the while the determinism of natural science reinforces the assumption that society causes its own evils. A French jurist, for example, says that in order to understand crime we must first brush aside all ideas of Responsibility. He means the criminal's and takes for granted that of society. The murderer kills because reared in a broken home or, conversely, because at an early age he witnessed his parents making love. Out of such cases, which make pathetic reading in the literature of modern criminology, is born the abolitionist's state of mind: we dare not kill those we are beginning to understand so well.

If, moreover, we turn to the accounts of the crimes committed by these unfortunates, who are the victims? Only dull ordinary people going about their business. We are sorry, of course, but they do not interest science on its march. Balancing, for example, the sixty to seventy criminals executed annually in the United States, there were the seventy to eighty housewives whom George Cvek robbed, raped and usually killed during the months of a career devoted to proving his virility. "It is too bad." Cvek alone seems instructive, even though one of the law officers who helped track him down quietly remarks: "As to the extent that his villainies disturbed family relationships, or how many women are still haunted by the specter of an experience they have never disclosed to another living soul, these questions can only lend themselves to sterile conjecture."

The remote results are beyond our ken, but it is not idle to speculate about those whose death by violence fills the daily two inches at the back of respectable newspapers—the old man sunning himself on a park bench and beaten to death by four hoodlums, the small children abused and strangled, the middle-aged ladies on a hike assaulted and killed, the family terrorized by a released or escaped lunatic, the half-dozen working people massacred by the sudden maniac, the boatload of persons dispatched by the skipper, the mindless assaults upon schoolteachers and shopkeepers by the increasing horde of dedicated killers in our great cities. Where does the sanctity of life begin?

It is all very well to say that many of these killers are themselves "children," that is, minors. Doubtless a nine-year-old mind is housed in that 150 pounds of unguided muscle. Grant, for argument's sake, that the misdeed is "the fault of society," trot out the broken home and the slum environment. The question then is, What shall we do, not in the Utopian city of tomorrow, but here and now? The "scientific" means of cure are more than uncertain. The apparatus of detention only increases the killer's antisocial animus. Reformatories and mental hospitals are full and have an understandable bias toward discharging their inmates. Some of these are indeed "cured"—so long as they stay under a rule. The stress of the social free-for-all throws them back on their violent modes of self-expression. At that point I agree that society has failed—twice: it has twice failed the victims, whatever may be its guilt toward the killer.

As in all great questions, the moralist must choose, and choosing has a price. I happen to think that if a person of adult body has not been endowed with adequate controls against irrationally taking the life of another, that person must be judicially, painlessly, regretfully killed before that mindless body's horrible automation repeats.

I say "irrationally" taking life, because it is often possible to feel great sympathy with a murderer. Certain *crimes passionnels* can be forgiven without being condoned. Blackmailers invite direct retribution. Long provocation can be an excuse, as in that engaging case of some years ago, in which a respectable carpenter of seventy found he could no longer stand the incessant nagging of his wife. While she excoriated him from her throne in the kitchen—a daily exercise for fifty years—the husband went to his bench and came back with a hammer in each hand to settle the score. The testimony to his character, coupled with the sincerity implied by the two hammers, was enough to have him sent into quiet and brief seclusion.

But what are we to say of the type of motive disclosed in a journal published by the inmates of one of our Federal penitentiaries? The author is a bank robber who confesses that money is not his object:

> My mania for power, socially, sexually, and otherwise can feel no degree of satisfaction until I feel sure I have struck the ultimate of submission and terror in the minds and bodies of my victims. . . . It's very difficult to explain all the queer fascinating sensations pounding and surging through me while I'm holding a gun on a victim, watching his body tremble and sweat. . . . This is the moment when all the rationalized hypocrisies of civilization are suddenly swept away and two men stand there facing each other morally and ethically naked, and right and wrong are the absolute commands of the man behind the gun.

This confused echo of modern literature and modern science defines the choice before us. Anything deserving the name of cure for such a man presupposes not only a laborious individual psychoanalysis, with the means to conduct and to sustain it, socially and economically, but also a re-education of the mind, so as to throw into correct perspective the garbled ideas of Freud and Nietzsche, Gide and Dostoevski, which this power-seeker and his fellows have derived from the culture and temper of our times. Ideas are tenacious and give continuity to emotion. Failing a second birth of heart and mind, we must ask: How soon will this sufferer sacrifice a bank clerk in the interests of making civilization less hypocritical? And we must certainly question the wisdom of affording him more than one chance. The abolitionists' advocacy of an unconditional "let live" is in truth part of the same cultural tendency that animates the killer. The Western peoples' revulsion from power in domestic and foreign policy has made of the state a sort of counterpart of the bank robber: both having power and neither knowing how to use it. Both waste lives because hypnotized by irrelevant ideas and crippled by contradictory emotions. If psychiatry were sure of its ground in diagnosing the individual case, a philosopher might consider whether such dangerous obsessions should not be guarded against by judicial homicide *before* the shooting starts.

I raise the question not indeed to recommend the prophylactic execution of potential murderers, but to introduce the last two perplexities that the abolitionists dwarf or obscure by their concentration on changing an isolated penalty. One of these is the scale by which to judge the offenses society wants to repress. I can for example imagine a truly democratic state in which it would be deemed a form of treason punishable by death to create a disturbance in any court or deliberative assembly. The aim would be to recognize the sanctity of orderly discourse in arriving at justice, assessing criticism and defining policy. Under such a law, a natural selection would operate to remove permanently from the scene persons who, let us say, neglect argument in favor of banging on the desk with their shoe. Similarly, a bullying minority in a diet, parliament or skupshtina would be prosecuted for treason to the most sacred institutions when fists or flying inkwells replace rhetoric. That the mere suggestion of such a law sounds ludicrous shows how remote we are from civilized institutions, and hence how gradual should be our departure from the severity of judicial homicide.

I say gradual and I do not mean standing still. For there is one form of barbarity in our law that I want to see mitigated before any other. I mean imprisonment. The enemies of capital punishment—and liberals generally—seem to be satisfied with any legal outcome so long as they themselves avoid the vicarious guilt of shedding blood. They speak of the sanctity of life, but have no concern with its quality. They give no impression of ever having read what it is certain they have read, from Wilde's *De Profundis* to the latest account of prison life by a convicted homosexual. Despite the infamy of concentration camps, despite Mr. Charles Burney's remarkable work, *Solitary Confinement*, despite riots in prisons, despite the round of escape, recapture and return in chains, the abolitionists' imagination tells them nothing about the reality of being caged. They read without a qualm, indeed they read with rejoicing, the hideous irony of "Killer Gets Life"; they sigh with relief instead of horror. They do not see and suffer the cell, the drill, the clothes, the stench, the food; they do not feel the sexual racking of young and old bodies, the hateful promiscuity, the insane monotony, the mass degradation, the impotent hatred. They do not remember from Silvio Pellico that only a strong political faith, with a hope of final victory, can steel a man to endure long detention. They forget that Joan of Arc, when offered "life," preferred burning at the stake. Quite of another mind, the abolitionists point with pride to the "model prisoners" that murderers often turn out to be. As if a model prisoner were not, first, a contradiction in terms, and second, an exemplar of what a free society should not want.

I said a moment ago that the happy advocates of the life sentence appear not to have understood what we know they have read. No more do they appear to read what they themselves write. In the preface to his useful volume of cases, *Hanged in Error*, Mr. Leslie Hale, M.P., refers to the tardy recognition of a minor miscarriage of justice— one year in jail: "The prisoner emerged to find that his wife had died and that his children and his aged parents had been removed to the workhouse. By the time a small payment had been assessed as 'compensation' the victim was incurably insane." So far we are as indignant with the law as Mr. Hale. But what comes next? He cites the famous Evans case, in which it is very probable that the wrong man was hanged, and he exclaims: "While such mistakes are possible, should society impose an irrevocable sentence?" Does Mr. Hale really ask us to believe that the sentence passed on the first man, whose wife died and who went insane, was in any sense *revocable*? Would not any man rather be Evans dead than that other wretch "emerging" with his small compensation and his reasons for living gone?

Nothing is revocable here below, imprisonment least of all. The agony of a trial itself is punishment, and acquittal wipes out nothing. Read the heart-rending diary of William Wallace, accused quite implausibly of having murdered his wife and "saved" by the Court of Criminal Appeals—but saved for what? Brutish ostracism by everyone and a few years of solitary despair. The cases of Adolf Beck, of Oscar Slater, of the unhappy Brooklyn bank teller who vaguely resembled a forger and spent eight years in Sing Sing only to "emerge" a broken, friendless, useless, "compensated" man—all these, if the dignity of the individual has any meaning, had better have been dead before the prison door ever opened for them. This is what counsel always says to the jury in the course of a murder trial and counsel is right: far better hang this man than "give him life." For my part, I would choose death without hesitation. If that option is abolished, a demand will one day be heard to claim it as a privilege in the name of human dignity. I shall believe in the abolitionist's present views only after he has emerged from twelve months in a convict cell.

The detached observer may want to interrupt here and say that the argument has now passed from reasoning to emotional preference. Whereas the objector to capital punishment *feels* that death is the greatest of evils, I *feel* that imprisonment is worse than death. A moment's thought will show that feeling is the appropriate arbiter. All reasoning about what is right, civilized and moral rests upon sentiment, like mathematics. Only, in trying to persuade others, it is important to single out the fundamental feeling, the prime intuition, and from it to reason justly. In my view, to profess respect for human life and be willing to see it spent in a penitentiary is to entertain liberal feelings frivolously. To oppose the death penalty because, unlike a prison term, it is irrevocable is to argue fallaciously.

In the propaganda for abolishing the death sentence the recital of numerous miscarriages of justice commits the same error and implies the same callousness: what is at fault in our present system is not the sentence but the fallible procedure. Capital cases being one in a thousand or more, who can be cheerful at the thought of all the "revocable" errors? What the miscarriages point to is the need for reforming the jury system, the rules of evidence, the customs of prosecution, the machinery of appeal. The failure to see that this is the great task reflects the sentimentality I spoke of earlier, that which responds chiefly to the excitement of the unusual. A writer on Death and the Supreme Court is at pains to point out that when that tribunal reviews a capital case, the judges are particularly anxious and careful. What a left-handed compliment to the highest judicial conscience of the country! Fortunately, some of the champions of the misjudged see the issue more clearly. Many of those who are thought wrongly convicted now languish in jail because the jury was uncertain or because a doubting governor commuted the death sentence. Thus Dr. Samuel H. Sheppard, Jr., convicted of his wife's murder in the second degree is serving a sentence that is supposed to run for the term of his natural life. The story of his numerous trials, as told by Mr. Paul Holmes, suggests that police incompetence, newspaper demagogy, public envy of affluence and the mischances of legal procedure fashioned the result. But Dr. Sheppard's vindicator is under no illusion as to the conditions that this "lucky" evader of the electric chair will face if he is granted parole after ten years: "It will carry with it no right to resume his life as a physician. His privilege to practice medicine was blotted out with his conviction. He must all his life bear the stigma of a parolee, subject to unceremonious return to confinement for life for the slightest misstep. More than this, he must live out his life as a convicted murderer."

What does the moral conscience of today think it is doing? If such a man is a dangerous repeater of violent acts, what right has the state to let him loose after ten years? What is, in fact, the meaning of a "life sentence" that peters out long before life? Paroling looks suspiciously like an expression of social remorse for the pain of incarceration, coupled with a wish to avoid "unfavorable publicity" by freeing a suspect. The man is let out when the fuss has died down; which would mean that he was not under lock and key for our protection at all. He *was* being punished, just a little—for so prison seems in the abolitionists' distorted view, and in the jury's and the prosecutor's, whose "second-degree" murder suggests killing someone "just a little."*

If, on the other hand, execution and life imprisonment are judged too severe and the accused is expected to be harmless hereafter—punishment being ruled out as illiberal—what has society gained by wrecking his life and damaging that of his family?

What we accept, and what the abolitionist will clamp upon us all the more firmly if he succeeds, is an incoherence which is not remedied by the belief that second-degree murder merits a kind of second-degree death; that a doubt as to the identity of a killer is resolved by commuting real death into intolerable life; and that our ignorance whether a maniac will strike again can be hedged against by measuring "good behavior" within the gates and then releasing the subject upon the public in the true spirit of experimentation.

These are some of the thoughts I find I cannot escape when I read and reflect upon this grave subject. If, as I think, they are relevant to any discussion of change and reform, resting as they do on the direct and concrete perception of what happens, then the simple meliorists who expect to breathe a purer air by abolishing the death penalty are deceiving themselves and us. The issue is for the public to judge; but I for one shall not sleep easier for knowing that in England and America and the West generally a hundred more human beings are kept alive in degrading conditions to face a hopeless future; while others—possibly less conscious, certainly less controlled—benefit from a premature freedom dangerous alike to themselves and society. In short, I derive no comfort from the illusion that in giving up on manifest protection of the law-abiding, we who might well be in any of these three roles—victim, prisoner, licensed killer—have struck a blow for the sanctity of human life.

---

*The British Homicide Act of 1957, Section 2, implies the same reasoning in its definition of "diminished responsibility" for certain forms of mental abnormality. The whole question of irrationality and crime is in utter confusion, on both sides of the Atlantic.

QUESTIONS

1. Is Barzun's substitution of the phrase "judicial homicide" for "capital punishment" justified? Or is it merely a euphemism?

2. What is the difference between a slogan and a considered proposition? Provide examples.

3. According to Barzun, how do psychiatry and moral liberalism go hand in hand?

4. How do ideas "give continuity to emotion"?

5. How convincing is Barzun's argument that it is better to be executed than imprisoned by mistake?

SUGGESTED ACTIVITIES

1. Discuss Barzun's basic paradox that the sanctity of human life can require taking human life.

2. Discuss the differences in Barzun's and Orwell's views on capital punishment. Identify the weaknesses and strengths in each position.

3. Write an essay making a case for your position on this complex issue.

MARTIN LUTHER KING, Jr.

Letter from Birmingham Jail

The preeminent leader of the civil rights movement in the fifties and sixties, King was a Baptist minister, the president of the Southern Christian Leadership Conference, and winner of the Nobel Peace Prize in 1964. He was, not coincidentally, among the greatest American orators of the twentieth century. In the midst of his varied activities he authored several books, among them Stride Toward Freedom *(1964). In this famous letter, King, combines powerful detail with equally powerful logic to justify civil disobedience.*

MY DEAR FELLOW CLERGYMEN:

While confined here in the Birmingham city jail, I came across your recent statement calling my present activities "unwise and untimely." Seldom do I pause to answer criticism of my work and ideas. If I sought to answer all the criticisms that cross my desk, my secretaries would have little time for anything other than such correspondence in the course of the day, and I would have no time for constructive work. But since I feel that you are men of genuine good will and that your criticisms are sincerely set forth, I want to try to answer your statement in what I hope will be patient and reasonable terms.

I think I should indicate why I am here in Birmingham, since you have been influenced by the view which argues against "outsiders coming in." I have the honor of serving as president of the Southern Christian Leadership Conference, an organization operating in every southern state, with headquarters in Atlanta, Georgia. We have some eighty-five affiliated organizations across the South, and one of them is the Alabama Christian Movement for Human Rights. Frequently we share staff, educational, and financial resources with our affiliates. Several months ago the affiliate here in Birmingham asked us to be on call to engage in a nonviolent direct-action program if such were deemed necessary. We readily consented, and when the hour came, we lived up to our promise. So I, along with several members of my staff, am here because I was invited here. I am here because I have organizational ties here.

But more basically, I am in Birmingham because injustice is here. Just as the prophets of the eighth century B.C. left their villages and carried their "thus saith the Lord" far beyond the boundaries of their home towns, and just as the Apostle Paul left his village of Tarsus and carried the gospel of Jesus Christ to the far corners of the Greco-Roman world, so am I compelled to carry the gospel of freedom beyond my own home town. Like Paul, I must constantly respond to the Macedonian call for aid.

Moreover, I am cognizant of the interrelatedness of all communities and states. I cannot sit idly by in Atlanta and not be concerned about what happens in Birmingham. Injustice anywhere is a threat to justice everywhere. We are caught in an inescapable network of mutuality, tied in a single garment of destiny. Whatever affects one directly, affects all indirectly. Never again can we afford to live with the narrow, provincial "outside agitator" idea. Anyone who lives inside the United States can never be considered an outsider anywhere within its bounds.

You deplore the demonstrations taking place in Birmingham. But your statement, I am sorry to say, fails to express a similar concern for the conditions that brought about the demonstrations. I am sure that none of you would want to rest content with the superficial kind of social analysis that deals merely with effects and does not grapple with underlying causes. It is unfortunate that demonstrations are taking place in Birmingham, but it is even more unfortunate that the city's white power structure left the Negro community with no alternative.

In any nonviolent campaign there are four basic steps: collection of the facts to determine whether injustices exist; negotiation; self-purification; and direct action. We have gone through all these steps in Birmingham. There can be no gainsaying the fact that racial injustice engulfs this community. Birmingham is probably the most thoroughly segregated city in the United States. Its ugly record of brutality is widely known. Negroes have experienced grossly unjust treatment in the courts. There have been more unsolved bombings of Negro homes and churches in Birmingham than in any other city in the nation. These are the hard, brutal facts of the case. On the basis of these conditions, Negro leaders sought to negotiate with the city fathers. But the latter consistently refused to engage in good-faith negotiation.

Then, last September, came the opportunity to talk with leaders of Birmingham's economic community. In the course of the negotiations, certain promises were made by the merchants—for example, to remove the stores' humiliating racial signs. On the basis of these promises, the Reverend Fred Shuttlesworth and the leaders of the Alabama Christian Movement for Human Rights agreed to a moratorium on all demonstrations. As the weeks and months went by, we realized that we were the victims of a broken promise. A few signs, briefly removed, returned; the others remained.

As in so many past experiences, our hopes had been blasted, and the shadow of deep disappointment settled upon us. We had no alternative except to prepare for direct action, whereby we would present our very bodies as a means of laying our case before the conscience of the local and the national community. Mindful of the difficulties involved, we decided to undertake a process of self-purification. We began a series of workshops on nonviolence, and we repeatedly asked ourselves: "Are you able to accept blows without retaliating?" "Are you able to endure the ordeal of jail?" We decided to schedule our direct-action program for the Easter season, realizing that except for Christmas, this is the main shopping period of the year. Knowing that a strong economic-withdrawal program would be the by product of direct action, we felt that this would be the best time to bring pressure to bear on the merchants for the needed change.

Then it occurred to us that Birmingham's mayoral election was coming up in March, and we speedily decided to postpone action until after election day. When we discovered that the Commissioner of Public Safety, Eugene "Bull" Connor, had piled up enough votes to be in the run-off, we decided again to postpone action until the day after the run-off so that the demonstrations could not be used to cloud the issues. Like many others, we waited to see Mr. Connor defeated, and to this end we endured postponement after postponement. Having aided in this community need, we felt that our direct-action program could be delayed no longer.

You may well ask, "Why direct action? Why sit-ins, marches, and so forth? Isn't negotiation a better path?" You are quite right in calling for negotiation. Indeed, this is the very purpose of direct action. Non-violent direct action seeks to create such a crisis and foster such a tension that a community which has constantly refused to negotiate is forced to confront the issue. It seeks so to dramatize the issue that it can no longer be ignored. My citing the creation of tension as part of the work of the nonviolent-resister may sound rather shocking. But I must confess that I am not afraid of the word "tension." I have earnestly opposed violent tension, but there is a type of constructive, nonviolent tension which is necessary for growth. Just as Socrates felt that it was necessary to create a tension in the mind so that individuals could rise from the bondage of myths and half-truths to the unfettered realm of creative analysis and objective appraisal, so must we see the need for nonviolent gadflies to create the kind of tension in society that will help men rise from the dark depths of prejudice and racism to the majestic heights of understanding and brotherhood.

The purpose of our direct-action program is to create a situation so crisis-packed that it will inevitably open the door to negotiation. I therefore concur with you in your call for negotiation. Too long has our beloved Southland been bogged down in a tragic effort to live in monologue rather than dialogue.

One of the basic points in your statement is that the action that I and my associates have taken in Birmingham is untimely. Some have asked: "Why didn't you give the new city administration time to act?" The only answer that I can give to this query is that the new Birmingham administration must be prodded about as much as the outgoing one, before it will act. We are sadly mistaken if we feel that the election of Albert Boutwell as mayor will bring the millennium to Birmingham. While Mr. Boutwell is a much more gentle person than Mr. Connor, they are both segregationists, dedicated to maintenance of the status quo. I have hoped that Mr. Boutwell will be reasonable enough to see the futility of massive resistance to desegregation. But he will not see this without pressure from devotees of civil rights. My friends, I must say to you that we have not made a single gain in civil rights without determined legal and nonviolent pressure. Lamentably, it is an historical fact that privileged groups seldom give up their privileges voluntarily. Individuals may see the moral light and voluntarily give up their unjust posture; but, as Reinhold Niebuhr has reminded us, groups tend to be more immoral than individuals.

We know through painful experience that freedom is never voluntarily given by the oppressor; it must be demanded by the oppressed. Frankly, I have yet to engage in a direct-action campaign that was "well timed" in the view of those who have not suffered unduly from the disease of segregation. For years now I have heard the word "Wait!" It rings in the ear of every Negro with piercing familarity. This "Wait" has almost always meant "Never." We must come to see, with one of our distinguished jurists, that "justice too long delayed is justice denied."

We have waited for more than 340 years for our constitutional and God-given rights. The nations of Asia and Africa are moving with jetlike speed toward gaining political independence, but we still creep at horse-and-buggy pace toward gaining a cup of coffee at a lunch counter. Perhaps it is easy for those who have never felt the stinging darts of segregation to say, "Wait." But when you have seen vicious mobs lynch your mothers and fathers at will and drown your sisters and brothers at whim; when you have seen hate-filled policemen curse, kick, and even kill your black brothers and sisters; when you see the vast majority of your twenty million Negro brothers smothering in an airtight cage of poverty in the midst of an affluent society; when you suddenly find your tongue twisted and your speech stammering as you seek to explain to your six-year-old daughter why she can't go to the public amusement park that has just been advertised on television, and see tears welling up in her eyes when she is told that Funtown is closed to colored children, and see ominous clouds of inferiority beginning to form in her little mental sky, and see her beginning to distort her personality by developing an unconscious bitterness toward white people; when you have to concoct an answer for a five-year-old son who is asking, "Daddy, why do white people treat colored people so mean?"; when you take a cross-country drive and find it necessary to sleep night after night in the uncomfortable corners of your automobile because no motel will accept you; when you are humiliated day in and day out by nagging signs reading "white" and "colored"; when your first name becomes "nigger," your middle name becomes "boy" (however old you are) and your last name becomes "John," and your wife and mother are never given the respected title "Mrs."; when you are harried by day and haunted by night by the fact that you are a Negro, living constantly at tiptoe stance, never quite knowing what to expect next, and are plagued with inner fears and outer resentments; when you are forever fighting a degenerating sense of "nobodiness"—then you will understand why we find it difficult to wait. There comes a time when the cup of endurance runs over, and men are no longer willing to be plunged into the abyss of despair. I hope, sirs, you can understand our legitimate and unavoidable impatience.

You express a great deal of anxiety over our willingness to break laws. This is certainly a legitimate concern. Since we so diligently urge people to obey the Supreme Court's decision of 1954 outlawing segregation in the public schools, at first glance it may seem rather paradoxical for us consciously to break laws. One may well ask: "How can you advocate breaking some laws and obeying others?" The answer lies in the fact that there are two types of laws: just and unjust. I would be the first to advocate obeying just laws. One has not only a legal but a moral responsibility to obey just laws. Conversely, one has a moral responsibility to disobey unjust laws. I would agree with St. Augustine that "an unjust law is no law at all."

Now, what is the difference between the two? How does one determine whether a law is just or unjust? A just law is a man-made code that squares with the moral law or the law of God. An unjust law is a code that is out of harmony with the moral law. To put it in the terms of St. Thomas Aquinas: An unjust law is a human law that is not rooted in eternal law and natural law. Any law that uplifts human personality is just. Any law that degrades human personality is unjust. All segregation statutes are unjust because segregation distorts the soul and damages the personality. It gives the segregator a false sense of superiority and the segregated a false sense of inferiority. Segregation, to use the terminology of the Jewish philosopher Martin Buber, substitutes an "I-it" relationship for an "I-thou" relationship and ends up relegating persons to the status of things. Hence segregation is not only politically, economically, and sociologically unsound, it is morally wrong and sinful. Paul Tillich has said that sin is separation. Is not segregation an existential expression of man's tragic separation, his awful estrangement, his terrible sinfulness? Thus it is that I can urge men to obey the 1954 decision of the Supreme Court, for it is morally right; and I can urge them to disobey segregation ordinances, for they are morally wrong.

Let us consider a more concrete example of just and unjust laws. An unjust law is a code that a numerical or power majority group compels a minority group to obey but does not make binding on itself. This is *difference* made legal. By the same token, a just law is a code that a majority compels a minority to follow and that it is willing to follow itself. This is *sameness* made legal.

Let me give another explanation. A law is unjust if it is inflicted on a minority that, as a result of being denied the right to vote, had no part in enacting or devising the law. Who can say that the legislature of Alabama which set up that state's segregation laws was democratically elected? Throughout Alabama all sorts of devious methods are used to prevent Negroes from becoming registered voters, and there are some counties in which, even though Negroes constitute a majority of the population, not a single Negro is registered. Can any law enacted under such circumstances be considered democratically structured?

Sometimes a law is just on its face and unjust in its application. For instance, I have been arrested on a charge of parading without a permit. Now, there is nothing wrong in having an ordinance which requires a permit for a parade. But such an ordinance becomes unjust when it is used to maintain segregation and to deny citizens the First-Amendment privilege of peaceful assembly and protest.

I hope you are able to see the distinction I am trying to point out. In no sense do I advocate evading or defying the law, as would the rabid segregationist. That would lead to anarchy. One who breaks an unjust law must do so openly, lovingly, and with a willingness to accept the penalty. I submit that an individual who breaks a law that conscience tells him is unjust, and who willingly accepts the penalty of imprisonment in order to arouse the conscience of the community over its injustice, is in reality expressing the highest respect for law.

Of course, there is nothing new about this kind of civil disobedience. It was evidenced sublimely in the refusal of Shadrach, Meshach, and Abednego to obey the laws of Nebuchadnezzar, on the ground that a higher moral law was at stake. It was practiced superbly by the early Christians, who were willing to face hungry lions and the excruciating pain of chopping blocks rather than submit to certain unjust laws of the Roman Empire. To a degree, academic freedom is a reality today because Socrates practiced civil disobedience. In our own nation, the Boston Tea Party represented a massive act of civil disobedience.

We should never forget that everything Adolf Hitler did in Germany was "legal" and everything the Hungarian freedom fighters did in Hungary was "illegal." It was "illegal" to aid and comfort a Jew in Hitler's Germany. Even so, I am sure that, had I lived in Germany at the time, I would have aided and comforted my Jewish brothers. If today I lived in a Communist country where certain principles dear to the Christian faith are suppressed, I would openly advocate disobeying that country's anti-religious laws.

I must make two honest confessions to you, my Christian and Jewish brothers. First, I must confess that over the past few years I have been gravely disappointed with the white moderate. I have almost reached the regrettable conclusion that the Negro's great stumbling block in his stride toward freedom is not the White Citizen's Counciler or the Ku Klux Klanner, but the white moderate, who is more devoted to "order" than to justice; who prefers a negative peace which is the absence of tension to a positive peace which is the presence of justice; who constantly says, "I agree with you in the goal you seek, but I cannot agree with your methods of direct action"; who paternalistically believes he can set the timetable for another man's freedom; who lives by a mythical concept of time and who constantly advises the Negro to wait for a "more convenient season." Shallow understanding from people of good will is more frustrating than absolute misunderstanding from people of ill will. Lukewarm acceptance is much more bewildering than outright rejection.

I had hoped that the white moderate would understand that law and order exist for the purpose of establishing justice and that when they fail in this purpose they become the dangerously structured dams that block the flow of social progress. I had hoped that the white moderate would understand that the present tension in the South is a necessary phase of the transition from an obnoxious negative peace, in which the Negro passively accepted his unjust plight, to a substantive and positive peace, in which all men will respect the dignity and worth of human personality. Actually, we who engage in nonviolent direct action are not the creators of tension. We merely bring to the surface the hidden tension that is already alive. We bring it out in the open, where it can be seen and dealt with. Like a boil that can never be cured so long as it is covered up but must be opened with all its ugliness to the natural medicines of air and light, injustice must be exposed, with all the tension its exposure creates, to the light of human conscience and the air of national opinion, before it can be cured.

In your statement you assert that our actions, even though peaceful, must be condemned because they precipitate violence. But is this a logical assertion? Isn't this like condemning a robbed man because his possession of money precipitated the evil act of robbery? Isn't this like condemning Socrates because his unswerving commitment to truth and his philosophical inquiries precipitated the act by the misguided populace in which they made him drink hemlock? Isn't this like condemning Jesus because his unique God-consciousness and never-ceasing devotion to God's will precipitated the evil act of crucifixion? We must come to see that, as the federal courts have consistently affirmed, it is wrong to urge an individual to cease his efforts to gain his basic constitutional rights because the quest may precipitate violence. Society must protect the robbed and punish the robber.

I had also hoped that the white moderate would reject the myth concerning time in relation to the struggle for freedom. I have just received a letter from a white brother in Texas. He writes: "All Christians know that the colored people will receive equal rights eventually, but it is possible that you are in too great a religious hurry. It has taken Christianity almost two thousand years to accomplish what it has. The teachings of Christ take time to come to earth." Such an attitude stems from a tragic misconception of time, from the strangely irrational notion that there is something in the very flow of time that will inevitably cure all ills. Actually, time itself is neutral; it can be used either destructively or constructively. More and more I feel that the people of ill will have used time much more effectively than have the people of good will. We will have to repent in this generation not merely for the hateful words and actions of the bad people, but for the appalling silence of the good people. Human progress never rolls in on wheels of inevitability; it comes through the tireless efforts of men willing to be co-workers with God, and without this hard work, time itself becomes an ally of the forces of social stagnation. We must use time creatively, in the knowledge that the time is always ripe to do right. Now is the time to make real the promise of democracy and transform our pending national elegy into a creative psalm of brotherhood. Now is the time to lift our national policy from the quicksand of racial injustice to the solid rock of human dignity.

You speak of our activity in Birmingham as extreme. At first I was rather disappointed that fellow clergymen would see my nonviolent efforts as those of an extremist. I began thinking about the fact that I stand in the middle of two opposing forces in the Negro community. One is a force of complacency, made up in part of Negroes who, as a result of long years of oppression, are so drained of self-respect and a sense of "somebodiness" that they have adjusted to segregation; and in part of a few middle-class Negroes who, because of a degree of academic and economic security and because in some ways they profit by segregation, have become insensitive to the problems of the masses. The other force is one of bitterness and hatred, and it comes perilously

close to advocating violence. It is expressed in the various black nationalist groups that are springing up across the nation, the largest and
best-known being Elijah Muhammad's Muslim movement. Nourished
by the Negro's frustration over the continued existence of racial discrimination, this movement is made up of people who have lost faith
in America, who have absolutely repudiated Christianity, and who
have concluded that the white man is an incorrigible "devil."

I have tried to stand between these two forces, saying that we need
emulate neither the "do-nothingism" of the complacent nor the hatred
and despair of the black nationalist. For there is the more excellent
way of love and nonviolent protest. I am grateful to God that, through
the influence of the Negro church, the way of nonviolence became an
integral part of our struggle.

If this philosophy had not emerged, by now many streets of the
South would, I am convinced, be flowing with blood. And I am further
convinced that if our white brothers dismiss as "rabble-rousers" and
"outside agitators" those of us who employ nonviolent direct action,
and if they refuse to support our nonviolent efforts, millions of Negroes
will, out of frustration and despair, seek solace and security in black-
nationalist ideologies—a development that would inevitably lead to a
frightening racial nightmare.

Oppressed people cannot remain oppressed forever. The yearning
for freedom eventually manifests itself, and that is what has happened
to the American Negro. Something within has reminded him of his
birthright of freedom, and something without has reminded him that
it can be gained. Consciously or unconsciously, he has been caught up
by the *Zeitgeist*, and with his black brothers of Africa and his brown
and yellow brothers of Asia, South America, and the Caribbean, the
United States Negro is moving with a sense of great urgency toward
the promised land of racial justice. If one recognizes this vital urge
that has engulfed the Negro community, one should readily understand why public demonstrations are taking place. The Negro has
many pent-up resentments and latent frustrations, and he must release
them. So let him march; let him make prayer pilgrimages to the city
hall; let him go on freedom rides—and try to understand why he must
do so. If his repressed emotions are not released in nonviolent ways,
they will seek expression through violence; this is not a threat but a
fact of history. So I have not said to my people, "Get rid of your
discontent." Rather, I have tried to say that this normal and healthy
discontent can be channeled into the creative outlet of nonviolent direct
action. And now this approach is being termed extremist.

But though I was initially disappointed at being categorized as an extremist, as I continued to think about the matter I gradually gained a measure of satisfaction from the label. Was not Jesus an extremist for love: "Love your enemies, bless them that curse you, do good to them that hate you, and pray for them which despitefully use you, and persecute you." Was not Amos an extremist for justice: "Let justice roll down like waters and righteousness like an everflowing stream." Was not Paul an extremist for the Christian gospel: "I bear in my body the marks of the Lord Jesus." Was not Martin Luther an extremist: "Here I stand; I cannot do otherwise, so help me God." And John Bunyan: "I will stay in jail to the end of my days before I make a butchery of my conscience." And Abraham Lincoln: "This nation cannot survive half slave and half free." And Thomas Jefferson: "We hold these truths to be self-evident, that all men are created equal. . . ." So the question is not whether we will be extremists, but what kind of extremists we will be. Will we be extremists for hate or for love? Will we be extremists for the preservation of injustice or for the extension of justice? In that dramatic scene on Calvary's hill three men were crucified. We must never forget that all three were crucified for the same crime—the crime of extremism. Two were extremists for immorality, and thus fell below their environment. The other, Jesus Christ, was an extremist for love, truth, and goodness, and thereby rose above his environment. Perhaps the South, the nation, and the world are in dire need of creative extremists.

I had hoped that the white moderate would see this need. Perhaps I was too optimistic; perhaps I expected too much. I suppose I should have realized that few members of the oppressor race can understand the deep groans and passionate yearnings of the oppressed race, and still fewer have the vision to see that injustice must be rooted out by strong, persistent, and determined action. I am thankful, however, that some of our white brothers in the South have grasped the meaning of this social revolution and committed themselves to it. They are still all too few in quantity, but they are big in quality. Some—such as Ralph McGill, Lillian Smith, Harry Golden, James McBride Dabbs, Anne Braden, and Sarah Patton Boyle—have written about our struggle in eloquent and prophetic terms. Others have marched with us down nameless streets of the South. They have languished in filthy, roach-infested jails, suffering the abuse and brutality of policemen who view them as "dirty nigger-lovers." Unlike so many of their moderate brothers and sisters, they have recognized the urgency of the moment and sensed the need for powerful "action" antidotes to combat the disease of segregation.

Let me take note of my other major disappointment. I have been so greatly disappointed with the white church and its leadership. Of course, there are some notable exceptions. I am not unmindful of the fact that each of you has taken some significant stands on this issue. I commend you, Reverend Stallings, for your Christian stand on this past Sunday, in welcoming Negroes to your worship service on a non-segregated basis. I commend the Catholic leaders of this state for integrating Spring Hill College several years ago.

But despite these notable exceptions, I must honestly reiterate that I have been disappointed with the church. I do not say this as one of those negative critics who can always find something wrong with the church. I say this as a minister of the gospel, who loves the church; who was nurtured in its bosom; who has been sustained by its spiritual blessings and who will remain true to it as long as the cord of life shall lengthen.

When I was suddenly catapulted into the leadership of the bus protest in Montgomery, Alabama, a few years ago, I felt we would be supported by the white church. I felt that the white ministers, priests, and rabbis of the South would be among our strongest allies. Instead, some have been outright opponents, refusing to understand the freedom movement and misrepresenting its leaders; all too many others have been more cautious than courageous and have remained silent behind the anesthetizing security of stained glass windows.

In spite of my shattered dreams, I came to Birmingham with the hope that the white religious leadership of this community would see the justice of our cause and, with deep moral concern, would serve as the channel through which our just grievances could reach the power structure. I had hoped that each of you would understand. But again I have been disappointed.

I have heard numerous southern religious leaders admonish their worshipers to comply with a desegregation decision because it is the law, but I have longed to hear white ministers declare: "Folow this decree because integration is morally right and because the Negro is your brother." In the midst of blatant injustices inflicted upon the Negro, I have watched white churchmen stand on the sideline and mouth pious irrelevancies and sanctimonious trivialities. In the midst of a mighty struggle to rid our nation of racial and economic injustice I have heard many ministers say: "Those are social issues, with which the gospel has no real concern." And I have watched many churches commit themselves to a completely otherworldly religion which makes a strange, un-Biblical distinction between body and soul, between the sacred and the secular.

I have traveled the length and breadth of Alabama, Mississippi, and all the other southern states. On sweltering summer days and crisp autumn mornings I have looked at the South's beautiful churches with their lofty spires pointing heavenward. I have beheld the impressive outlines of her massive religious-education buildings. Over and over I have found myself asking: "What kind of people worship here? Who is their God? Where were their voices when the lips of Governor Barnett dripped with words of interposition and nullification? Where were they when Governor Wallace gave a clarion call for defiance and hatred? Where were their voices of support when bruised and weary Negro men and women decided to rise from the dark dungeons of complacency to the bright hills of creative protest?"

Yes, these questions are still in my mind. In deep disappointment I have wept over the laxity of the church. But be assured that my tears have been tears of love. There can be no deep disappointment where there is not deep love. Yes, I love the church. How could I do otherwise? I am in the rather unique position of being the son, the grandson, and the great-grandson of preachers. Yes, I see the church as the body of Christ. But, oh! How we have blemished and scarred that body through social neglect and through fear of being nonconformists.

There was a time when the church was very powerful—in the time when the early Christians rejoiced at being deemed worthy to suffer for what they believed. In those days the church was not merely a thermometer that recorded the ideas and principles of popular opinion; it was a thermostat that transformed the mores of society. Whenever the early Christians entered a town, the people in power became disturbed and immediately sought to convict the Christians for being "disturbers of the peace" and "outside agitators." But the Christians pressed on, in the conviction that they were "a colony of heaven," called to obey God rather than man. Small in number, they were big in commitment. They were too God-intoxicated to be "astronomically intimidated." By their effort and example they brought an end to such ancient evils as infanticide and gladiatorial contests.

Things are different now. So often the contemporary church is a weak, ineffectual voice with an uncertain sound. So often it is an archdefender of the status quo. Far from being disturbed by the presence of the church, the power structure of the average community is consoled by the church's silent—and often even vocal—sanction of things as they are.

But the judgment of God is upon the church as never before. If today's church does not recapture the sacrificial spirit of the early church, it will lose its authenticity, forfeit the loyalty of millions, and be dismissed as an irrelevant social club with no meaning for the twentieth century. Every day I meet young people whose disappointment with the church has turned into outright disgust.

Perhaps I have once again been too optimistic. Is organized religion too inextricably bound to the status quo to save our nation and the world? Perhaps I must turn my faith to the inner spiritual church, the church within the church, as the true *ekklesia*[1] and the hope of the world. But again I am thankful to God that some noble souls from the ranks of organized religion have broken loose from the paralyzing chains of conformity and joined us as active partners in the struggle for freedom. They have left their secure congregations and walked the streets of Albany, Georgia, with us. They have gone down the highways of the South on tortuous rides for freedom. Yes, they have gone to jail with us. Some have been dismissed from their churches, have lost the support of their bishops and fellow ministers. But they have acted in the faith that right defeated is stronger than evil triumphant. Their witness has been the spiritual salt that has preserved the true meaning of the gospel in these troubled times. They have carved a tunnel of hope through the dark mountain of disappointment.

I hope the church as a whole will meet the challenge of this decisive hour. But even if the church does not come to the aid of justice, I have no despair about the future. I have no fear about the outcome of our struggle in Birmingham, even if our motives are at present misunderstood. We will reach the goal of freedom in Birmingham and all over the nation, because the goal of America is freedom. Abused and scorned though we may be, our destiny is tied up with America's destiny. Before the pilgrims landed at Plymouth, we were here. Before the pen of Jefferson etched the majestic words of the Declaration of Independence across the pages of history, we were here. For more than two centuries our forebears labored in this country without wages; they made cotton king; they built the homes of their masters while suffering gross injustice and shameful humiliation—and yet out of a bottomless vitality they continued to thrive and develop. If the inexpressible cruelties of slavery could not stop us, the opposition we now face will surely fail. We will win our freedom because the sacred heritage of our nation and the eternal will of God are embodied in our echoing demands.

---

[1] The Greek New Testament word for the early Christian church.

Before closing I feel impelled to mention one other point in your statement that has troubled me profoundly. You warmly commended the Birmingham police force for keeping "order" and "preventing violence." I doubt that you would have so warmly commended the policemen if you were to observe their ugly and inhumane treatment of Negroes here in the city jail; if you were to watch them push and curse old Negro women and young Negro girls; if you were to observe them, as they did on two occasions, refuse to give us food because we wanted to sing our grace together. I cannot join you in your praise of the Birmingham police department.

It is true that the police have exercised a degree of discipline in handling the demonstrators. In this sense they have conducted themselves rather "nonviolently" in public. But for what purpose? To preserve the evil system of segregation. Over the past few years I have consistently preached that nonviolence demands that the means we use must be as pure as the ends we seek. I have tried to make clear that it is wrong to use immoral means to attain moral ends. But now I must affirm that it is just as wrong, or perhaps even more so, to use moral means to preserve immoral ends. Perhaps Mr. Connor and his policemen have been rather nonviolent in public, as was Chief Pritchett in Albany, Georgia, but they have used the moral means of nonviolence to maintain the immoral end of racial injustice. As T.S. Eliot has said, "The last temptation is the greatest treason: To do the right deed for the wrong reason."

I wish you had commended the Negro sit-inners and demonstrators of Birmingham for their sublime courage, their willingness to suffer, and their amazing discipline in the midst of great provocation. One day the South will recognize its real heroes. They will be the James Merediths, with the noble sense of purpose that enables them to face jeering and hostile mobs, and with the agonizing loneliness that characterizes the life of the pioneer. They will be old, oppressed, battered Negro women, symbolized in a seventy-two-year-old woman in Montgomery, Alabama, who rose up with a sense of dignity and with her people decided not to ride segregated buses, and who responded with ungrammatical profundity to one who inquired about her weariness: "My feets is tired, but my soul is at rest." They will be the young high school and college students, the young ministers of the gospel and a host of their elders, courageously and nonviolently sitting in at lunch counters and willingly going to jail for conscience' sake. One day the South will know that when these disinherited children of God sat down at lunch counters, they were in reality standing up for what is best in the American dream and for the most sacred values in our Judaeo-Christian heritage, thereby bringing our nation back to those great wells of democracy which were dug deep by the founding fathers in their formulation of the Constitution and the Declaration of Independence.

Never before have I written so long a letter. I'm afraid it is much too long to take your precious time. I can assure you that it would have been much shorter if I had been writing from a comfortable desk, but what else can one do when he is alone in a narrow jail cell, other than write long letters, think long thoughts, and pray long prayers?

If I have said anything in this letter that overstates the truth and indicates an unreasonable impatience, I beg you to forgive me. If I have said anything that understates the truth and indicates my having a patience that allows me to settle for anything less than brotherhood, I beg God to forgive me.

I hope this letter finds you strong in the faith. I also hope that circumstances will soon make it possible for me to meet each of you, not as an integrationist or a civil-rights leader but as a fellow clergyman and a Christian brother. Let us all hope that the dark clouds of racial prejudice will soon pass away and the deep fog of misunderstanding will be lifted from our fear-drenched communities, and in some not too distant tomorrow the radiant stars of love and brotherhood will shine over our great nation with all their scintillating beauty.

Yours for the cause of Peace and Brotherhood,
MARTIN LUTHER KING, JR.

QUESTIONS

1. Why does King hope his terms will be patient as well as reasonable?

2. What kinds of strategies does King employ to refute the charge of "outside agitator"?

3. What is the difference between violent and nonviolent tension?

4. What is King's acid test of whether a law is just or unjust? Is it specific or general? Subjective or objective? Why does he—at that point in the essay—invoke and quote so many theologians and philosophers? Is the strategy effective? How so? Why not?

5. How does King justify his "extremism"? Is his justification effective? How so? Why not?

6. How can "right defeated" be stronger than "evil triumphant"?

SUGGESTED ACTIVITIES

1. Write about Niebuhr's observation cited by King: "groups tend to be more immoral than individuals."

2. In your own terms, argue in support of King's assertion that "one has a moral responsibility to disobey unjust laws." Now argue against it.

3. Calling on personal experience, compare "lukewarm acceptance" with "outright rejection."

4. Explain in writing the lines by T. S. Eliot quoted by King: "The last temptation is the greatest treason: To do the right deed for the wrong reason."

THOMAS JEFFERSON

The Declaration of Independence

Thomas Jefferson needs no introduction. Neither does the Declaration of Independence. *For purposes of comparison and to understand better the benefits of revision, an early rough draft—as it probably read when Jefferson first submitted it to Benjamin Franklin—is followed by the final draft.*

The Rough Draft

A DECLARATION BY THE REPRESENTATIVES OF THE
UNITED STATES OF AMERICA, IN GENERAL
CONGRESS ASSEMBLED.

When in the course of human events it becomes necessary for a people to advance from that subordination in which they have hitherto remained, & to assume among the powers of the earth the equal & independent station to which the laws of nature & of nature's god entitle them, a decent respect to the opinions of mankind requires that they should declare the causes which impel them to the change.

We hold these truths to be _^ ~~sacred and undeniable~~; that all men
are created equal & independent; that from that equal creation they
derive ~~in~~ rights inherent & inalienable, among which are the preservation of life, & liberty, & the pursuit of happiness; that to secure
these ends, governments are instituted among men, deriving their just
powers from the consent of the governed; that whenever any form of
government shall become destructive of these ends, it is the right of
the people to alter or to abolish it, & to institute new government,
laying it's foundation on such principles & organizing it's powers in
such form, as to them shall seem most likely to effect their safety &
happiness. prudence indeed will dictate that governments long established should not be changed for light & transient causes: and accordingly all experience hath shewn that mankind are more disposed to
suffer while evils are sufferable, than to right themselves by abolishing
the forms to which they are accustomed. but when a long train of
abuses & usurpations, begun at a distinguished period, & pursuing
invariably the same object, evinces a design to ~~subject~~ reduce them to
arbitrary power, it is their right, it is their duty, to throw off such
government & to provide new guards for their future security. such
has been the patient sufferance of these colonies; & such is now the
necessity which constrains them to expunge their former systems of
government. the history of his present majesty is a history of unre-
mitting injuries and usurpations, among which no one fact stands
single or solitary to contradict the uniform tenor of the rest, all of
which have in direct object the establishment of an absolute tyranny
over these states. to prove this, let facts be submitted to a candid
world, for the truth of which we pledge a faith yet unsullied by falsehood.
he has refused his assent to laws the most wholesome and necessary
    for the public good:
he has forbidden his governors to pass laws of immediate & pressing
    importance, unless suspended in their operation till his assent should
    be obtained; and when so suspended, he has neglected utterly to
    attend to them.
he has refused to pass other laws for the accommodation of large
    districts of people unless those people would relinquish the right of

representation∧, a right inestimable to them & formidable to tyrants only:
    in the legislature

he has dissolved Representative houses repeatedly & continually, for
opposing with manly firmness his invasions on the rights of the
people:

~~he has dissolved,~~ he has refused for a long space of time to cause
others to be elected, whereby the legislative powers, incapable of
annihilation, have returned to the people at large for their exercise,
the state remaining in the meantime exposed to all the dangers of
invasion from without, & convulsions within:

he has endeavored to prevent the population of these states; for that
purpose obstructing the laws for naturalization of foreigners; refusing to pass others to encourage their migrations hither; & raising
the conditions of new appropriations of lands:

he has suffered the administration of justice totally to cease in some
of these colonies, refusing his assent to laws for establishing judiciary powers:

he has made our judges dependent on his will alone, for the tenure of
their offices, and amount of their salaries:

he has erected a multitude of new offices by a self-assumed power, &
sent hither swarms of officers to harrass our people & eat out their
substance:

he has kept among us in times of peace standing armies & ships of
war:

he has affected to render the military, independent of & superior to
the civil power:

he has combined with others to subject us to a jurisdiction foreign to
our constitutions and unacknowledged by our laws; giving his assent
to their pretended acts of legislation, for quartering large bodies of
armed troops among us;

    for protecting them by a mock-trial from punishment for any
murders∧ they should commit on the inhabitants of these states;
        which

    for cutting off our trade with all parts of the world;

    for imposing taxes on us without our consent; for depriving us of
the benefits of trial by jury;

    for transporting us beyond seas to be tried for pretended offenses;

for taking away our charters, & altering fundamentally the forms
of our governments;

for suspending our own legislatures & declaring themselves invested
with power to legislate for us in all cases whatsoever:

he has abdicated government here, withdrawing his governors, &
declaring us out of his allegiance & protection:

he has plundered our seas, ravaged our coasts, burnt our towns &
destroyed the lives of our people:

he is at this time transporting large armies of foreign mercenaries to
compleat the works of death, desolation & tyranny, already begun
with circumstances of cruelty & perfidy unworthy the head of a
civilized nation:

he has endeavored to bring on the inhabitants of our frontiers the
merciless Indian savages, whose known rule of warfare is an undistinguished destruction of all ages, sexes, & conditions of existence:

he has incited treasonable insurrections of our fellow citizens, with
the allurements of forfeiture & confiscation of our property:

he has waged cruel war against human nature itself, violating it's most
sacred rights of life & liberty in the persons of a distant people who
never offended him, captivating & carrying them into slavery in
another hemisphere, or to incur miserable death in their transpor-
tation thither. this piratical warfare, the opprobrium of *infidel* powers, is the warfare of the *Christian* king of Great Britain. [deter-
mined to keep open a market where MEN should be bought & sold,]
he has prostituted his negative for suppressing every legislative attempt
to prohibit or to restrain this execrable commerce: and that this
determining to keep open a market where MEN should be bought and sold:
∧
assemblage of horrors might want no fact of distinguished die, he
is now exciting those very people to rise in arms among us, and to
purchase that liberty of which *he* has deprived them, by murdering
the people upon whom *he* also obtruded them: thus paying off
former crimes committed against the *liberties* of one people, with
crimes which he urges them to commit against the *lives* of another.
in every stage of these oppressions we have petitioned for redress
in the most humble terms; our repeated petitions have been answered
by repeated injury. a prince whose character is thus marked by every

act which may define a tyrant, is unfit to be the ruler of a people who mean to be free. future ages will scarce believe that the hardiness of one man, adventured within the short compass of twelve years only, on so many acts of tyranny without a mask, over a people fostered & fixed in principles of liberty.

Nor have we been wanting in attentions to our British brethren. we have warned them from time to time of attempts by their legislature to extend a jurisdiction over these our states. we have reminded them of the circumstances of our emigration & settlement here, no one of which could warrant so strange a pretension: that these were effected at the expence of our own blood & treasure, unassisted by the wealth or the strength of Great Britain: that in constituting indeed our several forms of government, we had adopted one common king, thereby laying a foundation for perpetual league & amity with them: but that submission to their parliament was no part of our constitution, nor ever in idea, if history may be credited: and we appealed to their native justice & magnanimity, as well as to the ties of our common kindred to disavow these usurpations which were likely to interrupt our correspondence & connection. they too have been deaf to the voice of justice & of consanguinity, & when occasions have been given them, by the regular course of their laws, of removing from their councils the disturbers of our harmony, they have by their free election re-established them in power. at this very time too they are permitting their chief magistrate to send over not only soldiers of our common blood, but Scotch & foreign mercenaries to invade & deluge us in blood. these facts have given the last stab to agonizing affection, and manly spirit bids us to renounce forever these unfeeling brethren. we must endeavor to forget our former love for them, and to hold them as we hold the rest of mankind enemies in war, in peace friends. we might have been a free & a great people together; but a communication of grandeur & of freedom it seems is below their dignity. be it so, since they will have it: the road to ~~glory &~~ happiness ⟨& to glory⟩ is open to us too; we will climb it ~~in a separately state~~ ⟨apart from them⟩, and acquiesce in the necessity which ⟨de⟩ pronounces our ~~everlasting Adieu!~~ eternal separation!

We therefore the representatives of the United States of America in General Congress assembled do, in the name & by authority of the good people of these states, reject and renounce all allegiance & subjection to the kings of Great Britain & all others who may hereafter claim by, through, or under them; we utterly dissolve and break off all political connection which may have heretofore subsisted between us & the people or parliament of Great Britain; and finally we do assert and declare these colonies to be free and independent states, and that as free & independent states they shall hereafter have ^{full}power to levy war, conclude peace, contract alliances, establish commerce, & to do all other acts and things which independent states may of right do. And for the support of this declaration we mutually pledge to each other our lives, our fortunes, & our sacred honour.

The Final Draft

THE UNANIMOUS DECLARATION OF THE THIRTEEN UNITED STATES OF AMERICA.

When in the Course of human events, it becomes necessary for one people to dissolve the political bands which have connected them with another, and to assume among the powers of the earth, the separate and equal station to which the Laws of Nature and of Nature's God entitle them, a decent respect to the opinions of mankind requires that they should declare the causes which impel them to the separation.—We hold these truths to be self-evident, that all men are created equal, that they are endowed by their Creator with certain unalienable Rights, that among these are Life, Liberty and the pursuit of Happiness.—That to secure these rights, Governments are instituted among Men, deriving their just powers from the consent of the governed,—That whenever any Form of Government becomes destructive of these ends, it is the Right of the People to alter or to abolish it, and to institute new Government, laying its foundation on such principles and organizing its powers in such form, as to them shall seem most likely to effect their Safety and

Happiness. Prudence, indeed, will dictate that Governments long established should not be changed for light and transient causes; and accordingly all experience hath shewn, that mankind are more disposed to suffer, while evils are sufferable, than to right themselves by abolishing the forms to which they are accustomed. But when a long train of abuses and usurpations, pursuing invariably the same Object evinces a design to reduce them under absolute Despotism, it is their right, it is their duty, to throw off such Government, and to provide new Guards for their future security.— Such has been the patient sufference of these Colonies; and such is now the necessity which constrains them to alter their former Systems of Government. The history of the present King of Great Britain is a history of repeated injuries and usurpations, all having in direct object the establishment of an absolute Tyranny over these States. To prove this, let Facts be submitted to a candid world.—He has refused his Assent to Laws, the most wholesome and necessary for the public good.—He has forbidden his Governors to pass Laws of immediate and pressing importance, unless suspended in their operation till his Assent should be obtained; and when so suspended, he has utterly neglected to attend to them.—He has refused to pass other Laws for the accommodation of large districts of people, unless those people would relinquish the right of Representation in the Legislature, a right inestimable to them and formidable to tyrants only.—He has called together legislative bodies at places unusual, uncomfortable, and distant from the depository of their public Records, for the sole purpose of fatiguing them into compliance with his measures.–He has dissolved Repres $\overset{en}{\wedge}$ tative Houses repeatedly, for opposing with manly firmness his invasions on the rights of the people.—He has refused for a long time, after such dissolutions, to cause others to be elected; whereby the Legislative powers, incapable of Annihilation, have returned to the People at large for their exercise; the State remaining in the meantime exposed to all the dangers of invasion from without, and convulsions within.— He has endeavoured to prevent the population of these States; for that purpose obstructing the Laws for Naturalization of Foreigners;

refusing to pass others to encourage their migrations hither, and raising the conditions of new Appropriations of Lands.—He has obstructed the Administration of Justice, by refusing his Assent to Laws for establishing Judiciary powers.—He has made Judges dependent on his Will alone, for the tenure of their offices, and the amount and payment of their salaries.—He has erected a multitude of New Offices, and sent hither swarms of Officers to harrass our people, and eat out their substance.—He has kept among us, in times of peace, Standing Armies without the Consent of our legislatures.—He has affected to render the Military independent of and superior to the Civil power.—He has combined with others to subject us to a jurisdiction foreign to our constitution, and unacknowledged by our laws; giving his Assent to their Acts of pretended Legislation.—For quartering large bodies of armed troops among us:—For protecting them, by a mock Trial, from punishment for any Murders which they should commit on the Inhabitants of these States:—For cutting off our Trade with all parts of the world:—For imposing Taxes on us without our Consent:—For depriving us in many cases, of the benefits of Trial by Jury:—For transporting us beyond Seas to be tried for pretended offenses:—For abolishing the free System of English Laws in a neighboring Province, establishing therein an Arbitrary government, and enlarging its Boundaries so as to render it at once an example and fit instrument for introducing the same absolute rule into these Colonies:—For taking away our Charters, abolishing our most valuable Laws, and altering fundamentally the Forms of our Governments:—For suspending our own Legislatures, and declaring themselves invested with power to legislate for us in all cases whatsoever.—He has abdicated Government here, by declaring us out of his Protection and waging War against us.—He has plundered our seas, ravaged our Coasts, burnt our towns, and destroyed the lives of our people.—He is at this time transporting large Armies of foreign Mercenaries to compleat the works of death, desolation and tyranny, already begun with circumstances of Cruelty & perfidy scarcely paralleled in the most barbarous ages, and totally unworthy the Head of a civilized nation.— He has constrained our fellow Citizens taken Captive on the high

Seas to bear Arms against their Country, to become the executioners of their friends and Brethren, or to fall themselves by their Hands.— He has excited domestic insurrections amongst us, and has endeavoured to bring on the inhabitants of our frontiers, the merciless Indian Savages, whose known rule of warfare, is an undistinguished destruction of all ages, sexes and conditions. In every stage of these Oppressions We have Petitioned for Redress in the most humble terms: Our repeated Petitions have been answered $\wedge$ by repeated injury. A Prince whose character is thus marked by every act which may define a Tyrant, is unfit to be the ruler of a free people. Nor have We been wanting in attentions to our British brethren. We have warned them from time to time of attempts by their legislature to extend an unwarrantable jurisdiction over us. We have reminded them of the circumstances of our emigration and settlement here. We have appealed to their native justice and magnanimity, and we have conjured them by the ties of our common kindred to disavow these usurpations, which would inevitably interrupt our connections and correspondence. They too have been deaf to the voice of justice and of consanguinity. We must, therefore, acquiesce in the necessity, which denounces our Separation, and hold them, as we hold the rest of mankind, Enemies in War, in Peace Friends.—

We, therefore, the Representatives of the United States of America, in General Congress, Assembled, appealing to the Supreme Judge of the world for the rectitude of our intentions do, in the Name, and by Authority of the good People of these Colonies, solemnly publish and declare, That these United Colonies are, and of Right ought to be Free and Independent States; that they are Absolved from all Allegiance to the British Crown, and that all political connection between them and the State of Great Britain is and ought to be totally dissolved: and that as Free and Independent States, they have full Power to levy War, conclude Peace, contract Alliances, establish Commerce, and to do all other Acts and Things which Independent States may of right do.—And for the support of this Declaration, with a firm reliance on the protection of divine Providence, we mutually pledge to each other our Lives, our Fortunes and our sacred Honor.

SUGGESTED ACTIVITY

Choose any five of the rough-draft revisions and explain what Jefferson accomplished by making them.

Copyrights and Acknowledgments

Rhetorical Table
for Readings

Index to Rhetoric

Because this Index is intended to be practical, it is keyed to the Rhetoric only. In addition to all of the terms contained in the Table of Contents, the Index includes alternative terms, technical terms, and the titles to specific reference works not provided in the Table of Contents. There are no names of authors or their writings. This is, then, a supplement and a cross-reference to the Table of Contents. By using the Index and the Table of Contents, you can locate in a moment any topic discussed in the Rhetoric.